Charles Seale-Hayne Library
University of Plymouth
(01752) 588 588
LibraryandITenquiries@plymouth.ac.uk

Music, Art, and Metaphysics

Essays in Philosophical Aesthetics

Jerrold Levinson

OXFORD
UNIVERSITY PRESS

OXFORD

UNIVERSITY PRESS

Great Clarendon Street, Oxford OX2 6DP

Oxford University Press is a department of the University of Oxford.
It furthers the University's objective of excellence in research, scholarship,
and education by publishing worldwide in

Oxford New York

Auckland Cape Town Dar es Salaam Hong Kong Karachi
Kuala Lumpur Madrid Melbourne Mexico City Nairobi
New Delhi Shanghai Taipei Toronto

With offices in

Argentina Austria Brazil Chile Czech Republic France Greece
Guatemala Hungary Italy Japan Poland Portugal Singapore
South Korea Switzerland Thailand Turkey Ukraine Vietnam

Oxford is a registered trade mark of Oxford University Press
in the UK and in certain other countries

Published in the United States
by Oxford University Press Inc., New York

British Library Cataloguing in Publication Data

Data available

Library of Congress Cataloging in Publication Data

Data available

Typeset by SPI Publisher Services, Pondichery, India
Printed in Great Britain
on acid-free paper by
MPG Books Group, Bodmin and King's Lynn

ISBN 978-0-19-959663-8 (Hbk)
 978-0-19-959662-1 (Pbk)

1 3 5 7 9 10 8 6 4 2

Contents

Preface

This book brings together the bulk of my work in aesthetics to date, spanning a bit more than a decade. It consists of twelve previously published essays, plus four new ones appearing here for the first time. Some remarks on the new essays in relation to the old ones are in order. Chapter 10, "What a Musical Work Is, Again," offers further reflections on some of the issues raised in its predecessor, in the course of responding to discussions and criticisms which that paper has attracted. Chapter 11, "The Concept of Music," originally composed as the introduction to a reader in philosophy of music destined never to see light, has links with the definitional enterprise of Chapters 1 and 3, as well as with the other explicitly musical essays of Part Three. Chapter 14, "Hope in *The Hebrides*," is loosely continuous with Chapter 13, addressing aspects of emotional expression in music there presupposed without being directly examined. Finally, Chapter 16, "Authentic Performance and Performance Means," although composed in response to a particular essay by another writer, can be seen as a natural development and partial fusion of concerns present in several of the preceding essays, especially Chapters 4 and 15.

The reprinted essays appear with little alteration. There have been minor changes of wording throughout, but no real cuts (with the exception of a short concluding section dropped from "Aesthetic Supervenience"). Some footnotes have been shortened, some lengthened, and some superfluous ones eliminated altogether. To nine of the reprinted essays I have appended "Additional Notes." This seemed a good medium for accommodating a modicum of latter-day thoughts, while also affording me the opportunity briefly to situate those papers in relation to work that has appeared subsequently.

My justification for reprinting the previously published essays with minimal alterations is twofold. First, I have not substantially changed my views since writing them, and those views are, as far as their author can tell, more or less of a piece. Second, the essays have, as scrutinized texts, already begun to acquire a small life of their own, and my leaving them largely intact, for better or worse, is a recognition of that.

Most of the essays in this volume, old and new, are situated at the intersection of aesthetic and metaphysical concerns: how the category of art in general is to be circumscribed in a way that is both extensionally adequate and illuminating of the act of art making ("Defining Art Historically" and "Refining Art Historically"), how the nature and proper interpretation of an art form cannot be detached from issues about its roots or causal origins ("Hybrid Art Forms"), how entrenched modes of aesthetic experience and aesthetic discourse entail or enjoin certain conclusions about the ontology of art ("What a Musical Work Is," "Autographic and Allographic Art Revisited," "Titles," and "What a Musical Work Is, Again"), how the aesthetic and artistic content of a work of art relates to the nonaesthetic structure on which it is erected, be it in sound, word, paint, or stone ("Aesthetic Uniqueness" and "Aesthetic Supervenience"), and how this content, though historically determined, does not fundamentally evolve over time ("Artworks and the Future").

An important second focus of the essays as a whole is a special concern with the art of music. This means, in particular, both (1) examination for their own sake of aesthetic problems peculiar to music, and (2) illumination of problems of wider aesthetic import seen through the lens of that particular art form. In the first category I would place "The Concept of Music," "Truth in Music," "Hope in *The Hebrides*," "Evaluating Musical Performance," and "Authentic Performance and Performance Means"; in the second category, perhaps, "What a Musical Work Is" together with its sequel, and "Music and Negative Emotion."

If one were to characterize my position in art theory as a whole, it would emerge, I think, as a historicist and contextualist objectivism. This melding of historicist and contextualist considerations with a fairly thoroughgoing objectivism about aesthetic content, artistic meaning, and the concept of art in effect stands as a third thematic pole of the collection; more specifically, the idea that artworks are onto-logically, interpretively, and evaluatively bound up with their histories of production, the art-historical situations in which they come to be, and the history-involving intentions of their makers is a central theme of the three essays in Part One and of a number of those in Parts Two and Three as well.

In rough fashion, then, this accounts for the tripartite grouping of the essays. Those in Part One emphasize above all the historicity of art making. Those in Part Two explore metaphysical issues—as to the nature of art objects, art properties, art causation, and art identity—most prominently. And those in Part Three, while usually evincing historicist and metaphysical concern in some fashion, are predomi-nantly contributions to the rather specific metatheory of musical ap-preciation and criticism. That said, it is clear that on thematic grounds alone, and a somewhat different weighing of the substance of each essay, Chapters 9 and 11 might reasonably have landed in Part One, Chapters 4 and 10 in Part Three, and Chapter 2 in Part Two. But I was also concerned that essays be placed in proximity to those they pre-suppose or to which they crucially refer, and that chronological order be preserved, if possible, for the reprinted essays. These additional desiderata, together with the obvious thematic ones, determined the final grouping.

Finally, as the essays will make plain, I generally stand opposed, in style as well as substance, to sociological, relativist—and more nar-rowly, deconstructivist—approaches to the realm of art which have been fashionable of late. This is meant neither as apology nor as defiance; rather, as a *caveat lector.*

I thank particularly four individuals who have had most to do with these essays being written: Kendall Walton, for first having shown me how aesthetics could be both rigorous and imaginative, and for a core of insights I have tried to add to in my own work; Peter Kivy, for having early shown an interest in my work on music, and for enriching it by his sometimes dogged opposition; Richard Wollheim, for his philosophical example and encouragement, and his unselfish praise of my efforts beyond what they deserved; and last, Nicholas Wolterstorff, whose specific choice of philosophical subjects is one I found myself somewhat paralleling, beginning with my early work in general metaphysics and continuing with my shift to aesthetics. What is of worth in these essays is partly due to them.

I thank next Lydia Goehr and Jenefer Robinson, who read through the entire manuscript, offering many valuable suggestions. I thank my editor, John Ackerman, for his unfailing encouragement and his staff at Cornell University Press for their very professional assistance.

I also express my appreciation to all of the following who—sometimes unknowingly, though usually quite deliberately—have made helpful comments on various essays at various stages, contributing to their improvement: Dennis Ahern, John Bennett, Baruch Brody, John Brown, Malcolm Budd, Noël Carroll, James Celarier, Gregory Currie, Stephen Davies, Douglas Dempster, Mark De Bellis, Richard Eldridge, Kit Fine, Michael Gardner, Norman Gillespie, Joshua Halberstam, Göran Hermerén, Terry Horgan, Warren Ingber, Gary Iseminger, David Luban, Jack Meiland, Michael Slote, Kim Sterelny, Lawrence Stern, Joseph Tolliver, Alan Tormey, and Susan Wolf. I thank my colleagues in the Maryland philosophy department for their support and stimulation over the past fourteen years. Finally, I owe a special debt to my wife, Karla Hoff, who was an inspiration to me in at least two respects. As a much harder worker than I am, and as a better editor than I will ever be, she helped bring this book to fruition earlier than would otherwise have been the case, had I had only my own company to dwell in and only my own reflection to observe.

Two last debts: to Michael Eckersley, for design of the illustration in Ch. 6, and to Leonard Meyer, whose collection *Music, the Arts, and Ideas* (1967) provided the model for my own title.

JERROLD LEVINSON

College Park, Maryland

Acknowledgments

I thank the editors and publishers who have kindly granted permission to reprint essays appearing in this volume. The places of original publication are as follows:

"Defining Art Historically," *British Journal of Aesthetics*, 19 (1979): 232–50.

"Hybrid Art Forms," *Journal of Aesthetic Education*, 18 (1984): 5–13. (Copyright © 1984 Board of Trustees of the University of Illinois.)

"Refining Art Historically," *Journal of Aesthetics and Art Criticism*, 47 (1989): 21–33.

"What a Musical Work Is," *Journal of Philosophy*, 77 (1980): 5–28.

"Autographic and Allographic Art Revisited," *Philosophical Studies*, 38 (1980): 367–83. (Copyright © 1980 by D. Reidel Publishing Company, Dordrecht, Holland.)

"Aesthetic Uniqueness," *Journal of Aesthetics and Art Criticism*, 38 (1980): 435–49.

"Aesthetic Supervenience," *Southern Journal of Philosophy*, 22 Supplement (1983): 93–110. (Copyright © 1983 by Department of Philosophy, Memphis State University.)

"Titles," *Journal of Aesthetics and Art Criticism*, 44 (1985): 29–39.

"Artworks and the Future," in *Aesthetic Distinction*, ed. T. Anderberg, T. Nilstun, and I. Persson (Lund: Lund University Press, 1987), pp. 56–84.

"Truth in Music," *Journal of Aesthetics and Art Criticism*, 40 (1981): 131–44.

"Music and Negative Emotion," *Pacific Philosophical Quarterly*, 63 (1982): 327–46. (Copyright © 1982 by University of Southern California.)

"Evaluating Musical Performance," *Journal of Aesthetic Education*, 21 (1987): 75–88. (Copyright © 1987 Board of Trustees of the University of Illinois.)

Introduction

When the present volume appears it will be two decades since the original publication of *Music, Art, and Metaphysics,* and about eight years since it was allowed to go out of print. Though I believe there are good reasons to reissue it now, which I will mention in a moment, I should say that without the urging of various friends and colleagues, most notably David Davies and Andrew Kania, and that of Peter Momtchiloff at Oxford University Press, I might, nevertheless, not have taken the steps necessary to bring the reissue about. For it is hard to revisit one's past, whether academic or personal, and thus to confront one's former self. Though it is only twenty years since the publication of *Music, Art, and Metaphysics,* some of the essays in the book first appeared over thirty years ago, and the thinking in them, as far as that is concerned, goes back to my graduate studies of almost forty years ago.

In any event, what are the reasons, alluded to above, for reissuing *Music, Art, and Metaphysics*? The first reason, I suppose, is that many of the essays have had a significant influence on the direction and character of analytic aesthetics, beginning naturally in the English-speaking sphere, but exerting an influence eventually also outside that sphere, in Scandinavia, France, Italy, Spain, Portugal, Germany, and other countries. The essays continue to be referred to and commented on with regularity, most notably "What a Musical Work Is," "Defining Art Historically," "Music and Negative Emotion," and "Hope in *The Hebrides,*" but also, if to a lesser extent, "Titles," "Hybrid Art Forms," "Artworks and the Future," and "The Concept of Music." The second reason for reissue, not unrelated to the first, is to make the essays, especially those not so widely reprinted in anthologies of aesthetics, readily available to current and future generations of students and scholars.

As for this Introduction, it affords me an opportunity to briefly describe and situate the essays for the benefit of those who encounter them for the first time, and to remark further on some of the issues that they address. But most enjoyably, for me, is the occasion here afforded to recall and share aspects of the genesis of certain of the essays that may be of interest to others.

In commenting briefly on the essays, a task to which I now turn, I address them more individually than I did in the volume's original preface, which follows this Introduction, where I was mainly concerned to justify how the essays were grouped and to foreground broad lines of connection among them. Here, by contrast, I simply indicate in a straightforward manner what each essay is about, what philosophical question it engages, what philosophical problem it seeks to illuminate.

The Essays: Summaries and Remarks

Two of the essays, "Defining Art Historically" and its sequel "Refining Art Historically," are concerned with the problem of the definition of art in the most general sense, one covering all art, of whatever genre, in whatever culture, whether actual or merely possible. The account offered in the first essay, and defended and elaborated in the second, places the accent on the connection that an art maker must effect between his or her activity and pre-existing art by the manner in which what is made is projected for regard. It thus offers an account in which both the intention of a maker and the concrete history of art play an essential role in securing for something the status of artwork; in short, an intentional-historical theory of art. The account was developed against the background of traditional formalist, expressionist, and aestheticist accounts of arthood, which it clearly rejects, but also in contradistinction to functionalist and institutional accounts of arthood, from which it more subtly distances itself.[1]

"Hybrid Art Forms" is concerned with exploring the concept of an art form that in some way fuses, straddles, or blurs the boundaries between two or more pre-existing art forms. As both the biological label and the gloss just given may already suggest, the concept of a hybrid art form is argued to be an essentially historical one, making ineliminable reference to the artistic hybrid's antecedents, and not a concept analyzable entirely in formal or structural terms. The essay also provides a rough taxonomy of hybrid art forms according to the manner in which aspects or elements of preceding art forms have been combined in the hybrid in question, and draws some lessons for the proper appreciation of works in such art forms.

The ontology of music is manifestly the focus of both "What a Musical Work Is" and its sequel "What a Musical Work Is, Again", which explicitly restrict themselves to the ontology of the standard work of classical music. At issue is what is to be understood as comprised in or as partly constituting such a work, apart from the sound structure that is its most salient feature. For instance, are any of these essential to the identity of such a work: its creator; its title; its time of composition; its aesthetic properties; the artistic intentions governing it; its context of origination; its specified instrumentation; its performing history; its critical reception? Underlined throughout is that the grasp of a musical work's ontological status and character is relevant to aesthetic appreciation of it, and that a work is misunderstood where such grasp is absent, distorted, or incomplete.[2]

---

[1] Much subsequent work on the philosophical definition of art engages with the theory presented in those essays. Some of the most important such works, often critical of the account or proposing modifications of it, is that of Noël Carroll, Gregory Currie, Stephen Davies, Berys Gaut, Aaron Meskin, Alessandro Pignocchi, and Robert Stecker.

[2] A happy development in recent philosophical aesthetics is much more attention to the methodology of ontological inquiry, to what might be called *meta-ontology*. More generally, for the increased sophistication now brought to questions about the ontology of music and other forms of art, much is owed to the important contributions of Peter Alward, Ben Caplan, David Davies, Stephen Davies, John Dilworth, Julian Dodd, Simon Evnine, Lydia Goehr, Robert Howell, Sherri Irvin, Andrew Kania, Robert Kivy, Carl Matheson, Charles Nussbaum, Stefano Predelli, Guy Rohrbaugh, Robert Stecker, and Amie Thomasson.

"Autographic and Allographic Art Revisited" is a sort of corollary to the two essays just discussed, though the field of inquiry is widened from that of music to that of the arts as a whole. The central target is the famous distinction, proposed by Nelson Goodman, between *autographic* art forms, those clearly admitting of forgery, such as painting and drawing, and *allographic* art forms, those putatively not admitting of forgery, such as music and poetry. What I aimed to show was that Goodman's way of drawing this distinction was flawed, and that it is not so much a work's susceptibility to forgery or essential connection to an artist and a time that characterizes the class of autographic arts Goodman had in mind, but rather, a work's not comprising a structure defined, either wholly or in part, by a notation. In short, Goodman's characterization of the autographic arts will not work, since given the considerations advanced in "What a Musical Work Is" and "What a Musical Work Is, Again," musical works turn out to exhibit such an essential connection and so are, after a fashion, as forgeable as paintings.

The main objective of "Titles" was twofold, the first relatively simple, the second more complicated. The first objective was to characterize *true* artwork titles, that is, verbal expressions that are actually parts of works as constituted by their creators, as opposed to nicknames, definite descriptions, museum catalog designations, and the like. The second objective was to defend and illustrate the claim that a work's true title is always *relevant* to its understanding and appreciation, even in cases where the meaning-constituting potential of titling appears to have been declined or neutralized, as with a title such as "Untitled".

The issue in "Aesthetic Uniqueness" is the uniqueness of individual artworks, as regards aesthetic properties, artistic properties, expressiveness, meaning, and experience offered. Might two distinct artworks ever display identical aesthetic, including expressive, characters? Might they ever possess all and only the same aesthetic properties, or all and only the same artistic properties? Whether or not they might possess all the same aesthetic and artistic properties, might they ever give appreciators the very same aesthetic experiences? And if so, does that possibility hold only for works within the same art form, or might it even hold for works in different art forms, for instance, a charcoal drawing and a piano prelude? This essay remains perhaps the least remarked on of the essays in *Music, Art, and Metaphysics*, and yet the issue with which it is concerned is one I continue to regard as fascinating.[3]

"Aesthetic Supervenience," which was written for a Spindel Conference at Memphis State University, is concerned with the nature of aesthetic properties and their underlying bases in non-aesthetic properties, and the conceptual and causal relations between the non-aesthetic and aesthetic properties of an artwork.[4] My main objectives

---

[3] I hope to fruitfully revisit the issue in a projected essay on the possibility of expressive equivalences between abstract painting and instrumental music.

[4] Of important subsequent work on aesthetic properties and aesthetic supervenience, I would note especially the contributions of John Bender, Malcolm Budd, Gregory Currie, Rafael De Clercq, Alan Goldman, Peter Lamarque, Roger Pouivet, and Nick Zangwill.

in the essay were these: to offer useful characterizations of the supervenience, or asymmetrical dependence, of an artwork's aesthetic properties on its non-aesthetic properties; to relate my reflections on aesthetic supervenience to Frank Sibley's and Monroe Beardsley's groundbreaking work on the manner and degree to which aesthetic properties are or are not conditioned by non-aesthetic properties, emphasizing Beardsley's often-overlooked distinction between *application* conditions for aesthetic terms and *occurrence* conditions for aesthetic properties; to defend a loosely *objectivist* and *emergentist* view of aesthetic properties, and aesthetic content more generally; and to argue against the extreme physicalist claim of the existence of *a priori* physicophenomenal laws that would permit the deduction of phenomenal and aesthetic properties from physical ones. In the last part of the essay, the notion of aesthetic supervenience is given concrete application through case studies of the aesthetic content of an abstract painting by Mondrian and a keyboard prelude by J. S. Bach.

The focus of the rather lengthy essay "Artworks and the Future" is the nature of artistic content and meaning, and its degree of stability over time. Does the passage of time, the emergence of new audiences, the arising of new contexts, necessarily induce alteration in the artistic content or meaning of works of art? I argued, in opposition to a postmodern article of faith in support of the inevitability of such alteration, that such meaning and content, rightly understood, does *not* change over time, even if the situation-relative *significance* of a work and its meaning does. As it happens, I returned to the theme of this essay in a subsequent essay, in which I was led to qualify its "no change in content or meaning over time" thesis, at least for the special case of works within the oeuvre of a given artist, where it seems that later works may in some cases subtly affect the content or meaning of earlier ones.[5]

"The Concept of Music" is concerned with the problem of defining music, of characterizing it as a specific art form distinct from other forms of art. The definition arrived at proposes two features as essential to the art form of music: one, the employment and organization of sound; two, a certain projected reception, involving enrichment of experience through attention to organized sounds as such. The aim was to characterize music in such a way that instances of music of any style or any culture would be covered, but not every instance of organized sound, excluding those organized for purposes not recognizable as musical.[6]

"Music and Negative Emotion" and "Hope in *The Hebrides*" are both concerned with emotion in relation to music. The former focuses on the *evocation* of emotion *by* music, whether in literal or imagined mode, and the latter focuses on the *expression* of emotion *in* music, though the issues are of course related, in that emotional evocation *by* music is most often the result of the listener's awareness of and sensitivity to

---

[5] "Work and Oeuvre," in *The Pleasures of Aesthetics* (Ithaca: Cornell University Press, 1996).

[6] Some important subsequent work on the concept of music has been done by Stephen Davies, Andy Hamilton, Andrew Kania, and Roger Scruton.

emotional expression *in* music. The more specific focus of "Music and Negative Emotion" is the ostensibly paradoxical phenomenon of negatively expressive music, whose tendency to induce negatively emotional states in attentive and responsive listeners would seem to make it the sort of music one would go out of one's way to avoid, and yet this is manifestly not the case, such music often being the most earnestly sought after and prized. After initial presentation of the paradox and some clarifications on the nature of emotions, much of the remainder of the essay explores ways to defuse the paradoxical appearance of pursuing emotion of a negative sort from darkly expressive music, issuing in a number of rewards that one might plausibly reap from such a pursuit. The more specific focus of "Hope in *The Hebrides*" is the question of whether purely instrumental music might be capable of expressing higher, cognitively complex emotions, such as shame, pride, regret, or contempt. As its title suggests, the specific higher emotion chosen for illustration in this essay is hope, and a case, both philosophical and musical, is made for its expression by a particular passage in Mendelssohn's famous overture.[7]

"Evaluating Musical Performance" and "Authentic Performance and Performance Means" are both concerned with what makes a performance a performance of a given musical work *at all*, with what makes it a *correct* or *authentic* performance of that work, and with what makes it a *good* performance of that work–three ideas which, though logically connected, are scarcely equivalent. The former essay is more pragmatically oriented, and considers performance evaluation from a variety of involved perspectives, including those of listeners, performers, critics, and composers, while the latter essay has more theoretical objectives in sight, on the one hand, providing philosophical ammunition for what is sometimes called the "historical authenticity" movement in music performance, and on the other hand, offering further support for the instrument-essentialist view of standard musical works defended in "What a Musical Work Is" and "What a Musical Work Is, Again."

Of the essays in *Music, Art, and Metaphysics* it is "Truth in Music" that I now harbor the most reservations about. Certainly I would not approach the topic that way today, nor would I be likely to defend the thesis that I there settle on. But what I was trying to do was find some plausible and interesting sense in which a passage of purely instrumental music, unconnected to any text or narrative, might be said to be true or false. I did manage to find something—that such a passage might be thought of as true to the extent that its sequence of emotional expressions was one that had some psychological plausibility in reality—but from my present vantage point this seems even more strained to me than it did at the time. What I now think is that if there is an important sense in which music is true, that lies not so much in the verisimilitude of such a sequence of

---

[7] Of important subsequent work on emotional expression and evocation in music, and the bearing of music's emotional dimension on its value as music. I would note especially that of Jeanette Bicknell, Paul Boghossian, Malcolm Budd, Stephen Davies, Peter Kivy, Derek Matravers, Aaron Ridley, Jenefer Robinson, Roger Scruton, and Robert Sharpe.

expressions, but rather more in the nature or character of the expressiveness achieved in individual passages of music.[8]

The Essays: Anecdotes and Reminiscences

"Titles." The nature and significance of artwork titles was my first idea for a doctoral thesis while in graduate school at the University of Michigan in the early 1970s, during which time my interest was roughly equally divided between aesthetics, which I studied with Kendall Walton, and metaphysics, which I studied mainly with Jaegwon Kim. When I aired this idea I was told—with justice, I eventually saw—that that was perhaps too narrow and specialized a topic for a dissertation in philosophy. So I ended up writing one in metaphysics instead, on the nature of attributes, which became the source of my first two published essays in philosophy, "Properties and Related Entities" (*Philosophy and Phenomenological Research* 1978) and "The Particularization of Attributes" (*Australasian Journal of Philosophy* 1980). Anyway, not long after, I returned to the topic of titles and devoted an article to it, which format suited what I had to say about titles, I am sure, rather better than a dissertation would have.

"Aesthetic Uniqueness." This essay was in effect my first full-fledged effort in aesthetics. The story connected with its genesis may be of some interest, and perhaps of inspiration to those who may be tempted prematurely to abandon philosophy for some financially surer pursuit. In the spring of 1976 I found myself nearing the end of a second one-year position with no clear future, at a private university in New Jersey that shall remain nameless. One fine spring day I received a call from Samuel Gorovitz, then chair of the philosophy department at the University of Maryland, asking me if I remained interested in the post they were trying to fill for a philosopher of art, and whether I had a paper in aesthetics I was willing to present to them. Since at that time most of my work in philosophy, including my dissertation, represented me as a metaphysician, it was reasonable for Gorovitz to inquire whether I also really was as well, or was at least prepared to become, an aesthetician. I replied that I was indeed still interested in the post, and that I was more than willing to present an appropriate paper to the department. But the fact is that I *hadn't* yet written the paper in question, though the ideas for it were pretty clearly worked out in my mind. Anyway, within a week the paper was written, and was apparently good enough to secure me the post, which I have occupied happily now for thirty-four years, and, for the most part, as an aesthetician. The paper I gave then was an early version of "Aesthetic Uniqueness."

"Music and Negative Emotion." The essay begins with a lurid and melodramatic image of the music lover who fancies music of starkly distressing emotional character as some sort of masochist whose listening room thus appears in the guise of a torture chamber. I leave to it readers to discover the rhetorical purpose of that attention-getting

---

[8] For some hints in this vein see my "Musical Profundity Misplaced," *Journal of Aesthetics and Art Criticism* 50 (1992).

device, but what I want to add here, more soberly, is that that image remotely derives from my practice—at least in early years, when I was in the first blush of my inordinate passion for music—of listening to recorded music in seclusion, in the dark, eyes closed, and in a reclined or semi-reclined position. For it seemed that it was in such conditions, which facilitated total attention to and immersion in the music, that music had its most powerful effects on me emotionally, both positive and negative, and however those effects are best analyzed from a philosophical perspective. There was, to my ritual of seriously listening to music, an undeniable aspect of submission, of opening myself up to the power of music to ravish, entrance, and overpower, for better or worse. It thus took little tweaking to convert that practice into the overheated image with which "Music and Negative Emotion" endeavors to ensnare the reader.

"What a Musical Work Is." This essay takes as an exemplar of the standard notated classical composition Beethoven's Quintet for Piano and Winds, op. 16. The choice of Beethoven was natural, since he occupies in both the popular and the learned mind the place of classical composer *par excellence*. The choice of the Quintet as an illustration was rather more arbitrary, except that I wanted a piece that was not too well known, that used a number of instruments, and that used them distinctively. Plus, I was quite fond of it. Ironically, however, though the crucial role of instrumentation in the identity of such a work was a main theme of my essay, in the essay's original appearance in the *Journal of Philosophy* I had incorrectly given the instrumentation as piano, *flute*, oboe, clarinet, and horn—instead of piano, oboe, clarinet, horn, and *bassoon*—a mistake my keenest philosophical adversary on this issue, Peter Kivy, was only too happy to point out. Yet a subsequent development convinced me that my choice of that piece to illustrate my ideas on musical ontology was not so random as all that, but had, perhaps, been guided by an unseen providence. For when my daughter Melanie was born, on the very last day of 1989, what was playing on the sound system of the delivery room but that very piece of relatively obscure chamber music...

"Hope in *The Hebrides*" has the curious distinction of having had a poem written in its honor by another philosopher, a poem that appears to contain a gentle critique of its main thesis—though since it is a poem it is a little hard to tell with assurance. The poem is by Roger Scruton, is entitled simply "Hope", and can be found in a recent collection of the philosopher's incidental writings.[9] I will not quote the poem in full, but this excerpt will give a fair idea of its good natured and witty flavor:

> The cellos ride B minor, and charm it into D;
> Young Felix wrote no finer theme, and if it hopes then hope exists in melody.
>
> Just make your boat of music-staves, for then you'll float
> On waves of sound; those dancing naiads are really triads,
> And every sea-change, just a key-change, your ballast just a note.

---

[9] *Gentle Regrets* (London: Continuum, 2006). Note that not all line breaks and capitalizations have been retained in this excerpt, so interested readers are encouraged to consult the original in the source cited.

> But can I steer this ship to port and find the thing I hope?
> The answer's clear: yes sure, in thought; but in the real world, nope.

My last reminiscence concerns both "Defining Art Historically" and "What a Musical Work Is," which continue to be my most often cited and reprinted papers. Early in my philosophical career certain thinkers who loomed large in the philosophy of art naturally exerted an important personal influence on me. Most significant among those thinkers was my graduate school mentor in aesthetics, Kendall Walton, and a second, unofficial mentor in aesthetics that I acquired later in Richard Wollheim. (Walton's essay "Categories of Art" remains probably the single most important influence on my various forays in aesthetic theory, while Wollheim's *Art and Its Objects* was the first book in aesthetics I was completely taken with.) In addition to Walton and Wollheim there were then also Nicholas Wolterstorff and Peter Kivy, two excellent aestheticians with whom I had personal contact early on, and whose research specifically in philosophy of music was of particular inspiration to me.

Arthur Danto, on the other hand, a formidable art critic and art theorist as well as a philosopher of worldwide renown, and thus an unavoidable presence in aesthetics, was not someone with whom I was particularly close. Still, we became acquainted not long after my first publications in the field, and I remember asking his opinion, on some occasion or other, of the two essays of mine that had begun to attract some attention, namely "Defining Art Historically" and "What a Musical Work Is," essays that I thought he was likely to have taken note of, since he was indirectly a target of the critique of prevailing theories of arthood advanced in the former, and belonged to the editorial board of the journal that had published the latter.

His response, which I quote as best I can, remains engraved in my memory thirty years on: "What I think, Jerry, is that the paper on defining art is probably correct, but not interesting. Whereas the paper on musical works is so interesting, it hardly matters whether or not it is correct." I leave to others to assess the justice of those judgments, but as may be imagined, that was not the sort of comment, coming from someone of Danto's stature, that was easily forgotten by one just beginning to make his way in the field.

Jerrold Levinson
College Park, Maryland
September 2010

PART ONE

ART AND HISTORY

1 *Defining Art Historically*

The question of what makes something art is probably the most venerable in aesthetics. What is the artness of an artwork? Wherein does it reside? We would certainly like to know. We would certainly be interested to learn what ties together Dickens's *Oliver Twist,* Tallis's *Spem in alium,* Flavin's *Pink and Gold,* Balanchine's *Variations for a Door and a Sigh,* Wilson and Glass's *Einstein on the Beach,* the Parthenon, and countless other unknown and unsung objects under the common banner of art. After rejecting the many proposals made by philosophers from Plato to the present on grounds of narrowness, tendentiousness, inflexibility, vagueness, or circularity, one would appear to be left with no answer to the question at all, and perhaps a suspicion that it is unanswerable. Nevertheless, the question has been taken up in recent years and given a new sort of answer: the institutional theory of art, adumbrated by Arthur Danto and propounded explicitly by George Dickie. In short, the theory is that artworks are artworks because they occupy a certain place, which they must be given, in a certain institution, that of Art.[1]

---

[1] Dickie's definition of art runs as follows: "A work of art in the classificatory sense is (1) an artifact (2) a set of the aspects of which has had conferred upon it the status of candidate for appreciation by some person or persons acting on behalf of a certain social institution (the art-world)" *Art and the Aesthetic* (Ithaca: Cornell University Press, 1974), p. 34.

I

In this essay I would like to begin to develop an alternative to the institutional theory of art, albeit one that is clearly inspired by it. What I will retain from that theory is the crucial idea that artworkhood is not an intrinsic exhibited property of a thing, but rather a matter of being related in the right way to human activity and thought. However, I propose to construe this relation solely in terms of the *intention* of an *independent individual* (or individuals)—as opposed to an overt *act* (that of conferring the status of a candidate for appreciation) performed in an *institutional setting* constituted by many individuals— where the intention makes reference (either transparently or opaquely) to the *history of art* (what art has been) as opposed to that murky and somewhat exclusive institution, the *artworld*. The core of my proposal will be an account of what it is to regard-as-a-work-of-art, an account that gives this an essential historicity.[2] It is this which will do the work in my theory which the notion of artworld is supposed to do in the institutional theory. That art is necessarily backward-looking (though in some cases not consciously so) is a fact that the definition of art must recognize. To ignore it is to miss the only satisfying explanation of the unity of art across time and of its inherently continuous evolution— the manner in which art of a given moment must *involve*, as opposed to merely *follow*, that which has preceded it.

II

Before sketching my view in some detail, I want to remark on two major difficulties with the institutional theory. (I pass over the often-made charges that the theory is uninformative, and that the key notions of 'artworld' and 'conferral of status' are vague and artificial.)[3]

---

[2] The suggestions that regarding-as-a-work-of-art may be a primary notion and that the nature of art must be located in its historical development can be found in Richard Wollheim's *Art and Its Objects* (New York: Harper & Row, 1971), sections 40 and 60–63, respectively. It is those remarks that first prompted me to work out the view I am trying to present. I might add here that I use 'regard' in this essay as a broad term covering whatever is done in relation to an object so as to experience or interact with it.

[3] For useful criticism of the institutional theory see R. Sclafani, "Art as a Social Institution: Dickie's New Definitions," *Journal of Aesthetics and Art Criticism*, 32

The first problem is the implication that art making must involve a certain *cultural performance,* a ceremony or quasi ceremony, a kind of hand waving that draws into the fold. One must do something outwardly, and one must do it in relation to a certain social institution. On the contrary, I would urge that there can be private, isolated art that is constituted as art in the mind of the artist—and on no one's behalf but his or her own and that of *potential* experiencers of it. (I assume that *just that* is not enough to make the artworld, or else the notion becomes trivial and otiose.) Although in my scheme an art maker will *typically* have art and an existing society of art consumers in mind when producing an art object, this is not necessary. In no case *must* one invoke or accord with the shadowy infrastructure of the artworld to make what one makes into art. Consider the farmer's wife at a Nebraska country fair who sets an assemblage of egg shells and white glue down on the corner of a table for folks to look at. Isn't it possible that she has created art? Yet she and the artworld exist in perfect mutual oblivion. Consider a solitary Indian along the Amazon who steals off from his nonartistic tribe to arrange colored stones in a clearing, not outwardly investing them with special position in the world. Might not this also be art (and, note, before any future curator decides that it is)? The institutional theory comes close to conflating art and *self-conscious* art, art and *socially situated* art, art and *declared* art.

The second and main problem I find with the institutional theory is that the artworld must do all the work in specifying the *way* in which an object has to be presented or treated in order for it to be a work of art, whereas the notion of *appreciation* (the point of the enterprise) is not specified at all or only in the most general terms.[4] That is to say, we are not told enough about what the art maker must envisage must be

---

(1973); R. Sclafani, "Art Works, Art Theory, and the Artworld," *Theoria,* 39 (1973); T. Cohen, "The Possibility of Art: Remarks on a Proposal by Dickie," *Philosophical Review,* 82 (1973); A. Silvers, "The Artworld Discarded," *Journal of Aesthetics and Art Criticism,* 34 (1976); K. Walton, "Review: Dickie: *Art and the Aesthetic,*" *Philosophical Review* (January 1977); M. Beardsley, "Is Art Essentially Institutional?" in *Culture and Art,* ed. L. Aagaard-Mogensen (Atlantic Highlands, N.J.: Humanities Press, 1976). I share many of the misgivings expressed by these authors.

[4] Which even then may be subject to counterexamples, as well as being unilluminating in any case (cf. Cohen, "Possibility of Art"). Dickie's extremely general suggestion for the meaning of 'appreciation' is: "in experiencing the qualities of a thing one finds them worthy or valuable" (Dickie, *Art and the Aesthetic,* pp. 40–41).

done with his or her object by potential spectators. It seems, though, that some kind of specification of this must be essayed if making art is to be distinguished from making nonart. I believe the key to an adequate and revealing definition of art is to specify what the art object must be *intended for,* what sort of *regard* the spectator must be asked to extend to the object—rather than designate an *institution* on behalf of which some such request can be made. The trick, of course, is to do so without describing an intended way of regard given by fixed characteristics (e.g., with full attention, contemplatively, giving special notice to appearance, with emotional openness). It has been sufficiently shown that *that* sort of definition is doomed to failure, given the impossibility of locating a single unitary aesthetic attitude or regard common to all the ways we approach and have approached works of art, and given the ways unthought of in which we will undoubtedly be approaching some works in the future. The definition I will offer does not hamstring the kinds of regard that may eventually be given to artworks, yet gives the art-making intention the content it sorely needs.

III

The above-mentioned content is to be found in the actual historical development of art. My idea is roughly this: a work of art is a thing intended for regard-as-a-work-of-art, regard in any of the ways works of art existing prior to it have been correctly regarded. In the absence of any identifiable 'aesthetic attitude', how else can 'regard-as-a-work-of-art' be understood? Obviously, in adopting this proposal we are not analyzing art completely in nonart terms. Rather, what we are doing is explicating what it is for an object to be art at a given time with reference to the body of past art taken as unproblematic. But what it is for a thing to be art at any time can eventually be exhibited in this manner, by starting with the present and working backward. New art is art because of this relation to past art, art of the recent past is art because of this relation to art of the not-so-recent past, art of the not-so-recent past is art because of this relation to art of the distant past . . . until one arrives presumably at the *ur*-arts of our tradition—those to which the mantle of *art* can be initially attached, but which are art *not* in virtue of any relation to preceding objects. (I will return to the *ur*-arts in section VII.) Before stating a more careful definition, let me further attempt to explain the motives for its introduction.

The concept of artwork is unlike that of other sorts of things that surround us—e.g., cars, chairs, persons. *Artwork* seems to lack antecedently defined limits in terms of intrinsic features, even flexible ones—as opposed to car, chair, person. There is no question of determining in all cases that something is art by weighing it against some archetype or other. The *only* clue one has is the particular, concrete, and multifarious population that art has acquired at any point (that is, assuming, as I do, the nebulousness and/or inessentiality of that institution, the artworld). It appears almost obvious, then, that for a prospective object to count as art must be for it to be related in some way to those objects that have already been decided or determined. For a thing to be art it must be linked by its creator to the repository of art existing at the time, as opposed to being aligned by him with some abstracted template of required characteristics. What I am saying is that currently the concept of art has no content beyond what art *has been*. It is this content that must figure in a successful definition.

Let me focus on the central case of art-aware art makers. In such cases making an artwork is a conscious act involving a conception of art. But what conception of art can all such art makers, existing at different times and places, have in common? It seems the only possibility is a conception of art tantamount to all or anything that has been art until now—a concrete conception not equivalent to any abstract principle or generalization drawn from a survey of art's past. Art-aware art makers are thus those who connect their creations to such a conception and, in so doing, make them art. If they do not do this—if their activities involve no reference whatsoever to the body of artworks preceding them—then I think we fail to understand in what sense they are consciously or knowingly producing art. Given the abandonment of special aesthetic attitudes and/or artistic purposes, some connection of some sort between current artworks and earlier ones must logically be demanded of the putative art maker. It looks as if there are three likely ways in which the connection might be established: (i) by making something that will be externally similar to previous art works; (ii) by making something that is intended to afford the same kind of pleasure/experience that previous artworks have afforded; (iii) by making something that is intended for regard or treatment as previous artworks have been regarded or treated.

The first suggestion, while the simplest, clearly will not do. It is useless unless respects of similarity are indicated, since just about anything would be externally similar to some past artwork in some respect. But aside from that, artworks are just not to any great extent bound together by external similarity. For example, certain welded iron sculptures resemble portions of junkyards more closely than they do the sculptures that were their predecessors. External similarity to artworks is neither necessary nor sufficient for being an artwork. The second suggestion is more promising, but it fails too. There are two reasons for this: (1) the pleasures/experiences derived from art are not necessarily unique to art; (2) it is the *manner* in which artworks afford their pleasures/experiences, the *ways* in which one approaches or engages them *so that* they give those pleasures/experiences, which characterize them as art. To illustrate these points, imagine a drug that when ingested would provide a pleasure/experience akin to what one can have by listening intently to Beethoven's Quartet in C-sharp Minor, op. 131. Such a drug would not thereby be an artwork, although it would be a handy thing to have around. Furthermore, to focus on the pleasures derived from artworks is to emphasize the passive and resultant in the situation, as opposed to the active and causative—i.e., the way of taking the object. It is more reasonable to hold that an artist directing an object toward potential spectators is concerned intentionally with what is to be *done* with the object, as opposed to what might be *got* out of it, since spectators can only *directly* adjust themselves or behave with respect to the former. So I think we are left with the third suggestion as the only one around with which to build an account of what it is to be art.

IV

A definition that preserves my basic idea, but adds certain qualifications, is the following:

(I) *X* is an artwork = df *X* is an object that a person or persons,

having the appropriate proprietary right
over *X*, nonpassingly intends for regard-
as-a-work-of-art, i.e. regard in any way
(or ways) in which prior artworks are or
were correctly (or standardly) regarded.

Several comments on this initial definition are in order. First, there is
the phrase 'intends for'. This is to be understood as short for 'makes,
appropriates or conceives for the purpose of', so as to comprehend
fashioned, found, and conceptual art. Second, there is the notion that
the intent must be fairly stable ('nonpassing'), as opposed to merely
transient. In other words, it is not enough to turn an object into art that
one momentarily considers it for regard-as-a-work-of-art. Third, I
have construed regard-as-a-work-of-art as equivalent to ways of regarding past art only in so far as they are or were *correct* (or *standard*)
ways. If one omits this qualification, or appeals instead to *common*
ways of regard, or even *rewarding* ways of regard, the definition will
go awry. The following case illustrates this point.

Italian Renaissance portraits are presumably artworks. Suppose
they come to be regarded in a new and unprecedented way—viz., they
begin to be used as thermal insulation, and are found to be quite
suitable for this. And suppose, through an amazing decline in taste or
an unparalleled need for insulation, this manner of regard becomes the
rule. If we omit 'correctly' from our definition, or replace it by 'commonly' or 'rewardingly', then given the case as described, it follows
from our definition that anything subsequently intended by its maker
for use as insulation (e.g., a sheet of Fiberglas) would be an artwork.
Why? Because Renaissance portraits are past artworks that are regarded, are commonly regarded, and are rewardingly regarded as
insulation. This must be wrong. It can't be possible to turn all tomor-
row's Fiberglas production into art simply through general misuse
today of a certain class of portraits. To avoid this unwanted consequence, we *must* appeal to some notion of *correct* regarding for artworks.[5] Using Renaissance portraits as insulation is manifestly not a

---

[5] The notion of correct regard for an artwork is a difficult one to make out, but surely
relevant to it are the following considerations: (1) how the artist *intended* his work to
be regarded; (2) what manner of regarding the work is *most* rewarding; (3) the kinds of

correct way of regarding them, no matter how widespread or satisfactory such a use might be. And so on our definition nothing can become art through intentional reference to such a prior way of regarding artworks.

Fourth, the definition includes a proprietary-right condition. What this amounts to is basically *ownership*—you cannot 'artify' what you do not own and thus have no right to dispose of. All your intentions will not avail in such a case, because another person's intention, that of the owner, has priority over yours. (Of course, if owners are not opposed to your intention, they can grant you permission to make their possessions into artworks.) One standardly attains the right in question by creating an object, but notice that this will not always suffice— for example, if the object is created under contract during working hours while in the employ of a metal tubing company. (On the other hand, neither is it necessary to create something in order to have the right to 'artify' it, as witnessed by found art.) It might be thought that the proprietary-right condition would rule out varieties of conceptual art, but this is not so. One must just avoid the mistake of taking the art object in such cases to be simply and solely what the artist has described or pointed to (e.g., Marilyn Monroe, the Empire State Building, a slice of the life of a family in Queens—things that the artist clearly has no proprietary right over), rather than a directed complex of the description and the object.

Given a proprietary-right condition, it is somewhat problematic whether curators, promoters, exhibitors can turn nonart objects of the past into art objects of the present as blithely as is usually allowed. Imagine an art museum having mounted for regard-as-a-work-of-art a strange ornate receptacle whose original purpose is unknown. The object comes from an ancient Mexican culture thought to have died out. However, a well-documented descendant of the tribe, armed with

---

regard *similar* objects have enjoyed; (4) what way of regarding the work is optimum for realizing the *ends* (e.g., certain pleasures, moods, awarenesses) which the artist envisaged in connection with appreciation; (5) what way of regarding the work makes for the most satisfying or coherent picture of its place in the *development* of art. (For an illuminating discussion of some of these factors, see Walton, "Categories of Art," *Philosophical Review*, 79 [1970].) Nothing in the present paper depends on the exact analysis of 'correct regard', however. To understand my account of art one only has to grant that *there are* correct ways of regarding past artworks, whatever that might amount to.

full knowledge of its customs and practices, appears and successfully demands the removal of the receptable from public view (it is apparently a sacred ritual object, used for nocturnal royal baptisms, and not in any sense for appreciation). I maintain that the object in question does not just revert to being nonart—it never was art at all, because our present art establishment unknowingly lacked the right to make it such. This sort of case may be more prevalent than is generally imagined.

It will be useful to distinguish three kinds of intention which can realize the condition expressed in the definition: *intending for regard-as-a-work-of-art*. The first would be the *specific art-conscious* intention: intending for regard in the specific way or ways some particular past artworks (or class of artworks) have been correctly regarded. An example of this would be intending for regard in the way wire sculptures are to be regarded. The second is the *nonspecific art-conscious* intention: intending for regard in whatever ways any past artworks have been correctly regarded, having no particular ones in mind. The third is the *art-unconscious* intention: intending for regard in some specific way ϕ characterized in terms of intrinsic features, where ϕ is *in fact* a way in which some past artworks have been correctly regarded, though this fact is not known to the intender. An example of this might be intending for listening to with attention to timbre.

The first and second kinds realize *intending for regard-as-a-work-of-art* on a referentially *opaque* interpretation of that notion, whereas the third kind satisfies a *transparent* interpretation of it. Given the notion as readable in both modes, my definition thus allows (via the art-unconscious intention) for art makers ignorant of all artworks, all art activities, and all institutions of art. Such persons can be seen to make art if they intend their objects for regard in ways that *happen to be*, unbeknown to them, in the repertory of aesthetic regards established at that time. In such a case there is the requisite link to the prior history of art, but it is one such art makers are unaware of, though they have in fact forged it.

So cases of naïve activity can be cases of art making if they accord with the development of art at that point in the manner sketched. And I would insist that a theory must account for these cases. From where we stand such persons (e.g., the Amazon Indian mentioned before) are clearly making art—and it is not our recognition that makes it so.

V

The definition presented in the preceding section conveys in a fairly perspicuous fashion what I believe it now means for something to be an artwork. However, at the expense of some perspicuity but in the name of greater precision and flexibility, I offer a second definition that makes explicit the time-dependence of the status of 'artwork', clarifies the interpretation of 'prior artworks', and indicates more exactly what sort of definition of art I am giving.

(I_t) X is an artwork at t = df X is an object of which it is true at t that some person or persons having the appropriate proprietary right over X, nonpassingly intends (or intended) X for regard-as-a-work-of-art—i.e., regard in any way (or ways) in which artworks existing prior to t are or were correctly (or standardly) regarded.

An object can be an artwork at one time and not another. This definition recognizes that an object may not be an artwork from the moment of its physical creation, but may only become an artwork at some *later* date. It also allows for an object that becomes an artwork even subsequent to its creator's intending it for a certain regard, and even subsequent to the death of its creator.[6]

The first sort of case is relatively common. Any piece of found art serves as an example. The snow shovel involved in Duchamp's *Snow Shovel*, or the bottle rack in his *Bottle Rack*, became works of art at a certain time owing to Duchamp's appropriating them with a certain intention, whereas they existed but were not works of art before that time. The same goes for driftwood mounted and displayed in someone's living room, or potsherds and door handles touched by cura-

[6]There are three times of importance that should be distinguished if we are to get clear on this issue. One is the time of physical creation of the object, t_p. A second is the time of intentioned-object creation, t_i—i.e., the time at which the brute object is structured or transformed by a certain intention concerning it. Every artwork is, strictly speaking, an intentioned object. A third is the time of art-becoming, t_a. In the typical or normal case of art production $t_p = t_i = t_a$; in the case of found art, t_p is earlier than t_i, and $t_i = t_a$; in the case of the naïve creator ahead of his time (discussed below), $t_p = t_i$, and t_a is later than t_i.

torial intent in a museum of primitive art. Another kind of example would be a canvas that is undertaken and completed merely as a technical exercise but which after a few days' reflection is then viewed by its creator as for regarding-as-a-work-of-art. These things are art only *after* a certain intentional decision has taken place. Definition I_t makes this plain.

The second sort of case is less common, but I think a completely adequate definition of art must be capable of handling it. An example would be the following: A naïve or art-unaware creator makes an object Z at t, which he intends for a kind of treatment or regard that is not a correct way of regarding any artworks existing prior to t_1. However, it is a kind of treatment or regard that *will be* correct for certain artworks θ existing 200 years after t_1. I think we want to say that the naïve creator's work is art beginning around t_2 ($= t_1 + 200$) but not before. That is to say, Z becomes art 200 years after its intentioned creation, when the history of art, so to speak, catches up with what Z's creator was engaged in. It would be hard to deny at t_2 that Z was art; for, after all, it was created and intended for just the sort of treatment that θ's, which are recognized artworks at t_2, are correctly accorded. Z is art at t_2 because it was intended for a kind of regard which (unknown to its creator) turns out to be in the stock of standard regards for artworks at t_2. Z at t_2 can be seen as projected for a kind of appreciative activity which had become part of artistic tradition. However, before t_2 this cannot be seen. There is no plausible ground for considering Z to be art prior to t_2. Something cannot be art from the outset *just* in virtue of its future redemption by the evolution of art—only actual redemption will turn the trick then and there.

Definition I_t handles this case as desired. Z is an artwork at t_2 (and thereafter) because it is an object of which it is true at t_2 that someone rightfully and nonpassingly intended it (at t_1) for regard in a way in which some artworks existing prior to t_2 are correctly regarded. However, Z is *not*, according to I_t, an artwork at t_1.

So what sort of definition of art have we given? In short, a definition that explains what it is to be art at a given time in terms of what is art at previous times. To be art at t is to be intentionally related in the required way to something that is art prior to t. The present state of art shows us that certainly nothing more can be required. On the other hand, nothing less than this can be required if we are to locate a conception of art which will cover equally Donatello's *David* and Carl Andre's *Lever,* Mozart's *Jupiter* Symphony and Stockhausen's *Momente,* Shelley's "Ode to the West Wind" and John Berryman's *Dream Songs.* If there is now a univocal sense of 'art' in which all six items count as art, and count as such from the time of their creation, then I believe this sense is given (more or less) by definition I_t.

I can almost see readers shake their heads at this point and ask: But does this definition *really tell* me what art is? Doesn't it seem that I have to *know* what art is in order to use it? In fact, isn't the definition simply *circular,* in that it defines art in terms of art? This response is perfectly understandable, but it is nonetheless mistaken. True, there is something reflexive about the definition, in that it exhibits art as essentially referring to itself. But to eliminate this reflexiveness would be to eviscerate the term 'art' of the only universal content it now retains. If artworks at one time are essentially intentionally related to artworks at an earlier time, then on the assumption that definitions attempt to give essences, how could a definition of art fail to explicate artworks—to put it bluntly—in terms of artworks? Thus the *appearance* of circularity.

But, strictly speaking, I_t is *not* circular. What it does is define the *concept*: *being art at a given time* by reference to the *actual body of things* that are art prior to that time. True, one cannot tell what counts as art at *t* without its being granted what things count as art prior to *t*—but this is in fact just the way art itself works. Furthermore, and this also conforms to the reality of art, to the extent that it is unclear which objects *prior to t* are artworks, it will be equally unclear which objects *at t* count as art. True, one cannot use the definition to tell, all at once, what has, does, and will count as art at all times, but this is because the applicability of 'art' at any stage is always tied to its concrete, historical realization at that stage. That the definition is not circular if properly understood can be seen by reflecting that one doesn't have to know what 'artwork at *t*' *means* in order for I_t to *tell* you; one only has to grant that there is a set of things which are artworks prior to *t*—*whatever* they are and *whatever* that (viz., 'artwork') might mean.

The last point suggests another way of expressing the analysis of art that I offer, a way I think that removes any lingering suspicion of circularity. Basically, what I have proposed is that the *meaning* of 'art now' involves the extension of 'art previously'—that the *meaning* of 'art at *t*' is to be given in terms of the *extension* of 'art prior to *t*'. Formulating a variant of I_t to make this explicit, we have:

(I'_t) X is an artwork at t = df X is an object of which it is true at t that some person or persons, having the appropriate proprietary right over X, nonpassingly intends (or intended) X for regard-as-a-work-of-art—i.e., regard in any way (or ways) in which objects in the extension of 'artwork' prior to t are or were correctly (or standardly) regarded.[7]

It is clear that the *meaning* of 'artwork' is not involved in the right-hand side of this definition, but only its past *extension* at some point. Thus, I maintain that I'_t or I_t captures our present concept of art—and without presupposing that concept in doing so.

VI

On the view I have presented, which makes art a necessarily backward-looking affair, one may wonder how the *revolutionary* aspect of art can be accommodated. Surely, one might say, if art is continually looking to the rear, how can it change or advance? Won't it always remain the same? To begin to answer this let me first distinguish revolutionary from merely new or original art. A new artwork is simply one non-identical to any previously existing artwork. An original artwork is a new one significantly different in structural or aesthetic properties from any previously existing artwork. The production of original art could continue indefinitely without there being any additions to the stock of ways in which artworks are regarded. But by a revolutionary artwork I mean one for which any of the past ways of approaching art seems inadequate, inappropriate, pointless, or impossible; a revolutionary

---

[7]Note in this definition that when I speak of the extension of the term 'art work' at a time *t* this means the extension of the term at *t* as it is understood *now*—i.e., in its current usage.

artwork appears to be ultimately calling for a kind of regard which is totally *unprecedented*. It is plainly only revolutionary art that poses any difficulty for my analysis.[8]

Art that is revolutionary because it demands or requires a new approach to yield up its fruits to spectators is not per se a problem. A problem only arises for artworks—e.g., Dadaist ones—which are *intended* as revolutionary by their artists, that is to say, intended for treatment in a manner completely distinct from what has gone before. (Whether all intentionally revolutionary art is thereby revolutionary *simpliciter* is a complicated question I will not go into here.) Two strategies suggest themselves for reconciling my proposal to this important and characteristic mode of art making. One is to maintain that although consciously revolutionary artists desire that eventually their objects will be dealt with in unprecedented ways, to make them *art* they must initially direct their audiences to take them (or try taking them) in some way that art *has* been taken—otherwise, what can we make of the claim that they have given us *art*, as opposed to something else? The art-making intention of consciously revolutionary artists may thus have to be a covertly disingenuous one, somewhat along these lines: 'My object is for regarding in any way artworks have been regarded in the past (but with the expectation that this will prove frustrating or unrewarding, thus prodding the spectator to adopt some other point of view—this being my ultimate intention)'. The secondary intention embodies the true *aim* of such art, but the primary intention must be present to make it *art* at all.

A second strategy for dealing with this issue perhaps does less violence to the outward stance of the consciously revolutionary artist. This requires a liberalization of what regard-as-a-work-of-art amounts to. Instead of construing it as restricted to past correct ways of regarding artworks, broaden it to include completely unheralded types of regard so long as one is directed to adopt such regards in conscious op-

---

[8]Most movements in art are revolutionary in a *weak* sense, in that they ask for or involve *some* specific new ways of taking art objects, but few such movements (perhaps none before Dadaism) deny the applicability of *all* past ways of taking art objects. For example, Impressionist paintings certainly are and were to be approached in specific ways (e.g., synoptic vision from a distance) which were not in practice for previous paintings (e.g., those of the Neo-classicists). But there clearly remained ways in common in which they were to be regarded. Thus, weakly revolutionary art does not challenge the historicity of the art-making intention.

position to those past correct ways. The liberalized version of regard-as-a-work-of-art then reads as follows: regard in any way (or ways) in which prior artworks are or were correctly (or standardly) regarded, or *in some other way in contrast to and against the* background of those ways. (Call this 'regard-as-a-work-of-art*'.) If this second strategy is adopted, one simply substitutes 'regard-as-a-work-of-art *' for 'regard-as-a-work-of-art' in I, I_t, and I'_t to get definitions adequate to revolutionary art. Whereas the idea of the first strategy was that self-aware revolutionary artists must on one level intend the existing correct art regards, freeing them to intend on another level some entirely new regard, the present strategy does not insist that they should directly intend the existing ways at all, but only that they should project the new way *in relation* (albeit antagonistic relation) to its predecessors. If they fail to do even that, I think there are no grounds on which one could deny that they fail to make art. Of course it is open at that point for some other member of the art community, assuming they have the proprietary right, to appropriate the would-be artist's work at a later date with the right intention, and so bring it into the sphere of art. The point is, to get a revolutionary mode of activity to *be* art it is necessary that its creator (or the creator's subsequent proxy) should consciously nod in the direction of past artistic activity.

Which of the two strategies is ultimately preferable as a way of accommodating the historical definition of art to revolutionary art making is a question I will not attempt to settle here. However, for the sake of simplifying succeeding discussion, I will assume for the remainder of this essay the workability of the first strategy and tentatively adopt it. This means that definition I, I_t, I'_t, properly understood, will be viewed as adequate to revolutionary (as well as evolutionary) art.

VII

The view presented so far suggests the following picture of art's evolution. Artworks are objects projected for regard, at least in part, in ways past artworks have been standardly regarded. These artworks, if at all original, will differ from those of the past more or less markedly, and will therefore optimally call for ways of regard (which the artist has usually envisaged) somewhat different from ones already in practice. But then *those* ways will become part of the tradition of art appreciation, allowing for newer works to be constituted as art by reference to *them*, and so on. There is thus a deeper continuity in the development of art than is generally noted. Artworks of a given period do more than *follow* their predecessors. They are even more than causally *descended* from them, more even than testimonies to the influence of style, medium, and subject matter. Rather, those predecessors are *necessarily involved* (via the ways in which they have been regarded) in the intentional structure which determines their successors as art. What art becomes depends conceptually, not just causally, on what art has been.

Definition I_t analyzes being art at a given time in terms of what is art prior to that time. The definition can be applied at the present time, and then at as many times back into the past as one chooses, until one at last reaches the origins of art[9] itself (i.e., the *ur*-arts). Having reached that terminus, however, we could then use it as the starting point of another kind of definition of art, one that begins with the hypothesized origins of art and yields serially all that has sprung from it up to the present. This would be a *recursive* definition and would reveal art as a recursive domain. Before giving one, let me tell a somewhat oversimplified tale.

The time predates the beginning of art. Certain societies are thriving in which various activities are going on. In some of these activities objects (including events) are produced and then treated in a certain manner. These activities can be identified retrospectively as the *ur*-arts of our tradition. At some point, new activities arise wherein objects of a different sort are produced which are intended for treatment as objects of some *ur*-art are. The new activity then becomes associated with that of the *ur*-art, under a wider category, that of *art*. At this stage, an activity of object making can only become art by relating itself to the purposes of some (or possibly more than one) *ur*-art; the objects of the activity can only be artworks by being thought of in connection with the ends toward which the objects of some *ur*-art were directed. Once a new activity and its objects are established as art, *further* activities and objects now enter the realm of art through intentional

[9] That is, *art* as understood in present-day Western culture.

connection with *them*. Eventually one arrives at art as we find it today.[10] Let me state the definition suggested by this tale:

(II) Initial Step: Objects of the *ur*-arts are artworks at t_o (and thereafter).[11] Recursive Step: If X is an artwork prior to t, then Y is an artwork at t if it is true at t that some person or persons, having the appropriate proprietary right over Y, nonpassingly intends (or intended), Y for regard in any way (or ways) in which X is or was correctly regarded.

I believe this definition very nearly generates all and only those things that have been, are, or could be artworks, given the concept of art we presently have.[12] And yet, it is easy to understand how the definition might strike one as inoperative or incomplete. For recursion depends on the initial step, the initial step speaks of the *ur*-arts—but one has not been told what the *ur*-arts *are*! I would be happy to supply their description if I knew what they were, but I don't. Nor does anyone. Is there, then, a way to save II from this charge of having merely programmatic status?

I think there is. Our explanation of the *idea* of an *ur*-art given earlier in this section can be turned to provide a method in principle for *actually identifying* the *ur*-arts. Basically, one just has to ask, of objects at points successively farther into the past, and until the questioning

[10] The story I tell here is consonant with a remark made in passing by Walton, "Review: Dickie," concerning the historical development of art. I should also emphasize that the story is told from the point of view of art as the production of artworks for appreciation by spectators, and not from the point of view of art as the release of psychic energy or the expression of artistic impulses by creators. As should be apparent, it is only the former idea of art that this essay is concerned to elucidate.

[11] Let t_0 be the time roughly at which the *ur*-arts begin spawning non-*ur*-art artworks.

[12] Wollheim, in section 60 of *Art and Its Objects*, mentions the possibility of a general *method* of identifying all works of art which would be recursive in form. He concludes that as a method of identification it would not work, the reason being the inability to formulate rules of transformation adequate to the concrete evolution of art in the distant and also the recent past. He has in mind rules that would operate on given structures or styles and spew out altered ones according with the direction taken by art at a given juncture. The problem is especially acute for the modern period: "whereas earlier changes in art affected only the more or less detailed properties of a work of art, e.g., painterly vs. linear, in the art of our day one work of art generates another by the supersession of its most general properties . . . e.g., hard-edge painting as the successor

process terminates, "What makes this count as art?" More formally, and relying on definition I for simplicity of exposition, the procedure would be as follows: Begin with a group of related recent artworks, A. Then by I, A consists of objects that were *intended* for regard R, where R is the manner of regard *in fact* standardly accorded certain earlier artworks, A'. Now focus on A'. By I, A' consists of objects that were intended for regard R', R' being the regard in fact standardly given an even earlier set of artworks, A''. A, A', A'' . . . thus form a backward-reaching series of artworks whose principle of continuation should be clear. Eventually one arrives at a set of objects, A_0, which are such that objects succeeding them are intended for regard as A_0's are standardly regarded, but there are no objects X preceding A_0 such that A_0's were intended to be regarded as X's in fact standardly were. A_0 is then one set of *ur*-artworks. Of course to put this method into practice would be exceedingly difficult. It would require a great deal of knowledge of artists' intentions and actual appreciative practices of societies to perform successfully the backward trace on an initial sample. And one would have to do this for many such samples in order to unearth all the *ur*-arts of Western culture. However, *if* one did carry out this procedure for a wide, well-chosen variety of current paradigm artworks, one would have pretty good reason to be confident that all of the *ur*-arts had been ferreted out from their historical hiding places. At that point, if one liked, one could substitute for the place-holder '*ur*-arts' in II a specification in *intrinsic* terms of the activities that archaeological investigation had revealed to be *in fact* the roots of Western art. This would in effect 'complete' the recursive definition of art.

It is important to note that while the basic definition (I_t) is put forward as capturing the general concept of art which we now employ, the recursive definition aims only at displaying in a revealing way the *extension* of that concept. The basic definition explains the shared sense in which Donatello's *David* is art in 1420, Shelley's "Ode to the

---

of abstract expressionism" (p. 126).

Granted that Wollheim is right about this, I think the possibility of a definition such as I propose is unaffected. The definition does not depend on rules of stylistic change but, rather, simply on the rule I have argued for as constraining the intention that makes something art. The definition, unlike Wollheim's projected method, does not of course generate all works of art in terms of their intrinsic observable features, but only in terms of certain external intentional relations they bear to other objects.

West Wind" is art in 1820, and Stockhausen's *Momente* is art in 1970. The recursive definition, though, does *not* explain the sense of 'artwork'. It would be implausible to maintain that our conception of artwork entails that all such things have ultimate ancestors of the sort that the *ur*-arts are. Surely the notion of *ur*-arts, whether characterized positionally or intrinsically, is not part of the content of a judgement that something is an artwork. What the recursive definition does, though, is to generate all artworks by a method that closely parallels and illuminates the actual historical process of the evolution of art.[13]

VIII

Having spelled out the theory I have to offer, in which the concrete history of art replaces the institutional network of art at center stage, I wish to remark further on certain issues over which my theory and the reigning institutional one differ. In particular, two issues that can be put in the form of questions: (1) Is art making in essence an *internal* (intention) or *external* (conferral) matter? (2) Need a person have a special *position* in the artworld to create certain sorts of artworks? I will consider these briefly in turn.

(1) Consider an object made by an artist, and intended for regard-as-a-work-of-art, but not offered, not placed, not mounted, not circumscribed, advertised, or sold—in short, not 'done with' in any way. Isn't

---

[13]The recursive definition justifies perhaps more strongly than the basic definition my titular claim to be 'defining art historically.' Of course, I am not defining art simply as that which has a history; just about any activity has a history. But neither am I defining it simply as that activity whose historical source is the *ur*-arts. For some of the ultimate ancestors of art (viz., the *ur*-arts) may in fact also be ultimate ancestors of activities other than art. If that is so, does our recursive definition unwantedly generate those nonart activities as well as that of art? No, because in order to be art something must not only have an *ur*-art as ancestor but must also be descended from it in a particular fashion—namely, via intentional relations invoking previous standard regards. It is a good bet that even if there *are* other activities which have *ur*-arts as ultimate ancestors, they do not exhibit *that* principle of descent.

Now that we have concluded our discussion of the *ur*-arts as they figure in the recursive definition, it might be observed that objects of the *ur*-arts are artworks that do *not* conform to our basic definition of the meaning of 'artwork', namely I_t (or I'_t). For there are no artworks and correct regards prior to the *ur*-arts. I_t (or I'_t) thus strictly speaking only tell one what it means for any thing *apart from an ur-art object* to be an artwork. Objects of the *ur*-arts are, by contrast, simply stipulated to be artworks.

this still an artwork? The institutionalist might argue that having the intention *just is* conferring a certain status, and no other 'action' is necessary. But if having the intention is always *thereby* conferring status, while any overt conferring must *anyway* include the requisite intention (or else it is mere sham, 'playing the artist'), then this seems to me tantamount to admitting that intention is really all that is essential to art making. This is not to say that art makers are very *likely* to *just* intend an object for regard-as-a-work-of-art. It is highly unlikely that they will fail to act so as to draw attention to their works. Artists naturally try to increase the chances of their works getting the regard they intend (both for their benefit and for ours).

On the other hand, the fear that taking everything outward away from the essentials of art making would mean a world pullulating with artworks of the unfashioned kind, generated at every turn of thought—that fear is groundless. It is relatively easy, natural, and common to summon the requisite nonpassing intention in connection with an object one has made, but difficult, unnatural, and rare to form such an intention in connection with an object one has not made—it takes a certain courage and occasionally perversity to convince oneself of the right or point of so appropriating what nature or another person has already fashioned. Only if one overlooks the fact that these intentions are not gong to arise in many people will one suppose the need for an art maker to perform an action on behalf of the artworld, in order to account for the observation that not one person in a hundred has transformed his or her kitchen stove into a work of art.

(2) Arthur Danto gives an answer to question two in speaking of 'the making of artworks out of real things'—i.e., the appropriation/minimal-fashioning mode of art. "It is analytically true that artworks can only be *by* artists, so that an object, however much (or exactly) it may resemble an artwork is not *by* whoever is responsible for its existence, unless he is an artist. The mere object [e.g., a brass bushing] perhaps does not lie outside their [viz., non artists'] powers. But as an artwork it does." [14] If 'artist' in these remarks meant only 'person who at some time makes an artwork' then I would have no trouble agreeing that an artwork can be brought into being by nobody other than an

---

[14] A. Danto, "Artworks and Real Things," *Theoria*, 39 (1973): 14.

artist. However, the context makes it clear that 'artist' means there something more like 'person with an established position in the art-world, one of whose main concerns is the making of artworks' (call this 'artist*'). Danto believes that tracing a 'real thing' to someone who is not an artist* defeats any claim it might have to be art. I cannot accept this. I do not believe the 'conventions of ascribing'[15] the predicate 'is art' are like that at all. The only reason I see why one would maintain they are is based on confusing *established* or *professional* art with *all* art. I am willing to admit that commanding a special position or having a certain background may be relevant to making brass bushings into *recognized* art, or making them into *significant* art, or into artworks that will affect the *development* of art—but *not* to making them into art *simpliciter*. The wittiest riposte of the season is presumably utterable *only* by a member of high society; art per se no more operates on this level than philosophy does.

IX

The concept of art has certainly changed over time. There is no doubt of that. It is thus worth emphasizing in this final section that my analysis is aimed just at capturing what the concept of art is *at present*—that is, what it *now* means for an object created *at any time* (past, present, or future) to count as art at that time, rather than what it meant at the time of the object's creation.[16] Claiming that the analysis indicates what it means, say, for something created in 1777 to be an artwork thus does not entail or require that the concept-of-art$_{1977}$ is identical with concept-of-art$_{1777}$. Presumably these two concepts would classify the field of objects into art and nonart somewhat differently. And calling Rembrandt's *Night Watch* a work of art in 1777 undoubtedly meant something different from what is meant by calling it that in 1977. However, given my analysis of it, I think the only part of concept-of-art$_{1977}$ that could unarguably be held to have been *missing*

---

[15] Ibid., p. 12.

[16] This is the distinction, difficult to grasp firmly, between: (i) what it *means at present* for something to *be art at the time of its creation*, and (ii) what it *meant at the time of its creation* for something to *be art at that time*.

from concept-of-art$_{1777}$ is the permissibility of objects as art which are unfashioned or only minimally fashioned by their creators.[17] Whereas concept-of-art$_{1977}$ associates *The Night Watch* with former stainless steel bars, coat racks, cardboard cartons, and goats' heads, concept-of-art$_{1777}$ served in part to differentiate *The Night Watch* from such things. This major conceptual changeover occurred, as we know, around 1920 as a result of the Dadaist movement.

I have already noted that the historical definition of art provides a powerful and direct explanation of the inherent unity and continuity of the development of art. In short, for something to be an artwork at any time is for it to be intentionally related to artworks that precede it—no more and no less. And the historical definition, if accepted, helps to dispel the lingering effects of the so-called 'intentional fallacy' understood as a claim about the irrelevance of artists' intentions to correct or full appreciation of their works. For if artists' intentions are recognized as central to the difference between art and nonart, they are not so likely to be offhandedly declared irrelevant to an understanding of artworks once seen as so constituted. In particular, the historical definition indicates the overwhelming importance for appreciation of those past artworks/genres/ways of regard/modes of treatment which artists connect to their current productions through their art-making intentions.

The historical definition of art also casts a useful light on the fact that in art anything goes, but not everything works. The reason anything goes is that there are no clear limits to the sorts of things people may seriously intend us to regard-as-a-work-of-art. The reason not everything works is that regarding-something-as-a-work-of-art necessarily involves bringing the past of art to bear on what is being offered as art in the present. That the present object and past regards will mesh is not guaranteed.[18] The interaction of the two sometimes satisfies imme-

---

[17]On the other hand, it seems clear that there was much in the concept-of-art$_{1777}$ that is missing from the concept-of-art$_{1977}$. Concept-of-art$_{1777}$ was surely more restrictive than its 1977 counterpart; one could reasonably maintain that it included specification of structural features, technical requirements, purposes, ends, and even minimum aesthetic effectiveness. Thus, to get from concept-of-art$_{1777}$ to concept-of-art$_{1977}$ one must delete all such artistic specifications, while broadening the sphere of creation beyond that of fashioning; what is retained throughout is the common thread of reference by art at any time to the sort of treatment earlier art was accorded.

[18]Thus it is clear that the historical theory of art leaves room for the sense of 'conceptual strain' accompanying some works of art (e.g., *Bottle Rack*) that Anita

diately, sometimes only after an interval. Sometimes we are shocked and unsettled, but recover and are illuminated. Sometimes we are forcibly impelled to adopt new modes of regard, leaving old ones aside. But sometimes we are simply bewildered, bored, bothered—or all three—and in a manner that is never transcended. In such cases we have artworks, all right, but such works don't work.

In conclusion, let me say that I do not mean to deny that there is a common practice of art, and a group of people bound together under that umbrella, nor do I deny that artworks need to be understood in relation to their cultural situation. What I do deny is that the institutions of art in a society are essential to art, and that an analysis of arthood must therefore involve them. The making of art is primary; the social frameworks and conventions that grow up around it are not. While the sociology of art is of great interest, the essence of art does not lie there but instead in art's relation to its contingent history. The theory I offer sketches in its main outlines what this relation is.

Silvers ("The Artworld Discarded") accuses the institutional theory of eliminating. The strain arises from the clash between the *nature* of the object and the *kinds of regard* typically accorded earlier artworks, which regards had to be invoked in making the object in question art.

2 *Hybrid Art Forms*

Not all art forms are pure or thoroughbred. Some are hybrids. This is a distinction artists and their audiences are attuned to and which seems to have some creative and critical significance. In this essay I will begin to examine the notion of hybrid art form. My opening query is the natural one: What exactly are hybrid art forms, i.e., when do we count an art form as hybrid?

First, some examples. These will serve as intuitive data, though revisable in light of subsequent reflection. Collage, kinetic sculpture, shaped canvas painting, musical installations, concrete poetry, opera (particularly Wagnerian music drama), music with color sequences (such as Scriabin envisaged), mime with musical accompaniment, calligraphic dance, cliché-verre,[1] sound film, happenings, the Wilson and Glass form of "opera," and a whole variety of mixed-media activities that can be loosely grouped together as "theater."

The wrong sort of answer to the question of why we think of these as hybrid art forms is that works belonging to them are complex and contain structural elements of various kinds. Rembrandt's or Raphael's paintings are complex and operate in several respects at once: two-

---

[1] Nineteenth-century technique combining drawing and photography: drawing on transparency through which a photographic plate is then exposed to light.

dimensional patterning, three-dimensional depth, disposition of bodies and movements, and psychological interaction. Yet no one thinks of such paintings, however much they seem to be doing, as hybrid artworks. A somewhat more tempting, though ultimately unsatisfactory, answer is that we think of art forms as hybrid when they can be decomposed, conceptually, into two or more distinct artistic activities or ostensible media. This is not right, however, because with ingenuity, almost any art form can be conceived so as to appear the combination of simpler artistic strands. String quartet composition can be thought of as writing for trios coupled with writing for solo violin. Full-figure sculpture becomes the coupling of head sculpting and body sculpting. Pottery is analyzed as an art of shaping clay joined to art of glazes and finishes. Traditional poetry becomes the generation of proselike sequences of words joined to a craft of rhyme and metrical stress. Traditional painting is decomposable in thought into activities of drawing and coloring or, alternatively, figuring and backgrounding. Dance falls out as silent bodily movement joined to rhythmic music.

I think it is probable that the common notion of a hybrid art form is not a purely structural one. It is not the intrinsic features of works in a hybrid form that mark them as such—or at least it is not *only* such features. The dimensional multiplicity or conceptual decomposability of the works in an art form does not itself establish hybrid status; nor does the employment of two or more clearly different sorts of materials.

Rather, hybrid status is primarily a *historical* thing, as is, in a way, being a biological hybrid. An art form is a hybrid one in virtue of its development and origin, in virtue of its emergence out of a field of previously existing artistic activities and concerns, two or more of which it in some sense combines. Hybrid artworks always manifest significant structural or dimensional complexity to be sure, but *that* they are hybrid works, and what *manner* of hybrids they are (i.e., what they are hybrids *of*), can be made clear only by reference to historical conditions at the time of creation and in terms of media that have already been constituted as such. The components of a putative hybrid must be locatable somewhere in the preceding culture and must be plausibly seen as having come together in the result. In short, hybrid art forms are art forms arising from the *actual* combination or interpenetration of earlier art forms. Art forms that have *not* so arisen, though they may be intellectually analyzable into various possible or actual structural or mediumistic components, are not hybrids in the primary sense. (We might call them *Gedanken* hybrids.) As I remarked above, European figurative painting is not normally considered a hybrid art. But note that if it had derived developmentally from an art of two-dimensional ornamental patterning gradually grafted on to an already established technique of representing empty three-dimensional spaces through perspective grids, then one might be inclined to think of that familiar art as a hybrid one.

The distinction between true hybrids and *Gedanken* hybrids has some importance, I believe, for appreciation. Roughly, it is this. If works are artistic hybrids, in the primary sense, they must be understood in terms of and in light of their components; if they are only *Gedanken* hybrids, then they *need not* and, in most cases, *should not* be so understood. If art form *C* has emerged as a combination of *A* and *B*, then we appropriately understand or gauge the *A*-aspect of a *C*-work (e.g., the painterly aspect of a Cubist collage) against a background of norms, styles, and concerns attaching to the preexisting practice of art *A*. With a *Gedanken* hybrid, there is no appropriate appreciative background carried by the components so distinguished.

The lesson I am stressing here is that the history of development of an art form remains relevant in understanding works in the form as it currently exists; the fictitious history of a *Gedanken* hybrid is, on the contrary, of virtually no relevance. One more illustration. It would generally be more apt and revealing critically to note photographic or theatrical effects in a silent film than to be on the lookout for calligraphic ones, given the actual genesis of the film medium. Of course, film *might have somehow* (!) evolved in virtue of greater and greater figurativeness, depth, and animation in what was originally calligraphy as we know it—but it *did not*, and that is the point. How germane comparisons and references are is not independent of developmental background.

Looking back at our opening list, we can recognize traditional opera as a combination of song and drama, shaped canvas as a combination of painting and sculpture, concrete poetry as a combination of poetry and graphics, kinetic sculpture as (perhaps) a combination of sculpture and dance, and the Wilson and Glass operas as a combination of song, drama, painting, dance, mime, and possibly other arts as well. These are not just "theoretical" breakdowns of the complex arts in each case; rather, they denote real antecedents, existing independently of and prior to the hybrid in question, which are brought into interaction through the work of artists. In most cases artists are explicitly aware of the combinations they are effecting, but we need not hold this as a necessary feature of hybrids so long as there are preexisting artistic media or modes that can be plausibly identified as contributors to the resulting art form.[2]

At this point the reader may be forgiven for believing that I have gone back on an earlier conclusion. I have just allowed that hybrid art forms can be thought of as art forms that display two or more media in combination. But is medium not a structural category, so that hybrid status is after all a purely structural affair, determinable by mere inspection? No, for *medium* in the present context is *not* equivalent to *material* or *physical dimension*. Rather, by a *medium* I mean a developed way of using given materials or dimensions, with certain entrenched properties, practices, and possibilities.[3] 'Medium' in this sense is closer to 'art form' than to 'kind of stuff'. Hybrid art forms, which merge different media, *may not* involve different materials or dimensions (e.g., prose-poems, "fusion" jazz), and art forms that *do* clearly involve different materials or dimensions, *may not* be ones we normally recognize as hybrid (e.g., ceramics, folk song).[4] Only a historically informed analysis, not a purely material or dimension-individuating one, will capture the aesthetically important notion of hybrid art in actual use. A hybrid art form is an art form with a "past,"

---

[2] I might note in passing that though I have characterized hybrid art forms as ones in which two distinct *arts* are combined, there are artistic phenomena we might call hybrid in which an existing art and some preexisting technological process or semi-artistic activity are brought together; for example, neon and laser sculpture, computer music, computer graphics, video installations, earthworks (the latter joining sculpture to a body of construction skills).

[3] One might point out that distinct arts can share a common material and still represent different media—e.g., stone sculpture vs. stone architecture.

[4] To spell this out, prose-poetry combines two verbal media, "fusion" jazz two musical media—symphonic and improvisatory. Ceramics employs two materials, clay and glazes, while song has two dimensions, music and words. Ceramics and traditional song are complex but nonhybrid arts. Of course, this does not prevent us from ahistorically viewing traditional song as a combination of poetry and music, a perspective that fits nineteenth-century lieder, however, better than Appalachian ballads or Balinese chant.

and it is its miscegenetic history that makes it hybrid, not just the complex "face" it presents.

We are now, curiously, in a position to characterize what a pure, or thoroughbred, art form is in contrast to a hybrid one. A thoroughbred art form is simply one that has *not* arisen from the interpenetration or interaction of previously existing art forms. So put, two things are immediately evident. One, the notion of a thoroughbred art form is logically secondary to that of a hybrid, being in fact the notion of a nonhybrid. Two, the ordinary categorization of an art form as thoroughbred or nonhybrid will usually be a relative or limited one, not positing an absolute purity reaching back to the dawn of Western art. For example, to call a current art form nonhybrid will usefully be to say that with respect to its *recent* or *critically relevant* past it has been constituted as an art form in a fairly stable fashion, as opposed to having lately evolved from other activities in the artistic environment. There may indeed be some *absolutely* pure or nonhybrid arts, but the important distinction seems to be between arts whose antecedents are still evident in them, and appropriately taken into account in critical response, and those whose artistic predecessors, if there are any, have long since receded from the appreciative or interpretive picture.

II

The art forms on our opening list are all hybrids, then, in displaying a complex character in virtue of derivation from two or more earlier forms (or media) of art, but they are manifestly not all the same *sort* of hybrid. I have used the word "combination" to cover the relation of hybrid to antecedents in general, but we should now recognize that several logically distinct varieties of combination are involved. What varieties are there? It seems to be there are three important ones, which can be labeled *juxtaposition* (or addition), *synthesis* (or fusion), and *transformation* (or alteration).

In juxtaposition or addition the objects or products of two (or more) arts are simply joined together and presented as one larger, more complex unit. The individual components are recognizably the same as in their pure manifestation and retain their identities as instances of their respective art forms—though the particular shape and quality of each would in many cases be inexplicable without reference to the other. Artistic products explicitly described as involving *accompaniment* are invariably of this sort—e.g., song accompanied by guitar, mime accompanied by flute, silent film accompanied by piano roll. But also included would be dance inspired by and viewed along with calligraphic drawings, symphonies performed simultaneously with light shows, music/sculpture installations, and, for the most part, the Wilson and Glass *Einstein on the Beach*. In all such cases, the contributing elements are distinct and separable from one another; they form a whole by summation and not by merging or dissolution of individual boundaries. Juxtapositional hybrids consist of elements imaginable in isolation from the others to which they are joined and which, so isolated, would count as bona fide (if peculiar) instances of the arts entering into the hybrid. This is not at all to deny that in such hybrids the whole is often (aesthetically) "more than" the sum of its parts, but only to point out the recognizable allegiance the parts still owe to their artistic origins. Most (though not all) artistic entities described as multi- or mixed-media phenomena would be what I am labeling juxtapositional hybrids.

In synthesis or fusion the objects or products of two (or more) arts are brought together in such a way that the individual components to some extent lose their original identities and are present in the hybrid in a form significantly different from that assumed in the pure state. When A is *fused with*, as opposed to merely *added to*, B, the resulting hybrid object cannot be said to contain isolatable elements or parts that are *strictly speaking* instances of A or of B, and so cannot be viewed as basically the linear addition of such elements or parts. When A and B are fused, each is modified by the other so that the result neither is nor contains anything that can be comfortably recognized as an A or a B in the original sense. Opera of the Wagnerian sort, viewed as a synthesis of song and drama, is a prime example of this. If Wagnerian opera were a juxtapositional hybrid, what it might amount to would be some players performing self-contained songs with orchestra and other players acting out a theatrical drama at the same time or in regular alternation. But Wagnerian opera is not a drama *plus* song—it is sung drama or dramatic song. In Wagnerian opera the same players are both singing and acting—they sing while acting and act through singing. No part of what is taking place on stage is *strictly* an instance of either dramatic art or the art of lieder, yet the relation of such opera to these antecedents remains unmistakable.

Somewhat different examples of the synthetic sort of hybrid, involving nontemporal arts, are concrete poetry and shaped canvases. Concrete poetry is clearly a hybrid deriving from ordinary poetry and graphic art. But a concrete poem, although it has a poetry *aspect* and a graphic *aspect,* is not itself an ordinary poem or a straightforward example of graphic art, nor does it contain parts which are. It is not a matter of a poem merely *joined* to a picture; it is a *single* object that is *as much* a picture as it is a poem, but, again, is not strictly assignable to either in terms of traditional categories. Rather, it is a poem-picture. We can say that it is *partly* a poem and *partly* a graphic work—but not, in contrast to juxtapositional hybrids, that it has *parts* that straightforwardly count as poems or graphic works.

The phenomenon of shaped canvases, such as Frank Stella has produced, can be regarded similarly. They are not comfortably denominated paintings, because their irregular, nonrectilinear, attention-demanding boundaries are contrastandard for paintings and not comfortably considered sculptures because of features—flatness, one-sidedness, wall-mounting—which are contrastandard for sculpture. Nor, on any natural division, do they contain *parts* that are straightforwardly paintings or sculptures, although they can be aptly described as partly paintings, partly sculptures. Painting and sculpture are fused in the genre of shaped canvases—as one could argue they are fused in a different manner in collage or assemblage (Schwitters, Rauschenberg, Johns)—and not simply added together. The result is a painting-sculpture. A juxtapositional hybrid of the two arts, on the other hand, would be something like this: a painting and a related sculpture considered as an artistic unit and viewed together. This would be painting plus sculpture, an art form that does not at present exist.[5]

A third variety of hybrid art form, which I label transformational, is closer to the synthetic model than to the juxtapositional one, but differs from the former in that the arts combined do not contribute to the result in roughly the same degree. A transformational hybrid of *A* with *B* is not *halfway* between *A* and *B*; it is basically *A* transformed in

[5] Except in the context of ballrooms and palace hallways.

a *B*-ish direction. A good example of this sort of hybrid is kinetic sculpture. Kinetic sculpture can be seen as ordinary sculpture modified in the direction of dance. It is not an equal fusion of the two, but rather an incorporation of some of the special or distinctive *characteristics* of dance into what remains recognizably *sculpture,* though in an extended sense. The result could not reasonably be called an instance of dance, even in an extended sense—though of course it might be so *metaphorically.* Contrast this with synthetic cases—e.g., concrete poetry, shaped canvas. In a synthetic hybrid of *A* and *B* the result can be described as a (nonstandard) *A* with *B*-ish features (e.g., a pictorial poem) or *with roughly equal claim* as a (nonstandard) *B* with *A*-ish features (e.g., a poemlike picture). A certain parity or symmetry is involved. But not in a transformational hybrid. A kinetic sculpture is a terpsichorean sculpture, but not (except metaphorically) a sculptural dance. Whether a synthetic or transformational hybrid results from the combination of two arts would seem to be largely a function of how similar the arts were antecedently in respect of materials, temporal status, and other characteristics. The more similar, the more likely there will be fusion instead of alteration.

Note that in both synthetic and transformational cases, some *essential* or *defining* feature of one or both arts is challenged, modified, or withdrawn. Thus a shaped canvas painting is no longer (automatically) *rectangular,* a kinetic sculpture is not longer *stationary.* This marks a difference between transformational hybrids and a wide spectrum of cases of *influence* of one art form on another. For example, Stuart Davis's paintings of the 1940s, with their jazz-inspired visual rhythms, are not transformational hybrids of paiting and jazz because they remain wholly and unequivocally paintings, with all standard features intact. Of course, this weaker sort of artistic cross-fertilization is equally fascinating and worthy of analysis as the phenomenon of hybridization, but it is, I think, distinguishable from it.

As a final illustration, let us consider how silent film might be categorized with respect to the typology I have loosely sketched. Taking it to be a hybrid, most significantly of theater and photography, is it a synthesis of the two, or is it a transformation of the photograph in a theatrical (or narrative) direction? Even though the early description "moving pictures" supports the latter suggestion, it is not conclusive. For "photographed theater" seems just as apt. In defense of a synthesis classification, a silent film is in extended senses perhaps both a kind of photograph (a kinetic one) and a kind of theater (a nonbodily one).

III

One striking and central significance hybrid art forms have, and which partly explains their appeal to and pursuit by artists, is this. Hybrid art forms, and the works they encompass, tend to be *symbols of creativity itself*, of forcefully and purposively putting things together, of welding items previously disparate and unconnected into new and more complex unities. To create is typically to reorganize and recombine pre-existing materials into unprecedented wholes. The hybridization of art forms does precisely this, not at the level of single works and their components, but at the level of artistic categories and their antecedents. Thus individual hybrid artworks, in virtue of the arts they display in combination, acquire a significance as emblems of creative activity in general.

The interaction of the separate components or strands in a hybrid artwork—whether harmonious, antagonistic, synchronic, or anarchic—is surely the most obvious feature of attention in such works. This seems particularly so when the hybrid involved is a juxtapositional hybrid of two purer temporal arts—e.g., music, mime, dance, abstract color film. Artists and audiences are interested in how the two sequences of events will be related to each other—whether they will unfold in parallel fashion, in explicit opposition, or in an apparently sublime indifference. We are on watch for sparks of similarity and contrast to be struck from events in different realms occurring simultaneously. One question that arises regarding this central feature is the following: How is the relation between the two developing patterns—e.g., a musical one and a mimetic one—in such a hybrid different from the relation between different structural aspects in paradigm non-hybrid arts—e.g., meaning and sound in a poem, melody and bass in a baroque sonata? In giving only a brief answer to this broad question, two points seem worth noting. The first is that in hybrid works the patterns being related are usually in *physically* distinct media with very different propensities and histories. The second point is that the patterns in a hybrid are experienced as *purposely* combined and having been put together against some resistance—as opposed to the union being experienced as a natural fact or as having an origin so remote it does not impinge on the consciousness of the perceiver. We hear meaning and sound, or melody and bass, as individual components only by a special act of attention; by contrast, we can hardly remain unaware of the forceful combination of artistic elements which yield hybrids such as *Einstein on the Beach.*

One objective realizable in a temporal hybrid through a particular relating of the components is the stressing of common features or isomorphisms between two arts. In juxtaposing dance and calligraphic drawing in a certain way, the calligraphic aspect of dance and the dancelike aspect of calligraphy can be highlighted and our perception of each strand focused and oriented by the proximity of the other. We will tend to see different things in the dance if the drawings are not present, and vice versa. Juxtaposing A with B in an artistic hybrid may, in Nelson Goodman's terms, change the properties that A or B exemplifies in the joint context, relative to what it would exemplify on its own, or at least affect the prominence of what each so exemplifies.[6]

In closing, I want to remark on perhaps the most intriguing thing about hybrid art forms, particularly those that draw from several artistic sources. It is that there seem to be basically *two* sorts of overall effect that such hybrids achieve—but these effects are almost diametrically opposed. We can label these effects the *integrative* and the *disintegrative.* In the former case the multiple hybrid presents an image of richness and complexity, but one in which individual elements work together or cooperate toward a common end, so that we are, as it were, made to see the one in the many. Hybrids that are formally *synthetic,* in the sense explained above, will naturally incline toward this effect— for example, Wagnerian opera, with its ideal of a complete, all-encompassing experience, achieved through an intimate union of symphony, song, drama, and stagecraft. In the other case—the disintegrative— the complexity and richness function in service of an ideal not of unity, but of complete fragmentation and rampant uncoordination. Works that achieve this sort of effect—a natural one for *juxtapositional* hybrids, in which individual artistic contributions do not formally

---

[6]Cf. Nelson Goodman, *Languages of Art* (Indianapolis: Bobbs-Merrill, 1968), chap. 2.

meld with their neighbors—do so through a kind of cognitive overload. There is too much going on, too much to deal with, more disconnection than one can hope to overcome through one's own integrative efforts at appreciation. We are forced to see the many, as the one is nowhere to be found. Disintegrative effects—which characterize, for example, portions of *Einstein on the Beach*—often seem symbolic or allusive of the psychological fragmentation, informational bombardment, and pervasive anomie of contemporary urban life. This makes them fascinating, though also a bit depressing. Which do you prefer—an honest and at times transfiguring image of our present disunified condition, or a heroic presentation of a unity that perhaps remains outside our grasp in ordinary life? Wilson and Glass or Wagner? But there may be no need to choose.

Additional Notes

1. I have pursued an investigation of one (or rather, two) of the hybrid art forms mentioned in passing in section II, in my "Song and Music Drama," in *What Is Music?* ed. P. Alperson (New York: Haven Publications, 1987), pp. 283–301.

2. Apropos of my remarks on *Einstein on the Beach* in section III, it now appears that there is nothing essential to Glass's developing style which constrains it to the production of artworks of predominantly disintegrative effect. One in which—to my limited experience, confined to CDs—it is integrative effects that are more to the fore is Glass's "opera" *Akhnaten*, written eight years after *Einstein*. Naturally enough, the underlying themes may have something to do with this divergence—the religious unification of a people around a credo of sun-based monotheism, rather than the explosive implications of humankind's having wrenched secrets from the depths of the universe regarding its fragile construction. Musically, much of *Akhnaten* is less frenetic and more lyrical than *Einstein*, and textually, it is more straightforward and communicative. *Akhnaten* appears less juxtapositional, and more synthetic, in its employment of the recognizable individual media it brings together. For example—judging from illustrations at least—stage movement, costumes, and sets are in less overt tension with the work's concurrent musical and textual elements. (This may have something to do with the fact that *Akhnaten* is more totally Glass's in conception, whereas *Einstein* was a fairly equal collaboration with Robert Wilson.) In any event, *Akhnaten*, like *Einstein*, is a marvelous achievement and eloquent testimony to the power of "hybrids."

3 *Refining Art Historically*

I

Recent aesthetics has seen much critical discussion of intentionalist and of institutional theories of art.[1] Concurrently we have witnessed the rise of historicist accounts of art.[2] As a related development, attention has been drawn to the idea that the concept of art is somehow indexical, or that it involves rigid designation.[3] Finally, although

[1] See Richard Wollheim, *Art and Its Objects* (Cambridge: Cambridge University Press, 1980), supplementary essay 1; Monroe Beardsley, "Redefining Art," in *The Aesthetic Point of View* (Ithaca: Cornell University Press, 1982); Göran Hermerén, *Aspects of Aesthetics* (Lund: Gleerup, 1983); Ben Tilghman, *But Is It Art?* (Oxford: Basil Blackwell, 1984); Timothy Bartel, "Appreciation and Dickie's Definition of Art," *British Journal of Aesthetics*, 19 (1979); Robert MacGregor, "Art—Again," *Critical Inquiry*, 5 (1979); Jeffrey Wieand, "Can There Be an Institutional Theory of Art?" *Journal of Aesthetics and Art Criticism*, 39 (1981); Susan Feagin, "On Defining and Interpreting Art Intentionalistically," *British Journal of Aesthetics*, 22 (1982); George Todd, "Art and the Concept of Art," *Philosophy and Phenomenological Research*, 44 (1983); Randall Dipert, "Art, Artifacts, and Regarded Intentions," *American Philosophical Quarterly*, 23 (1986); George Dickie, *The Art Circle* (New York: Haven Publications, 1985), and my review of it in *Philosophical Review*, 96 (1987). I stress that this is a very partial list.

[2] See Arthur Danto, "Artworks and Real Things," *Theoria*, 39 (1973), and *The Transfiguration of the Commonplace* (Cambridge: Harvard University Press, 1981); Anita Silvers, "The Artworld Discarded," *Journal of Aesthetics and Art Criticism*, 34 (1976); Graham McFee, "The Historicity of Art," *Journal of Aesthetics and Art Criticism*, 38 (1980).

[3] See James Carney, "Defining Art," *British Journal of Aesthetics*, 15 (1975), and "What Is a Work of Art?" *Journal of Aesthetic Education*, 16 (1982); Peter Kivy,

37

this latter will not be my concern, as a backlash to all the above there has been a noticeable resurgence of attempts to define art in the traditional way, that is, aesthetically.[4]

Against this bewildering array of theoretical offerings, I wish to raise my voice, once again, in defense of my own suggestion on this matter, offered some years back.[5] I have found that my view of the issue has puzzled those who took note of it because of its peculiar way of fusing certain of the above tendencies, of locating itself within the logical spaces of these various orientations. At least, that is what I suspect. My own view can be described as intentionalist *and* historicist, *non*institutional, and what might be called *internally* indexical. I am taking pains to air it again, with some refinement, for one reason. It still strikes me, nine years later, as superior to any other view that has been put forward, judged on the two grounds of extensional adequacy and insight into the nature of art today. No other view I am aware of seems as close to capturing the only thing it can now mean to make something art.

What, then, is the view? In short, it is that an artwork is a thing (item, object, entity)[6] that has been seriously intended for regard-as-

---

"Aesthetic Concepts: Some Fresh Considerations," *Journal of Aesthetics and Art Criticism*, 37 (1979); Robert Matthews, "Traditional Aesthetics Defended," *Journal of Aesthetics and Art Criticism*, 38 (1979); Joseph Margolis, *Art and Philosophy* (Atlantic Highlands, N.J.: Humanities Press, 1980); Catherine Lord, "Indexicality, Not Circularity: Dickie's New Definition of Art," *Journal of Aesthetics and Art Criticism*, 45 (1987). The idea that art is a rigidly designated natural kind is justly criticized in Thomas Leddy, "Rigid Designation in Defining Art," *Journal of Aesthetics and Art Criticism*, 45 (1987). Although I recognize a certain indexical element in one mode of art making, I hasten to add that it is no part of my view that art is anything like a natural kind.

[4]Monroe Beardsley, "An Aesthetic Definition of Art," in *What Is Art?* ed. H. Curtler (New York: Haven, 1983); William Tolhurst, "Toward an Aesthetic Account of the Nature of Art," *Journal of Aesthetics and Art Criticism*, 42 (1984); George Schlesinger, "Aesthetic Experience and the Definition of Art," *British Journal of Aesthetics*, 19 (1979); Harold Osborne, "What Is a Work of Art?" *British Journal of Aesthetics*, 21 (1981); Richard Eldridge, "Form and Content: An Aesthetic Theory of Art," *British Journal of Aesthetics*, 25 (1985). Schlesinger's account is interestingly criticized by Douglas Dempster in "Aesthetic Experience and Psychological Definitions of Art," *Journal of Aesthetics and Art Criticism*, 44 (1985), and the retreat to aesthetic theories in general is effectively criticized by Noël Carroll in "Art and Interaction," *Journal of Aesthetics and Art Criticism*, 45 (1986).

[5]See Chapter 1, above.

[6]I include the terms in parentheses partly in response to a complaint registered by Göran Hermerén that my theory as stated "cannot handle post-object art" (*Aspects of*

a-work-of-art—i.e., regard[7] in any *way preexisting artworks are or were correctly regarded.*[8]

As explained in my earlier essay, this formula is to be understood as allowing for either a transparent or an opaque reading of the embedded underlined phrase, corresponding to two rather different modes of art making, two rather different ways of realizing the art-making intention. On the one reading, someone can be making art in virtue of directly intending an object for a complex of regards (approaches, attitudes) such as: ⟨with close attention to form, with emotional openness, with awareness of symbolism⟩ without having in mind or invoking intentionally any particular past artworks, genres, movements, traditions. On the other reading, someone can be making art precisely in virtue of directly intending an object for regard *as some particular* past artwork or artworks are or were correctly regarded, without having in mind or invoking intentionally any specific regards or sets of regards intrinsically characterized.[9] In the first instance, we

---

Aesthetics, p. 62). I never meant for "object" in my definition to be understood narrowly, as restricted, for example, to those medium-sized bits of drygoods you can get your hands on. By "object" I meant, and mean, *any thing whatsoever.* Thus, material objects are of course comprised, but also words, thoughts, structures, events, situations—whatever is in some way identifiable, indicatable, able to be picked out, at least in thought.

[7] It should be understood that *regard,* in this formulation, has a sense larger than merely *view,* or even *consideration,* encompassing more active modes such as *taking, treatment, approach, engagement with,* and so on. It is meant widely enough to cover, in the abstract, any mode of interaction with an object that could be proper to some work of art. In invoking an umbrella notion of regard-as-a-work-of-art, I am, as indicated in my earlier essay, following Wollheim's lead in section 40 of *Art and Its Objects.* The reading I give this phrase, however, as just explained, is probably broader than what Wollheim had in mind.

[8] In my original essay (see Chapter 1, above) I develop this basic definition in three variants: a simple and uncluttered one, similar to what has been given here; a second in which the status of being an artwork at a given time is explicitly introduced; and a third, which makes manifest the manner in which the analysis renders the meaning of "artwork" at a time in terms of the extension of "artwork" at an earlier time. I have made one change in the wording of the simple formula I will work with in this essay. The phrase "nonpassingly intends" in my original definition has been replaced by the phrase "seriously intends," this being less of a strain on the English language. In any case, whichever phrase is used the idea I insist on is not sobriety of character, but rather firmness, stability of intent—i.e., actually meaning it. It is no part of my proposal to exclude joking, whimsical, sardonic, or irreverent works of art, or acts of art making.

[9] It should be noted that (i) regarding something *as* a work of art is subtly different from (ii) regarding something *as if it were* a work of art (when one believes/knows it is not); and thus, *intending* something for regard of the first sort is not the same as

might say, certain intended regards make something art because they
happen to be regards past artworks were properly accorded. In the
second instance, by contrast, the intended regards make something art
because they are *explicitly* of the form: regards such and such past
artworks were properly accorded—whatever those might turn out to
be, characterized in themselves. For future reference we can call the
two modes or intentions of art making I have been contrasting the
intrinsical and the *relational* ones.

I said above that this view is intentionalist, historicist, indexical after
a fashion, and noninstitutional. It's intentionalist because it gives priority to an individualist, agent-based notion of what art is and how it
comes to be, insisting that a certain intentional orientation of persons
toward their products or activities is a sine qua non of the status of art.
It's historicist because it acknowledges directly the manner in which
art making at a given time is essentially connected with and logically
presupposes art making at preceding times, so that options for art
making at later dates are necessarily conditioned or affected by options
for art making at earlier ones. It's indexicalist in the limited sense that
it recognizes as one of two primary modes of art making the relating of
a given thing intentionally to other things that are merely indexically
or demonstratively invoked (e.g., "as artworks *before now* were correctly regarded," "as *those things* were appropriately taken"). Finally,
it's noninstitutional because although it grants that a certain sort of
background or context must minimally exist for art making to occur,[10]
its conception of this is rather spare—roughly, a preceding history of
human activities of the right sort to which an agent can refer in
intention, in whole or in part, knowingly or unknowingly. In any
event, the background or context required need not be institutional or
practicelike, in Dickie's or Danto's full-blown senses. It needn't be
an *artworld*, which I take to be at least a type of social structure

---

intending it for regard of the second sort. Though I cannot investigate this difference
here, I wish it to be clear that it is only the first sort of intent that I hold to be definitive
of art making.

   [10] This is somewhat complicated by the matter of those items that turn out to be the
ur-artworks of all subsequent histories or traditions of art. (See Chapter 1, above.) If
they *themselves* are counted among the artworks—and it is arguable whether they
should be, it being perhaps a matter for stipulation—then at least certain temporally
remote artworks are art *not* in virtue of *any* connection to a preceding context of
activities, however minimal.

or community; an art *history*—meaning just any prior art activity—uninstitutional and unselfconscious even, will suffice.

Although I cannot here recall all the considerations that led me to this view, I will try to reproduce something of the basic motivation involved. If one reflects on the varieties of art and art making in the past half century, one cannot help but be struck by the fact that, intrinsically speaking, there are simply no holds barred. Anything, seen from the outside as it were, *can* be art. At the same time, that hardly means that everything now *is* art, that there is no distinction worth capturing, and yet we would be profoundly dissatisfied to learn that all that remained of arthood was a purely trivial marker such as the condition of having been *called* or *dubbed* "art." Still, on the other hand, the return to a traditional notion of aesthetic aim or aesthetic experience seems blocked by the undeniable evolution of art beyond this sort of contemplative, perceptually based conception, as evidenced by Conceptual art, Minimal art, Performance art. So it seems we must seek something more substantial than the merely verbal default notion of art, but less restrictive than classical accounts with respect to the intrinsic character of both the entities that can be art and the kinds of engagement they are envisaged to receive, and yet, unlike what institutional theories offer, something that can plausibly be seen to be an essential aspect of art making from its earliest phases, in or out of social contexts, through all periods of art making, from the most traditional and paradigmatic to the most outré and avant-garde.

In company with others, I suggest that this essential aspect presents itself most clearly in the stripped-down activities of present-day artists of the latter sort. So consider such an ostensible artist, Jaspers. Jaspers directs our attention to a pile of wood shavings on the floor, a green three-by-five index card tacked to his wall, and the fact that Montgomery is the capital of Alabama. He names this set of things *John*. He then *says* that this is his latest artwork. We, however, not willing to acquiesce in the merely verbal notion of arthood, take the matter as not yet settled. We ask him what does he *mean* by saying that assortment is an artwork. He might reply that he doesn't mean *anything* in so saying. If that's *true,* then very probably it isn't an artwork. But suppose he does mean something, but he's not sure what. We try to help him out. Perhaps he is projecting this assortment for aesthetic delectation? No, he's not interested in that. Perhaps he is trying to make a statement?

No, he doesn't think so, and in any case, why wouldn't he just put an announcement in the newspaper? Perhaps he is simply acknowledging that in designating this assortment he is acting as an agent of the artworld? No, unlikely as it might seem, he has no connections with the artworld, has never read art criticism, and is innocent of art theory in any robust sense.

Running out of ideas, we press him to consider *why* he calls *John* art, and finally hit upon this form of the question: What does *John* have to do with all those other things that are art—i.e., that have been antecedently acknowledged as art? In other words, what is the connection between *John* and all prior art? Surely there must be some connection, or else we are at a loss to understand what could be meant by *John's* being art. Jaspers's eyes light up. We sense we are on the right track. Perhaps he thinks of his item as intrinsically resembling some earlier art? No, Jaspers very decidedly thinks of *John* as fresh, bold, original— really different from other things he's seen. Perhaps he believes it will offer experiences similar to what some earlier art provided. No, once again, Jaspers feels *John* has something unprecedented to offer, that it will affect people in a wholly new way—if approached, of course, in the right fashion. Aha, we exclaim, what fashion is that? There are two moves Jaspers could make at this stage, it seems. He could try to describe, in intrinsic terms, how he would like *John* to be approached, or he could just say that he would like *John* to be more or less approached, at least at the outset, as certain other indicated things are or have been approached. In the first case, if the approach described is one we can identify as properly attaching to some preexisting art, then we will be satisfied we understand what Jaspers meant in calling *John* art. And in the second case, if the indicated things are some selection out of, or even the entire body of, preexisting art, then we will be again satisfied that we have located a nontrivial sense for Jaspers's utterance. The connection looked for has been established: Jaspers would in effect be saying, "This is to be dealt with, at least initially, as you have dealt with (all or some of) that." If there is another plausible way of securing a connection, subject to the restraints on analyzing the concept of art reviewed above, I do not see what it could be. Nor, I suspect, do Jasper or any of his confreres. Yet the connection proposed in this case is arguably one that, in one form or another, can be located in any recognizable case of art making, at any historical moment.

The account is an intentional one, as I have stressed. Like several of its competitors, it sees the large nugget of truth in the notion that, in the current cultural situation, art is anything that is intended to be art,[11] and attempts to transmute this insight into something less circular and uninformative. Now, the appeal to human intentions in this context, as in many others, is often thought to be problematic because it is thought, variously, that the objectivity of art and its meanings will be jeopardized, that one is having truck with unverifiable entities, that the publicness of artworks will be undermined, and so on. But to appeal to intentions—or intentionality—in explicating the concept of art making is not to commit oneself to any particular view of how an individual's intentions are embodied in the world, or the part of the world that is the particular situation at hand. Intentions are, I suppose, psychological states or properties of the individuals who have them, but nothing constrains us to construe them as psychic occurrences or flashes of will. It is, in principle, possible to get at the intentions governing a given work, particularly that which determines whether the effort in question *is* art. In most cases, this is suggested by the outward face of the object, its context of creation, the process by which it came about, the genre it appears to belong to. It is fairly infrequently that skepticism about the manner in which an object is *really* being projected will push us beyond surface features and situational clues in search of a veritable intention that is at odds with them. But if and when it does, we are hardly at a total loss. People can be queried, journals consulted, outside pronouncements attended to, subsequent behavior studied, the remainder of a corpus considered. So I will take it that if being intended to be dealt with in a certain manner is in fact what makes something art, we need not worry that this would make arthood an occult thing.[12]

One last proviso of a general nature. Wittgenstein's attack against essentialism, and thus against efforts to give classical analyses of ordinary concepts by displaying their elements and how they are logically put together, has persuaded many philosophers of art, beginning with

[11] Not, of course, to be confused with the cruder and emptier slogan "Art is anything that is *called* art," which is aptly criticized by Beardsley in "Redefining Art" (p. 313).

[12] For some helpful remarks on the embodiment of intentions in artistic situations, see Stephen Davies, "The Aesthetic Relevance of Author's and Painter's Intentions," *Journal of Aesthetics and Art Criticism*, 41 (1982).

Morris Weitz and Paul Ziff, to pack up their tents and retreat when faced with matters of definition.[13] The skeptical warnings here were a useful corrective, but it seems that Wittgensteinians in art, as elsewhere, exaggerate the extent to which cultural concepts fail to have extractable, fairly serviceable, essences. That a concept may *change* over time is certainly no reason not to try to discern what it basically amounts to at any given time. That a concept may lack *strictly* necessary and sufficient conditions of application, which is probably the case for all save those explicitly introduced in a formal context, is not reason enough to totally abandon the attempt to theorize in a definitional vein—if seasoned with a grain of salt—as to the nuclear operating conditions of the concept. Surely we can aspire to say more than that a concept is elusive, contextual, or open to the future. We may provisionally assume, at least, that it's not a case of hopelessly diffuse strands of similarity—shards of sense—and accordingly try to tease out the most central core of meaning we can discover.

II

My suggestion, again, is that an artwork, as the term is used today, is a thing that has been seriously intended for regarding-as-a-work-of-art—i.e., regard in any way preexisting or prior artworks are or were correctly regarded. When the formula is read in its transparent guise, so that it affirms as art certain items intended for intrinsically characterized regards that an agent has in mind, it is subject to a certain kind of misconstrual, which I will now try to ward off. The problem is that the formula may easily be thought to be *too broad,* since it seems that many nonartworks (e.g., traffic signals) are indeed regarded, and were intended to be regarded, in some way (e.g., with attention to color) that some prior artworks (e.g., Impressionist paintings) are and were correctly regarded.

The solution to this problem is that only *relatively complete or total* ways of regarding are to be allowed as substitution instances of this formula: not *single, isolated* ways of regarding, as we would ordinarily

[13]See Richard Eldridge, "Problems and Prospects of Wittgensteinian Aesthetics," *Journal of Aesthetics and Art Criticism,* 45 (1987), for a judicious review and assessment of the force of Wittgensteinian qualms about art theorizing.

individuate them, but only *complexes* or *ensembles* of such. Thus, ⟨with attention to color⟩ would not *by itself* count as a way some past artworks have been correctly regarded, but only as *part* of some rather more fully characterized orientation toward an object; otherwise, of course, the definition would indeed end up inadvertently embracing, in addition to traffic signals, political maps, rug samples, graphic displays, microscope specimen slides, and so on. Something closer to a comprehensive way of regard properly brought to bear on, say, almost any easel painting would be this constellation: ⟨with attention to color, with attention to painterly detail, with awareness of style, with awareness of art-historical background, with sensitivity to formal structure and expressive effect, with an eye to representational seeing, with willingness to view patiently and sustainedly . . .⟩ Anything now intended for more or less *this* complex treatment or way of regard, we may be sanguine, would have difficulty not counting as an artwork.

Someone can make something art by intentionally projecting it for a sort of regard earlier art was in fact properly accorded. But we see that these must be *integral* regards if the formula is to be valid. The backward-looking invocation must be not just to a single *part* or *element* in the complex way some preceding art was correctly regarded, but to a *total package or overall approach*. This means that a would-be art maker, envisaging kinds of object-treatment intrinsically conceived, must have a fairly filled-out notion that *as a whole* matches, or meshes with, some treatment in the preexisting register of ways artworks were correctly approached. One who intends an object for ⟨looking at⟩ does not automatically make an artwork even though paintings are, indeed, correctly looked at. One only effects artwork status in this mode by intending, and thus implicitly adverting to, a relatively *inclusive* way of regard which was, as it happens, correctly carried to some earlier art—though one might be typically unable to articulate explicitly all the elements of the complex regard intended.[14]

---

[14] A worry that might arise here is whether the complex way of regard (call it γ) correctly accorded some past art will need to have been *uniquely* accorded to those or other artworks, if the problem currently under discussion is not to resurface. In other words, suppose that very complex was also properly, and commonly, brought to bear on another class of things, zorks, which do not appear to be artworks. Then if I now seriously intended an object for regard as zorks are correctly regarded, and thus for γ, would that make the object art? Would it also serve, in revisionary fashion, to make all zorks into art? Though I have gone along with these questions so far, in truth I do not

Finally, we should recall that the sort of misfiring of the definition I have been here concerned to forestall is an issue only for one of the two modes of art making recognized on my analysis, that involving an intrinsical (or art-*unconscious*) intention as opposed to a relational (or art-*conscious*) intention. In the first mode, agents and potential artists can be oblivious of art, in general and in particular, having no objects or tradition or history in mind that they strive to relate themselves to, but only certain ways they envisage what they are making being taken, being done with, being for.[15] As we have seen, if these as a whole are *in fact* in the repertoire (i.e., that of past art regards), then such making *is* art making and must be recognized to be. In the second mode, on the other hand, where agents have explicitly in mind particular past artworks, or art genres, or art forms, or art movements, or even art as a whole, and make their own efforts art by intentionally relating it to these, in the manner prescribed, then the problem of misfiring does not arise. Anything proposed for regard *explicitly* as some identified chunk of the artistic past, near or remote, was properly regarded, pretty clearly counts as art in this post-Duchampian age—and does so, it would seem, with little room for contest.

Two more points about this contrast of art-making modes deserve to be noted. First, the relational, art-conscious mode is undoubtedly the more *common*, statistically speaking, as one would discover by surveying in mind the history of art making in our world—i.e., the number of art makers *completely* oblivious to all preceding and surrounding artistic efforts, who do not mentally relate what they are doing to *anything* done before them with certain aims, is no doubt fairly small, represented mainly by isolated (H. Rousseau-like, or R. Crusoe-like) cases here and there, and probably a larger cluster toward the murky beginnings (the cave paintings of Lascaux and Altamira?) of anything one could reasonably call art in a sense connecting them (those beginnings) to the various traditions of art we have now. Historical survey

---

think they pose a genuine problem. *Could* there really be, for instance, nonart objects that as a matter of fact are properly regarded or taken in the *full, complete* way abstract Expressionist paintings (say) are, but which remain, nevertheless, *non*art? I suggest not.

[15] My account is here in strong contrast to Danto's, whose theory makes all art making *necessarily* into art-conscious art making. This strikes me as rather the wrong sort of contemporary-art-centered art theorizing.

aside, the art-conscious mode of art making is even more obviously the dominant mode *today*. In particular, it fits naturally with the reflexive, self-referential, self-conscious tendency of all *modernist* art, though, if I am right, it is more fundamental than that specific tendency of modernism (which, as Steinberg and others have stressed, itself yields a special kind of content),[16] and instead characterizes the vast majority of artistic makings at all times.

Second, making art in which one envisages ways, intrinsically conceived, that one's effort is to be regarded, can easily *coexist* with the making of art through the conscious relating of one's effort to some preceding artistic context. It's clear that in such cases, surely the most usual of all, the explicit backward historical acknowledgment guarantees the effort its art status, preempting or sidelining whatever status the intrinsically characterized intended regards would have secured for the effort on their own account. This "mixed" case—mixed in that both intrinsic and relational thoughts concerning intended treatment are present in agents' attitudes toward their creations—falls for me under the rubric of the art-conscious art-making intention, since the relational element (the thought of prior art) itself assures the art status of what is made.

III

In this section I discuss a second objection that can be lodged against my proposal. Rather than being thought too *broad* on the grounds that many correct past art regards were also purposely accorded many clearly nonart objects, the analysis may be thought to founder because the notion of *correct* art regards cannot itself be made out within the prescribed terms of the analysis. Monroe Beardsley has registered this objection as follows:

> "The notion of correct regard for an artwork is a difficult one to make out," Levinson concedes in a footnote. But it is one of the crucial elements of the definiens. Since he makes it clear that 'commonly' or 'rewardingly' cannot be substituted for 'correctly', I am inclined to

[16] Leo Steinberg, "Other Criteria," in *Other Criteria* (London: Oxford University Press, 1978).

fear a dilemma here. Either we give a general account of 'correctly' in terms of some version of taking an aesthetic interest in X or else we make an open-ended list of specific 'ways of regarding' that have been permitted in the past and that will among them probably permit just about anything in the future. In the end, this definition may [not be] usable.[17]

One is not surprised to find Beardsley seeking to show that any viable definition of art will need to fall back on aesthetic interest at some point. But I submit that his specific charge mistakes the basic idea of the account I was developing, which was to undisguisedly sidestep characterization of art or correctness of regard in qualitative terms. Just as the intrinsic nature of the objects that are art at any time develops historically, so do the modes of interaction or approach that count as correct for them as artworks; they vary and evolve from one period to another, from one art form to another, from one genre to another. Certainly this latter cannot now be confined to *aesthetic* appreciation, in anything like its classic sense, for that is simply too constricting given the variety of appropriate treatments, for art recent and remote, which need to be comprehended.[18] Indeed, I still think the question of what are correct—admissible, valid, appropriate—ways of dealing with art at a given time is a difficult, and important, one. But it was not then, nor is it now, my aim to essay a full-scale answer to it. My attempt at a rough sketch of considerations that correctness of art treatment in general might involve, in the footnote Beardsley alludes to (note 5), was perhaps misleading insofar as it suggested that the validity of my analysis of art (or artwork) presupposed the adequacy of that sketch or some refinement of it. I don't think it does.

The way I see the matter is rather this. Possibly there is no general analysis to be given of what correct ways of regarding art end up being at any given phase in art history, for any specified group of artworks. All I require is that there is a *fact* to the effect that such and such are (were) the correct ways of regard for those works at that period, just as

[17] *The Aesthetic Point of View*, p. 302.

[18] This has been well argued by a number of contemporary writers. See George Dickie, *Art and the Aesthetic* (Ithaca: Cornell University Press, 1974); Timothy Binkley, "Piece: Contra Aesthetics," *Journal of Aesthetics and Art Criticism*, 35 (1977); Robert Schultz, "Does Aesthetics Have Anything to Do with Art?" *Journal of Aesthetics and Art Criticism*, 36 (1978); Noël Carroll, "Art and Interaction."

there is a *fact* that so and so objects are (were) the artworks of a given past period. Then what my analysis claims is that being an artwork *now,* say, consists in no more and no less than being intentionally related to *those prior objects* and/or *those prior ways* in the manner I have described. This can come about by either of two routes: through a directly indexical act of art making, invoking preceding art in an explicit manner, and thence the correct regards associated with it, or through an art-making intention effective because explicitly directed on a way of regard that in fact figures in a rather large, though concrete, set—that of all prior correct art regards that have emerged up to the present.

Is it not part of the historical record, at *some* point, that during a given *earlier* period, certain things are artworks—taken, accepted, certified, and known to be artworks—and certain ways of dealing with them acknowledged as correct ones, correct for them as art?[19] Let this be granted. Then my analysis tells you what it is for something to be art *subsequently* in relation to that historical record—that descriptive account of the preceding art scene—as given. An analogy comes to mind here. Suppose you want to find out who are the present-day descendants of Charlemagne. Well, it must first be granted that there *was* a Charlemagne, that some particular person was he, around 800, presumably. You might then be able to ascertain his progeny in the immediately succeeding years if you had very good sources. But now return to the present. You could tell who among us now are the descendants of Charlemagne if you knew—if it were granted you— who counted as descendants in the *preceding* generation. And you could ascertain who in that preceding generation were descendants if you were granted who among the *still preceding* generation were descendants, and so on. At each stage you can say who the descendants of Charlemagne are, how to pick them out, if you are vouchsafed who they are in the previous period.

---

[19]The notion of correct regard that I need must indeed be understood with the *as art* proviso, if matters are not to go awry in virtue of the existence of regards correctly carried (in some sense) to paintings, say, *as investments.* But this is no more of a problem than before because all I presuppose is that this notion has an *extension,* not what its *analysis* might be. Whatever it *means* to say that, at some time, such and such were regards properly carried to artworks *as art,* clearly this was *true* for some such regards and not others.

It is the same, I am suggesting, with the concept of art at the point to which it has now evolved. It is an *almost purely historical* notion, where what is essential to being art is having the right sort of (intentional, as it turns out) relation to one's artistic predecessors—and the same can be said, if pressed, of those predecessors, and of their predecessors, and so on.[20] The series presupposes, it is clear, that at any time there is a truth of the matter, however muzzy around the edges, of what counted as artworks and correlative proper art regards at preceding times. The muzzier that fact is for any given time, the muzzier will be the limits of what can end up counting as art at a subsequent time. This is a consequence I accept, since it strikes me as true to how things are.

In my original essay, "Defining Art Historically," the way I tried to make the point I have been laboring here was to stress that the analysis lays bare what it *means* to be an artwork at a given time in terms of what *were* artworks, and the ensemble of ways they were correctly interacted with, at preceding times. More formally, that the *intension* of "artwork at *t*" is to explicated in terms of the *extension* of "artwork," and of "ways artworks are correctly regarded *as art*," for times prior to *t*. The idea that not only earlier artworks themselves, but also their associated proper modes of engagement, had to be granted, in extension, for the analysis (of *art now* in terms of *art until now*) to be effective was indeed not clearly brought out in my original discussion. I am grateful to Beardsley's criticism for prodding me to make this plainer.

Returning, then, to the dilemma that Beardsley poses for me, I am in a sense accepting the second horn but rejecting two of the implications he feels attach to it. One is the responsibility to provide either a general analysis of what a correct regard for an artwork is, or else an exhaustive list of all correct regards up to a given time. I hope what I have said so far indicates why this is unnecessary. On my analysis, the meaning

---

[20] Of course, *at* those earlier times, say 1800, being art was, and was conceived to be, *more* than just proper intentional relation to one's predecessors. It might then have involved, perhaps, imaginative representation of life, expression of sentiment, moral import, and so on as required features, or close to it. But it would have *also* involved the minimal feature or condition I have identified. The point to keep in mind is that we are after a *univocal* notion of art, applicable in the present, with respect to which all art, present and past, can be seen to be encompassed.

of "artwork at *t*" does not involve either the contents of any such analysis or any explicit conception of what the members of such a list are; it requires only that there *be,* potentially, such a list, and, of course, the even more basic list of (what are acknowledged to be) artworks up to that point. The other implication rejected is that my formulation will ultimately permit as admissible art-making intentions "just about anything in the future." I claim this is not so if only relatively replete regards are adhered to in applying the formula, ways of regard conceived as complex wholes, as explained in the previous section. Of course, the definition allows that just about any *thing* or *item* might become art in the future, but *that* cannot be a worry any art theorist can take seriously anymore.

Last, there is the matter raised by Beardsley of the *usability* of a definition of art. It's not clear to me what demand this represents. Practical use, in any event, does not seem germane where philosophical definitions are concerned. No one needs a conceptual analysis of *person,* say, in order to be able to recognize people and distinguish them from apes, mannequins, and IBM PCs. Perhaps what is required, then, is that a definition of art provide a way of telling *in principle* if a randomly offered item is an artwork. One form this requirement can take is the so-called "warehouse test":[21] could someone, armed only with the definition and his or her senses, reliably sort the various objects in a warehouse into artworks and nonartworks? But I think it must be evident that I do not accept, and see no reason to accept, such a test as a criterion of adequacy; in fact, I would go further and say that any definition of art *passing* such a test would thereby show itself to be *inadequate,* most obviously to recent art of this century. On the other hand, if a philosophical definition need only provide a way of telling, or rule for determining, whether a particular item is an artwork *given* a complete description of the object and the teleological, cultural, historical context in which it arises, then it seems the definition meets this standard as well as any other. Finally, one might ask of a philosophical definition that it be usable in the sense of being theoretically *fertile.*

---

[21] See William Kennick, "Does Traditional Aesthetics Rest upon a Mistake?" *Mind,* 57 (1958); Douglas Dempster, "Aesthetic Experience and Psychological Definitions of Art." Dempster cautions incidentally that defining "artwork" is not quite the same task as defining "art," a point I am in agreement with, though it has not been my concern to mark that distinction in the present essay.

Whether the intentional-historical definition is such still remains to be seen.

IV

I now consider certain objections Richard Wollheim has recently registered against the Institutional theory of art, since they could be thought
to have force against my own theory, similar as it is in some ways.[22]
Wollheim characterizes as Institutional any theory of art according to
which art is defined "by reference to what is said or done by persons or
bodies of persons whose roles are social facts" (157). Though hardly
miles off, it is evident that this characterization does not properly fit my
view, particularly in two respects. First, I emphasize not outward
action—saying and doing—but instead intentional stance, however
embodied, as crucial to making something art. Second, I do not require,
but instead deny, that art makers must occupy certain social roles, roles
in that shadowy infrastructure Institutionalists call the artworld. Still,
it is worth looking at Wollheim's thoughtful reservations about Institutional theory (IT), since they are clearly of relevance to my own as well.
   As I make it out, his reservations are basically four in number. (1) IT
violates the intuition that there be an *interesting connection* between
being an artwork and being a good artwork, that is, something beyond
the former's serving as a logical presupposition of the latter. (2) IT
violates the intuition that art making be an *important* activity, apart
from the artistic value, if any, of what is made. (3) IT makes Duchampian art making *central*, whereas a theory of art should exhibit
such as a *special case*, both ironic and provocative in relation to
normal or ordinary art. (4) Finally, IT must respond to the question
whether proposers of candidates for appreciation need have *good
reasons*, or any understandable reasons, for doing so, but either way it
responds proves unsatisfactory. If a proposer has good reasons, then it
seems the holding of those reasons would be, or could be made, itself a
virtually adequate account of arthood. Yet if a proposer need have no
such reasons—which is the more likely Institutionalist response—

---

[22] *Art and Its Objects,* supplementary essay 1. Wollheim himself appears to regard
my account as a variant of the Institutional theory (see his Bibliography, p. 269).

then an epistemic difficulty arises, that of how we could ever justifiably *believe* of such an agent "that, in drawing our attention to a certain artifact, he is putting it forward for appreciation, unless we can also attribute to him some idea of what it is about the artifact that we should appreciate, and further, believe that it is because of this that he is drawing our attention to it" (165).

I take these reservations in turn. Intuition (1) is admittedly a deep-rooted one. What can my theory offer in homage to it? Well, there is a connection, although it is not of the sort that, in traditional theories, allows concrete standards of evaluation to be derived from criteria of membership. The connection is this. A *good* work of art is one with properties and potentials that make it *worthy* of having been inten-tionally projected for the kind of treatment earlier art had properly received (which treatment, by and large, is such as to make engage-ment with this earlier art *worthwhile*). A *good* work of art is thus one that is *fittingly* connected to the tradition that, in being purposely fitted to the work, sustains it as a work of art at all. If new art is necessarily connected, by intentional invocation, to the enduring art that has preceded it, then we have a powerful explanation and justification of our standard procedure of assessing present art, at least initially, with reference to the aims and achievements of past art. If new art, in virtue of being art, is necessarily to be approached—at least at the outset—in *something like* the ways old art rightly is, then no question is more natural than to ask whether doing so for the new offers rewards comparable to those obtained from the old.[23] This seems to me a welcome consequence and a sufficient homage to the intuition at hand.

Intuition (2), while equally venerable, is vaguer, and I shall have less to say in response to it. I don't see why art cannot be important, particularly at this point in art history, in virtue of its *typical* or *traditional* modes of pursuit, in virtue of its *possibilities* and *prospects,* rather than in virtue of its *defining conditions*. Art is important, per-

---

[23]The point can be usefully restated with reference to the case of Jaspers, discussed above. By linking his object in the requisite way to those of its predecessors that were art, Jaspers in an important sense brings his object into the purview of art: It is not just to be *called* art, but is to be *approached* as (some) art has been. But if so, then it is naturally and appropriately subject to a standard of evaluation akin to that accorded earlier art: how well does *it*, at its historical juncture, reward regarding-as-a-work-of-art, for some realization of that, compared with its *predecessors* at theirs?

haps, because of the kind of thing that can be done within it, and the kind of experience that may be engendered as a result, and the kind of life that can issue from devotion to it, rather than because of what must *necessarily* be true of anything falling in its ambit. But if pressed for a strand of importance that owes to art's essential nature, on my account of it, there is this we could offer. If any art making is necessarily a relating of a present activity to an artistic past, then it has the humble, though not insignificant, virtue of constituting part of what we mean by *culture*, that network of human activities characterized by learning and storing, tradition and preservation, community and continuity—in short, by reference and remembrance. That should be enough to appease Wollheim's second intuition.

Third, the matter of an account's appearing to place Duchampian art making at center stage (3). What I would say in my defense (and, mutatis mutandis, Dickie's as well) is that this appearance is the inevitable upshot of trying to distill out the *minimum* essence of art making in the present situation. It is not meant to imply that most art making *has* consisted in, or *does* consist in, a bare intentional-historical act of positioning. No, art is usually much more: mastery of physical media, expression of emotion, vehicle of social statement, solution of artistic problems. But it is none of those things irreducibly and essentially—not anymore, at least.

In addition, I would respond to this third worry with a counter-observation. We must distinguish between demands reasonably made of (a) a general theory of art, and demands reasonably made of (b) a basic definition of art. We cannot hold (b) to account for all that we would hold (a) to account for. A more appropriate wider demand on (b), beyond adequacy and insight on its own terms, is only that it be *satisfyingly integratable* into (a), when and where it develops. The irony and provocativeness of Duchampian art making, one might hope, would reemerge in the context of a comprehensive art theory, taking from and bordering on art history and sociology of art, even if not displayed in an analytic definition of our current concept of art.

Wollheim's last reservation (4) is probably the weightiest and prompts me to consider whether something hasn't, analogously, been left out of my own account. Need one have good, or even any, reasons for intending something for regard-as-a-work-of-art if one's doing so is to count as making art? Well, *implicit* in the notion of intending something for such regard, perhaps, is the supposition that an intender believes it will be *worthwhile* doing so, that an intender has *some* reason for so prescribing, a reason that might be put most generally as that the experience had by following the prescription would be *valuable* in some way. The possibility, in principle, of coming up with or ferreting out such a reason is what enables us to believe, *vide* Wollheim, that an agent has in fact intended us to regard some item as a work of art. The question is whether this implicit supposition needs or merits explicit mention in a definition of art.[24]

I find myself of two minds about this. On the one hand, there seems reason to resist such cluttering of the definition in the name of little more than a reminder of art making, like other aspects of culture, must be conceived as fundamentally a *rational* activity—not an insane or pointless one. In other words, it would just underscore that art making is an *intelligible* phenomenon, adding nothing that is distinctive of art making as opposed to other purposeful human activities. But furthermore, it is worth noting that reasons can, in many cases, be thought of as *already comprised in* the modes of regard toward which art makers project their offerings. In my original essay, "Defining Art Historically," I distinguished between art theories that focus on how candidate artworks are to be *regarded* or *taken,* and those that focus on the experiences they are supposed to *offer,* or the responses they are designed to *elicit.* Though I argued for and elected the former strategy, there is indeed something to be said for the latter. What is valid in it can, I think, be legitimately subsumed under the other, as follows. What it is, typically, to intend something for treatment as earlier artworks were properly treated is to intend that the thing be approached in certain (neutrally designated) ways so as to derive certain rewards therefrom. That is to say, the expected experiential rewards of so attending to a work could be understood, at least in typical cases of art making, as *part of* or *integral to* the fully characterized mode of regard or treatment that art makers intend their efforts to receive and implicitly recommend to their potential audiences. An example of this would be intending a film or novel for: ⟨interpretive play so as to provide cognitive pleasure⟩, an artistically valid mode of regard figuring in many total art-making intentions.[25]

---

[24]The idea that making art involves a presupposition of worthwhileness for the intended recipients is interestingly explored in Jeffrey Wieand, "Quality in Art," *British Journal of Aesthetics,* 21 (1981).

[25]As stressed recently by Noël Carroll, "Art and Interaction."

On the other hand, if we cannot claim that such built-in reasons are to be found in the specific ways of regard projected in *every* admissible case of art making (and we cannot), and yet feel that the *underlying* rationality of art making should be explicitly captured in a definition, then we could easily add to my basic formulation a clause to this effect.

The result would be this: An artwork is a thing (item, etc.) that has been seriously intended for regard-as-a-work-of-art—i.e., regard (treatment, etc.)—in any way preexisting artworks are or were correctly regarded, *so that an experience of some value be thereby obtained.*[26]

Whether this really constitutes an improvement of the definition I will leave to others to decide.

V

I come now to the last of the challenges with which I will here try the resources of my account, one that is in many ways the most interesting.[27] It consists in the criticism that all relational theories of art are fundamentally mistaken, at least insofar as they attempt to furnish necessary conditions of arthood, because certain intrinsic qualities of objects indeed suffice to make them artworks, regardless of the intentional context or purposive background of the object. Case in point: Kafka's novels.

It is well known that Kafka, while still in reasonable health, left written instructions for Max Brod, his friend and literary executor, forbidding posthumous publication of any of his extant manuscripts, suggesting in fact that they be burned. These included the manuscripts of *The Trial* and *The Castle*. Let us, then, posit that it was Kafka's express dying wish that those *textes inédits* be utterly destroyed upon his death. Now, a literary death wish of this sort appears to be clearly incompatible with serious intent that one's writings be regarded or taken in some way preceding literature was—appears in fact to be

[26] An alternate, more specific, form this clause could take would be: so that an experience with value in some way similar to what earlier art afforded will be thereby obtained.

[27] I owe the impetus of this challenge, and the central example discussed in connection with it, to Daniel Kolak.

pretty clearly incompatible with intent that they be regarded in any way whatsoever! Yet these writings of Kafka—which, fortunately, have survived—just as clearly are literary art, and of a very high order. The upshot would seem to be that, contrary to what I maintain, art intent is *not* necessary to make something art, is *not* necessary for something to exist as art.

As usual, a number of responses suggest themselves as ways of dealing with this arresting case. First, it can be observed that there undoubtedly was art-intent at many points prior to, during, and perhaps even after the period of composition. One might ask whether final expressed intentions are automatically to be given priority in deciding art status.

Second, even if this were granted, it could be questioned whether the direction to burn the manuscripts is absolutely inconsistent with the persistence of art-intent on Kafka's part. Kafka may have been deeply conflicted, harboring contradictory intentions or wishes, in which a need for communication vied with an anxious perfectionism. Or else he may have intentionally projected his work for certain ideal readers (whom he would have wanted to regard his writings in such and such a fashion), but believing them not to exist among his likely readers, and not likely to exist in near future, was resigned to having the work consigned to the flames.

Third, if we declined to avail ourselves of the above gambits, we might choose to view the case as one of those anomalous ones where, owing to the exceptional potential literary value at stake, we recognize that the community of readers and critics can in effect justifiably *appropriate* certain texts and project them for literary regard, thus overruling, unusually, a creator's considered intent. The text becomes literature, as it were, "willy-nilly." The conditions of his happening, though, are special. In order for the literary community itself to so override a creator's sincere disavowal of literary-intent I suggest it would have to at least be the case that the text was (a) *inordinately* valuable taken as literature, (b) *unsuited* to other employment, and (c) something we could scarcely *help taking* as literature. Kafka's possibly ill-intended (though luckily not ill-fated) texts do certainly meet these conditions.

Last, the Kafka case can serve as a reminder that the notion of art I have been at pains to analyze, one I would insist is the central one in

contemporary usage and thought, is that for which experiencers, spectators, audiences are a sine qua non. That is to say, it is a notion that
descends from, though superseding, that according to which art is in
some fashion the production of artworks for appreciators. We might,
though, wish to recognize a *secondary* notion of art, centered on
creative process rather than appreciative aim, according to which
something is art if its making was the outcome of one of a class of
impulses identified as artistic, or if its making resulted in the attainment of certain states or the release of certain energies on the part of
the maker.[28] Clearly, on this sort of process-based (and rather Colling-
woodian) conception of what it is to be an artwork, Kafka's texts sail
through untroubled, irrespective of any intentions that may have pre-
dated or postdated their appearance. Recognizing this should help us
see, from yet another angle, that Kafka-like cases do not really cast
doubt on the adequacy of a relational analysis, appealing to intentionality, of our current *central* notion of art.

VI

I will end with a point of emphasis. My view, which requires a certain
intention or purposive orientation of a would-be art maker, is not
committed to the idea that such makers need formulate these intentions explicitly, nor that they must be consciously aware of having
them, nor that their relation to prior art be something transparent to
them (*pace* Danto). My view does, however, entail a sort of rock-
bottom test that could be expressed thus. If would-be art makers will
not themselves acknowledge having the sort of intent I posit—that is,
if we ask them point blank whether their objects are intended, at least
initially, to be regarded in some way past art was, and they deny it, nor
admit of any other intended regard that we can identify to be in the
class of past art regards—and if we can see no grounds for attributing
such intent to them on their behalf, then my account says what they are

---

[28] If one wanted to pursue this, one could even give a relational-historicist form to an
analysis of this process-centered notion of art: Something is an artwork if made in the
same *way* that any earlier art was made, or out of the same *impulses,* or offering the
same *satisfaction* in making.

doing *cannot* be art.[29] And if an agent with no announced claim of making art yet intends something for unequivocal regard-as-some-past-art-is-correctly-regarded, in either the transparent or opaque construal of that notion, then my account says that what he or she is doing *must* be art. I submit that this is the only thing it can now mean for something to be an artwork.[30]

[29] In entailing a definite judgment of this sort my view differs from the superficially similar, institutional view of Timothy Binkley, developed in his "Piece: Contra Aesthetics," that an artwork is merely something that has been *indexed* as an artwork, according to the conventions of the artworld. Binkley's view pointedly excludes acknowledging that how an item is intended to be taken or treated has *anything* to do with whether it can count as art; this, I suggest, is a grave flaw. I would also hope that, unlike Binkley, I cannot be accused of simply dodging the problem of apparent circularity in the analysis offered.

[30] Two discussions of the present essay have recently appeared: Crispin Sartwell, "A Counter-Example to Levinson's Historical Theory of Art" and Daniel Kolak, "Art and Intentionality," both in the *Journal of Aesthetics and Art Criticism,* 48:2 (1990). My response, "A Refiner's Fire: Reply to Sartwell and Kolak," is in the following issue, 48:3 (1990). See also Victor Haines, "Refining Not Defining Art Historically," *Journal of Aesthetics and Art Criticism,* 48:3 (1990), and my response, "Further Fire: Reply to Haines," in the next issue.

PART TWO

METAPHYSICS OF ART

4 *What a Musical Work Is*

What *exactly* did Beethoven compose? That is the question with which I will begin. Well, for one, Beethoven composed a quintet for piano and winds (oboe, clarinet, horn, bassoon) in E-flat, op. 16, in 1797. But what sort of thing is it, this quintet which was the outcome of Beethoven's creative activity? What does it consist in or of? Shall we say that Beethoven composed actual *sounds*? No, for sounds die out, but the quintet has endured. Did Beethoven compose a *score*? No, since many of those who are familiar with Beethoven's composition have had no contact with its score.[1]

Philosophers have long been puzzled about the identity or nature of the art object in nonphysical arts, e.g., music and literature. In these arts—unlike painting and sculpture—there is no particular physical "thing" that one can plausibly take to be the artwork itself. This puzzlement has sometimes led philosophers (e.g., Croce) to maintain that musical and literary works are purely mental—that they are in fact private intuitive experiences in the minds of composers and poets. But this does not seem likely, since experiences can be neither played nor read nor heard. More generally, the Crocean view puts the objectivity of musical and literary works in dire peril—they become inaccessible and unsharable. Fortunately, however, there is a way of accepting

[1] There are of course several other objections to these proposals, and to the Crocean proposal mentioned below. I do not mean to suggest that those I recall are clearly decisive by themselves.

the nonphysicality of such works without undermining their objectivity.

Those familiar with recent reflection on the ontological question for works of art will know of the widespread consensus that a musical work is in fact a variety of abstract object—to wit, a structural type or kind.[2] Instances of this type are to be found in the individual performances of the work. The type can be heard through its instances, and yet exists independently of its instances. I believe this to be basically correct. A piece of music is *some* sort of structural type, and as such is both nonphysical and publicly available. But *what* sort of type is it? I aim in this essay to say as precisely as I can what structural type it is that a musical work should be identified with.

The most natural and common proposal on this question is that a musical work is a *sound* structure—a structure, sequence, or pattern of sounds, pure and simple.[3] My first objective will be to show that this proposal is deeply unsatisfactory, that a musical work is more than just a sound structure per se. I will do this by developing three different objections to the sound-structure view. In the course of developing these objections, three requirements or desiderata for a more adequate view will emerge. The rightness—or at least plausibility—of those requirements will, I think, be apparent at that point. My second objective will then be to suggest a structural type that does satisfy the requirements, and thus can be identified with a musical work.[4]

At the outset, however, I should make clear that I am confining my inquiry to that paradigm of a musical work, the fully notated "classi-

---

[2] See, for example, C. L. Stevenson, "On 'What Is a Poem?' " *Philosophical Review*, 66 (1957): 329–62; J. Margolis, *The Language of Art and Art Criticism* (Detroit: Wayne State University Press, 1965); R. Wollheim, *Art and Its Objects* (New York: Harper & Row, 1968).

[3] It should be understood at the outset that sound structure includes not only pitches and rhythms, but also timbres, dynamics, accents—that is, all purely audible properties of sound. (See Additional Note 2, below.)

[4] This essay is indebted to two recent theories of the musical work: Nicholas Wolterstorff, "Toward an Ontology of Artworks," *Noûs*, 9 (1975): 115–42; and Kendall Walton, "The Presentation and Portrayal of Sound Patterns," *In Theory Only* (1977): 3–16. These writers are certainly aware of some of the considerations that I adduce pointing to the complexity of a musical type. However, I believe they do not take them seriously enough, and thus are inclined to acquiesce in the view that musical works *are* or *may be* just sound structures. In this essay I aim squarely to reject that view and to formulate one more adequate.

cal" composition of Western culture, for example, Beethoven's Quintet for piano and winds in E-flat, op. 16. So when I speak of a "musical work" in this paper it should be understood that I am speaking only of these paradigm musical works, and thus that all claims herein regarding musical works are to be construed with this implicit restriction.

I

The first objection to the view that musical works are sound structures is this. If musical works were sound structures, then musical works could not, properly speaking, be created by their composers. For sound structures are types of a pure sort which exist at all times. This is apparent from the fact that they—and the individual component sound types[5] that they comprise—can always have had instances.[6] A sound event conforming to the sound structure of Beethoven's Quintet op. 16 logically could have occurred in the Paleozoic era.[7] Less contentiously, perhaps, such an event surely could have taken place in 1760—ten years before Beethoven was born. But if that sound structure was capable of being *instantiated* then, it clearly must have *existed* at that time. Beethoven's compositional activity was not necessary in order for a certain sound-structure type to exist. It was not necessary to the possibility of certain sound events occurring which would be instances of that structure. Sound structures per se are not created by being scored—they exist before any compositional activity. Sound structures predate their first instantiation or conception because they are possible of exemplification *before* that point.[8] So, if composers truly create their works—i.e., bring them into existence—then musical works cannot be sound structures.

[5]E.g., F-sharp minor triad, three-note French-dotted rhythmic figure, middle C of bassoon timbre.

[6]This point is made by Wolterstorff, "Toward an Ontology," p. 138.

[7]Though of course lack of suitable production facilities made this impossible in some nonlogical sense.

[8]Someone might hold that in saying that a certain novel sound instance is possible at *t*, all we are committed to is that the sound structure of which it *would be* an instance might possibly *come into existence* at *t,* simultaneously with its first instance. But I do not think this is a plausible view; in saying that a certain sound event could occur at *t* we are saying something stronger than that the structure it would exemplify might come into existence—we are saying that that structure is right then available.

We can also defend the preexistence of pure sound structures (i.e., existence prior to any instantiation or conception) in a somewhat different manner. We need only remind ourselves that purely sound structures are in effect mathematical objects—they are *sequences* of sets of sonic elements. (Sonic elements are such as pitches, timbres, durations.) Now if the preexistence of simple sonic element types be granted—and I think it must be—it follows automatically that all sets and all sequences of sets of these elements also preexist. Therefore pure sound structures are preexistent. But if pure sound structures preexist, then it is not open for them to be objects of creational activity. So again, if composers are truly creators, their works cannot be pure sound structures.[9]

But why should we insist that composers truly create their compositions? Why is this a reasonable requirement? This question needs to be answered. A defense of the desideratum of true creation follows.

The main reason for holding to it is that it is one of the most firmly entrenched of our beliefs concerning art. There is probably no idea more central to thought about art than that it is an activity in which participants create things—these things being artworks. The whole tradition of art assumes art is creative in the strict sense, that it is a godlike activity in which the artist brings into being what did not exist beforehand—much as a demiurge forms a world out of inchoate

---

[9]Some who yet resist the idea that pure sound structures preexist compositional activity possibly fail to distinguish between *structure* and *construction*. It is true that constructions need to have been constructed in order to exist; it does not follow that structures need to have been constructed—i.e., actually put together from parts—in order to exist. The Brooklyn Bridge is a construction and embodies a structure. The Brooklyn Bridge did not exist before its construction. But the geometrical structure it embodies, which required and received no construction, has always existed.

Given there will still be philosophers who are attracted to the view that pure sound structures are in some way created by composers, presumably through mental activity, and that these are their works, I take this occasion to point out briefly two untoward consequences of such a view. The first is that instances of pure sound structures can always have been sounded accidentally before any composer thinks them into existence by directing his or her attention on the realm of sounds. In which case we would then be countenancing compositions that have instances before those compositions begin to exist. The second is that persons who conceive or sketch sound structures new to them have no (logical) assurance that they have in fact composed *anything*. For if composing is bringing sound structures into existence, one may fail to do so in writing a score, provided someone else has conceived the same structure earlier. Notice that this is not a matter of the latecomer having composed the *same* work as a predecessor, but rather— what the latecomer and we would surely find incredible—a matter of the latecomer having composed *no* work at all.

matter. The notion that artists truly *add* to the world, in company with cake bakers, house builders, lawmakers, and theory constructers, is surely a deep-rooted idea that merits preservation if at all possible. The suggestion that some artists, composers in particular, instead merely *discover* or *select* for attention entities they have no hand in creating is so contrary to this basic intuition regarding artists and their works that we have a strong prima facie reason to reject it if we can. If it is possible to align musical works with indisputably creatable artworks such as paintings and sculptures, then it seems we should do so.

A second, closely related reason to preserve true creation vis-à-vis musical works is that some of the status, significance, and value we attach to musical composition derives from our belief in this. If we conceive of Beethoven's Fifth Symphony as existing sempiternally, before Beethoven's compositional act, a small part of the glory that surrounds Beethoven's composition of the piece seems to be removed. There is a special aura that envelops composers, as well as other artists, because we think of them as true creators. We marvel at a great piece of music *in part* because we marvel that, had its composer not engaged in a certain activity, the piece would (almost surely) not now exist; but it does exist, and we are grateful to the composer for precisely that. Ecclesiastes was wrong—there *are* ever some things new under the sun, musical compositions being among the most splendid of them— and splendid, at least in part, in virtue of this absolute newness.

Shall we then accept the creatability requirement as suggested? Before we do so a last qualm should be addressed. It is open for someone to admit the importance of musical composition being characterized by true creation and yet waive the creatability of works themselves. Such a person will point to entities associated with the compositional process that composers unequivocally bring into existence—e.g., thoughts, scores, performances—and claim that true creation need be extended no further. Now it is certainly true that these entities are strictly created, and we may also accord composers some recognition of their creativity in regard to these things. But the fact of the matter remains that *works* are the main items, the center and aim of the whole enterprise, and that since musical works are not identical with scores, performances, or thoughts,[10] if those are the only things actually

---

[10]Though composers compose their works *by* writing scores, having thoughts, or, less typically, producing performances.

created, then much is lost. "Composers are true creators" acquires a hollow ring; creation in music shrinks to an outer veneer with no inner core.

I propose, then, that a most adequate account of the musical work should satisfy the following requirement, that of *creatability*:[11]

> (Cre) Musical works must be such that they do *not* exist prior to the composer's compositional activity, but are *brought into* existence *by* that activity.

II

The second objection to the view that musical works are sound structures is this. (1) If musical works were just sound structures, then, if two distinct composers determine the same sound structure, they necessarily compose the same musical work. (2) But distinct composers determining the same sound structure in fact inevitably produce different musical works.[12] Therefore, musical works cannot be sound structures *simpliciter*. The rest of this section is devoted to supporting and elucidating the second premise of this argument.

Composers who produce identical scores in the same notational system with the same conventions of interpretation will determine the same sound structure. But the musical works they thereby compose will generally not be the same. The reason for this is that certain attributes of musical works are dependent on more than the sound structures contained. In particular, the aesthetic and artistic attributes of a piece of music are partly a function of, and must be gauged with

---

[11] It would be well to note here that, even if one rejects the requirement of creatability, abandonment of the sound-structure view in favor of something like the view I eventually propose will be demanded by the second and third requirements developed. And those requirements strike me as being nonnegotiable.

[12] Notice that if we assume that composing musical works is strictly creating them, it follows immediately that two composers cannot compose the very same musical work (no matter what sound structures they determine) unless they are either composing jointly or composing independently but simultaneously. This is just a consequence of the fact that the same thing cannot be created both at t and at a later time t'. (The same goes for a single composer on temporally separate occasions; if composing is creating, a composer cannot compose the same work twice.) I will not, however, in this section assume that composing is strict creation.

reference to, the total musico-historical context in which the composer is situated while composing his piece. Since the musico-historical contexts of composing individuals are invariably different, then even if their works are identical in sound structure, they will differ widely in aesthetic and artistic attributes. But then, by Leibniz's law, the musical works themselves must be nonidentical; if W_1 has any attribute that W_2 lacks, or vice versa, then $W_1 \neq W_2$.

I will not attempt to give a strict definition of musico-historical context, but will confine myself to pointing out a large part of what is involved in it. The total musico-historical context of a composer P at a time t can be said to include at least the following: (a) the whole of cultural, social, and political history prior to t,[13] (b) the whole of musical development up to t, (c) musical styles prevalent at t, (d) dominant musical influences at t, (e) musical activities of P's contemporaries at t, (f) P's apparent style at t, (g) P's musical repertoire[14] at t, (h) P's oeuvre at t, (i) musical influences operating on P at t. These factors contributing to the total musico-historical context might be conveniently divided into two groups, a–d and e–i. The former, which we could call the *general* musico-historical context, consists of factors relevant to anyone's composing at t; the latter, which we could call the *individual* musico-historical context, consists of factors relevant specifically to P's composing at t. In any event, all these factors operate to differentiate aesthetically or artistically musical works identical in sound structure, thus making it impossible to identify those works with their sound structures. I now provide several illustrations of this.[15]

[13] Cf. J. L. Borges, "Pierre Menard, Author of the Quixote," in *Labyrinths* (New York: New Directions, 1962), for a fictional demonstration of the dependence of artistic meaning on historical context of creation.

[14] Cf. Wollheim, *Art and Its Objects*, pp. 48–54, for a discussion of the dependence of a work's expression on the artistic repertoire of the artist. The notion of "repertoire" is roughly that of a set of alternative decisions or choices within which an artist appears to be operating in creating his works. Wollheim extracts this idea from E. H. Gombrich's discussions of artistic expression in *Art and Illusion* and *Meditations on a Hobby-Horse*.

[15] The convincingness of these examples depends crucially on accepting something like the following principle: "Works of art *truly have* those attributes which they *appear* to have when *correctly* perceived or regarded." I cannot provide a defense of this principle here, but it has been well argued for by C. Stevenson, "Interpretation and Evaluation in Aesthetics," in W. E. Kennick, *Art and Philosophy* (New York: St.

(1) A work identical in sound structure with Schoenberg's *Pierrot Lunaire* (1912) but composed by Richard Strauss in 1897 would be aesthetically different from Schoenberg's work. Call it *Pierre Lunaire**. As a Straussian work, *Pierrot Lunaire** would follow hard upon Brahm's *German Requiem,* would be contemporaneous with Debussy's Nocturnes, and would be taken as the next step in Strauss's development after *Also Sprach Zarathustra.*[16] As such it would be more *bizarre,* more *upsetting,* more *anguished,* more *eerie* even than Schoenberg's work, since perceived against a musical tradition, a field of current styles, and an oeuvre with respect to which the musical characteristics of the sound structure involved in *Pierrot Lunaire* appear doubly extreme.[17]

(2) Mendelssohn's *Midsummer's Night Dream* Overture (1826) is admitted by all to be a highly *original* piece of music. Music of such elfin delicacy and feel for tone color had never before been written. But a score written in 1900 detailing the very same sound structure as is found in Mendelssohn's piece would clearly result in a work that was surpassingly *unoriginal.*

(3) Brahms's Piano Sonata op. 2 (1852), an early work, is strongly

---

Martin's, 1964), and Walton, "Categories of Art," *Philosophical Review,* 66 (1970): 334–67, among others.

[16] It is a mistake to regard this illustration as concerned with what *Pierrot Lunaire* would have been like if *it* had been composed by Strauss. (I am not even sure what *that* supposition amounts to.) The illustration rather concerns a possible musical work that possesses the same sound structure as *Pierrot Lunaire,* but is composed by Strauss in 1897. This work would be distinct from *Pierrot Lunaire* because aesthetically divergent. But if musical works were identified with sound structures, it could *not* be distinct.

[17] Another way of casting the argument using this example would be as follows. Consider a possible world Q in which both Schoenberg's *Pierrot Lunaire* and Strauss's *Pierrot Lunaire** exist, and call the sound structure they have in common K. In Q, the works diverge aesthetically and hence are nonidentical. Clearly, the works cannot both be identified with their common sound structure, but to so identify only one of them would be perfectly arbitrary. So in Q, *Pierrot Lunaire* $\neq K$. But then in the actual world as well, *Pierrot Lunaire* $\neq K$. Why? Owing to the necessity that attaches to identity and difference. If two things are nonidentical in any possible world, they are nonidentical in every possible world in which they exist. Put otherwise, statements of identity and difference involving rigid designators are necessary. 'Pierrot Lunaire' and 'K' designate rigidly; they are proper names, not definite descriptions. Thus 'Pierrot Lunaire $\neq K$' is necessarily true, since true in Q. Therefore, in the actual world, *Pierrot Lunaire* $\neq K$. (The argument can be recast in this way, mutatis mutandis, for illustrations (2)–(5) as well.)

Liszt-influenced, as any perceptive listener can discern. However, a work identical with it in sound structure, but written by Beethoven, could hardly have had the property of being Liszt-influenced. And it would have had a visionary quality that Brahms's piece does not have.

(4) The symphonies of Johann Stamitz (1717–1757) are generally regarded as seminal works in the development of orchestral music. They employ many attention-getting devices novel for their time, one of which is known as the "Mannheim rocket"—essentially a loud ascending scale figure for unison strings. A symphony of Stamitz containing Mannheim rockets and the like is an *exciting* piece of music. But a piece written today which was identical in sound structure with one of Stamitz's symphonies, Mannheim rockets and all, would not be so much exciting as it would be exceedingly *funny.* Stamitz's symphony is to be heard in the context of Stamitz's earlier works, the persistence of late Baroque style, the contemporary activities of the young Mozart, and the Napoleonic wars. "Modern Stamitz's" symphony would be heard in the context of "Modern Stamitz's" earlier works (which are probably dodecaphonic), the existence of aleatory and electronic music, the musical enterprises of both Pierre Boulez and Elton John, and the threat of nuclear annihilation.

(5) One of the passages in Bartok's Concerto for Orchestra (1943) satirizes Shostakovitch's Seventh Symphony (*Leningrad*) of 1941, whose bombast was apparently not to Bartok's liking. A theme from that symphony is quoted and commented on musically in an unmistakable manner. But notice that if Bartok had written the very same score in 1939, the work he would then have composed could not have had the same property of satirizing Shostakovitch's Seventh Symphony. Nor would the work that would have resulted from Shostakovitch's penning that score in 1943.

These examples should serve to convince the reader that there is always some aesthetic or artistic difference between structurally identical compositions in the offing in virtue of differing musico-historical contexts. Even small differences in musico-historical context—e.g., an extra work in *P*'s oeuvre, a slight change in style dominant in *P*'s milieu, some musical influence deleted from *P*'s development as a composer—seem certain to induce some change in kind or degree in some aesthetic or artistic quality, however difficult it might be in such cases to pinpoint this change verbally.

For example, suppose there had been a composer (call him "Toen-burg") in 1912 identical with Schoenberg in all musico-historical respects—e.g., birth date, country, style, musical development, artistic intentions, except that Toenburg had never written anything like *Ver-klarte Nacht* though he had in his oeuvre works structurally identical with everything else Schoenberg wrote before 1912. Now suppose simultaneously with Schoenberg he sketches the sound structure of *Pierre Lunaire*. Toenburg has not produced the same musical work as Schoenberg, I maintain, if only because his work has a slightly different aesthetic/artistic content owing to the absence of a *Verklarte Nacht*-ish piece in Toenburg's oeuvre. Schoenberg's *Pierrot Lunaire* is properly heard with reference to Schoenberg's oeuvre in 1912, and Toenburg's *Pierrot Lunaire* with reference to Toenburg's oeuvre in 1912. One thus hears something in Schoenberg's piece by virtue of resonance with *Verklarte Nacht* which is not present in Toenburg's piece. (Perhaps a stronger whiff of Expressionist sighs?)

Before formulating a second requirement of adequacy, as suggested by the fatal problem that contextual differentiation poses for the equation of musical works with pure sound structures, I must confront an objection that may be lurking in the wings. The objection in short is that the aesthetic and artistic differences I have been discussing are not really an obstacle to equating works and sound structures, because these supposed differences between *works* due to compositional con-text really just boil down to facts about their *composers* and are not attributes of works at all. The objection is understandable, but I find it unconvincing for several reasons, which I will briefly detail.

(1) Artistic and aesthetic attributions made of musical works are as direct and undisguised as attributions typically made of composers. It seems to be as straightforwardly true that the *Eroica* Symphony is noble, bold, original, revolutionary, influenced by Haydn, and reflec-tive of Beethoven's thoughts about Napoleon, as it is that Beethoven had certain personal qualities, was a genius, changed the course of Western music, studied with Haydn, and at one point idolized Napo-leon. (2) Whereas we may admit some plausibility to reducing artistic attributions (e.g., 'original', 'influenced by Haydn') to attributes of persons, there is no plausibility in so reducing aesthetic attributions; it is absurd to maintain that "W is scintillating," for example, is just a way of saying "W's composer is scintillating." (3) Finally, in the case of

artistic attributions, not only do they appear as entrenched and legitimate as parallel attributions to composers, but, if anything, they often seem to be primary. Consider originality, for example, and imagine a composer and oeuvre that possess it. Surely the composer is original because *his works* are original; his works are not original because *he is*.

I thus propose a second requirement—that of *fine individuation*—to which any acceptable theory of the musical work should conform:

(Ind) Musical works must be such that composers composing in different musico-historical contexts[18] who determine identical sound structures invariably compose distinct musical works.

III

The third objection to the view that musical works are sound structures is this. If musical works were simply sound structures, then they would not essentially involve any particular means of performance. But the paradigm musical works that we are investigating in this essay—e.g., Beethoven's Quintet op. 16—clearly *do* involve specific means of performance, i.e., particular instruments, in an essential way. The instrumentation of musical works is an integral part of those works. So musical works cannot be simply sound structures per se. Arguments in defense of the claim that performance means are an essential component of musical works now follow.

(1) Composers do not describe pure sound patterns in qualitative terms, leaving their means of production undiscussed. Rather, what they directly specify are means of production, through which a pure sound pattern is indirectly indicated. The score of Beethoven's Quintet op. 16 is not a recipe for providing an instance of a sound pattern per se, in whatever way you might like. Rather, it instructs one to produce an instance of a certain sound pattern through carrying out certain operations on certain instruments. When Beethoven writes a middle C for the oboe, he has done more than require an oboelike sound at a certain pitch—he has called for such a sound as emanating from that

[18]This includes a single composer on separate occasions.

quaint reed we call an "oboe." The idea that composers of the last three hundred years were generally engaged in composing pure sound patterns, to which they were usually kind enough to append suggestions as to how they might be realized, is highly implausible. Composers are familiar with tone colors only insofar as they are familiar with instruments that possess them. We do not find composers creating pure combinations of tone color, and then later searching about for instruments that can realize or approximate these aural canvases; it would obviously be pointless or at least frustrating to do so. Composers often call for complex sounds that they have never heard before and can scarcely imagine—e.g., the sound of two trombones and three piccolos intoning middle C while four saxophones and five xylophones intone the C-sharp a half step above; it is obvious here that what is primarily composed is not a pure untethered sound but an instrumental combination.[19]

(2) Scores are generally taken to be definitive of musical works, at least in conjunction with the conventions of notational interpretation assumed to be operative at the time of composition. It is hard to miss the fact that scores of musical works call for specific instruments in no uncertain terms. When we read in Beethoven's score the demand 'clarinet' (rather, 'Klarinett'), we may wonder whether a clarinet of 1970 vintage and construction will do as well as one of 1800, but we have

[19]It is inevitable someone will object at this point that certain composers, in certain periods, did not compose with definite instruments in mind and did not make specific instrumentation integral to their works. This may be true to some extent. But two points must be noted. First, I have set out to characterize the nature of the *paradigmatic* musical composition in Western culture, of which Beethoven's Quintet op. 16 is an example. It is enough for my purpose that most "classical" compositions, and effectively all from 1750 to the present, integrally involve definite means of performance. Second, even in regard to J. S. Bach, where controversy has long existed as to exactly what performing forces Bach intended, called for, or would have allowed in such compositions as *The Well-Tempered Clavier* or the *Brandenburg* Concerto no. 2, it is clear there are still restrictions as to performing forces which must be considered part of those compositions. Thus, *The Well-Tempered Clavier* may not be a work belonging solely to the harpsichord (as opposed to the clavichord or fortepiano), but it is clearly a work for *keyboard,* and a performance of its sound structure on five violins would just for that reason not be a performance of *it.* And although the performance component of the *Brandenburg* Concerto no. 2 may be indeterminate between a trumpet and a natural horn in that prominent instrumental part, it certainly excludes the alto saxophone. Finally, a composition such as Bach's *Art of the Fugue,* for which perhaps no means of sound production are either prescribed or proscribed, is in this context merely the exception that proves the rule.

still been given a fairly definite idea of what sort of instrument is required. There is nothing in scores themselves that suggests that instrumental specifications are to be regarded as optional—any more than specifications of pitch, rhythm, or dynamics. Nor does the surrounding musical practice of the time encourage such a way of regarding them.[20] If we are not to abandon the principle that properly understood scores have a central role in determining the identity of musical works, then we must insist that the Quintet op. 16 without a clarinet is not the same piece—even if all sound-structural characteristics (including timbre) are preserved. To feel free to disregard as prominent an aspect of scores as performing means is to leave it open for someone to disregard any aspect of a score he or she does not wish to conform to—e.g., tempo, accidentals, accents, articulation, harmony—and claim that one nevertheless has the same work.[21] The only way it seems one could justify regarding performing-means specifications as just optional features of scores is to simply *assume* that musical works are nothing but sound structures per se.

Consider a sound event aurally indistinguishable from a typical performance of Beethoven's Quintet op. 16, but issuing from a versatile synthesizer, or perhaps a piano plus a set of newly designed wind instruments, two hundred in number, each capable of just two or three notes. If performance means were not an integral aspect of a musical work, then there would be no question that this sound event constitutes a performance of Beethoven's Quintet op. 16. But there is indeed such a question. It makes perfect sense to deny that it is such a performance on the grounds that the sounds heard did not derive from a piano and four standard woodwinds. We can count something as a performance of Beethoven's Quintet op. 16 only if it involves the participation of the instruments for which the piece was written—or better, of the instruments that were written into the piece.

(3) To regard performing means as essential to musical works is to maintain that the sound structure of a work cannot be divorced

---

[20]This should not be confounded with the fact that many composers were ready and willing to adapt their works in response to exigencies—in short, to license transcriptions.

[21]This is not to say that *everything* found in scores is constitutive of musical works. Some markings do not fix the identity of a work but are instead of the nature of advice, inspiration, helpful instruction. However, the suggestion that instrumental specifications are of this sort is totally insupportable.

from the instruments and voices through which that structure is fixed, and regarded as the work itself. The strongest reason why it cannot be so divorced is that the aesthetic content of a musical work is determined not only by its sound structure, and not only by its musico-historical context, but also in part by the actual means of production chosen for making that structure audible. The character of a musical composition—e.g., Beethoven's Quintet op. 16 for piano and winds— is partly a function of how its sound structure relates to the potentialities of a certain instrument or set of instruments designated to produce that structure for audition. To assess that character correctly one must take cognizance not only of the qualitative nature of sounds heard but also of their source or origin. Musical compositions, by and large, have reasonably definite characters; that is to say, we can and do ascribe to them many fairly specific aesthetic qualities. But if prescribed performing forces were not intrinsic to musical compositions, then those compositions would not have the reasonably definite characters we clearly believe them to have. The determinateness of a work's aesthetic qualities is in peril if performing means are viewed as inessential so long as exact sound structure is preserved.

Consider a musical work W with specified performing means M which has some fairly specific aesthetic quality ϕ. The sound structure of W as produced by different performing means N, however, will invariably strike us either as not ϕ at all, or else as ϕ to a greater or lesser degree than before. Therefore, if means of sound production are not regarded as an integral part of musical works, then W cannot be said determinately to have the attribute ϕ. So if we wish to preserve a wide range of determinate aesthetic attributions, we must recognize performing means to be an essential component of musical works. I now provide two illustrations of this point.[22]

(a) Beethoven's *Hammerklavier* Sonata is a sublime, craggy, and heaven-storming piece of music. The closing passages (marked by ascending chordal trills) are surely among the most imposing and awesome in all music. However, if we understand the very sounds of the *Hammerklavier* Sonata to originate from a full-range synthesizer, as opposed to a mere eighty-eight-key piano of metal, wood, and felt, it not longer seems so sublime, so craggy, so awesome. The aesthetic

[22]Cf. Walton, "Categories of Art," pp. 349–50, for related examples.

qualities of the *Hammerklavier* Sonata depend in part on the strain that its sound structure imposes on the sonic capabilities of the piano; if we are not hearing its sound structure *as* produced by a piano, then we are not sensing this strain, and thus our assessment of aesthetic content is altered. The closing passages of the *Hammerklavier* are awesome in part because we seem to hear the piano bursting at the seams and its keyboard on the verge of exhaustion. On a ten-octave electronic synthesizer those passages do not have quite that quality, and a hearing of them with knowledge of source is an aesthetically different experience. The lesson here applies, I believe, to all musical works (of the paradigm sort). Their aesthetic attributes always depends, if not so dramatically, in part on the performing forces understood to belong to them.

(b) Consider a baroque concerto for two violins, such as Bach's Concerto in D Minor, BWV 1043. In such pieces one often finds a phrase (A) assigned to one violin, which is immediately followed by the *very same* phrase (B) assigned to the other violin. Now when one hears such passages *as* issuing from *two* violins (even if in a given performance there are no discernible differences between A and B in timbre or phrasing), a sense of question and answer, of relaxation and unhurriedness, is communicated. But if one were to construe such passages as issuing from a *single* violin, that quality would be absent, and in its place the passages would assume a more emphatic, insistent, and repetitive cast.

(4) The dependence of aesthetic attributes on assumed or understood performing forces should now be apparent. The dependence of artistic attributes is even more plain. (a) Consider Paganini's Caprice op. 1, no. 17. This piece surely deserves and receives the attribution 'virtuosic'. But if we did not conceive of the Caprice no. 17 as essentially for the violin, as inherently a *violin piece* (and not just a *violin-sounding piece*), then it would not merit that attribution. For, as executed by a computer or by some novel string instrument using nonviolinistic technique, its sound structure might not be particularly difficult to get through. (b) Imagine a piece written for violin to be played in such a way that certain passages sound more like a flute than they do like a violin. Such a piece would surely be accounted *unusual,* and to some degree *original* as well. Understood as a piece for violin and occasional flute, however, it might have nothing unusual or origi-

nal about it at all. Retaining the sound structure while setting actual performance means adrift completely dissolves part of the piece's artistic import.

(c) According to one respected critic, Beethoven in the Quintet op. 16 was interested in solving problems of balance between piano and winds—a nominally incompatible array of instruments—and succeeded in his own individual way.[23] It is not hard to agree with this assessment; thus, 'solves the problem of balance between piano and winds' is an attribution true of Beethoven's quintet. It is difficult to see how this would be so if the quintet is purely a sound structure, if piano and winds are not strictly part of the piece at all.[24]

I thus propose a third requirement for any account of the musical work: *inclusion of performance means.*

(Per) Musical works must be such that specific means of performance or sound production are integral to them.

IV

If musical works are not sound works *simpliciter*, then what are they? The type that is a musical work must be capable of being created, must be individuated by context of composition, and must be inclusive of means of performance. The third desideratum is most easily met, and will be addressed first.

I propose that a musical work be taken to involve not only a pure sound structure, but also a structure of performing means. If the sound structure of a piece is basically a sequence of sounds qualitatively defined, then the performing-means structure is a parallel sequence of performing means specified for realizing the sounds at each point. Thus a musical work consists of at least two structures. It is a compound or conjunction of a sound structure and a performing-means structure. This compound is itself just a more complex structure; call it an "S/PM" structure, for short.[25] Beethoven's op. 16 Quintet is at base

23 James Lyons, liner notes, phonograph record Nonesuch 71054.
24 The best one could say would be that the quintet achieved a satisfactory blending of pianoish sounds and woodwindish sounds.
25 One could alternatively speak of a single structure that, construed rightly, entails both the required sounds and the required means of sound production. This would be a

an S/PM structure; the means of producing the sounds belonging to it are no more dispensable to its identity as a composition than the nature and order of those sounds themselves. This satisfies requirement (Per).

To satisfy the first and second requirements of adequacy we arrived at, it is necessary to realize that a musical work is not a structure of the *pure* sort at all, and thus not even an S/PM structure *simpliciter.* An S/PM structure is no more creatable or context-individuated than a sound structure is. I propose that we recognize a musical work to be a more complicated entity, namely this:

(MW) S/PM structure-as-indicated-by-X-at-*t*

where X is a particular person—the composer—and t is the time of composition. For the paradigmatic pieces we are concerned with, the composer typically indicates (fixes, determines, selects) an S/PM structure by creating a score. The *piece* he thereby composes is the S/PM structure-as-indicated by him on that occasion.

An S/PM structure-as-indicated-by-X-at-*t,* unlike an S/PM structure *simpliciter,* does not preexist the activity of composition and is thus capable of being created. When a composer θ composes a piece of music, he indicates an S/PM structure ψ, but he does not bring ψ into being. However, through the act of indicating ψ, he does bring into being something that did not previously exist—namely, ψ-as-indicated-by-θ-at-t_1. Before the compositional act at t_1, no relation obtains between θ and ψ. Composition establishes the relation of indication between θ and ψ. As a result of the compositional act, I suggest, the world contains a new entity, ψ-as-indicated-by-θ-at-t_1. Let me call such entities *indicated structures.* And let me represent indicated structures by expressions of form "S/PM$^* x^* t$." It is important to realize that indicated structures are entities distinct from the pure

---

structure of *performed sounds,* as opposed to "pure" sounds. For example, one such *performed sound* would correspond to the following specification: "Middle C of half-note duration played on oboe." Clearly this implies both a certain sound qualitatively defined and a means of producing it.

The main reason I favor the S/PM formulation is that it is more transparent. It preserves some continuity with the sound-structure view that it supersedes, and displays more clearly than the performed-sound formulation that, although a musical work is *more* than a sound structure, it most definitely *includes* a sound structure. (But see Chapter 10, section XIV, below.)

structures per se from which they are derived. Thus, in particular, $\psi^* \theta^* t_1$ is *not* just the structure ψ with the accidental property of having been indicated by θ at t_1—$\psi^* \theta^* t_1$ and ψ are strictly nonidentical, though of course related. $\psi^* \theta^* t_1$, unlike ψ, can be and is created through θ's composing. Thus requirement (Cre) is satisfied.

Indicated structures also serve to satisfy our second requirement (Ind). If musical works are indicated structures of the sort we have suggested, then two such works, $\psi^* \theta^* t_1$ and $\alpha^* \phi^* t_2$, are identical iff (i) $\psi = \alpha$, (ii) $\theta = \phi$, and (iii) $t_1 = t_2$—i.e., the sound structures, persons, and times involved are identical. But if musical works are necessarily distinct if composed either by different people or at different times, then it certainly follows that works composed in different musico-historical contexts will be distinct, since any difference of musico-historical context from one work to another can be traced to a difference of composer or time or both. Put otherwise, musico-historical context (as explained in section II) is a function of time and person; given a time and person, musico-historical context is fixed. So requirement (Ind) is satisfied. That it is satisfied by our proposal with something to spare is a matter I will return to in section V. I now endeavor to increase the reader's grasp of what indicated structures are.

Indicated structures are a different class of type from pure structures. Types of the latter class we may call *implicit* types, and those of the former class *initiated* types. Implicit types include all purely abstract structures that are not inconsistent—e.g., geometrical figures, family relationships, strings of words, series of moves in chess, ways of placing five balls in three bins. By calling them "implicit types" I mean to suggest that their existence is implicitly granted when a general framework of possibilities is given. For example, given that there is space, there are all the possible configurations in space; given there is the game of chess, there are all the possible combinations of allowed moves. Sound structures *simpliciter* are clearly implicit types. Given that there are sounds of various kinds, then all possible patterns and sequences of those sounds must be granted existence immediately as well. For a sound structure, in company with all pure structures, is always capable of instantiation before the point at which it is noticed, recognized, mentioned, or singled out. And thus its existence must predate that point. The same goes for a performance-means structure *simpliciter*. Given performing means (i.e., instruments) of various kinds, then all possible combinations and sequences of such means exist as well. The compound of these two, a sound/performance means structure, thus of course also counts as an implicit type.

The other class of types, *initiated* types, are so called because they begin to exist only when they are initiated by an intentional human act of some kind. All those of interest can, I think, be construed as arising from an operation, like indication, performed upon a pure structure. Typically, this indication is effected by producing an exemplar of the structure involved, or a blueprint of it. In so indicating (or determining) the structure, the exemplar or blueprint inaugurates the type that is the *indicated* structure, the structure-as-indicated-by-*x*-at-*t*. All indicated structures are, perforce, initiated types.

Initiated types include such types as the Ford Thunderbird, the Lincoln penny, the hedgehog. The Ford Thunderbird is not simply a pure structure of metal, glass, and plastic. The pure structure that is embodied in the Thunderbird has existed *at least* since the invention of plastic (1870); there could certainly have been instances of it in 1900. But the Ford Thunderbird was created in 1957; so there could not have been instances of the Thunderbird in 1900. The Ford Thunderbird is an *initiated* type; it is a metal/glass/plastic structure-as-indicated (or -determined) by the Ford Motor Company on such and such a date. It begins to exist as a result of an act of human indication or determination. The instances of this type are more than just instances of a pure structure—they are instances of an indicated structure. The Lincoln penny is similarly not a pure structure, an abstract pattern *tout court,* but a structure-as-indicated, a pattern-as-denominated-by-the-U.S. government. Objects conforming to the pattern *tout court* but existing in A.D. 100 in Imperial Rome would not be instances of the Lincoln penny. Even the hedgehog is probably best understood not as a pure biological structure, but rather as a biological structure-as-determined-or-fixed by natural terrestrial evolution at a particular point in history. The creatures we call "hedgehogs" possess a certain structure and stand in certain causal relations to some particular creatures that came into existence at a given past date. The biological structure of the hedgehog might have been instantiated in the Mesozoic era, or on Uranus, but nothing existing at that time, or at that place, could be an instance of the hedgehog as we understand it. Musical works, as I have suggested, are indicated structures too, and thus types that do not already exist but must instead be initiated. The same is true of poems, plays, and novels—each of these is an entity more individual and temporally bound than the pure verbal structure embodied in it.

The distinction between indicated structure and pure structure can perhaps be made clearer by analogy with the distinction between sentence and statement long enshrined in the philosophy of language. These distinctions are motivated in similar ways. Statements were recognized partly in response to the need for entities individuated in some respects more finely than sentences, in order to provide bearers for the varying truth values that turned up in connection with a given sentence on different occasions.[26] Just so, indicated structures are recognized in response to the need for entities more finely individuated than pure structures, in order to provide bearers for various incompatible sets of aesthetic, artistic, cultural, semantic, and genetic properties. We allow that a given sentence can make different statements when uttered in different circumstances. Similarly, we realize that a given sound/performance means structure yields different indicated structures, or musical works, when indicated in different musico-historical contexts.[27]

V

I have proposed that musical works be identified with rather specific indicated structures, in which a particular person and time figure ineliminably. The proposal MW was made, recall, in order to satisfy the creatability and individuation requirements. However, as I noted at that point, MW satisfies the individuation requirement with logical room to spare. Perhaps both requirements can be satisfied without invoking types that are quite so particularized. The obvious alternative is that a musical work is this sort of type:

(MW′) S/PM structure-as-indicated-in-musico-historical-context-C

[26] See, for example, J. L. Austin's "Truth," *Proceedings of the Aristotelian Society*, supplementary volume 24 (1950): 111–28.

[27] The analogy might even be reversed, so as to illuminate the nature of statements. If musical works are structures-as-indicated . . . , then possibly statements just are: sentences-as-uttered . . .

Such types would be both creatable and sufficiently individuated. A type of this sort, like an MW type, comes into existence through some *actual* indication of an S/PM structure by a person at a time—a person who at that certain time is situated in a particular context. But the type's identity is not inherently tied to that of any individual as such. Thus, two composers composing simultaneously but independently in the same musico-historical context who determine the same S/PM structure create *distinct* MW types, but the *same* MW′ type.

Given these two proposals, then, which satisfy all our desiderata, do we have reason to prefer one or the other? I will discuss one consideration in favor of MW′ and three considerations in favor of MW.

(1) On the MW′ proposal, it is at least logically possible for a musical work to have been composed by a person other than the person who actually composed it. If *A* is the actual composer of a musical work, ψ-as-indicated-in-C_1, then all we need imagine is that someone other than *A* was the person to first indicate the S/PM structure ψ in musico-historical context C_1. On the MW proposal, however, it becomes *logically impossible* for a work to have been composed by other than its actual composer. Could someone else have composed Beethoven's Quintet op. 16, according to MW? For example, could Hummel have done so? No, because if ψ is the S/PM structure of the Quintet op. 16, then all that Hummel might have composed is ψ-as-indicated-by-Hummel-in-1797, and not ψ-as-indicated-by-Beethoven-in-1797.[28] It must be admitted to be somewhat counterintuitive for a theory to make the composer of a work essential to that work.

(2) We can turn this consequence upside-down, however. One might cite as a virtue of the MW proposal that it gives composers *logical insurance* that their works are their very own, that no one else has or ever could compose a work identical to any of theirs. If *A*'s musical work is an MW type, then even a fellow composer situated in an identical musico-historical context determining the same S/PM structure composes a distinct musical work. It seems to me this is a desirable consequence, from the point of view of preserving the uniqueness of compositional activity. Why should composers have to fear, however abstractly, that their works are not exclusively theirs any more than

[28] I am assuming, of course, that Hummel could not possibly have *been* Beethoven. If he *could* have, then I suppose that, even on MW, Hummel might have composed Beethoven's quintet.

painters painting paintings or sculptors sculpting sculptures need be
troubled about whether their works are at least numerically distinct
from anyone else's? Why not adopt a construal of 'musical work' (and
of 'poem', 'novel', 'dance', and so on) which, while maintaining musical works as abstract types, guarantees this individuation by artist for
them as well? Considerations (1) and (2) thus appear to fairly well
cancel each other out.

(3) A more decisive reason, however, for ensuring by proposal MW
that composers A and B who determine the same S/PM structure in the
same musico-historical context yet compose distinct works W_1 and
W_2, is that, although W_1 and W_2 do not, it seems, differ structurally or
aesthetically or artistically at the time of composition t, differences of
an artistic sort are almost certain to develop after t. So, unless we wish
to embrace the awkwardness of saying that two musical works can be
identical when composed but nonidentical at some later point, we have
a strong incentive to adopt MW. W_1 and W_2 will almost certainly
diverge artistically because of the gross improbability that A and B will
continue to be subject to the exact same influences to the same degree
and that A's and B's oeuvres will continue to appear identical after the
composition of W_1 and W_2. If A's and B's artistic careers do exhibit
these differences after t, then W_1 and W_2 will acquire somewhat
different artistic significance, since W_1 will eventually be seen properly
against A's total development, and W_2 against B's total development.
W_1 may turn out to be a *seminal work*, whereas W_2 turns out to be *a
false start*. Or W_1 may turn out to be *much more influential* than W_2,
owing to the fact that A comes to be much better known than B. In any
case, there will be *some* divergence in artistic attributions, if not always
so marked, unless A and B remain artistic duplicates of each other
throughout their lives (and thereafter). Since circumstances subsequent
to a work's composition are not comprised in musico-historical context of composition, proposal MW' leaves us open for the awkwardness mentioned above. MW forestalls this problem completely.[29]

---

[29]I will take this opportunity to point out that although aesthetic and artistic
attributes have played a large role in this essay, I have not insisted on them as *essential*
to musical works, but only as relevant—in common with all other attributes—to
individuating them. The argument has nowhere required as a *premise* that such attributes are essential attributes. It has assumed only that aesthetic/artistic attributes
truly belong to works in a *reasonably determinate* fashion. As for what attributes *are*
essential to musical works, given MW, it seems that certain structural and genetic

(4) A last consideration inclining us to MW comprises certain intuitions concerning what would count as a performance of what. It seems that, in order for a performance to be a performance *of W*, not only must it fit and be intended to fit the S/PM structure of *A*'s work *W*; there must also be some *connection*, more or less direct, between the sound event produced and *A*'s creative activity. Whether this is primarily an intentional or causal connection is a difficult question,[30] but, unless it is present, I think we are loath to say that *A*'s work has been performed. Consider two composers, Sterngrab and Grotesteen, who compose quartets with identical S/PM structures; suppose even that they share the same musico-historical context. Now imagine that the Aloysious Ensemble, who are great friends of Sterngrab, give the ill-attended premiere of Sterngrab's Quartet op. 21. Clearly, the Aloysious have performed Sterngrab's Quartet op. 21—but have they also performed Grotesteen's Quartet op. 21? I think not. Why? For several reasons: they don't know Grotesteen; they weren't using Grotesteen's scores; they didn't believe themselves to be presenting Grotesteen's work—in short, there was no connection between their performance and Grotesteen the creator. Grotesteen's creating his op. 21 Quartet had nothing whatever to do with the sound event produced by the Aloysious Ensemble on the afore-mentioned occasion. Now, if Sterngrab's quartet has performances that Grotesteen's does not, and vice versa, then, again by Leibniz's law, Sterngrab's and Grotesteen's quartets cannot be identical. On proposal MW', Sterngrab and Grotesteen have composed the same musical work; on proposal MW, their works are distinct. That MW squares with this intuition regarding identification of performances is thus one more point in its favor.

I therefore rest with the account of musical works represented by

---

attributes would have to be admitted: S/PM structure, composer, date of composition. But it is not obvious that aesthetic/artistic attributes will turn out to be essential—i.e., possessed by a work in all possible worlds it inhabits. Consider a possible world in which Schoenberg determines the S/PM structure of *Verklarte Nacht* during 1899 but in which Wagner had never existed. The resultant work might still be *Verklarte Nacht*, though some of its aesthetic/artistic attributes would be subtly different. On the other hand, were we to adopt MW', then aesthetic attributes might arguably become essential, since the appreciative contexts fixing them would be so.

[30] Quandaries arise when these considerations conflict, which I will not attempt to deal with here. For example, suppose the Aloysious Ensemble are actually reading copies of Grotesteen's score while believing themselves to be playing Sterngrab's score. Do they perform Sterngrab's quartet, Grotesteen's quartet, or both? (For more on this, see Chapter 5, below.)

MW. In the next section I offer some remarks on performances and transcriptions in light of this account.

VI

(1) On my view, the following must all be distinguished: (a) instances of W; (b) instances of the sound structure of W; (c) instances of the S/PM structure of W; (d) performances of W. An *instance* of a musical work W is a sound event that conforms *completely* to the sound/performance means structure of W and which exhibits the required connection [31] to the indicative activity wherein W's composer A creates W. An instance of W is typically produced, either directly or indirectly, from a score that can be causally traced and is intentionally related by the performer, to the act of creation of W by A. Thus, all instances of W are instances of W's sound structure, and instances of W's S/PM structure—but the reverse is not the case.

Instances are a subclass of the set of performances of a work. A *performance* of a musical work W is a sound event that is *intended* to instantiate W—i.e., represents an attempt to exemplify W's S/PM structure in accordance with A's indication of it[32]—and which *succeeds to a reasonable degree.*[33] Since one cannot instantiate a musical work—an S/PM structure-as-indicated-by-X-at-t—without intending to, because instantiating *that* demands conscious guidance by instructions, memories, or the like which one regards as deriving from A's indicative act at t, it follows that the instances of W are all to be found among the performances of W. However, not all performances of W count as instances of W; many if not most attempts to exemplify S/PM structures fail by some margin. So these cannot count as instances of W, but they *are* performances—namely *incorrect* performances. (Of

---

[31] I will assume here that the required connection is primarily, if not wholly, intentional.

[32] And thus an attempt to exemplify an S/PM-as-indicated-by-X-at-t.

[33] What constitutes a "reasonable degree," and thus what differentiates poor or marginal performance from nonperformance, is for many compositions perhaps marked by the ability of an informed and sensitive listener to grasp, at least roughly, *what* S/PM structure is struggling to be presented. For example, even an especially informed and sensitive listener would grasp approximately nothing of the *Hammerklavier* Sonata from *my* attempt to present its structure, since my facility at the piano is next to nil—no performance (much less an instance) of the *Hammerklavier* Sonata can issue from me or my ilk.

course, that they are strictly incorrect by no means entails that they are bad.) There are not, however, any incorrect *instances* of W; the *correct* performances of W are its instances, and no others.[34]

Finally, let me note that musical works as I understand them *can* be heard in or through their performances. One *hears* an S/PM structure-as-indicated-by-X-at-*t* whenever one hears an instance of that S/PM structure produced by performers who, roughly speaking, are guided by X's indication of the S/PM structure in question. And one *knows* precisely what musical work—i.e., structure-as-indicated—one is hearing if one knows what creative act is in effect the guiding source of the sound event being produced.

(2) On my view of what a musical work (of the paradigm sort) is, it follows immediately that a transcription of a musical work is a distinct musical work, whether it involves alteration of the sound structure (the normal case), or *even* of just the performance-means structure. It is a virtue of my view that it gives a clear answer to this question, which is often thought to be only arbitrarily decidable. If we want such pieces to have the definite aesthetic qualities we take them to have, instrumentation must be considered inseparable from them. Thus, we need not rely, in endorsing the distinctness position on transcriptions vis-à-vis original works, merely on the principle of fidelity to the composer's intended instrumentation. Rather we are also constrained by higher-order considerations of preserving the aesthetic integrity of such pieces.

In conclusion, let me stress some obvious consequences of accepting the theory of the musical work that I have proposed. First, composers would retain the status of creator in the strictest sense. Second, musical composition would be revealed as necessarily personalized. Third, musical composition could not fail to be seen as a historically rooted activity whose products must be understood with reference to their

---

[34] Thus I am in opposition to Wolterstorff's suggestion, in "Toward an Ontology of Artworks," that musical works be construed as norm-kinds—i.e., as having correct and incorrect, or proper and improper, or standard and defective instances. What we say about musical works can, I think, be more perspicuously interpreted in terms of the distinction between instance and performance. Further, construing instance as requiring full conformity to score (i.e., as an all-or-none proposition) has the virtue, as Nelson Goodman pointed out in *Languages of Art* (Indianapolis: Bobbs-Merrill, 1968), of assuring preservation of a work's identity from work to instance and from instance to work. But by also distinguishing between instance and performance (which Goodman does not do) one can sweeten the judgment, say, that Rubinstein's playing of the Chopin Ballade no. 3 with two mistakes is not an *instance* of the work, with the willing admission that it is surely a *performance* of it (and possibly a great one).

points of origin. Fourth, it would be recognized that the pure sound structure of a musical work, while graspable in isolation, does not exhaust the work structurally, and thus that the underlying means of performance must be taken into account as well if the work is to be correctly assessed.[35]

[35] It is worth observing that, if the position developed in this paper is correct, it has interesting implications not only for the identity of other sorts of art work (this I take to be obvious) but for the identity of abstract cultural objects of various sorts—e.g., scientific theories, speeches, laws, games. A physical theory, for example, can't be *simply* a set of sentences, propositions, or equations *if* it is in fact the possessor of properties such as brilliance, revolutionariness, derivativeness, immediate acceptance. For that very set of sentences, propositions, or equations might be found in another theory occurring fifty years earlier or later which lacked those properties.

Additional Notes

1. A highly condensed exposition of the theory defended here, and a situating of it in relation to competing theories, can be found in my article "Ontology of Music," in *Handbook of Metaphysics and Ontology* (Munich: Philosophia Verlag, 1990).
2. I must caution that by *sound structure* throughout this essay I did not mean anything more abstract than "this complex sound followed by this one, followed by this one," that is to say, a specified *sequence* of sounds, with all audible characteristics comprised. In particular, I didn't mean to identify a musical work with any sort of *reductive* structure, such as a Schenkerian diagram displays, or a Babbitian set-theoretic analysis posits, nor with any class of such structures. My "structures" are the highly particular on-the-surface patterns that are directly determined by the score and its associated conventions of interpretation.

    And I want to stress that *sound structure* includes all standardly specified audible features, including not just melodic, rhythmic, and harmonic ones, not even just timbral, dynamic, articulational ones as well, but also *tempo*. This last has sometimes been excluded from the relevant hearable structure of a musical work, notably by Goodman, but this is in my view a mistake. Tempo, even when broadly specified (e.g., allegro), is a real part of the kind of sounding event designated, and is squarely comprised in sound structure. To play the score of the finale (allegro con brio) of Beethoven's Seventh Symphony at a clear adagio speed, but otherwise note-perfectly, is *not* to realize its sound structure, on my usage.
3. In argument (4) for proposal MW as against MW', in section v, I spoke of the artistic divergences between W_1 and W_2 after they are composed in ways that are a little at odds with the argument against change of artistic content over time advanced in "Artworks and the Future" (Chapter 9, below), written later. The discrepancies will be minimized if one puts the emphasis on those works *exhibiting* (already implicit) artistic differences over time, rather than *coming* (newly) *to possess* such differences, and if one remembers that not all sorts of subsequently acquired significances—relevant though they all are to issues of logical individuation—are accounted part of artistic *content* in the later essay.

5 Autographic and Allographic Art Revisited

There is an important difference between some art forms and others which is pointed to by the observation that works in some forms (e.g., painting) admit of forgery in the ordinary sense, while works in other forms (e.g., music) do not. If we consider these six central art forms—painting, carved sculpture, cast sculpture, printmaking,[1] music, and poetry—we intuitively regard the first four as subject to forgery but not the last two. In chapter 3 of *Languages of Art*, Nelson Goodman introduces a distinction between autographic and allographic (= non-autographic) art which is intended to capture this difference between intuitively forgeable and nonforgeable arts and to divide the six art forms above in the manner indicated.[2]

In this essay I argue the following concerning Goodman's making of the distinction: (1) that the explicit definition of 'autographic' in chapter 3, section 3, does not divide the above six arts in the desired manner; (2) that there is an alternative definition[3] of 'autographic' suggested in chapter 3, section 4, based on the identification of the allographic with a further feature N; (3) that although Goodman

[1] Including woodcut, engraving, etching, mezzotint, dry-point, etc.
[2] Indianapolis: Bobbs-Merrill Company, 1968.
[3] The text need not be construed as proposing another *definition* of 'autographic/allographic', but only as noting a second *distinction* and claiming it to be *coextensive* with 'autographic/allographic' as originally defined. I find it instructive to present the issue in terms of alternate definitions. On either construal my points remain unaffected, since my critique rests entirely on extensional grounds.

believes these definitions or ways of making the distinction are extensionally equivalent, they are not; and (4) that the alternate (implicit)
definition completely fails to divide the six arts in the desired manner
(all turn out to be autographic according to it).

I then propose a definition of 'autographic' which makes use of the
important concept (N) involved in the alternate definition of chapter 3
but which allows music and poetry to remain allographic arts. My
primary aim in this essay is to show that Goodman is able to regard his
two conceptions of autographic art as equivalent only because he
ignores the historically and contextually bound nature of artworks in
the intuitively nonforgeable arts, music and poetry.

I

Goodman introduces and explicitly defines the notion of autographic
art as follows:

(1t) "Let us speak of a work of art as *autographic* if and only if the
distinction between original and forgery of it is significant; or
better, *if and only if even the most exact duplication of it does
not thereby count as genuine.*"[4]

First, I think that by 'it' in this definition one should understand 'the
work or its (genuine) instances'. Goodman takes the definition to be
applicable to multiple as well as singular art forms, yet it is not all that
clear what it would be to duplicate a woodcut or a symphony, rather
than an *impression* of one or a *performance* of the other.[5]

But second, and more important, it appears that the definition as it
now reads fails to include printmaking and cast sculpture as autographic arts. Given a genuine impression of some woodcut, I *can*
produce a duplicate of it which will be genuine; all I need to do is locate
the original block and take another impression from it. Similarly, there
can be exact duplicates of instances of a cast sculpture which count as
genuine; namely, additional ones cast from the original mold.

---

[4] *Languages of Art*, p. 113.
[5] Even duplicating the printing block of the woodcut is not so clearly duplicating the
woodcut itself, since even in the case of the original the woodcut (= the work of art) is
not identical with the block.

Goodman is fully aware of this point. Speaking of etching he says: "But even the most exact copy produced otherwise than by printing from that plate counts not as an original but as an imitation or forgery."[6] The trouble is that there is nothing in the explicit definition that answers to the qualification "produced otherwise than by printing from that plate," which qualification is needed to keep printmaking an autographic artform. A similar qualification ("produced otherwise than by casting from that mold") is needed to keep cast sculpture properly autographic.[7]

I now propose modifications of (1t) which serve clearly to mark off as autographic all and only the 'fine arts'. What we are after is the notion of an art for which *at most* only a certain *kind* of exact duplication counts as genuine.

The most straightforward way of modifying the definition to deal with the problem would be this. In the multiple autographic arts there is always some unique physical object (e.g., plate, block, mold) essentially involved in the process of production for genuine instances and which imparts to those instances a certain common structure. Call such an object where it exists an 'arch form'. A duplicate of a bronze or an etching made without employing the appropriate arch form is thus automatically inauthentic. Making use of this notion, the definition of autographic, clarified and emended, looks like this:

(1a) A work of art (and the art form it belongs to) is autographic(a) *iff* even the most exact duplication of the work or its genuine instances which does not employ the *appropriate arch form* does not count as genuine.[8]

---

[6] *Languages of Art*, p. 114.

[7] Richard Wollheim has pointed out to me that the qualifications I develop in this section may in effect be covered by the word "thereby" in Goodman's definition. That is, one can read (1t) as proposing that a work is autographic *iff* exact duplications of it (or its instances) do not count as genuine *simply in virtue of being* exact duplications. If this is the intended reading, then the qualifications I introduce are indeed unnecessary to keep printmaking and cast sculpture autographic. But as I will show in section III, if the definition is read in that manner, it embraces all of the arts from the outset, and not just the ones Goodman has it in mind to capture as autographic. It is thus useful to have a specification of (1t) which *does* effectively separate off the fine arts from the others. And this is provided by any of (1a), (1b), or (1c).

[8] The definition should of course be read so that painting counts as autographic. Since there *is* no arch form associated with a painting, no duplicate can employ it, and thus no duplicate can be genuine.

Unlike (1t), this definition manages to at least sort our six arts in the proper manner.

A less narrow attempt to emend (1t) would employ the notion of 'direct transcription'. I mean by 'direct transcription' a general kind of duplication process—one that in particular excludes duplication via an existing arch form. The idea of *directly transcribing* an artwork (or instances thereof) is that one observes, inspects, assesses, the artwork (or instance) and then attempts to produce something resembling it employing only the *standard tools* and *raw materials* of the medium. Direct transcription involves reproducing the object from scratch; it is a matter (à la Gombrich) of looking, and then making and matching. Thus, to directly transcribe a painting one looks hard and takes up a brush and oils and applies them to a canvas. To directly transcribe a woodcut one looks hard and takes up a block and a chisel and eventually, paper for impressions. The notion of directly transcribed duplicates is also applicable to poetry and music. To directly transcribe a copy of a poem one takes up pen, typewriter, or printing press, and a fresh piece of paper, and then produces with them the same configuration of words.[9] Directly transcribing a performance of a piano sonata is simply sitting down at the keyboard and playing what one has just heard. The difference between poetry and music on the one hand, and painting and printmaking on the other, is that directly transcribed duplicates can count as genuine in the former arts but not in the latter.

So a second emendation of (1t) would be this:

(1b) A work of art (and the art form it belongs to) is autographic(b)
      iff even the most exact duplication of the work or its genuine
      instances *by direct transcription* does not count as genuine.[10]

Since a duplication by direct transcription is always a duplication not employing the appropriate arch form, but not vice versa, 'auto-

---

[9] Not all intentional duplications of a copy of a poem would count as direct transcriptions. For example, if instead of typing out a copy of Shelley's "Ozymandias" from a book I own I were to go to the press responsible for the edition and have them print another copy for me from the original linotype, this would *not* be a directly transcribed copy in the sense I intend. Of course, copies of a poem produced *either* way are genuine, which distinguishes poetry from printmaking.

[10] Painting is, again, emphatically autographic on this definition: since *no* duplication of a painting counts as genuine, a fortiori no duplication by direct transcription does.

graphic(b)' is intensionally somewhat broader than 'autographic(a)'; i.e., being autographic(b) does not logically entail being autographic(a). For example, there could be a work of art in an art form in which certain duplicates not made from an arch form are genuine (thus making the work allographic(a)), but these duplicates are not directly transcribed ones, and moreover all directly transcribed duplicates are nongenuine (thus making the work allographic(b)). A work in the imaginary art form of serendicubes, which begins with an original aluminum cube and counts as further genuine instances of the work all and only cubical objects of the same size *discovered but not fashioned* within a radius of five miles, would be such a work (autographic(b) but not autographic(a)). Although autographic(a) and autographic(b) are not intensionally equivalent, they are very nearly so. The farfetched nature of the above example probably makes this clear; it is difficult to think of duplicates not made from arch forms which would not be directly transcribed ones. However, these two formulations of the autographic are certainly extensionally equivalent; that is to say, any existing art form is autographic(a) *iff* it is autographic(b).

There is, finally, a way of emending (1t) without explicitly invoking arch forms or direct transcription. The problem, recall, is that *some* exact duplicates of a print or cast sculpture *do* count as genuine, yet we still want these arts to be autographic. Now those duplicates only count as genuine because of *how they were made*. In order to capture this idea we don't have to prescribe or proscribe *specific* paths of duplication as such. In the multiple autographic art forms some duplicates are genuine but *no* duplicate is a genuine instance of a work *irrespective of its actual physical means of production*. So that if there are exact duplicates of a given work which count as genuine *regardless* of how they were physically produced, then that work and art form fail to be autographic. Our third emendation of (1t) would then be:

(1c) A work of art (and the art form it belongs to) is autographic(c) *iff* even the most exact duplication of the work or its genuine instances does not count as genuine *irrespective of the particular physical means of production involved.*[11]

[11] Note the emphasis on *physical means* of production. Definition (1c) does not say a work is autographic if *no* duplicate is genuine irrespective of its *history of production as a whole*. (If it did, then, as we shall see, it would count music and poetry as autographic.)

Clearly printmaking counts as autographic(c), whereas poetry does not. A candidate impression cannot be a genuine instance of print X regardless of what particular physical object was used to make it, whereas a candidate copy of poem Y may count as genuine regardless of what-if-any-pen was used to inscribe it.[12] The relation between autographic(c) and autographic(b) is complex. There are logically possible art forms that are autographic(c) but not autographic(b). Consider the art of quasipainting, which is like painting except that genuine instances in addition to the 'original' include paintings roughly reproducing the appearance of the 'original' which are painted with the *very same* brush and paints as were used in making the 'original'. Quasipainting is autographic(c) but neither autographic(b) nor autographic(a). Probably there could also be art forms that are autographic(b) but not autographic(c). Nevertheless, (1c), (1b), and (1a) are clearly close enough to be considered only slightly variant formulations of a single conception of the autographic. 'Autographic(c)' and 'autographic(b)' (and hence 'autographic(a)') are certainly extensionally equivalent; all existing arts (and in particular our six paradigms) are sorted by each definition into autographic and allographic in just the same way.

I cannot say which of the three modification of (1t) would most accord with Goodman's considered intention. However, there is no need to decide this. Since my objective in the remainder of this essay is to contrast this conception of the autographic, which separates the visual arts from the others, with a somewhat different conception also implicit in Goodman's chapter 3, I will ignore the differences between (1a), (1b), and (1c) and consider them as definitive of roughly a single notion of autographicity. I will refer to this as 'autographic(1)'. When unpacking is required I will incline to use formulation (1b).

II

Goodman makes the autographic/allographic distinction in chapter 3, section 3 of *Languages of Art*. In section 4 Goodman sets out to

---

[12] Music is also allographic(c) in that a duplicate of a performance of a piano sonata may be genuine (i.e., belong to the work) regardless of what particular piano is involved in the duplication—though not, of course, regardless of whether a piano is involved at all.

explain *why* some arts are autographic and others are allographic. The reason, according to Goodman, is that autographicity results when the sphere of the genuine for a given work is wholly circumscribed by notational correctness and not by physical origin.

Thus, poetry and music are allographic because all that is required for items to be genuine instances of sonnets or symphonies is that they be, in the one case, spelled correctly, and in the other case, compliant with the spelling in a certain score.

> All that matters for genuine instances of a poem is what may be called *sameness of spelling*: exact correspondence as sequences of letters, spaces, and punctuation marks.[13]

> The constitutive properties of a performance of the symphony are those prescribed in the score . . . there is a theoretically decisive test for compliance with the score . . . and a performance . . . is or is not strictly a performance of that work, according as it does or does not pass this test.[14]

A little later on, Goodman in effect identifies the allographic and the notational: "an art seems to be allographic *just insofar* as it is amenable to notation."[15] The impression of identification is strengthened in chapter 5 of *Languages of Art* and in some of Goodman's later comments in *Problems and Projects*.[16]

Let us say that works in a given art form are *notationally identifiable iff* identity of genuine instances of works is *solely* a matter of identity of character in a notation (e.g., poems) or compliance with a character in a notation (e.g., musical compositions). Roughly this is to say that in a notationally identifiable art form, structure, and nothing else, determines genuineness. What Goodman is proposing, then, is that the root of allographicity is notational identifiability, that the notions are in effect coextensive. Directly transcribed duplicates of a work or its instances are genuine when and only when the work is notationally identifiable.

We can thus see in section 4 the suggestion of an alternate, more fundamental concept of the autographic, one that Goodman takes to

[13] *Languages of Art*, p. 115.
[14] Ibid., pp. 117–18.
[15] Ibid., p. 121.
[16] Indianapolis: Hackett Publishing Co., 1972, pp. 128 and 136.

be extensionally equivalent to that of section 3. So as not to imply that Goodman is guilty of defining a single term in two different ways, let us explicitly label the alternate conception 'autographic(2)', and define it as follows:

> (2) A work of art (and the art form it belongs to) is autographic(2) *iff* the work is not notationally identifiable.[17]

Now, Goodman clearly believes that works of art are autographic(2) just in case they are autographic(1). He believes that, with respect to existing art forms, 'autographic(2)' and 'autographic(1)' cover exactly the same ground. In particular, he holds that music and poetry are allographic on either conception, whereas painting, printmaking, and sculpture are autographic.

The claim implicit in Goodman's discussion which I wish to challenge can now be put nicely as follows:

> (C) For any work *W* in an existing art form, *W* is notationally identifiable *iff* some duplication of *W* by direct transcription counts as genuine.[18]

In the next section I will show that (C) is false, and that Goodman's de facto equation of autographic(1) and autographic(2) is a mistake. This mistake will help us to see that poetry and music are not as different from painting and sculpture in a certain respect as is generally thought.

III

If musical compositions were simply pure sound structures and poems were simply pure verbal structures, such works would be neither auto-

---

[17]In a footnote in sec. 3, Goodman says about his explicit definition of 'autographic' that it is "a preliminary version of a difference we must seek to formulate more precisely" (p. 113). This promissory note is presumably cashed out in the meticulous theory of notation in chap. 4. But if the theory of notation is to make the notion of autographicity more precise, the autographic and notational must themselves be connected. This is, of course, accomplished in (2) above, and thus supports the idea that Goodman meant for something like (2) to supplant his initial conception of autographicity, while remaining coextensive with it.

[18]C is simply '*W* is allographic(2) *iff* *W* is allographic(1)' spelled out.

graphic(1) nor autographic(2). 'Autographic(1)' and 'autographic(2)' might then have been extensionally equivalent. But that is *not* what musical compositions and poems are. A musical work of the standard sort *contains* a pure notationally defined structure, but is not to be *identified* with that structure. I have recently argued elsewhere[19] that the standard musical work is not a *pure* structure at all, but an *indicated* structure—a pure structure of sounds and performance means-as-indicated-by-a-person-at-a-particular time.[20] Thus, Brahms's Piano Trio in C, op. 101, is not simply a sequence of sounds performed on a piano, violin, and cello, but rather that sequence-as-indicated-by-Brahms-in-the-summer-of-1880. The reasons for this more complex identification are primarily two: pure structures cannot be created, whereas musical works regularly are; and more important, pure sound/performance means structures cannot be the bearers of the determinate and fine-grained aesthetic and artistic attributes that musical works possess. The latter is true, in brief, because the aesthetic and artistic attributes of a work are not fixed solely by the relevant sound/performance means structure. This precludes identifying such works with the pure structures comprised in them.

For much the same reasons, a poem is certainly not just a given word sequence. A poem is the product of a particular individual at a specific time and place, with a reasonably definite meaning and aesthetic character that is in part a function of that time and place. A word sequence per se, on the other hand, existing as long as the relevant language has existed, cannot be the creation of a given person and possesses neither the sort of meaning nor the aesthetic character a poem bears in its context. By analogy with my proposal for musical works, I would be inclined to regard a poem of the standard sort as a word structure-as-indicated-by-X-at-t.[21] The poet typically indicates

---

[19] "What a Musical Work Is" (Chapter 4, above).

[20] In "What a Musical Work Is," I considered a closely related proposal, that a musical work is an S/PM (sound/performance means) structure-as-indicated-in-musico-historical context C, but concluded that it was not preferable to the proposal invoked here. Yet a combination of the two may be preferable to either of them. That is, understand a musical work as an S/PM structure-as-indicated-by-P-at-t-in-musico-historical context C. An additional virtue of this proposal is that it rightly counts as distinct identically scored works produced simultaneously by a single individual working in two different musical traditions or styles at once. (However, the essentialist implications at which some balk are thereby increased; see Chapters 8 and 10, below).

[21] My motivation here is similar to that of William Tolhurst in "On What a Text Is and How It Means," *British Journal of Aesthetics*, 19 (1979): 3–14. Tolhurst, seeking

a word structure—and thus (in the right circumstances) creates a structure-as-indicated—by setting down on paper an instance of that word structure.[22] This sort of entity—an indicated verbal structure—is both creatable and a possible possessor of the aesthetic and semantic properties that belong to the poem but cannot belong to the pure word structure included in it.

It remains to show how, if sonnets and sonatas are the sorts of entities I have proposed, 'autographic(1)' and 'autographic(2)' will fail to cut up the arts pie in the same way. Given a sonnet or sonata is a structure-as-indicated-by-X-at-t (i.e., an indicated structure) the instances of such a type are *more* than (though they must also be) instances of the associated pure word or S/PM structure. In order to be an instance of the indicated structure, an instance of the pure structure must in addition be *related in a certain way* to the dated act of indication (determination, fixation) of the pure structure by composer or poet which brings the sonata or sonnet into existence.

It would be difficult to state explicitly and perfectly generally what sort of relation this must be, although it is obvious that intentional and/or causal relatedness is involved. We can, however, give clear examples in which the appropriate relation is present and equally clear

---

likewise to block the identification of poem and word sequence, claims that a poem is an utterance of a word sequence on a particular occasion. The problem, though, is that Tolhurst regards an utterance as a string of word tokens (and thus as a *particular*) while also maintaining that a poem is a *type* that can have many instances. This seems to leave us with poems that both *are* and *are not* types. So far as I can see, Tolhurst does not succeed in resolving the metaphysical tension implicit in his view. While I think he is right to insist that the *meaning* of a poem is utterance *meaning*—i.e., the meaning of the utterance represented by the initial token of the poem—the *poem*, as a type, cannot actually *be* that particular utterance. It may, on the other hand, be a type of the unusual sort I suggest.

That aside, I am in complete accord with Tolhurst's arguments to the effect that literary works are not identical to pure verbal structures and have individualized meanings that those structures (word sequences) themselves do not.

[22]It is not clear that *every* act of indication directed on a pure structure results in the existence of an indicated structure. Perhaps certain conventions or cultural practices must be in effect before we will recognize indicated structures as the outcome of indication. But more clearly, not every indication of a word structure that *does* result in an indicated structure is a *literary work*. Obviously, artistic intent is required; A's newspaper article, B's physics paper, C's letter to *Time* magazine are indicated verbal structures but not literary works. For an account of what it is in general for an object—indicated structure, painted canvas, heap of doorknobs, or whatever—to be a work of art, see Chapters 1 and 3, above.

examples in which it is not. If Haydn pens a piano trio in 1789 and the Artaria publishing house sets up galleys based on Haydn's autographed manuscript in 1790 and some Viennese amateurs correctly produce an instance of the involved S/PM structure by reading from one of those Artaria editions in 1791, a genuine instance of Haydn's trio (an indicated S/PM structure) has been sounded. If John Ashbery invents a poem in his head in March, and then recites it to his amanuensis, who writes it down, photocopies it, and sends the photocopy to the *New Yorker*, who print it in the November issue, then that issue of the *New Yorker* contains a genuine instance of the work (an indicated verbal structure). If Schwartz listens to Milstein play the chaconne from Bach's Violin Partita in D Minor and subsequently (*mirabilu dictu!*) plays perfectly what he has just heard, Schwartz probably produces an instance of that work, even if he doesn't know what a chaconne is or who Bach is.

On the other hand, if simians at the typewriter eventually type at random the word sequence embodied in "Dover Beach," they have not produced a genuine copy of Arnold's poem; they have not instanced the indicated structure Arnold created. If instrumentalists on a planet of Aldebaran instantiate an S/PM structure just like that in Mendelssohn's Octet, this fails to count as a performance of the indicated structure that is Mendelssohn's creation—as does *any* instantiation of that S/PM structure *anywhere* which occurs before 1825. If I write out by hand a copy of Black's poem which has just appeared in the *Atlantic Review*, I have not produced a genuine copy of White's identically worded poem, which has coincidentally just appeared in the *Pacific Review*.[23]

---

[23] A more complex case in which intentional considerations vie with and seem to override more straightforward causal ones is this. Black and White publish poems containing identical word sequences in the same issue of a poetry review. Suppose I know Black and notice his poem in the review but don't know White and don't notice his poem. Then suppose I decide to copy out Black's poem by hand to send to another friend, but do this while unintentionally looking at the page of the review on which White's poem has been printed. My handwritten copy, I would maintain, is an instance of Black's poem and not White's, even though an instance of White's poem is the direct causal source of the copy in question. Or suppose I intend to play a famous waltz by Y I have not heard and have never seen the score of. Someone devilishly gives me a score of the Dadaistic composer Z's recent waltz, which strangely enough has the same S/PM structure as Y's waltz. I think that the sound event I produce is a performance of Y's waltz, not of Z's waltz. Yet there is no continuous causal chain running from Y's

What is present in the first set of examples but not in the second is the right sort of link or connection between copy or performance in question and the work itself as originating in an artist's creative activity on a particular occasion. To instantiate a historically rooted indicated structure such as a sonnet or a sonata it does *not* suffice merely to instantiate a certain pure structure. The genuineness of instances of sonatas and sonnets is thus *more* than a matter of structure or 'sameness of spelling'. *Not all* notationally correct duplicates count as genuine. The upshot, then, is that poems and musical compositions are *not* notationally identifiable—they are autographic(2), although allographic(1). This means that all six of our paradigm arts are autographic(2); none are strictly notationally identifiable.

It follows that 'autographic(1)' and 'autographic(2)' are not coextensive and that (C) is false. This is because poems and musical compositions, when correctly viewed, turn out to be just as historically tethered as paintings, prints, and sculptures. The difference is not, contra Goodman, that 'history of production' is irrelevant to genuineness in the former arts.[24] How a copy or performance has come about is as relevant to its authenticity as the provenance of an impression is to its belonging to a given print. The difference is rather that, in poetry and music, the notationality of structure permits genuine duplication without theoretical limit, and second, the origination conditions for genuineness are hardly ever in question and so are easily—though mistakenly—overlooked.

IV

We have now seen that the nonautographic (as originally defined) and the notationally identifiable do not in fact coincide. This is a simple consequence of the failure of any existing artwork to be notationally identifiable. No existing art forms are notationally identifiable because

creative act of indication to my performance of Y's waltz. This suggests that at least in some cases it is what you think you are producing or performing, not what copies or scores you are actually using, that determines what work the result belongs to—assuming the appropriate pure structure gets instantiated. I am inclined to believe that where intentional and causal criteria conflict, the former will generally determine the identity of the performance.

[24] Cf. *Languages of Art*, pp. 118 and 122.

there are not existing art forms in which created works can be regarded as pure rather than indicated structures, and no existing art forms in which historical factors are wholly irrelevant to the question of genuineness of work or instances. Furthermore, though I cannot undertake a defense of this here, I suspect that no such (completely ahistorical) art form is even possible—not if set against the complex background of interpretive and characterizing practices that has always framed artistic activity.

This is not to say that notationality does not in some fashion mark a very significant difference among the arts. The problem is that this difference, which Goodman explores so brilliantly throughout much of *Languages of Art,* is not to be expressed as the distinction between notationally identifiable (allographic(2)) arts and those that are not notationally identifiable (autographic(2)). As we have seen, 'allographic(2)' has null extension. What we want is a conception of the autographic framed in terms of notationality which *is* coextensive with the autographic as originally conceived ('no directly transcribed duplicate is genuine'), and which divides our six paradigm arts in the same fashion. I propose the following:

(3) A work of art (and the art form it belongs to) is autographic(3) *iff* the identity of genuine instances of the work is *not at all* determined by identity of character in a notation or compliance with a character in a notation.

An allographic(3) artwork (e.g., a ballad, a symphony, a dance, a play) is thus one in which genuineness of instances is *partly* determined by notational identity or compliance.[25]

I think it would be helpful at this point to review how our six paradigms stack up vis-à-vis each of conceptions of autographicity we have discussed.

autographic(1): painting, carved sculpture, cast sculpture, printmaking
autographic(2): painting, carved sculpture, cast sculpture, printmaking, poetry, music

---

[25] The alternation 'identity of character' or 'compliance with character' is needed because sonnets, say, are *in* a notation, while sonatas are only *defined* by a notation.

autographic(3): painting, carved sculpture, cast sculpture, printmaking

A review of the other arts will confirm that an art is either both
autographic(1) and autographic(3) or else both allographic(1) and
allographic(3). 'Autographic(1)' and 'autographic(3)' are thus distinct
pie cutters, but unlike 'autographic(1)' and 'autographic(2)', they effect only one division of the pie.

Recall that this division was to correspond to the distinction between the intuitively forgeable and intuitively nonforgeable arts. And
that it does. But we are now in a position to see that, *strictly speaking,*
forgery of literary and musical works is possible after all. This is
because facts of origin have a bearing on authenticity in those arts as
well as in all others. Remember that a forgery as Goodman defines it is
an object "falsely purporting to have the history of production requisite for the (or an) original of the work."[26] If I knowingly present a
copy of White's poem as if it were a copy of Black's (identically
worded) poem, forgery has occurred. If I knowingly give a performance of Z's waltz (from Z's score and with Z in mind) while presenting it as a performance of Y's (identically scored) waltz, this too is
forgery.[27] Furthermore, it is a forgery of a work, and not (*pace* Goodman) merely forgery of a *performance* of a work. If I indite a sonnet
myself and claim it is a long lost work of Keats, or if I compose a march
and attribute it to the fictitious eighteenth-century Polish composer
Dubacewski, this is forgery once again.[28] In all of the foregoing cases

[26] *Languages of Art*, p. 122.

[27] The following worry may arise in some reader's mind at this point. If what makes a
performance a performance of Z's waltz rather than Y's waltz is that the performer
intentionally relates the performance to Z and Z's creative activity, then how can this
performance serve as a forgery of Y's waltz? Wouldn't that require the performer to
think of the performance *as being of* Y's waltz as well, and if so, *wouldn't* it be of Y's
waltz, and hence *not* a forgery? The way out of this puzzle is to recognize that forgery
can occur in virtue of the difference between the *generation* of a performance as an
instance of a particular work and the *presentation* (or *labeling*) of the performance as
an instance of a particular (possibly different) work. To forge Y's waltz the performer
must deceitfully *put forward* the performance as being of Y's waltz; but the performer
need not and must not *think* of it as deriving from and relating to Y's creative activity.

[28] Fritz Kreisler's notorious presentations of his own archaically flavored violin
pieces as if they were compositions by Porpora, Boccherini, and the like are actual cases
of this kind of forgery. So are Edward Fitzgerald's presentation of *The Rubaiyat of*

the history of production of the object is other than what it purports to be, and other than what it needs to be for genuineness.

The preceding examples call attention to something that is rarely brought out in discussions of forgery. This is that forgeries are of *two* main types. We can call the first type *referential* forgery and the second type *inventive* forgery. Something is a referential forgery if it falsely purports to be the or an original of a particular *actually existing* work of art. Thus the copy of White's poem and the performance of Z's waltz are referential forgeries (of, respectively, Black's poem and Y's waltz). A referential example in painting would be a forgery of Giorgione's *Tempest*. In referential forgery, there always exists some genuine work which the forgery *is of* (and thus, in a loose sense, *refers* to). Something is an inventive forgery if it falsely purports to be the or an original of a work that *does not exist,* and whose ascribed artist may not exist either. Thus, the 'Keats' sonnet and 'Dubacewski' march are inventive forgeries. A well-known inventive example in painting would be the numerous 'Vermeers' of Van Meegeren.

Inventive forgery is a serious and troublesome matter in both autographic and allographic arts. It distorts our grasp of a given artist's oeuvre and style, or of a given period's characteristics, as well as disguising and misrepresenting the achievement of individuals.[29] Van Meegeren's 'Vermeers' and Kreisler's violin confections threaten our conceptions of eighteenth-century painting and eighteenth-century music and manipulate us to give credit where it isn't due. While an inventive forgery is not artistically inferior to its original (there being none), it is in most cases of much less worth artistically than we are led to believe.

But referential forgery, while serious and much noted in the autographic—that is, autographic(1) or (3)—arts, is an unnoted and, I think, relatively harmless possibility in the allographic arts. Why is this so? Why is a forgery of *The Tempest* deeply disturbing whereas a forgery of Black's poem or Y's waltz is only mildly disconcerting? Why is the distance between an original painting and a forgery of it so much

---

Omar Khayyam as entirely the work of that Persian poet, and James MacPherson's presentation of his own romantic prose poems as the work of the legendary third-century Irish bard Ossian.

[29]See Denis Dutton, "Artistic Crimes: The Problem of Forgery in the Arts," *British Journal of Aesthetics,* 19 (1979): 302–14.

greater than the distance between authentic and inauthentic instances of poems and musical compositions? I think there are two main reasons for this.

One is that we can assure ourselves that some forgeries of a given poem can serve as well as genuine copies for aesthetic appreciation, and the same is true of some forgeries of a musical work vis-à-vis genuine performances of it.[30] What we are directly interested in with a musical or literary work is its structure understood in the work's proper historical setting. Now, a forgery known to be such carries with it and implies an appreciative context different from that of the original. But *in principle* we can ignore this and sustain the context appropriate to the genuine article—that is to say, we can 'go along with' the forgery. Since a forgery can have the same essential structure as a genuine instance, and this is ascertainable, the result for aesthetic appreciation can be demonstrably the same. A forged copy of a poem which is nonetheless correctly spelled, or a forged performance of a waltz which has nonetheless been correctly sounded, works as well as a genuine copy or performance if it is simply regarded as if it were one.[31] On the other hand, consider an ostensibly perfect forgery of a painting—i.e., one that is at present perceptually indistinguishable from the original. We *cannot* assure ourselves that the forgery can serve as well as the original for aesthetic appreciation. Granted that *if* it were an absolutely perfect forgery and *if* we were to regard it or think of it as the original (e.g., as coming from the hand of Giorgione in 1505), *then* the appreciative experience would be the same. But we *cannot ever know* if we have got a perfect forgery of a painting. So we cannot ever know if the forgery would provide the same experience as the original were we to regard it as such. As Goodman has pointed out,

---

[30]Note that I am *not* saying the forgery would have the same aesthetic properties as a genuine copy. It wouldn't. Cf. Mark Sagoff, "The Aesthetic Status of Forgeries," *Journal of Aesthetics and Art Criticism*, 35 (1976): 169–80.

[31]I do not mean to suggest that we *should* do this—that when confronted with apparently perfect forgeries (of either autographic or allographic artworks) known to be such we *should* ignore their provenance and treat them *as if* they were the originals. To do this may make us accessories to 'artistic crimes' (cf. Dutton, "Artistic Crimes") and underminers of the real value originals possess (cf. Mark Sagoff, "On Restoring and Reproducing Art," *Journal of Philosophy*, 75 [1978]: 453–70). I leave it as an open and difficult question here in what cases, if any, we are justified in adopting toward an artistic object an appreciative stance that does not accord with its creational history.

the forgery cannot be ascertained to possess the same essential structure as the original—for the notion of essential structure is inapplicable to painting as it presently exists. There simply is no structure-capturing notation for painting.[32] Thus, whereas a forgery of a poem or a waltz can be certified to be aesthetically as serviceable as a genuine instance, given the same appreciative stance is taken to both, a forgery of a painting or other autographic artwork can't be so certified. With a forged poem or waltz I can convince myself that if I manage to regard it as genuine, my experience of it will be qualitatively the same as if it were genuine. With a forged painting, however, I cannot convince myself that if I simply treat it as the original, my experience of it will be the same as my experience of the original.

The second reason why forgery of existing paintings is more upsetting than forgery of existing poems or waltzes is that it clearly *is* easier to disregard the inauthenticity of a perfectly forged poem or waltz than to disregard the inauthenticity of a perfectly forged painting. And this, I think, is probably due to the differing sorts of relations which ground authenticity in poetry and music as opposed to visual art. Structural requirements aside, authenticity in poetry and music is primarily a matter of intentional relatedness, not causal relatedness. The identity of a performance, say, is more a matter of what work the performer has in mind, of how the performer conceives of what he or she is doing, than of what work is the causal source of the score or memory which directly guides the performer in producing the appropriate sound event. Now the fact is that intentional relatedness, though more wide-ranging, is just not as gripping as causal relatedness in this context; an authenticity that derives from the former seems less precious than one based on the latter.[33]

We seem to feel more deeply connected with the artist's creative

---

[32] Cf. *Languages of Art,* chap. 3 and chap. 5, sec. 4.

[33] Furthermore, even if there are cases (cf. the Bach-Milstein-Schwartz example above) where the identity of a performance as belonging to a given work seems to be adequately secured just by the presence of an appropriate causal chain from the origination of the work to the issuance of the sound event, that sort of causal relatedness—typically involving manuscript copying, typesetting, aural memory—includes intentional *links* and is significantly different from the direct material causality involved in the authenticity of works of visual art. (By the latter I mean roughly this: any genuine instance of a painting, sculpture, or print has been physically affected by the artist or has been in contact with some other object so affected.)

activity—and thus less willing and able to ignore inauthenticity—when genuineness is based on and reflects a direct causal relation to the artist. This is the case in painting, sculpture, and printmaking. Confronted with the forged *Tempest* we feel the absence of physical connection to Giorgione acutely. We can't easily substitute appreciative contexts and regard the forgery as we do the real *Tempest*. Confronted with a referential forgery of some poem or waltz, though, it seems we would find the absent intentional connection to be something we could overlook with relative ease. If an impression taken from a woodblock on which Breughel actually labored is inadvertently mixed up with an excellent (at this point indistinguishable) forgery, something very important to us may have become unrecoverable. But if a copy of Black's poem, a copy of White's poem, and a chimp-generated copy of no poem—all containing the same word sequence in the same typeface—get indistinguishably jumbled, the resulting ontological degradation would most likely be accepted with equanimity. Chains of thought connect us to particular people and things, all right, but they are not so treasured nor so carefully guarded as chains of material causation.

v

When we review the autographic/allographic distinction from the perspective we have now attained, what do we find? On the one hand, there are the crucial differences: in allographic arts, identity is partially determined notationally, and directly transcribed duplicates can be genuine. But on the other hand, there is an underlying similarity: authenticity in all the arts involves a relation to a unique, historically positioned creative act, and thus all the arts are subject, with varying degrees of gravity, to forgery. The authentic *Night Watch* is the one Rembrandt made on a definite occasion in 1642. An authentic *Capriccio no. 43* is one pulled directly from a plate on which Goya toiled in 1779. So too, an authentic copy of *Correspondences*, or an authentic performance of the *Tragic* Overture, is one that is intentionally (and usually also causally) linked to particular creative activities of Baudelaire and Brahms in 1845 and 1881, respectively. And this, as I have said, is because of what such works *are*—namely temporally bound indicated structures.

6 Aesthetic Uniqueness

Works of art[1] taken individually are often said to be unique. What does this amount to? Clearly it amounts to more than numerical uniqueness, a distinction that fails to distinguish WOAs from anything else. Presumably, it is aesthetic uniqueness that is meant.[2] WOAs differ from one another aesthetically, one might say, because of differences in structure, every difference in structure yielding an aesthetic difference. The question I consider in this essay is whether every structurally distinct WOA has a unique aesthetic content. By aesthetic content of a WOA I mean the set of all aesthetic attributes belonging or attaching to the work. I take the thesis of aesthetic uniqueness to be this:

[1] The phrase "work of art" will often be abbreviated by WOA in the course of this essay.

[2] Mary Mothersill, in "'Unique' as an Aesthetic Predicate," *Journal of Philosophy*, 58 (1961): 421–37, says that the significant sense of uniqueness for works of art is their being one of a kind in respect to form. In my terms, this is approximately structural uniqueness, not aesthetic uniqueness. In any event, nothing ensures the structural uniqueness of works of art, even putting forgeries to one side. For example, works of art from different cultures which were very different in meaning might be exactly the same in perceptible structure.

Nonstructural attributes in respect of which structurally identical works may differ include chemical composition, density, creatorship, ownership, monetary value, spatial location, country of origin, and minutely specific physical attributes—e.g., ones of length, height, color, pitch. (Cf. section II.)

(AU) Works of art that differ structurally differ aesthetically (or: Works of art that differ in structural attributes differ in aesthetic attributes).[3]

A few words on interpreting this claim are in order. First, AU should not be understood as a descriptive (de facto) generalization to the effect that all *existent* WOAS are in fact different aesthetically. AU should rather be understood to range over all possible, as well as actual, WOAS. The de facto generalization covering just the artworks that happen to exist would only be of interest if it were thought to point to or be grounded in the universal (de jure) generalization that AU represents. AU is thus the assertion of a lawlike connection between structure and aesthetic content.[4] It expresses the conviction, derived from experience and observation, that no structural change in a WOA can *help* inducing an aesthetic one. It will therefore serve to disprove AU if we can produce a pair of *possible* artworks which differ structurally but are aesthetically identical; a pair of actual artworks is not required. Or AU can be disproved by showing that certain structural changes *could* be made in some actual artwork with no resultant aesthetic change.

In thinking about the thesis of aesthetic uniqueness one must also be sure not to confuse it with another claim, more obviously false, according to which structurally distinct WOAS always differ in their *broadest* or *most general* aesthetic attributes. It scarcely needs mentioning that structural differences do not invariably make for overarching aesthetic differences. Change part of the mountain from blue to violet in Cézanne's *Mont Sainte-Victoire* and one still has a *calm* painting. Chopin's Prelude op. 28, no. 4, and the funeral march from Beethoven's *Eroica* are, for all their structural differences, both *sad*

[3] I use the general term "attribute" throughout this essay, covering both properties and qualities (e.g., being graceful, gracefulness). For more on that distinction, see my "Properties and Related Entities," *Philosophy and Phenomenological Research*, 39 (1978): 1–22.

Note that in this thesis only attributes of whole works, not parts of works, are intended. However, the latter are easily transposed into the former. For example, if the arm of the statue is graceful, the statue has a graceful arm; if the introduction to the sonata is adagio, the sonata has an adagio introduction. And so on.

[4] In other words, AU should be construed as supporting counterfactual conditionals—e.g., if there were two WOAS W_1 and W_2 of distinct structures S_1 and S_2, then W_1 and W_2 would be aesthetically divergent.

pieces of music. Aesthetic uniqueness is uniqueness of *aesthetic content,* which comprises all of a work's aesthetic attributes and not, say, only the most dominant, general, or salient ones.

Recent discussion in aesthetics has not really dealt with the question of whether AU is true, though its truth often seems to be unthinkingly assumed. On the other hand, somewhat related claims of a causal sort concerning structure and aesthetic content have been explicitly enunciated and defended. The most fundamental of these is the Causal Dependency thesis, and is quite uncontroversial:

(CD) The aesthetic attributes of a WOA depend causally on its non-aesthetic attributes.

Aesthetic attributes are not occult, untethered, but rather causally emergent on and determined by more basic kinds of attributes.[5] A second claim, which we can call the Fine Causal Dependency thesis, has become equally prominent:

(FCD) Aesthetic differences between WOAS may be occasioned by very small structural differences.

This thesis is also more or less aesthetic orthodoxy, and has been so since Frank Sibley's landmark article of 1959.[6]

It should be obvious, I think, that neither CD nor FCD *entails* AU. That aesthetic attributes depend on structural ones does not guarantee that every collection of structural attributes generates a *unique* set of

[5] Monroe Beardsley discusses the nature of this dependency in section I of his article "The Descriptivist Account of Aesthetic Attributions," *Revue Internationale dé Philosophie* (1974): 336–52. See also Frank Sibley's "Aesthetic and Non-Aesthetic," *Philosophical Review,* 74 (1965): 135–59.

[6] "Aesthetic Concepts," *Philosophical Review,* 68 (1959): 421–50: "The aesthetic quality depends upon exactly this individual or unique combination of just these specific colors and shapes so that even a slight change might make all the difference" (p. 432). More recent expressions of this thesis follow: "The presence or absence of an aesthetic quality is very often, and therefore *may* in any particular case be, at the mercy of extremely subtle variations in non-aesthetic qualities" (Beardsley, "The Descriptivist Account of Aesthetic Attributions," p. 343). "There is no guarantee that a slight change in color or shape will leave the aesthetic qualities of a painting unaffected, and this is why reproductions often have aesthetic qualities different from those of the original" (Timothy Binkley, "Piece: Contra Aesthetics," *Journal of Aesthetics and Art Criticism,* 35 [1977]: 270).

aesthetic ones. That very small structural differences *can* lead to aesthetic differences in no way assures that they *invariably* do so.[7] Neither
CD nor FCD provides a guarantee that to each artistic structure will
correspond a unique aesthetic content. It may turn out that there are
more possible structurally distinct works of art than there are complexes of aesthetic characteristics. Thus there would be a many-one
mapping between artistic structures and resultant aesthetic contents.

A concept that has been much investigated of late is that of the
condition-governedness of the aesthetic. I want to consider the relation
between this concept and AU. Recent literature makes a helpful distinction between *occurrence*-conditions of aesthetic *attributes* and
application-conditions of aesthetic *terms*.[8] To say aesthetic attributes
have occurrence-conditions is only to say that there are nonaesthetic
attributes that are *causally* responsible for any aesthetic attribute present in a WOA (which is what CD affirms). To say an aesthetic term ϕ has
application-conditions is to say that there are finite lists of nonaesthetic features such that one is *warranted* in judging ϕ to apply to a WOA if
the WOA is known to possess all the features on such a list. Alternatively, ϕ has application-conditions if there are sets of nonaesthetic
features the presence of which logically *entails* the applicability of ϕ.[9]

Is there a connection between AU, a thesis about the occurrence of
aesthetic attributes, and application-condition governedness? Well, if
AU were true, aesthetic content would always be perturbable by structural changes, however minute, and judgments of aesthetic content
could thus never be assured from less than a complete list of structural
attributes. For example, if W were aesthetically unique, then W^*,
differing from W in a single nonaesthetic feature, would diverge from
W in some aesthetic predicate, ψ. But then neither the set (S) of
nonaesthetic attributes common to W and W^*, nor any subset of that
set, could possibly be application-conditions for ψ, since given S the

[7]Furthermore, even if all *small* structural differences *do* eventuate in aesthetic differences, it remains open that some *large*, blatant structural differences do *not*. This will
turn out to be of importance later in this essay.

[8]See Sibley, "Objectivity and Aesthetics," *Proceedings of the Aristotelian Society,*
supplementary volume 42 (1968): 31–72; Beardsley, "The Descriptivist Account of
Aesthetic Attributions."

[9]For more on the matter of application-conditions, see Peter Kivy, "Aesthetic Concepts: Some Fresh Considerations," *Journal of Aesthetics and Art Criticism,* 37 (1979):
423–32.

applicability of ψ is undetermined. Does it *follow* then that ψ lacks application-conditions? Hardly, for some set of features unrelated to S might do the job. Application-conditions need only be sufficient, not necessary. The fact that ψ turns up in some works (e.g., W) in the *absence* of certain conditions C would not prevent C from being such that when C *is* present, so is ψ, and we are in addition *warranted* in ascribing ψ to W on the basis of C.

In the other direction, even if every aesthetic term lacked application-conditions, that would not imply the truth of AU. For there might be two works, structurally very similar, no list of their structural features being sufficient to justify the application of any aesthetic terms, but which *in fact* possessed all and only the same aesthetic attributes. There is nothing in the absence of condition governing for aesthetic terms that would in itself guarantee AU; it would still be a matter of seeing how things turned out with individual works (though "taste," or something like it, might be required to do so). In sum, it seems there is no entailment either way between AU and the noncondition-governedness of aesthetic terms.

In asking whether structurally different artworks always exhibit aesthetic differences I am naturally thinking of pairs of works in the same genre, art form, or tradition, calling for the same general perceptual set or manner of reading. For it has been amply demonstrated[10] that structurally *identical* works, if they belong to different genres, art forms, or traditions, will exhibit numerous aesthetic differences. But if structurally identical works of different genres differ aesthetically, then obviously structurally different works of different genres will do so as much or more. Clearly, then, it is only pairs of works *within* a given genre/art form/tradition which provide any likely challenge to AU. It is only for such works that we can reasonably entertain the possibility of aesthetic equivalence despite structural divergence.[11]

[10]See Kendall Walton, "Categories of Art," *Philosophical Review,* 79 (1970): 334–67, and Nelson Goodman, *Languages of Art* (Indianapolis: Bobbs-Merrill, 1968). The aesthetic attributes of a work of art depend not only on its structure but also (in Walton's terms) on the correct category of perception for the work, or (in Goodman's terms) on the symbol system it is taken to be a character in. A work's structural attributes are never the sole determinants of its aesthetic content. For another way of approaching this conclusion, see Mark Sagoff, "The Aesthetic Status of Forgeries," *Journal of Aesthetics and Art Criticism,* 35 (1976): 169–80.

[11]Since the problem of aesthetic uniqueness will call to mind for many readers Goodman's discussion of forgery in chap. 3 of *Languages of Art,* it is worth noting that

I take it that the intrinsic interest of AU will be granted. But let me highlight, before moving on, three implications of the truth or falsity of AU.

(1) Artworks are often accorded a special status or respect on the grounds that each is aesthetically unique. It is something of an unscrutinized dogma that every artwork will not fail to be one of a kind aesthetically, that every artwork is guaranteed to have something different and unduplicated to offer us as a work of art. If AU is false, then this special attitude toward artworks would be partly undermined.

(2) If AU is true, then no structural decision an artist makes in creating a work can fail to have aesthetic import; on the other hand, if AU is false, then some such decisions may have no aesthetic import.

(3) If AU is true, all of an artist's works will be aesthetically distinct; if AU is false, some of them could be aesthetically identical.

II

The literature on the notion of an aesthetic attribute is vast.[12] I do not undertake to recount it or improve upon it here. I take aesthetic

---

he is there out for different game than I am after. First, there is the fact that he construes "aesthetic difference" more broadly than I do. He is concerned to show that between perceptually indistinguishable pictures one of which is a forgery there is indeed an aesthetic difference, namely, the fact that one *may* in the future make a perceptual distinction between them. Goodman also considers an attribute of a work that determines how it is to be regarded (e.g., in some cases, who created it, where, or why) as an aesthetic one. Now, I am holding such differences and qualities to be *nonaesthetic* though I grant them to be *aesthetically relevant* differences and qualities. Second, in Goodman's usage, a perceptible difference between artworks is automatically an aesthetic one, his aim being to show that an imperceptible difference can be aesthetic as well, whereas in my framework a perceptible difference is not automatically an aesthetic one, the question being precisely whether the one kind of difference always guarantees the other. In my terminology, what Goodman shows in chap. 3 is that one cannot *assume* that two presently indistinguishable by perception paintings are not different in aesthetic attributes: Given an original and a presently indistinguishable forgery, there is an *aesthetically relevant* difference *now* between the two and there *may* be a difference in *aesthetic* attributes as well.

[12]See Sibley, "Objectivity and Aesthetics"; M. Freedman, "The Myth of the Aesthetic Predicate," *Journal of Aesthetics and Art Criticism*, 27 (1968): 49–55; M. Beardsley, "What Is an Aesthetic Quality?" *Theoria*, 39 (1973): 50–70; T. Cohen, "Aesthetic/Non-Aesthetic and the Concept of Taste," *Theoria*, 39 (1973): 113–52; P. Kivy, "What Makes 'Aesthetic' Terms Aesthetic," *Philosophy and Phenomenological Research*, 35 (1975): 197–211.

attributes to be the class of attributes Sibley and others have familiarized us with. We have a fairly good intuitive grasp on this class, even though a clear and noncircular explicit definition remains elusive. Garishness, unity, flamboyance, and febrility belong to it; redness, weight, price, and belonging to Napoleon do not. I will take it, though, that perceivability is a necessary feature of aesthetic attributes.

It remains to characterize the less familiar notion of a structural attribute before considering some attempts to demonstrate the truth of AU. I will understand structural attributes to be a subset of *non* aesthetic attributes.

Roughly speaking, the structural attributes of a WOA are those nonaesthetic attributes that are perceivable in the work;[13] a structural difference between two works is then the possession by one of some structural attribute not possessed by the other. I define structural attribute in this way so that judging of AU will be tantamount to answering the intuitive question, "Does every perceivable difference make for an aesthetic difference?" Structural attributes include those of line, shape, color, texture, shadow, tempo, pitch, rhythm, timbre, tempo, word order, rhyme, height, width. Such comprise the structure of WOAs as open to normal observation.

It is clear that the aesthetic attributes of a WOA depend on its structural ones, and that aesthetic changes in a given work would seem to require structural changes underpinning them. At least this is true in any instance I am familiar with. However, it is *conceivable* that the appearance of some aesthetic attribute in a work might not be attributable to any structural change as I have defined it, but only to a nonstructural one. For example, take a colored region in a painting the precise shade of which is altered by altering its chemical composition,

---

[13] An attribute is perceivable in a work if the work can be determined to have the attribute through appropriate experience of the work. The term "appropriate" is admittedly vague, but it would be neither useful nor easy to make the matter more precise in this context. What counts as appropriate perception for one work of art is very different from what counts as such for another. This will be determined in each case by the nature of the genre, the aims and intentions of the artist or school, and other factors. The range of viewing distances that is acceptable, the range of lighting that would be suitable, the sort of viewing perspective one should adopt, the admissibility of instruments as viewing aids—all this is variable and not specifiable in the abstract. (Think of a seventeenth-century Dutch still life, a large landscape by Sisley, a piece of Op-Art by Vasarely.) I mean to convey this flexibility by speaking of "appropriate perception"; in particular, one should not take this as equivalent to "unaided perception."

but which is not, in the context of the painting, a perceptibly different color than before. The difference in shade is only apparent by direct comparison of the original and altered regions with certain colored patches outside the painting; it would by hypothesis not be apparent in comparison of the original and altered regions with each other. This alteration in shade, since it does not involve the loss or gain of any attribute perceivable in the painting, is thus nonstructural. However, such a change *just might* bring it about that the painting was, say, harmonious in higher degree than before (e.g., very harmonious as opposed to rather harmonious). This would be a case of a nonstructural change resulting in an aesthetic change without involving a structural change. Nothing hinges for us on whether there actually are such cases or not. We may admit that nonstructural changes as well as structural changes *can* induce aesthetic ones. Our question, recall, is whether structural changes *always* induce aesthetic ones. The corresponding question for nonstructural changes, whether they always induce aesthetic ones, is so obviously to be answered in the negative as to be of no further concern.

I suggested above that structural attributes were nonaesthetic attributes of works that were perceivable in them. And by this I mean perceivable in a work under normal or appropriate conditions of perception for the work. Questions remain, though, about the perceivability of such attributes. A major problem is one of saying how finely *specific* an attribute still counts as perceivable in a work. It seems clear that *having a straight line* and *having a straight line 5 centimeters long* should count as perceivable in a painting, but what about *having a straight line 5.0005 centimeters long*? I want to say that the latter is *not* perceivable in a painting because one could not on normal viewing tell *that* a line in a painting was 5.0005 centimeters in length *as opposed* to 5.0006 centimeters (or tell a line of 5.0005 centimeters *from* one of 5.0006 centimeters). One way to capture what we want is to define structural attribute in terms of structural difference, rather than vice versa. Structural difference is actually the more basic notion and suffices for any of the issues discussed in this essay. But the notion of structural attribute is convenient, if ultimately dispensable. So let us take the following:

(SD) Structural difference: a perceivable difference that is not itself an aesthetic difference (i.e., a difference in regard to some aesthetic attribute).

(SA) *X* is a structural attribute of a work of art *W* *iff*: substitution or replacement of *X* in *W* by any attribute of the same sort and level of specificity amounts to a structural difference.[14]

This formulation makes it clear that 5 centimeters length is a structural attribute while 5.0005 centimeters length is not; if a 5 centimeter line in a painting is altered to 6 centimeters, that amounts to a structural difference, while alteration of a 5.0005 centimeter line to 5.0006 centimeters does not.[15]

Other illustrations are these. *Exemplifying the ratio 4/7* would be a structural attribute since one can distinguish between a painted or architectural rectangle that conforms to that proportion and one that conforms to the nearby proportion 3/5. But *exemplifying the ratio 999/2000* is not likely structural for a typical visual artwork since not distinguishable from exemplification of the ratio 1000/2000.[16] *Containing a right angle* is structural but not likely *containing an angle of 60° 30'. Being in the key of B* is structural, but not likely *being scored for exactly 105 violins in unison*; one will detect a change from B to B-flat but one might not detect a change from 105 to 104 violins.

It would at first seem that no attribute of a *literary* work could fail to be structural on the grounds of overspecificity; literary works are

[14]Note that on this pair of definitions, "structural difference" and "difference in some structural attribute" come out coextensive—which is not so on some alternate pairs.

[15]I do not think there is a corresponding problem about the perceivability of *aesthetic* attributes. The attributes that turn out to be aesthetic have no independent quantitative standard of mensuration, but are instead indicated and individuated in a wholly phenomenal manner. In other words, although there are attributes of the same sort as structural ones which are nonstructural because too finely specified, there are no attributes of the same sort as aesthetic ones which fail to be aesthetic for such a reason. For instance, if sadness$_3$ and sadness$_4$ are two specific degrees of sadness attaching to WOAS, and we are incapable of perceiving or apprehending any work as having sadness greater than sadness$_3$ but less than sadness$_4$, then there *is no* sadness attribute intermediate between them (and thus the question of its being aesthetic cannot arise).

[16]A trickier question would be whether *exemplifying the Golden Section* counts as structural or not. It would depend on how precisely "the Golden Section" is interpreted. If the attribute in question is tantamount to *exemplifying a ratio of exactly .616*, then it is probably not structural for many works. If it is rather the attribute *exemplifying a ratio approximating three to five*, then it is likely to be structural.

fundamentally just words, and no alteration in words would be un-detectable to normal experience of the work (i.e., reading). But what of an attribute of a novel such as *containing 12,345 h's* $(= A_1)$? This does not strike one as an attribute whose presence in contrast to *containing 12,346 h's* $(= A_2)$ would be noticeable within the normal mode of apprehending a novel. So perhaps there are attributes of literary works which, while intuitively part of structure, are not structural by (SA). However, note that attributes such as the ones just mentioned, even if nonstructural themselves, cannot be altered without inducing changes in *other* attributes that *are* structural. For example, replacing A_1 by A_2 would entail deletion of *some* attribute like the following, which is clearly structural: *containing the word "harmony" in its last sentence*.

III

What arguments are there in support of AU? As we noted above, there is no argument for AU from lack of application-conditions for aesthetic terms. To what, then, can the defender of AU appeal? One way of arguing for AU hinges on a possible gap between aesthetic attributes and their linguistic expression. Thus a defender of AU might offer the following: "It may be that two structurally distinct works are the same in all aesthetic attributes that can be *verbally indicated*. But there are always aesthetic attributes we cannot verbally indicate in which the works diverge."

To what extent are aesthetic attributes expressible through linguistic means? Clearly enough, there are now, and will be in future, aesthetic features that lack standard designators. Consider a highly specific aesthetic attribute of some work. It is likely to be nameless, with no recognized label, simply because it is so specific, or because it has not occurred before in any known work (or at least not often enough). Nothing would seem to prevent us, however, from christening it on the spot with an appropriate term (either neologistic or metaphorical), even though we may have no further use for the label outside of that particular work.[17]

But that is not the end of the matter. Such christening will not

[17]The exact "extent" of the attribute christened—i.e., just how specific it is—is perhaps only fixed or clarified by further applications of the term in other cases.

succeed unless we can uniquely fix the reference of the term we wish to introduce. If a WOA turns up with two or more new or unlabeled aesthetic attributes (which is quite likely) we will not adequately fix a reference by speaking of "*the* new specific aesthetic attribute apparent in the work." Or if we detect aesthetic differences in work *A* vis-à-vis a similar work *B*, speaking of "*the* specific aesthetic attribute present in *A* but not in *B*" will fail of its purpose if there is more than one specific differential attribute between them. Does this mean we will be unable to fix a label on newly recognized attributes in such cases? I think not. For surely there will be *some* previously recognized and named aesthetic attribute that is more akin to one of the new ones than it is to the others, and which could be invoked to give an identifying description of that particular new attribute, via the similarity.

In sum, I believe we need not fear that our linguistic resources will be inadequate to capturing aesthetic attributes and differences once they have been recognized. If we can tell with assurance that works differ in some aesthetic respect, then we *can* also refer to such differences identifyingly; there are no more recognizable aesthetic attributes than there are verbally expressible ones. Finally, *even* if there were aesthetic attributes that we could notice but not label, then though this widens the field for aesthetic divergence between structurally different WOAs, it hardly follows that there *must be* such unnameable attributes separating them in every case.

A second and more interesting line of argument for AU is this. Aesthetic uniqueness might be thought to be guaranteed if it is the case that every structural element in a WOA has associated with it a unique aesthetic *vector* or *tendency*. Or alternatively, if every structural element in a WOA makes a prima facie aesthetic contribution to the work which is uniquely its own. If so, then a given musical phrase will (in a given context) incline a piece to a specific aesthetic attribute A_1, and a given color patch will (in a given context) incline a painting to a specific aesthetic attribute A_2, and no other phrase or patch inclines in exactly the same directions.

Granted the implausibility of this atomistic view of the generation of aesthetic content, still, even if it or something like it is true, it does not entail AU. For even if structural elements all pull in unique aesthetic directions, when the elements of a work combine into a whole, aesthetic vectors may combine so as to yield an aesthetic content that is equally realizable by some other combination of elements and associated vectors. Suppose, for illustration, a diminutive piece of music consisting of two phrases, P_1 and P_2, with vectors toward, respectively, A_1 and A_2; let the resultant aesthetic attribute of P_1P_2 be A_5 (assume for simplicity that this one attribute is its whole aesthetic content). It is still open that two different phrases, P_3 and P_4, with vectors toward A_3 and A_4, could form a piece of P_3P_4 with the same aesthetic result, A_5. A chemical analogy suggests itself. Compounds V, W, X, Y might all be chemically distinct, with different characteristics, and yet the mixing of V and W and the mixing of X and Y might result in precipitates of exactly the same color and texture. Ordinary phenomenal attributes are emergent on physico-chemical ones, much as typical aesthetic attributes are emergent on ordinary phenomenal ones. (See Chapter 7, below.) And just as a given phenomenal characteristic (color, texture) may be realized through totally different chemical combinations, so a given aesthetic attribute is conceivably realizable by combinations of phenomenal attributes which have no members in common.

Consider a third argument for showing that AU is true. Two works differ aesthetically if there is just one aesthetic attribute had by one work but not the other. Now, one might claim that when it comes to aesthetic attributes of high enough specificity, no two structurally distinct works *ever* share any such. Then given that every WOA has some of these very highly specific aesthetic attributes, it would follow that no two structurally distinct WOAs could be aesthetically identical. One idea in support of this position is that for any general aesthetic attribute A, each WOA, if it has A, also has *its own* highly specific variety of A. For example, given two cheerful poems, the specific cheerfulness of the one would not be the specific cheerfulness of the other no matter how similar the poems were. Given two watercolors, one could not be moist and airy in just the same manner as the other. The cheerfulnesses, the moist-and-airinesses, are of different kinds. Even if two works shared the rather specific cheerfulness$_7$ or moist-and-airiness$_6$, there would still always be a more individualized cheerfulness and moist-and-airiness in which they differed, simply because they were different works.

How plausible is this position? Not very, I would say. Consider unity. Two paintings P_1 and P_2 could both be unified and quite similarly so, and yet when we said "the unity of P_1," "the unity of P_2" we might not mean the same quality (but rather unity$_1$ and unity$_2$, different types of unity). Let P_1 and P_2 be more and more similar though, and it will be unclear how far we can legitimately go in appealing to ever more subtle types of unity. Can we really conceptualize indefinitely fine species of unity? We might try to do it by use of the formula "unified in such and such a way," taking our cue for filling the latter part of the formula from the work at hand in each case. Is it not apparent that following such a suggestion we would end up with "individualized unities" that were no more than a cover for the individual set of structural qualities of each work? For instance, if we were to say painting A is unified-in-having-red-and-orange-verticals-in-opposition, whereas painting B is unified-in-having-blue-and-green-horizontals-in-opposition. Such differences in unity are surely ad hoc. One would not maintain that a 5-pound bass and a 5-pound lamp exhibited distinct 5-poundednesses. Nor that the one possessed 5-poundedness-in-a-bassish-way, and the other 5-poundedness-in-a-lampish-way. We will admit that the 5-poundedness of the bass is achieved in a manner different from that of the lamp (e.g., a pound of bass is softer than a pound of lamp), but this does not make their weights any different. As it was with unity, so I think it will be with any aesthetic attribute that we endeavor to force into fully individualized form: it simply will not go with any conviction.[18]

A fourth argument for AU is rather different from the preceding three and depends on certain assumptions about aesthetic attributes vis-à-vis valuation.[19] If one assumes that (a) some aesthetic attributions are partly evaluative, and that (b) a prescriptivist view of aesthetic evaluation is correct, then in addition to describing WOAs, some aesthetic attribute terms function to praise or dispraise, commend or disapprove

[18] Of course, if we appeal to "particularized" attributes—e.g., this billiard ball's very own (bit of) redness, distinct from that of any other billiard ball—then every artwork necessarily has its own "bit" of any quality it possesses. (For more on this idea, see my "The Particularisation of Attributes," *Australasian Journal of Philosophy,* 58 [1980]: 102–15.) But this is true of objects in general, not just art objects, and so presumably one would not want to invoke that concept here. For on that conception of quality *no* two objects could share *all* their qualities; nothing special is entailed for art objects and aesthetic qualities. Note that I have not said anything to rule out contingently individualized aesthetic attributes—i.e., ones that no other work *happens* to share, or that no other combination of structural attributes will *in fact* give rise to.

[19] Some strain may be noted at a few points in the following discussion (i.e., as when I speak of evaluative *parts* or *aspects* of attributes), which could have been avoided by speaking entirely of aesthetic terms.

those works. However, one must be able to provide a reason or basis for one's praising or dispraising. Now, structural attributes or differences *are* such a reason or basis; they can be pointed at to justify selective commendation. Therefore, if two works are structurally different there will be grounds for a given person for commendation/disapprobation of the one that are not found in the other, and thus grounds present in the one work but not the other for some aesthetic attribution (namely, of the partly evaluative kind). As an example, given two WOAs that both qualify descriptively for the attribution of *gracefulness* but differ in some small structural feature, one may choose to commend one for the presence of that feature and so allow *gracefulness* of it, while not choosing to commend the one lacking said feature, so denying *gracefulness* of it. On this judgment, one work possesses gracefulness while the other does not; if questioned "on what basis?" one has only to refer the questioner to the aforementioned structural difference—or to any other difference, for that matter. Aesthetic content, because partly consisting of prescriptive evaluations, thus becomes observer-relative, and AU must accordingly be understood as relativized to a given individual. In this way it could be claimed that structurally different WOAs are *never* aesthetically identical for a given person since differential structural attributes always provide the basis for differential commendations, and thus, given the assumptions (a) and (b) above, for differential aesthetic attributions.

There are several points at which one can attack this line of reasoning. In the first place, the fact that on the above view structural differences provide *potential* grounds for differential commendation (and, hence, aesthetic attribution) does not insure that they become *actual* grounds—i.e., that anyone *will* make them the basis for such. And if no one does so, then AU may still be false for each observer. In the second place, in a given case of structurally similar but not identical works, there is no guarantee that there *will be* some partly evaluative aesthetic attribute whose *descriptive* component fits both works and whose evaluative component can then be awarded to one but not the other on the basis of some structural difference between them. Of course, one could always construct a partly evaluative aesthetic attribute to fit the case, but that is not the same thing. Third, one can challenge assumption (a), that some aesthetic attributions are partly evaluative—i.e., are in themselves partly ascriptions of either goodness or badness to WOAs. One alternative is to allow that all aesthetic attributes are *value-tending* without allowing that any are in themselves valuations (i.e., without allowing that any aesthetic terms have "good" or "bad" as part of their meaning). Beardsley, for example, has argued vigorously for this alternative.[20] Fourthly, one can challenge assumption (b) that aesthetic value judgments are prescriptive. One can hold that ascriptions of goodness and badness to a WOA are objective, tied closely to observable features that serve as criteria, rather than subjectively variable, by prescribing individuals fixing on any structural features, no matter how minor or seemingly irrelevant.

In the fifth place, even if the prescriptivist view of aesthetic attribution *is* correct, and even if structural differences *are* always made the basis of differential commendations by someone, and even if there always *are* partly evaluative aesthetic attributes that descriptively fit any pair of structurally similar but not identical works, one could then restate AU in a modified form that would retain its real core and still remain an open question. Grant for the sake of argument that some or even most aesthetic attributes are partly evaluative and that the evaluative part consists in a commendatory or disapprobational force. For any aesthetic attribute A, let A_d be the descriptive component of A or, alternatively, the attribute A understood as purely descriptive, that is to say, divorced of any prescriptive aspect. To the extent that ascribing A to a work describes it, A_d is the content of that description. And by *descriptive aesthetic content* of a WOA let us mean the set of all attributes A_d belonging to the work. Then the thesis

(DAU) Works of art that differ structurally differ in descriptive aesthetic content.

is completely untouched by this fourth line of argument for AU we have been considering. If DAU and AU really are distinct (i.e., if some aesthetic attributes *are* partly evaluative), it is DAU we would like to see established, and that has not been done.

IV

If we have found no convincing argument for AU, perhaps that is because none is possible. I believe AU to be false, and in an unredeem-

[20]See "What Is an Aesthetic Quality?"

able way. I begin by presenting one kind of counterinstance to AU which seems conclusive.

Imagine two paintings of the same size, produced on the same type of canvas, with the same paints, and in the manner of Jackson Pollack, but laterally symmetrical about the center vertical. Now add that they are indistinguishable to careful normal viewing except for one thing—the first painting has a medium-sized round blue patch somewhere in its left half which is missing from the second painting, whereas the second painting has an exactly similar patch at the corresponding position in its right half which is missing from the first painting. In short, they are mirror images of each other; one has the extra patch on the left, the other has it on the right. Now, this *is* a structural difference, and not a particularly *minute* one. But it is hard to envision any grounds on which one could maintain that this difference generated an aesthetic one. To construct a similar but perhaps more striking example, imagine two rectangular color-field paintings each of which comprises two equal square regions side by side, and which are precisely similar except for the fact that in one painting the left square is blue and the right is white, while in the other painting the colors are reversed. Here is a structural difference that would be hard to miss, and yet no aesthetic difference seems to be in the offing as a result.[21]

Are these examples then conclusive? Perhaps not. For on reflection there are three factors in the artistic situation which could be appealed to as sources of aesthetic divergence. One is human physiology. It might be that there are physiological asymmetries in the human perceptual apparatus which make it the case that something seen on the left is perceived as having a different character from the same thing seen on the right. The most likely locus of this would be the left-brain/right-brain dichotomy ("logical" vs. "intuitive") to which Sperry's experiments on commissurotomized patients have drawn attention. A second factor is that of widespread cultural associations and practices. In our culture it is arguable that leftness carries with a suggestion of clumsiness, untrust-

---

[21] The reader should note the emphasis on *right/left* reversal. This is fully deliberate; I imply nothing concerning other sorts of reversals. In particular, I would not venture to suggest that any instances of top/bottom reversal in painting would ever be without aesthetic effect. The up/down dimension in art is too fraught with aesthetic potential from several sources (psychological, physical, cultural) to make such a suggestion plausible.

worthiness, and exclusion, stemming from associations that have developed around lefthandedness in persons. And perhaps the cultural fact that our writing goes from left to right and not vice versa influences us to scan paintings from left to right, thus making our impressions of a painting different from those of its mirror image. A third factor is symbolic functioning. It might be argued that right/left is an established symbolic element in the tradition of Western art, and always carries with it the force of *dexter* vs. *sinister* (i.e., roughly good vs. evil) dating from the heraldry of the Middle Ages, much as a white dove in religious paintings standardly symbolizes the Holy Spirit. Each of these three factors might be held to make for some difference in aesthetic attributes— e.g., boldness, mystery, disturbingness—between the artworks described above.

One response to the mention of these factors would be this. Physiologically based left/right asymmetry in visual perception is a possibility, but there is no firm demonstration or evidence of it. Nor does the left-brain/right-brain dichotomy automatically render it a priori plausible, since in a normal person (i.e., one with *corpus callosum* intact) there are nerve pathways connecting *each* eye to *both* halves of the brain. Concerning cultural associations and habits (e.g., those related to the handedness of persons or the direction of writing), it is not implausible to say either that they would not be activated in relation to fully abstract paintings such as were described above, or else that even though they did tend to be activated, the paintings are of a kind for which the correct mode of viewing would be one in which such associations and habits were ignored, suppressed, or disengaged as inappropriate. And in regard to the suggestion of a determinate symbolic import for right/left, though this may have operated as a convention in paintings of some earlier periods, it is implausible to claim that it is in force in regard to modern-day products of abstract expressionist or color-field art.

Remember that all we really need is a *single* instance in which these factors can be discounted. Let us, then, just assume that physiologically based visual right/left asymmetry does not exist (there is not much reason to think it does). Then we can surely conceive *some such* color-field or actionist painting that even *given* our cultural associations and symbolic traditions would be aesthetically unchanged under right/left reversal. Consider an abstract painter of the 1970s who asks us to view his work outside of any relation to the world, as an arena for pure interaction of colors in space. Suppose that that painter is the creator of the works described at the beginning of this section. It seems clear, then, that AU is falsified by them. For in those works symbolism has been omitted, and cultural associations are properly short-circuited. Which means that all plausible grounds of aesthetic divergence have been eliminated—the two paintings thus must be identical in aesthetic content.

One might consider the issue settled at this point. However, I will go on to explore a second sort of response to the factors we have been discussing. In the course of doing so, a weaker and more plausible reading of AU will emerge (AU$_S$), though as we shall see, it too does not lack for counterexamples.

The other response is this. We can modify our initial cases so as to remove any question of their falsifying AU. Grant the validity in the cases as described of at least one of the aforementioned three aesthetically differentiating factors. Then imagine the same pairs of paintings as before, but now add that they occur in an artistic tradition that assigns no symbolic import to right vs. left, and in a culture that has no acquired associations or habits in regard to right vs. left, and assume that their creators and appreciators are beings who (like us) experience no physiologically based asymmetry vis-à-vis right and left. Surely *these* artworks, in their context, do not differ aesthetically though they do structurally. We thus have a pair of *possible* WOAs that incontestably falsify AU. Structurally distinct WOAs *will not* always differ aesthetically.

Defenders of aesthetic uniqueness will likely not be quite ready to give up their position to this line of attack. They will maintain with some plausibility, that no one, themselves included, ever dreamt that AU—a very strong statement concerning all possible works of art in all possible societies—was true. One has always been willing to concede, they might say, that rules of interpretation could be hypothesized and cultural beliefs postulated which would allow for structurally different artworks with the same aesthetic content. Thus, the fact that in a society somewhat different from ours the pairs of left/right paintings I have described would be aesthetically the same is interesting, but not quite to the point. The claim actually intended by champions of aesthetic uniqueness, a claim more reasonable than AU, is rather just that *given* our society with its history, culture, artistic tradition, then against the background of *all that,* WOAS simply cannot differ structurally without differing aesthetically. After all, the idea that every perceivable difference makes an aesthetic difference is one that is based *only* on the experience of creating, appreciating and interpreting art in our society, and therefore it is not too cowardly to take it to be a principle only valid for artworks within our society as it and we actually exist. Such experience would hardly be solid ground for postulating a broader principle governing any conceivable object counting as art made by and intended for any conceivable persons with any conceivable heritage.

So let us state a modified version of AU that even a conservative uniquist should be willing to stand by. I include in this formulation an additional restriction beyond those already mentioned, namely, that the WOAS covered be only those in known art forms.

> (AU$_S$) In our society—given our physiology, cultural associations, artistic traditions—and within existing and recognized art forms, works of art that differ structurally differ aesthetically.

I maintain that unquestionable counterexamples to AU$_S$, as well as to AU, exist. Of course I have already argued, in my first response, that certain pairs of possible left/right reversible paintings made by certain sorts of artist in our present culture *do* count as such. But I offer now an example of a different kind, which seems almost immune to dispute— and which requires *no* particular assumptions concerning physiology or proper appreciation.

Imagine two paintings, each 3 by 3 feet. The canvas and paints used are of the same type in both cases. Each painting consists simply of a fairly dense array of hard-edged 1-inch diameter black and gray polka dots. Let the black and gray dots be equal in number and roughly uniformly distributed over the whole of each canvas. One might generate these paintings directly, or one might start with a vast field of polka dots in the pattern indicated (not unlike wallpaper) and then select two 3-feet-square regions at random (see Fig. 1).

Now, these paintings clearly differ in structural attributes—namely, in having differently colored dots in many (perhaps all) corresponding positions on the canvases. The differences in local coloration between them will be readily perceivable on casual inspection. However, I think

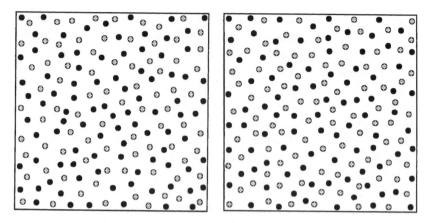

FIGURE 1. Visual distribution 1. 180 dots: 90 black, 90 gray.
Visual distribution 2. 180 dots: 90 black, 90 gray.

one can state confidently that *no* aesthetic difference between these
paintings—or at least *most* such paintings—can be forthcoming. And
this *given* our culture, traditions, and any plausible hypotheses one
likes concerning the human perceptual apparatus. There is simply not
enough *to* these paintings for aesthetic differences to result from the
structural differences we have left them. If the black and gray dots were
not equally numerous, if the dots were of different sizes, if there were
dot or color concentrations in one and not the other . . . but none of
these is the case. The discrepancies in dot positions which remain seem
to me to cancel out, provided the overall balance and distribution is the
same, so that the total aesthetic effect of both paintings is precisely
identical. I conclude, then, that AU_S, as well as AU, is false. Paintings
that are variants of one another in the manner just described provide at
least one falsification.[22]

[22]The reader may have wondered why the examples offered in this section hinged on
right/left or random distribution alterations in paintings, as opposed to much more
subtle and localized ones. The most obvious alterations of the latter persuasion would
be (a) slight changes in the position of single elements, or (b) slight changes in the
coloration of single elements. A little reflection enables one to see that the absence of
aesthetic change would be hard to *incontrovertibly* maintain in the face of these kinds
of alteration. For, assuming it is structural (i.e., perceivable), an (a) alteration changes
the spatial relations and a (b) alteration changes the color relations between the single
element and every element in the work. How can one hope to show, through argument,
that no aesthetic change will result? I am not saying there *aren't* falsifications of AU

Counterexamples to AU and AU$_S$ in the other arts are undoubtedly constructible, but I will not undertake to provide them here. One can envision sculptural and architectural examples using the devices invoked for painting—viz., right/left reversals, random homogeneous distributions. Admittedly, the temporal arts—e.g., literature and music, with their inherent directionality—would be more resistant to such devices. Perhaps small-scale local alteration would serve better in those cases. In any event, one interesting question concerning possible falsifications of AU and AU$_S$ is this . The examples we have considered, and others that are easily imagined, all involve pairs of works which differ in a small number of structural attributes. Could, however, two works of art that differed *widely* in structural attributes, or possessed *no salient* structural attributes in common, yet have the *same* aesthetic content? If such aesthetically identical pairs were possible, they would be like translations of one another into substantially different "structural languages." I will rest agnostic on this point.

I conclude this section with two observations. (1) The falsity of AU (and AU$_S$) can be related to the use of terms such as "tired," "stale," "worn out," "exhausted" to describe styles or genres. To say a style or genre was *worn out* or *exhausted* would mean that, despite structural differences between newly produced works and the body of already produced works, nothing new aesthetically was coming to the fore, all aesthetic content possible within the style or genre having already been brought into being. At such a stage, new works, though structurally clearly distinct from their predecessors, simply replay old aesthetic contents; the style or genre has reached its terminus. At a somewhat earlier stage, in which substantial structural variance from predecessors produces aesthetic contents only minimally different from those already achieved, one can speak of a style or genre as *tired* or *stale*. If AU were not false, no style or genre could ever become exhausted or worn out in the above sense. And if AU were not false, it would be less understandable for styles and genres to suffer the common fate of becoming even staler and more tired past a certain point in their development.

---

which are of this type. But it is unclear whether one can convincingly exhibit any by mere description, as opposed to actual creation and visual apprehension. The examples I did offer, on the other hand, I believe are such as *can* be grasped as counterexemplary to AU through conception informed by past viewing experience of a general sort.

(2) The falsity of AU (and AU$_S$) means that there are WOAs that are structurally distinct but aesthetically identical. Concerning such a pair of works, is it then true that the second would have nothing to offer us that the first did not offer us already? Not really. Granted, the second would fail to provide a single new aesthetic *feature,* but it would provide an *experience* different from that of the first. Structurally different works offer different experiences, perhaps even different *aesthetic* experiences.[23] I, for one, would wish to hear both of two Vivaldi allegros demonstrated to be aesthetically identical, simply because they would *sound* different. Or to view both of two Ellsworth Kelly paintings adjudged the same aesthetically, simply because they would *look* different. The very idea of a single aesthetic content being presented by two different-sounding pieces of music, or two different looking abstract paintings, would be of interest in itself.

V

I will here consider three ways proponents of aesthetic uniqueness would be likely to weaken their position so as to make it more defensible. None of these, however, is successful. (1) The first is to suggest that although not *every* structural difference results in an aesthetic one, every *large* structural difference does. What is a *large* structural difference? Most probably, one that is easily noticeable or observable. But on that score the structural difference between the blue/white and the white/blue square paintings of section IV is surely a large one. Or consider two absurdist Beckett-like plays that differ from each other in regard to whole lines at several places. This difference in structure would be easily noticeable by a reader or viewer, and thus count as a large one. But I think it safe to say that there would be at various places in such plays a range of alternative lines that yielded precisely the same

---

[23] The argument for this would be as follows: Experiences of listening to pieces by Vivaldi are usually aesthetic experiences. If they are different experiences from piece to piece, then they are, a fortiori, different aesthetic experiences. However, as we have seen, the works that occasion such experiences may not be aesthetically distinct, but only structurally distinct. In effect, what this comes down to is that two aesthetic experiences may be distinct while not *aesthetically* distinct—i.e., not distinct *in the aesthetic content they comprehend.*

aesthetic results, thus allowing for two easily distinguished plays that are aesthetically the same. There is no reason to think that large (readily noticeable) differences in structure, any more than small ones, will always cause aesthetic differentiation. If there is another interpretation of "large" which makes for a more plausible amendment of AU, I do not know it. Finally, if our uniquist retreats now only to the claim that works which differ in structure *widely* or in a *wholesale* way are always aesthetically different, then as noted before this may or may not be true, but it is in any event not a very bold assertion.

(2) The second is to suggest that although not every structural difference results in an aesthetic one, every *important* (or significant) structural difference does. What is an *important* structural difference? Two answers come quickly to mind, but neither is of any avail. Is an important structural difference one that is large? We have just seen where that leads. Is an important structural difference one that makes an aesthetic difference? Perhaps so, but the suggestion is clearly pointless in this context, for it would rescue AU only at the expense of making it an analytic truth of glaring triviality. Is there another construal of "important structural difference" which will fare better? Possibly, but again I do not know what it would be.

(3) The third way is to suggest that although not *every* work of art will be changed aesthetically if it undergoes structural change, still, every *good* work of art is such that a change in its structure changes its aesthetic content. Only *bad* or *faulty* WOAs can be altered without affecting them aesthetically; good WOAs are all aesthetically unique— i.e., have an aesthetic content not possessable or presentable by any other WOA. One compelling reason for believing this true would be a prior conviction in the equivalence: WOAs are good *iff* they are aesthetically unique. But what reason is there to believe that? Even if we allow that a WOA is *ceteris paribus* better if it is aesthetically unique (and I am not sure on what grounds), this is far from admitting aesthetic uniqueness to be either necessary or sufficient for aesthetic goodness. Why should a nonunique aesthetic content, because it is otherwise realizable, make its possessor automatically an inferior work of art? Aesthetic goodness, it seems, is in the main a function of the nature or quality of aesthetic content, and not of its nonduplicatability. Of WOAs that can be changed structurally without being changed aesthetically, there are surely good and excellent ones, as well as bad

and wretched ones. Consider any good abstract painting of a certain sort. There are, as noted before, right/left reversal and alternate random patterning operations that can be applied to it to yield structurally different but aesthetically identical paintings. And these variant paintings are, I presume, equally aesthetically good as the original. There is also little reason to doubt that many *good* novels, plays, films, symphonies, and so on have individual elements that can be altered without aesthetic upheaval. It is often said that in a *good* WOA every element has its place, that all elements fit together and balance one another precisely. But this may be so and yet some elements in a good work might switch places, and some elements might be replaced by ones not in the work, with no loss of fittingness or balance. To say that in a good work each element has its proper place need not presuppose or imply that *only that place* is proper to it, or that *only it* is proper to that place.

VI

Although the broad uniqueness thesis, even if qualified in the ways reviewed above, has been shown to be untenable, there may yet be *restricted* uniqueness in the realm of art. I want to raise the possibility of claims of aesthetic uniqueness considerably more limited in scope than AU. One idea that seems worth pursuing is that certain *parts* or structural *aspects* of works taken by themselves will always have unique aesthetic characters. A likely instance of such a part or aspect would be *melody* in music. (A likely candidate in drawing would be *the exact shape and configuration of any human face depicted.*) It is easy to believe that no two melodies considered in isolation, however similar, would have the very same aesthetic character. A change in a melody of just one interval or rhythmic value would seem certain to make it a little less or more jaunty, idyllic, yearning, grim . . . or what have you. Imagine a favorite theme with such a one-note alteration and perhaps you will be similarly convinced. But of course I have hardly *proved* this about melodies; where changing one note makes all the difference, changing three or four may bring one back to home base. There are indeed *actual* themes, structurally similar but nonetheless structurally different, between which one would be hard pressed to state a difference in aesthetic character. As an example, I would cite the rondo themes from Brahms's D Major and Bruch's G Minor Violin Concertos. However, an aesthetic difference is probably there for concerted reflection.

This claim, of the aesthetic uniqueness of melodies (or themes) *by themselves,* should not be confused with a related claim, that any two musical *works* that differ melodically (or thematically) will differ aesthetically. Nor is the second claim entailed by the first. Given that any two distinct melodies have different aesthetic characters, it does not strictly follow that works (even monothematic works) containing them will diverge in aesthetic content. Consider melodies M_1 and M_2, and two short piano preludes P_1 and P_2 built respectively on M_1 and M_2. It is still open that M_1 embedded in the musical (e.g., harmonic, textural) fabric of P_1 and M_2 embedded in that of P_2 would yield the same aesthetic result. However, since melody is of such paramount importance of weight in music (at least Western music), it can be admitted that the truth of the uniqueness claim for melodies would make the related claim for musical works very probable.

Another sort of limited uniqueness claim would focus not on parts or aspects of works of art, but on artworks within a certain *art* or *art form.* Of all the arts, *poetry* strikes me as the most plausible to essay such a claim for. It seems especially difficult to conceive of a structural change in a poem which would be absolutely without aesthetic repercussions. A change in a poem is a change in *words*[24]—additions, deletions, permutations—and words are what we are arguably most familiar with and most sensitive to. In the context of poetry, many more features of words than are usually taken note of are properly considered to be of possible aesthetic import—e.g., rhyme, alliteration, assonance, accentuation, literary allusiveness, etymology, cultural history, shades of synonymy and antonymy, spelling, soft or harsh sound, colloquial or formal tone. So given that the elements of poetry—viz., words—are so multifaceted in significance there, it is hard to imagine any word doing *quite* the poetic work of any other, or any arrangement of given words being identical in poetic effect to any other arrangement of them. Perhaps (only *just* perhaps) one can make aesthetically from

---

[24] I leave out of account poem-pictures, which are "poems" with graphic features understood as integral to the works (e.g., features such as word layout on page, kind of print face employed). Such works could be altered structurally without changing any of the words contained or their linear order.

theme A and harmony/texture B what one makes out of theme C and harmony/texture D, but it is even more doubtful one can make the exact aesthetic content of Wallace Stevens's "Peter Quince at the Clavier" (or that of any other poem) from any words except precisely those used, in just the order they occur. Thus, though a proof is clearly still wanting, all *poems* may be aesthetically unique, even if all works of art are not.[25]

[25] I observe, finally, that if one took the aesthetic content of a woa to be not simply the set of all its aesthetics attributes, but rather that set *as conveyed by a given structure,* then the question addressed in this paper could not substantially arise. On such a construal, AU would be a trivial analytic truth. Now, I don't wish to deny that we have an important aesthetic interest in the presentation of an aesthetic content (narrow sense) *by* a particular structure, as well as in the resultant aesthetic content itself. (Cf. the observation in the last paragraph of section IV.) If we denominate this more inclusive content of a woa its *experiential content,* then it is, of course, fair to say that distinct artworks have distinct experiential contents. In this light, then, the aim of this essay is to show that although structurally distinct woas necessarily differ in their experiential contents, there is no reason to believe in the necessary distinctness of their aesthetic contents.

Additional Notes

1. This is the first of my essays in aesthetics to have been written, around 1976. There are a number of things in it, both substantial and strategic, which I would handle differently if I were writing it today. A couple strike me in particular: (1) the somewhat unsystematic consideration of arguments for AU, and (2) the probable underestimation of sources of aesthetic differentiation that right/left reversal might provide, whether physiological or cultural in nature, and the bluntness of my attempt to bracket them off for the purposes of proceeding with the argument. As it happened, this essay never received the attention accorded some of my others, and so I have not been externally induced to reconsider it with a view to minimizing its infelicities. Of course, I still stand by the central conclusions, that AU is "unredeemably false," and that it is not a thesis of which art criticism or aesthetic theory has any need.

   I also regret that I did not include some discussion of Arnold Isenberg's important essay "Critical Communication," *Philosophical Review,* 58 (1949), which was arguably relevant to my theme. Isenberg advances an argument for the singularity and perhaps nonshareability of an artwork's aesthetic qualities, centered around El Greco's painting *Burial of Count Orgaz,* which is related to the third argument for AU I considered in section III, and it would have been useful to address it directly. However, I don't think there is anything in Isenberg's conclusion—that critical communicability of aesthetic qualities is in most cases only effective when the work itself as well as verbal description is used to guide perception and fix reference—that is damaging to my case against AU. (Isenberg's argument has, incidentally, lately been taken up and recast on a large scale, by Mary Mothersill, in *Beauty Restored* [London: Oxford University Press, 1984].)

2. In my remarks at the very end of section V I was thinking of Aristotle's organicist criterion of a good plot, offered in section 8 of his analysis of tragedy in the *Poetics*. He says a good plot is one in which, if you *interchange* any two incidents, or *remove* any one incident, the whole necessarily suffers aesthetically: "In poetry the story, as an imitation of action, must represent one action, a complete whole, with its several incidents so closely connected that the transposal or withdrawal of any one of them will disjoin and dislocate the whole. For that which makes no perceptible difference by its presence or absence is no real part of the whole" (trans. Ingram Bywater [London: Oxford University Press, 1966]). Now, while this may be true for *plots,* which model the unidirectionality and causal irreversibility of life as it is lived, if my discussion of AU in general is sound, such a principle cannot be generalized truly to cover all transposings of elements in *all* dimensions of works of art, particularly in nonlinear art forms.

7 Aesthetic Supervenience

I begin with the flat assertion that the aesthetic attributes of an object are supervenient on its nonaesthetic ones. Two issues that rear in the immediate wake of this pronouncement, assumings its truth, are these. One, what counts as an aesthetic attribute and, two, what particular form does the supervenience relation between aesthetic and nonaesthetic attributes take? I will not attempt to resolve the first issue, but will content myself with the usual enumerative induction to characterize the class with which we are concerned: gracefulness, mournfulness, balance, sublimity, garnishness, sobriety, flamboyance, gaiety, eerieness, and so on. I might also invoke a number of criteria that have been proposed in recent discussions of the question, though it is unclear whether any of these, either singly or jointly, are adequate to the class as intuitively circumscribed: require taste for discernment, have regional or gestalt nature, are value-relevant, are value-tending, are metaphorically attributed, figure in terminal descriptions.[1] It is the

[1] Various of these proposals can be found in writings of Sibley, Beardsley, Kivy, Hermerén, and Goodman. (For references, see Chapter 6, above, and Kivy, "What Makes 'Aesthetic' Terms Aesthetic?" *Philosophy and Phenomenological Research,* 35 [1975]: 197–211.) I am inclined to think the mark of *value-relevance* is the most nearly extensionally adequate of these. It covers univocally value-tending attributes, but also bivocally value-tending ones (sometimes positive, sometimes negative), and even some that are value-neutral in a given context, if they are the sort of attributes it could

second issue I will be concerned with here, namely, the *manner* in which paradigm aesthetic attributes are supervenient on their non-aesthetic bases. To investigate this will, of course, involve us in probing the nature of typical aesthetic attributes, whatever turns out to be the best criterion for membership in the class.

I take the thesis of aesthetic supervenience to be roughly this:

(AS) Two objects (e.g., artworks) that differ *aesthetically* necessarily differ *nonaesthetically* (i.e., there could not be two objects that were aesthetically *different* yet nonaesthetically *identical*: fixing the nonaesthetic properties of an object fixes its aesthetic properties).

Two comments are immediately in order. First, the necessity invoked in this claim should be understood to be a fairly strong one, approaching if not quite attaining logical necessity. Second, the nonaesthetic attributes on which an aesthetic attribute superveniently depends can be divided into three significant groups: structural, substructural, and contextual. By a *structural* attribute I mean roughly any perceivable, intrinsic, but nonaesthetic feature of an object (e.g., its particular shapes, lines, colors)—i.e., roughly anything composing the object on a fundamental level of observation. By a *substructural* attribute I mean any physical attribute that is *not* perceivable as such, that is, discernible from an alternative at the same level of specificity (e.g., having a line exactly 3.3333 centimeters long in the upper left corner).[2] By a *contextual* attribute I mean an appreciatively important relation of the object to the artistic context in which it occurs (e.g., being painted by Mondrian, being in a certain genre, being influenced by the *Mona Lisa*).[3]

It is clear that an aesthetic difference between two highly similar objects may have its roots in either a structural difference (i.e., a

---

conceivably make sense to cite as reasons for an evaluation. One can make a case for the good-tendingness and hence value-relevance of, for example, mournfulness in a violin sonata, an example Kivy is explicitly skeptical of, by observing that being mournful has the implied (and less desirable) contrast of having *no* emotional quality, or none that is *definite.*

[2] See Chapter 6, section II, above.

[3] On the significance of appreciative contexts, see Walton, "Categories of Art," *Philosophical Review*, 79 (1970): 334–67, and Chapter 4, above.

difference in discernible form), or a contextual difference (i.e., a difference in how the structure is appropriately taken/perceived/interpreted), or even, occasionally, a substructural one.[4] And, of course, it is possible for an aesthetic difference to be grounded in or on nonaesthetic differences of all three sorts simultaneously. What is not proven, but what I will assume for this discussion, is that the structural, the substructural, and the contextual exhaust the sorts of nonaesthetic attribute that are responsible for the issuance of aesthetic attributes. Once these attributes are fixed, the aesthetic content is fixed as well.

With the above distinctions in mind we may now formulate a special version (or corollary) of the thesis of aesthetic supervenience, one keyed more directly to the kinds of cases to be treated in this essay:

> (SAS) Two objects (e.g., artworks) that differ *aesthetically*, but neither contextually nor (purely) substructurally,[5] necessarily differ *structurally* (i.e., in some perceivable but nonaesthetic feature; that is, there could not be two contextually and substructurally identical objects that were aesthetically *different*, and yet structurally *identical*: fixing the structural properties of an object given its substructural and contextual ones already fixed, fixes its aesthetic properties).

This brings out the idea that aesthetic attributes are *centrally* supervenient on *structural* attributes. But how, exactly, is the aesthetic face erected upon the structural skeleton that supports it, and what is its logical connection to it once it is constituted? This is what I hope to illuminate.

[4] A specially nice instance of this comes from a psychological experiment in which it was discovered that subjects would standardly find one of a pair of virtually identical photographs of a woman's face more appealing or attractive than the other, but be unable to discern any particular structural difference between them. The difference between the photos was that one but not the other had undergone retouching to make the pupil's of the woman's eyes slightly larger. Not only did subjects in the experiment fail to note this directly, but they generally could not register it as such even when their attention was drawn to it. Yet an aesthetic difference was manifest nevertheless, as reflected in the decided preference of the majority of subjects for one photo rather than the other. (See R. Hess, "The Role of Pupil Size in Communication," *Scientific American*, 233 [1975]: 110–18.)

[5] Meaning by this, with respect to substructural differences that do not themselves eventuate in structural ones.

I note first that the special version of the aesthetic supervenience thesis has a rough converse, the thesis of aesthetic uniqueness, which has seemed to some to have considerable appeal:

(AU) Two objects (e.g., artworks) that differ structurally necessarily differ aesthetically as well.

Despite its plausibility, however, I believe AU is unredeemably false, as I argue at length in another place.[6] But this casts no shadow on SAS, of course, since many are the virtuous conditionals that conversion can deprave.

The main question that has lately agitated aestheticians with regard to aesthetic attributes, whose supervenience on structural attributes has generally been taken for granted, is whether aesthetic attributes are irreducibly *emergent on* and *distinct from* their structural bases, or whether they are in some sense *logical constructs* of them or *analytically tied* to them in virtue of the semantics of aesthetic description. Monroe Beardsley, following and clarifying Frank Sibley, casts the issue as one of whether aesthetic terms have *application-conditions,* that is to say, of whether aesthetic attributes are connected to structural ones in such fashion that, given certain structural attributes the ascription or denial of certain aesthetic attributes is logically justified or ensured. Beardsley's answer to this question is an unqualified negative; on his view, aesthetic features and structural features are only causally, and not at all conceptually, related.[7]

It will be helpful to sort out four positions on the specific relation of aesthetic attributes to the structural ones on which they supervene. Running from full-scale emergentism to what I will call *definist reductionism,* these positions differ with respect to the strength of concep-

---

[6] See Chapter 6, above.

[7] I will follow Beardsley ("The Descriptivist Account of Aesthetic Attributions," *Revue Internationale de Philosophie,* 28 [1974]: 336–52) in describing the determinative relation between structural properties and supervenient aesthetic ones as *causal.* In doing so, I recognize that I am using 'causal' more broadly than is usual. But I am mainly concerned to contrast (broadly) causal relations, which testify to some real empirical structure and organization of the world's properties, with semantic or conceptual relations, which do not. The contrast between "real" diachronic determination and "real" synchronic determination is not one I am out to highlight; both are *causal* on my usage.

tual connection they claim exists between the aesthetic level and the nonaesthetic (structural) one. The definist claims that one can give strict definitions of aesthetic attributes in nonaesthetic terms, that one can provide necessary and sufficient nonaesthetic conditions for any aesthetic attribution, and that these completely explicate the meaning of the attribution. Thus, the aesthetic definist might hold that gracefulness, say, just *is* having lines of a certain specifiable width, length, and curvature (or that "graceful" just *means* "has lines . . ."). It is not clear that any aesthetician would defend definist reductionism. One obvious problem with it is that airtight structural criteria such as the view posits do not seem to play the role one would expect in the application of aesthetic terms. The claim that strict nonaesthetic analyses capture the essence of aesthetic attributions seems mere rodomontade if even sophisticated attributers fail to be aware of this. Another, related, problem is that definist analyses would undercut the idea that there is anything distinctive about aesthetic qualities or aesthetic perception understood as the apprehension of aesthetic qualities. But third, it appears impossible to produce any definitions in terms of ordinary structural attributes that even approach extensional adequacy, let alone appear explicative of meaning. Surely it would be hard to fill out the definition of "gracefulness" initiated above with any plausibility, keeping in mind it is to be a general definition of that attribute, wherever and however it may appear.

A view less reductive than the definist's, holding only that there are structural conditions sufficient for the application of aesthetic predicates even though there are not strict and complete definitions of the latter via the former, we can call *positive condition-governing*. It is part of the meaning of aesthetic predicates, according to defenders of this view (of whom Peter Kivy is the most able and prominent),[8] that nonaesthetic (e.g., structural) descriptions are sometimes enough to logically ensure the applicability of an aesthetic description, that there are semantic rules in virtue of which an aesthetic feature must be said to be present if certain nonaesthetic structural features are present. Shifting from the linguistic to the metaphysical mode, the thesis of positive condition governing appears to suggest that aesthetic attributes are fundamentally just *complexes* of structural features, where

[8]See *Speaking of Art* (The Hague: Martinus Nijhoff, 1973).

what complexes a given aesthetic attribute comprises is not exhaustively specifiable in advance. For else how could structural features logically clinch the presence of an aesthetic feature, unless the aesthetic feature was understood as (logically) constituted by such features in that case (and others in other cases and so on)? Alternatively, the view in question suggests, rather, that there really aren't any aesthetic attributes as such, but only misleading semantic byproducts of certain nonaesthetic judgments which have the form of reference to a realm of distinct attributes.

Next along, we have the position of *negative condition governing*, maintained notably by Frank Sibley, who holds that there is a meaning connection between structural attributes and aesthetic ones only to the extent that certain structural descriptions can logically *preclude* certain aesthetic ones, even though structural descriptions are never sufficient to logically *ensure* the applicability of an aesthetic one.[9] Thus, for Sibley, a line may as thin, as smooth, as continuously curved as you like and none of this will conclusively mean that it is or must be *graceful* (as opposed to, say, anemic, or flat, or meandering); on the other hand, if we specify that a line is thick, short, broken, and rough, then according to Sibley it becomes impossible for it to be graceful, and even as a matter of semantics. This is what is meant by aesthetic terms being negatively, though not positively, governed in their application by the level of nonaesthetic description. On this view there remains a weak conceptual connection between aesthetic attributes and the nonaesthetic ones they supervene on, not a strong one as on the preceding (positive condition-governing) view, and certainly not the definitional connection of the first view detailed above. It is a bit hard to know what sort of picture this view entails of the metaphysical relation of aesthetic to structural attributes. It seems something like this: Aesthetic attributes are basically distinct from their structural bases and are not just complexes of them, though it might be that the *absence* of certain structural features (or the presence of certain *complementary* structural features, e.g., nonthickness) is partly constitutive of what the aesthetic attribute is, or what we understand it to be. (I will return to this interpretation of negative condition governing at the end of section IV.)

[9] See Sibley, "Aesthetic Concepts," *Philosophical Review*, 68 (1959): 42–50, and "Aesthetic and Non-Aesthetic," *Philosophical Review*, 74 (1965): 135–59.

The picture is not an altogether clear one, and that is one reason Beardsley and others have eschewed the negative condition-governing view that seems to generate it. Beardsley favors instead the position that there is *no* conceptual connection between nonaesthetic facts and aesthetic facts, that the latter specifically supervene upon the former in a purely causal and contingent fashion, though experience soon familiarizes us with the sorts of aesthetic effects that result from various sorts of nonaesthetic complexes.[10] I will call this position *emergentism*, as it holds that aesthetic attributes are ontologically distinct from whatever structural bases support them, and that they arise from them without in any sense including or comprising them in what they are. An emergentist allows, for example, that garishness appears to require bright, saturated colors for its emergence, but takes this to be a fact of nature or psychology, and not a matter of the semantics of "garish." Nor is it a conceptual matter, according to emergentism, that delicate arrays call for unsaturated colors, and graceful lines need generally to be curved. Rather, it is just that the effect doesn't happen to surface without those nonaesthetic conditions, not that it would be a contradiction or conceptual impossibility for it to surface in their absence.

II

Emergentism is the view I defend in this essay. Before I attempt to characterize emergence further, or look to some particular artworks as "case studies" in emergence, it will be helpful to consider how even simple sensible properties (e.g., straightness, yellowness, highness of pitch) stand to their physical bases. I think it will turn out that the relation between sensible properties and the physical ones they supervene on is not really all that different from the relation between aesthetic properties and the by and large sensible ones that *they* supervene on. (As I have defined structural property, it is roughly *equivalent* to sensible property *broadly construed*—i.e., so as to include perceptible relations among parts, perceptible positions, and so on).

What is it for a line to be *straight*, visually speaking? Well, of course there are *occurrence* conditions of this feature, in terms of molecular

[10]See Beardsley, "The Descriptivist Account of Aesthetic Attributions."

facts, or at a grosser and more readily expressible physical level, in terms of positions and relations of chemically specified miniregions of pigment. But straightness as a *visual feature* of a line is not *the same thing as* the satisfaction of various physical conditions whose disjunction may be biconditionally relatable to being visually straight. We do not and cannot mean by a line's being straight to the eye that its physical parts, whether fine or gross, have some geometrically specifiable set of interrelations (that is to say, the holding of such complex states of affairs is not part of the *application*-conditions for "visual straight line"). We neither initially grasp, nor do we subsequently undertake to employ, the idea of (visual) straight line by such criteria. Rather, what we do is record a certain kind of visual appearance, cognize a certain variety of visual impression, and it is this that provides the core meaning of straightness for visible lines. If we label that characteristic appearance or impression *looking-straight,* then straightness in lines might be understood as either the capacity to look-straight to a normal viewer in various standard and nondeceptive conditions, or else as that directly perceivable feature of a line that the sensation of looking-straight registers and informs one of (given standard, nondeceptive conditions). The alternate construals here correspond to two models of sensible properties that have some currency; the first we may call the *dispositional effect* model, and the second the *manifest appearance* model. These divergent models will be useful in our thinking about aesthetic properties a little further on.

If the visual straightness of lines is as I have suggested, a property fixed by or bound to a certain kind of phenomenal impression, then it should be possible for lines to be (correctly) adjudged visually straight which fall short on some more purely physicalist criterion. But we may note that this is indeed the case. A straight line, visually speaking, might be somewhat discontinuous in respect of material pigment, might have some pigmentation outside what are roughly the containing parallel boundaries of the line, might have gradual undulations along its length which cancel out to null effect, and so on. Also, given a certain visual context, it should be possible for lines that fail to be straight in a physical sense, even literally construed, to be visually straight in the midst of some configuration that causes them to present a straight-look to normal inspection of the object in question. It is important to emphasize that such a line, *in its fixed context,* though not physically straight, really *does* have the property of visual straight-ness, and not just the relativistic feature of, say, looking-straight to some person or other in some odd circumstances or other.

When we turn to a color quality, such as yellowness, the situation is very much the same. The occurrence-conditions of yellowness on a surface are a matter of certain kinds of molecular structure capable of differential absorption and reflectance of the component wavelengths of white light, where that absorbed least possesses a wavelength of roughly 5,500 angstroms. But, again, a surface's yellowness may be *determined* or *underlain* by its molecular light-emission propensities, but that is not what its yellowness *is*. Rather, its yellowness, as a visual quality, is something logically tethered to a certain sort of visual impression, namely, what we may call looking- or appearing-yellow. The yellowness of the ball is either (dispositional model) the disposi-tion of the ball to provide yellow-impressions under white light, or else (manifest model) a manifest way of appearing visually that our yellow-impressions in white light are indications or registrations of. The phenomenal aspect is central to the identity of the sensible property and cannot be purged from the picture without changing the subject. The truth condition of something's being yellow, on either the manifest or dispositional construal, is that it standardly appear yellow in white light, whatever that appearance or appearance-capacity may be super-venient on. The application-condition of "yellow" is primarily and ineliminably a matter of "looks yellow."

Moving to a simple aural property, highness of pitch, the story is expectedly not much different. High-pitchedness is supervenient on physical frequency of sound waves in air, but the quality that we are aware of in hearing is not that of having a wave frequency of such and such hertz. The high-pitchedness of the sound is directly a matter of its providing a certain sort of aural experience under standard conditions of audition. A sound—or perhaps, hearable phenomenon—that stan-dardly provided the right aural impression would be high-pitched even if, as seems physically impossible, it did not consist of air oscillations of 1000 hertz or more but rather of beta particles simulating a Navaho rain dance.

Now, it seems to me that in cases of sensible qualities of the kind we have been discussing—yellowness, high-pitchedness, straightness—there is an irreducible but nonanalytic and nonsemantic connection between the level of physical fact (fact stateable in the language of physics) and the level of phenomenal appearances, and thus that of sensible fact (i.e., instantiations of sensible qualities). Ordinary purely physical attributes (e.g., length, weight, magnetic flux) supervene on microphysical ones and may be coordinatable with them in such a way that the former are reduced to or seen as no more than conjunctions of the latter, and so that there are no ultimate laws of ordinary physical magnitudes not implicit in the laws of microphysics. But the relation between physical attributes (micro or macro) and sensible ones seems otherwise. Sensible attributes supervene on physical attributes, to be sure, but what phenomenal aspect—and thus what associated sensible attribute—will be correlated with what set of microphysical or macrophysical attributes appears to be a fundamental and undecomposable truth about the makeup of the world and, at the least, not something already comprised in the laws of physics proper.

Materialists who adopt the supervenience framework as an explication of their doctrine are wont to hold that if all worldly attributes are supervenient on physical ones, then physical facts and principles determine or fix all the facts.[11] But if I am right, then this is so only in a qualified sense. True, there can be no, say, sensible differences or alterations without underlying physical ones—this is just supervenience. But there are principles involved governing this connection which are *not* derivable or extractable from the laws interrelating physical magnitudes themselves. It seems that we must then acknowledge physico-phenomenal "laws" as playing an essential role in generating the world's complete face from the microphysical structure that is its supervenience base. Given a complete set of microphysical states and microphysical laws, the facts of the world would appear to be fixed, but *only* if we are also holding constant the physico-phenomenal correlations not included in the purely intraphysical workings of the universe.

Perhaps, though, a thoroughgoing materialist would suggest that the purely microphysical laws *themselves generate or yield* what I have called the physico-phenomenal laws or principles. But how could this be? Surely it is conceivable, and so presumably logically possible, that there obtain the purely microphysical laws we now have and yet there

[11]See, for instance, Terence Horgan, "Supervenience and Microphysics," *Pacific Philosophical Quarterly*, 63 (1982): 29–43, and "Supervenience and Cosmic Hermeneutics," *Southern Journal of Philosophy*, 22 supplement (1983): 19–38.

obtain different physico-phenomenal connections (e.g., a sound of high frequency having the hearable quality that a sound of low frequency now in fact carries). There is no question of conceptual relatedness, since the laws of physics do not and, strictly speaking, cannot make mention of colors, tastes, odors, timbres, or other items of that order, and so it is hard to see how the supposition of changed qualia with the same physics could be an inconsistent one. Perhaps the thoroughgoing materialist believes not that the physico-phenomenal principles are *entailed by* or *implicit in* the microphysical laws, but rather that it is part of the *overarching fabric of the world* that given a set of microphysical laws, a set of physico-phenomenal principles is fixed as well. Such a move would restore, less counterintuitively, the idea that specifying the microphysics of a world makes the total character of the world determinate.

This last suggestion, however, seems to presuppose a notion of possibility stronger than logical but weaker than physical on the *usual* construal—i.e., conformity to physical laws actually in effect in a world. If we label the usual notion *narrow physical possibility,* we can label the other *broad physical possibility.* It is broadly physically possible, let us say, that the actual laws of nature be somewhat different than they are—i.e., that what is now narrowly physically *impossible* be narrowly physically *possible,* or vice versa. (*Broad physical* possibility, we might note, is a conservative form of *metaphysical* possibility. We can perhaps make do with the notion of alternate worlds having roughly the same basic entities and physical magnitudes as ours, and at least governed by some recognizable and coherent set of laws, however divergent from ours; these worlds would then constitute the sphere of the *broadly* physically possible.)

If we now identify the 'broadly physically possible' with the 'overarching fabric of the world' invoked above, then what I had my thoroughgoing materialist saying about physico-phenomenal connections is that *in any broadly physically possible world,* a microphysical determination, laws and states, *by itself wholly determines everything,* including the phenomenal aspects of that world. Why, though, does he say this? Apparently because of the conviction that *however* the purely physical laws vary within the bounds of broad physical possibility, the *same* principles of physico-phenomenal correlation will obtain. And thus, since such correlations are part of the 'overarching fabric' of physical reality, they need not be independently specified in addition to microphysical laws in order to fully fix a world in all its qualitative glory.

If I have accurately plumbed the depths of the thoroughgoing materialist's psyche on this point, I confess that I am not sure why such philosophers readily entertain the possibility of *intraphysical* regularities different from those we have while holding that *physico-phenomenal* connections cannot (broadly physically) be other than they are. But no matter. For *even if they are right* in this conviction it is still hardly the case that the purely microphysical principles are the *only* fundamental ones: the physico-phenomenal principles are such too, logically and semantically underivable from those of the prevailing microphysics, even if they are *invariant* across (broadly) physically possible worlds.

Reverting to the example of yellow another time, I can make the point more concretely as follows. That yellow things typically look yellow may be a mere *analytic* truth, but that light of 5500 angstroms is critical to the experience we qualitatively and introspectively know as looking-yellow is *not*, but rather part of a set of contingent ultimate facts of the world, connecting microphysical conditions to phenomenal aspects (e.g., yellow-look) and thus to phenomenally tethered perceivable properties (e.g., being yellow).

III

The next question to address is whether phenomenal appearances and the phenomenal attributes tied to them (on either the manifest or dispositional construal) are *emergent,* as well as *supervenient,* on their physical bases. I would like to claim that they are, as I will similarly claim for aesthetic attributes relative to their structural bases. What do we mean by this?

First, we can state that emergence is to be compatible with supervenience, though not with definitional reductionism. Jaegwon Kim has shown[12] that if a property P is supervenient on a finite set of physical

---

[12] In "Supervenience and Nomological Incommensurables," *American Philosophical Quarterly,* 15 (1978): 149–56.

properties θ, then there is indeed a biconditional of coextension between *P* and and some logical construction, call it *C*, of properties in θ.
Thus, *P* will be present just in case the complex conjunctive/disjunc-
tive physical condition *C* is satisfied, and only then. This does not in
itself entail, however, any more than does the causal dependency of *P*
on θ, that *P* is really *nothing more than C*, that the manifestation of *P*
just is the holding of *C*. Coextensiveness, even necessary coextensiveness, does not establish property identity.[13] Furthermore, rather than
being in conflict with supervenience and the coextensive consequences
it carries, the idea of emergence seems to *require* a supporting and
correlatable substructure out of which, and in relation to, emergent
properties will do their emerging. Emergentism is not mysticism, after
all.

So far, then, properties of a given level are emergent on properties of
another level if they are supervenient on them, but not logically or
conceptually reducible to them. The latter point can be expanded so as
to bring out something important about emergence. It is that if a
property is regarded as emergent on a given underlying basis, it will be
conceivable that it might have emerged from a *different* underlying
basis, or that the underlying basis that in fact generates it might *not*
have done so. For example, it is readily imaginable that reflecting
wavelengths of 3,500 angstroms (the wavelength of violet light) would
have sufficed to make an object yellow, even holding our physiologies
and neurochemistries fixed, and that reflecting wavelengths of 5,500
angstroms would not have sufficed to make an object visible at all. And
this is because the *attribute* of yellowness is essentially tied to the
appearance yellow, while the latter is only contingently related to any
conditions physically specifiable.

The notions of emergent quality and regional (or gestalt) quality are
often associated, but I think we should resist making the latter a
necessary criterion of the former. Beardsley characterizes a regional
quality as a quality that a complex has as a result of the characters of
its perceivable parts and the relationships among them.[14] He has in
mind central aesthetic qualities such as unity, balance, sadness, gaiety,

[13] See Elliot Sober, "Why Logically Equivalent Predicates May Pick Out Different
Properties," *American Philosophical Quarterly*, 19 (1982): 183–89.

[14] *Aesthetics*, 2d ed. (Indianapolis: Hackett Publishing, 1981), p. xxix. I have inserted
the word "perceivable" since I think this is what Beardsley intends.

and tension, which clearly belong to a pattern as a whole in virtue of the interacting contributions of its elements. It is the whole configuration that has a certain look, feel, or force, and not any individual parts. The yellowness of a square patch, thus, is a local, not a regional, quality for Beardsley, since it is homogeneously distributed across the entire patch and belongs straightforwardly to each discriminable part of the patch as well. So if yellowness is an emergent phenomenal quality it is not a regional or gestalt one. The divergence comes out about, basically, because regionality or gestalthood is a feature of perceptual qualities vis-à-vis their more elementary perceptual conditions, whereas emergence, so far characterized, is a feature of qualities vis-à-vis their supervenience bases, which may not be perceptual ones.

An additional reason for not insisting that emergent qualities be regional in the above sense is that there may be graspable aesthetic qualities that are not regional, but which we would presumably want to recognize as emergent on their phenomenal underpinnings. I have in mind aesthetic qualities of simple colors and sounds, which are inherent in but distinct from the chromatic and sonic features themselves. Thus, a uniform patch of a saturated red may have a certain *vibrancy,* one of blue a certain *coolness,* while a violin's high E may be *steely* and a bassoon's low E-flat *woolly.* The vibrancy and coolness depend on the particular hue, saturation, and brightness of the colors but are not the same as them either individually or collectively; the steeliness and woolliness depend on the particular constellations of fundamental tones and overtones involved but are not simply identical to those distributions of pitch. The vibrancy, coolness, steeliness, and woolliness are not regional (or gestalt), since they attach to perceptually uniform elements and inhabit them throughout. A pure isolated tone or color typically has an aesthetic character that supervenes directly on its lower-level phenomenal specification, and since this is so, not all aesthetic emergence is of the regional (or perceivable-complex-involving) sort.

Furthermore, it appears that not all regional attributes are such as we would recognize as emergent. For example, if we take two 3-inch squares and conjoin them, the resulting object has an area of eighteen square inches, which neither of the two contributions possesses, though their respective areas, as related, are responsible for the area of the rectangles so formed. Such *summative* regional attributes as *being 18 square inches in area* are not happily construed as emergent on less extensive area-attributes—though they are clearly supervenient on them (together, perhaps, with positional attributes). The reason we rule this out as emergence seems to be that the regional attribute is not really *different* in nature or type from the subregional ones it supervenes on. In fact, in this and perhaps other such cases, it might even be an analytic implicate of them.

So emergent attributes are supervenient ones, logically and conceptually independent of their supervenience bases, often but not always involving regionality, and more than merely summative of the attributes they supervene on. The crucial idea for what follows is that emergent attributes have a certain *residual irreducibility* with respect to their lower-level bases, microphysical or otherwise. An upshot of this is that a complete account of the world's manifestation (what Terry Horgan calls the task of "cosmic hermeneutics"),[15] even given its ultimate supervenience on microphysical states, will require a number of fundamental *nonsemantic* principles *in addition to* purely microphysical ones. In the preceding section I discussed what I called physico-phenomenal principles in this light. I make the same claim, with perhaps a certain caveat, for what might be called *structuro-aesthetic* principles. In order to concretize the issue, and to explore the way in which typical aesthetic attributes emerge from perceivable structures nonaesthetically characterized, I consider two works by Mondrian and J. S. Bach in some detail as case studies.

IV

In surveying Mondrian's *Composition with Blue 1933* (hereafter, *CWB*) for the first time, it is hard to say whether its overall aesthetic effect strikes one before its dominant structural features or vice versa. One reason I choose this work for consideration is that its aesthetic effect is fairly unequivocal and its structural features few and easily detailed. The painting is 28 by 27 inches and consists of a light blue-gray background upon which is superimposed a grid of black lines about a half inch thick, one vertical and three horizontal, offset by a

---

[15] See the articles cited in n. 11, above.

square of saturated primary blue which sits to the right of the black vertical, almost resting on the bottom of the picture. The lowest of the three black horizontals runs across the north side of the square, and there are additional black line segments on the south and east sides, thus completing its outlining in black. The painting is an understated but masterly study in color and tone, line and mass, figure and ground. The resulting artwork has a pronounced air of *tranquility* and *strength*.

It is not difficult to pinpoint, from among *CWB*'s structural attributes, those that carry particular responsibility for its resultant aesthetic character. There is the rectilinearity of the primary lines and their extending from border to border. There is the strict parallelism or perpendicularity of all lines in the picture. There is the specific deep blue of the colored square, and its positioning relatively low in the picture. There is the slight off-centeredness of the colored square and of the main vertical line that forms its western face. There is the roughly two-to-one spacing ratio between the three horizontal lines. There is the particular shade of background gray on which the blue-black configuration rests, contrasting strongly with the black of the lines and gently echoing the cerulean blue of the square. All these are crucially relevant to the painting's achievement of tranquil strength, and to its avoidance, say, of dynamic density, gentle grace, or muted melancholy. Confirmation of the specific effectiveness of these features in the present case can be had by imagining alterations in them and trying to envisage the effect at the aesthetic level. There will invariably be such an effect. It would not be the same painting, aesthetically speaking, if there were minor lapses from rectilinearity, if the blue square were darker in hue or less saturated, if the square or dominant vertical were exactly on-center, and so on.

These salient structural attributes of *CWB* make their contribution to the resulting high-order strength and tranquility in part through intermediate-order aesthetic attributes that arise along the way, some local and some regional. Thus, the light gray-blue background carries with it a certain airiness, the deep blue square a decided coolness. Further, the structural relationship of the two colors yields a sense of harmony. Finally, the configuration of four lines and square, in its particular proportions and positionings, makes for a notable degree of stability and balance. All these aesthetic effects—the local airiness and coolness, the regional harmony, stability, and balance—somehow interact and coalesce, together perhaps with structural features I have not explicitly singled out, to give the overarching impression of tranquility and strength noted initially. And it is worth repeating that a viewer might accurately register that impression before registering its structural and lower-order aesthetic underpinnings, perhaps never consciously acknowledging or focusing those at all.

Bach's Prelude no. 12 from Book II of *The Well-Tempered Clavier* is a relatively simple affair, structurally speaking, though its emotional effect is of the rarest sort. I will deal only with the opening period, twenty-eight measures ending in a full cadence in A-flat. The basic key is F minor, which maintains its sway, more or less, through measure 19, despite a passing flirtation with F major in measures 4–8 and harmonic ambiguity in measures 16–19. At measure 20, A-flat, the relative major of F minor, surfaces firmly and continues to the double bar. The texture of the period is fairly light, almost purely homophonic through measure 19, then slightly denser during the A-flat ending, which contains an inner voice wending its way between arpeggiated chords above and a simple walking bass below. The dominant motivic feature of the period in the first twenty measures is a three-note figure consisting of a note repeated and then followed by a gentle half-step fall. Eighth-note rests between these figures make for a distinctive, halting rhythm.

There is more one could say on the structural level, especially as regards interrelations among local structural features—obvious phrase repetitions, a variant of the main motive being the inner voice of the A-flat section—but not much more. What is the aesthetic upshot of all this? Now music is so mercurial, so quickly changing in even the course of a few measures, that summary assessment is difficult. Yet overall I would characterize the effect as one of chaste and mildly elegiac *wistfulness*. Where does this come from? Well, being supervenient on them it comes, to be sure, from the structural features I briefly reviewed, as well as others I omitted to mention. But we can also see it arising, in intermediate fashion, from simpler aesthetic impressions more easily associatable with particular aspects of the music's perceptible structure. Thus, the main motive possesses a familiar sighing quality, the dominant rhythm an air of hesitancy and reserve, the open texture and soft dynamic level convey a certain delicacy, the alternation of dominant rhythm and faster arpeggiated one an effect of charm, while the

FIGURE 2. Johann Sebastian Bach, *The Well-Tempered Clavier*, Book II. Praeludium XII, measures 1–28.

basic F minor tonality and harmonic side-glance at F major generate a mild sense of tension or unease. These collectively produce the sort of wistfulness I gestured at above, though hardly as a matter of linear addition. Rather, it emerges.

Clearly, I have been telling these aesthetic stories from the emergentist point of view. What would a reductionist or condition-governist make of these cases? Consider just two of the intermediate local aesthetic attributes present in CWB—namely, the coolness of the blue square and the airiness of the background. Now, the reductionist view must be that coolness is just a kind of color quality, and that airiness is just another kind. In other words, that coolness is just equivalent to the disjunctive attribute: deep-blueness or dark-greenness or . . . , and airiness to the disjunctive attribute: light-grayness or light-blueness or hazy-yellowness or. . . . In a similar vein, a reductionist would presumably hold that bold or garish color combinations are just special subsets of bright ones, and that to say a given combination is bold or garish just means it is bright of a certain kind.

The inadequacy of the reductionist response here should be obvious. *What* kind of bright configuration is garish (or bold), and *which* disjunctive color quality does coolness (or airiness) amount to? How is garishness or coolness recognized and grasped? Why do we carve out certain sectors of the chromatic realm and give them particular designations? It seems the reductionist has no plausible answer here, or none as compelling as the simple admission of distinct, emergent higher-order perceptual features. If we consider, finally, the upper reaches of *CWB*'s aesthetic profile—e.g., its balance, stability, and tranquil strength—the idea that such attributions just connote sets of structural features seems quite bizarre. The tranquil strength derives from and depends on the lines, colors, and proportions, to be sure, but it is not *itself* just a certain range or class of these nonaesthetic features. To say a painting displays tranquil strength cannot reasonably mean that it boasts one of a certain number of structural configurations. No one could be made to understand, surely, what tranquil strength is by presenting it as in effect just a collective name for an array of disparate structures. The inadequacy of reductionism vis-à-vis the lower- and higher-level aesthetic attributes of *CWB* carries over fairly plainly, I think, to the hesitancy, unease, charm, and wistfulness of Bach's Prelude no. 12. These are not merely arbitrary disjunctions of rhythms, harmonies, and textures.

But is the condition-governist (or criteriological) view of aesthetic attributes really that much more plausible because it stops short of positing complete equivalence or definability? The condition-governist still holds there to be a strong meaning relation between aesthetic attributes and the structural features underlying them. In the case of *CWB*, for example, the condition-governist will want to say that its specific lines, widths, hues, and geometrically specifiable relations *just about* add up to its stability, that even though the stability it displays cannot be strictly *defined* in terms of such nonaesthetic features, it really is *no more than* the complex of them in this particular case. As far as *CWB*'s tranquil strength is concerned, the condition-governist seems to hold, in parallel fashion, that it is *more or less* just the juxtaposition of the coolness, stability, harmoniousness, and other lower order features present in the painting, that it is *conceptually implicated* in the aesthetic situation as already constituted.

It appears plain to me, however, that the coolness, stability, and so forth contribute to the effect of tranquil strength but without collapsing into that *sans* remainder. There is a distinct, holistic impression corresponding to this attribution, and that impression is separable from the simpler ones of stability and coolness, and so on, that stand right alongside it. The latter effects underlie the former one but do not swallow it up. The same can be said of the chaste wistfulness of the Bach prelude relative to its contributory lower-level hesitancy, delicacy, unease, and suspiriousness. These impressions can be distinguished in the mind and none of them is the linear sum of any of the others, nor would the admission of any number of them, it seems, ever logically clinch the applicability of a further one. That there are *meaning* rules, even of an open-ended and one-way sort, which dictate that of conceptual necessity a painting will exhibit tranquil strength, or a prelude chaste wistfulness, if certain sets of structural and lower-order aesthetic features are given, is a thesis that appears to fly in the face of the phenomenological facts.

Peter Kivy, a proponent of postive condition-governing, has argued against the purely emergentist conception of, say, garishness (wistfulness, tranquility) as follows: It is implausible that garishness should be like redness in having its ascribability directly tied to a certain kind of phenomenal impression, because whereas no feature of an object other than its perceived redness can be invoked in defending the ascription of "red" to it, in the case of garishness one can defend an ascription of "garish" by pointing to garish-tending (or garish-making) features of the object in question.[16]

I agree with Kivy that this is a difference between many aesthetic attributes and simple sensible ones, but it is far from clear that this

[16]"What Makes 'Aesthetic' Terms Aesthetic?"

difference has the upshot he favors. We may note, first, that this may
not be so much a matter of condition-governing or its absence as of
complexity versus *simplicity* in impressions. Second, although there
are what one might call garish-tending features of visual objects, these
are only so-*tending*; none of them *guarantees* or *ensures* a garish result
taken individually or—if emergentism is correct—even collectively.
Third, the possibility of rationally defending ascriptions of garishness
by appeal to lower-level perceivable features does not show that there
must be a conceptual connection between them; rather, a wide range
of empirical experience with manifestations of garishness on the part
of informed perceivers would be a perfectly adequate basis for such
defense.

This concludes what I have to say in rebuttal of the competing
condition-governist perspective on aesthetic attributes. But I want to
point out in addition that one unattractive consequence of both the
reductionist and the condition-governist positions on aesthetic properties is that they make it difficult to see, if aesthetic attributes are at base
no different from nonaesthetic ones (since they in effect collapse into
them), how it can be that the former are especially interesting, or
valuable, or worthy of careful discernment and contemplation. This
consequence strikes me as a greater drawback than the minimal ana-
lyzability, incomplete predictability, and difficulty of verification—if
they be accounted drawbacks—which attach to aesthetic attributes on
the emergentist stance.

I have been generally concerned to defend the emergent status of
aesthetic attributes, and thus the need, in the context of a project of
total world description, for fundamental and ineliminable structuro-
aesthetic (or phenomenal-aesthetic) principles tying aesthetic matters
ultimately to the microphysical bases they supervene on. Yet I confess
to some doubts as to whether all commonly discussed aesthetic attributes are *entirely* emergent, by the standard I have adopted of complete
conceptual independence. Some aesthetic attributes, on the face of it,
do seem connected rather closely to the nonaesthetic structural attributes that support them, in such a way that one is hard pressed to
conceive of the possibility of the former without the latter. (That is to
say, the thesis of at least *negative* condition governing has a strong
appeal in certain cases.) Can we imagine garishness appearing without
bright colors? Can we imagine unity inhabiting a configuration with-

out repeated or parallel structural elements? Can we imagine delicacy surfacing in a drawing without thinness of lines? If these skeptical queries are sound, then it would seem in these cases that garishness is perhaps after all *partly a matter of*, and not just *caused* or *subvened* by, brightness, and the same for unity vis-à-vis structural repetition/parallelism, delicacy vis-à-vis linear thinness.

What follows from the admission that some aesthetic attributes may *in part* consist in their structural bases? From a fundamentally emergentist point of view there seem to be two options. The first option is to recognize a *spectrum* or *continuum* among aesthetic attributes, some of which would then be said to be *more* wholly emergent than others, in inverse proportion to apparent conceptual involvement with supporting nonaesthetic structure. We might decide that this runs all the way from attributes with absolutely no conceptual allegiance to structural features (e.g., the poignancy of a melody), to attributes (perhaps on this account only pseudo-aesthetic) which reveal themselves as basically equivalent to conjunctions of two or three structural conditions. The second option is to jettison the requirement for emergence of *complete* conceptual independence from structural base, insisting only on some *substantial* measure of conceptual independence, reinforced perhaps by phenomenological separability. On this modification, any aesthetic attribute that is still conceptually and experientially *more* than its structural underpinnings, even if involving them to some extent, will count as emergent. Such attributes will be causal, and not merely semantical, derivatives of nonaesthetic structure.

Additional Notes

1. The topic of aesthetic supervenience is a large one, and I am conscious of not having covered all the bases, or even most of them, in this one outing. I focused, as is evident, more on the nature of aesthetic content and its emergence from nonaesthetic structure than on logical analysis of the supervenience relation per se. Some of the issues in need of attention have been addressed in two admirable essays that appeared subsequently: John Bender, "Supervenience and the Justification of Aesthetic Judgements," *Journal of Aesthetics and Art Criticism*, 46 (1987): 31–40, and Gregory Currie, "Supervenience, Essentialism, and Aesthetic Properties," *Philosophical Studies*, forthcoming 1990. The questions on which they focus are, respectively, these: Is supervenience *determination*, in an intuitive sense of what accounts for, and explains, a work's aesthetic content? (Bender), and: Is the supervenience base for aesthetic content properly a work's structural (and historical) attributes, or rather its *perceptual powers* vis-à-vis its appropriate perceivers? (Currie). Currie

explores, in addition, the matter of whether aesthetic supervenience is best thought of as *weak* supervenience—as bearing on the aesthetic indiscernibility of structural equivalents *within* a given possible world, or as *strong* supervenience—as bearing on the aesthetic indiscernibility of structural equivalents *across* possible worlds. (Jaegwon Kim has detailed this distinction generally in a series of papers on various aspects of supervenience; see, in particular, "Concepts of Supervenience," *Philosophy and Phenomenological Research*, 45 [1984]: 153–76. A useful general examination of the idea of supervenience and a consideration of its appropriate employment in different domains can be had in Simon Blackburn, "Supervenience Revisited," in *Essays on Moral Realism*, ed. G. Sayre-McCord, pp. 59–75 [Ithaca: Cornell University Press, 1988].)

In retrospect, the view I was defending in "Aesthetic Supervenience" can be seen to be a version of weak supervenience. That is to say, no invariance, in the way aesthetic content emerges from nonaesthetic conditions, is posited across metaphysically possible worlds, and I even refrain (see section 11) from positing it across narrowly physically possible worlds—i.e., from one such world to another—because I want to allow that in another possible world with exactly the same physical (that is to say, purely intraphysical) laws as this one, there might be different physico-phenomenal (i.e., physico-structural), and hence physico-aesthetic, correlations. (Currie, in "Supervenience, Essentialism, and Aesthetic Properties," incidentally ends up defending strong supervenience, but only where the supervenience base consists of perceptual powers, rather than ordinary perceptual properties and their contexts; he agrees that aesthetic content fails to strongly supervene on structural and historical properties.)

The most, then, that I commit myself to in this essay is that SAS, my central supervenience claim, is a principle valid *within*, though possibly not *beyond*, a given world, with whatever physics you like in place. This does not, admittedly, leave the thesis of aesthetic supervenience per se with all that much teeth. What SAS's content thus appears to come down to is that in a given possible world (e.g., this one) with a fixed set of physical laws, there will be a fixed set of physico-structural, and structuro-aesthetic, correspondence principles, so that within that world a given physical/structural complex will have a given aesthetic content—holding appreciative context constant, of course. In other words, SAS affirms that there will be a strict *function* from the structural to the aesthetic (modulo appreciative context, and leaving substructural wrinkles aside), and thus there can be no differences in aesthetic content not traceable back to and attributable to structural ones. Blackburn, in "Supervenience Revisited," suggests that in several cases (e.g., those of color, mental states) supervenience's cash value may just simply be the *necessitation*—possibly just nomological or causal—of higher-level by lower-level properties; in other words, the weak supervenience claim in aesthetics may be just a roundabout way of affirming that certain combinations of structural properties *nomologically* (*or causally*) *necessitate* certain aesthetic properties. From the vantage point of present reflections, the sort of aesthetic supervenience I was defending in my 1983 essay might amount to no more than that.

However, it strikes me that perhaps what is left out of aesthetic supervenience, when it is reduced to causal necessitation of the aesthetic by the lower-order perceptual, is that the special *relation* of the aesthetic with the perceptual generally is given no weight or recognition. For it is no *accident* that the aesthetic is nomologically tied—in some fashion or other, which may vary from one physically possible world to another—to the realm of perceptual properties generally, and not, say, to that of magnetic, electrochemical, economic, or social ones. It seems patent, rather, that *nothing other than* the totality of nonaesthetic perceptual properties—always holding appreciative context fixed—*could* be (and this might be a metaphysical "could") what nomologically necessitates aesthetic content. There is a very tight, quasi-conceptual connection between the aesthetic and the perceptual—the aesthetic *must*, it seems, be rooted in, based on the (nonaesthetic) perceptual, or else it couldn't be the sort of feature we call *aesthetic*. In other words, it may be metaphysically necessary that aesthetic content is causally tied, in a given world, to complexes of lower-level *perceptual* properties, even if those vary from world to world.

But why, after all, is this so? I think we can see, on a little reflection, a reason aesthetic content must be tied so closely to lower-level perceptual (i.e., structural) content so that, in a strong sense, there can be no aesthetic difference without structural difference (contextual and substructural complications aside, as before). And that is because the aesthetic properties of, say, a visual work of art are, on a higher level, simply *the way it looks*, just as are, on a lower level, its structural properties. We can hardly avoid thinking that the higher-level look of an object must strongly depend on its lower-level look, all other matters held constant. The higher-level look comes about *in virtue of* the particular interactions of components of its lower-level look, in conjunction with the fixed physical, physiological, and structuro-aesthetic principles prevailing at a given world. *What else*, one might ask, could possibly generate, or be responsible for, those higher-level looks? This, I think, is the root of the intuition that it may be, in some sense, metaphysically or quasi-conceptually impossible for there to be aesthetic without structural (phenomenal, perceptual) divergence in a given world situation. This is part, I take it, of what it means for aesthetic content to *emerge* from, and to overlay, its structural basis.

2. There is a tendency, especially in discussions of moral realism, to assimilate *aesthetic* and *moral* supervenience. I want to caution against this. Aesthetic supervenience, to my mind, has more in common with psychophysical supervenience, the supervenience of the mental on the physical, than it does with moral supervenience à la Hare. Aesthetic supervenience, as considered in this essay, is a relation between two classes of fundamentally or primarily *descriptive properties* (or, perhaps equivalently, between the lower-level perceptual powers of an object and its higher-level ones). Moral supervenience, on the other hand, concerns the relation between a person's or situation's relevant descriptive properties as a whole and straightforwardly moral evaluations made of the same. Whereas aesthetic supervenience— the supervenience of aesthetic features on nonaesthetic ones—is clearly in a broad sense a *causal*, or *world-structural* relation at base, moral supervenience might very well turn out (if, say, prescriptivism or projectivism in the moral domain is true) to be just a matter of the "logical grammar" of moral assessment. That is, it would turn out to be a kind of rational consistency requirement, to morally assess things the same which have been determined to be nonmorally the same. But this is quite another matter from the nomological-level dependencies within perceptual experience that are the crux of supervenience in the aesthetic case. (Terry Horgan relatedly takes to task the hasty assimilation of moral supervenience to *psychophysical* supervenience, in "Psychologistic Semantics and Moral Truth," *Philosophical Studies*, 52 [1987]: 357–70.)

Of course, if we were to consider the supervenience of aesthetic *evaluations* narrowly speaking ("this work is good [fine, excellent]") rather than that of aesthetic *properties*, then the parallel with moral supervenience, as that is usually taken, would be restored. But then *aesthetic value* supervenience, which is manifestly not the same as what I have labeled *aesthetic* supervenience, was not the subject of my essay. Alternatively, the parallel is partly restored if we focus, in the moral case, not on attributions of moral goodness and badness, right and wrong, but on narrower moral attributions, such as those concerning virtues (loyalty, charity, courage, kindness), which obviously have a large descriptive content, and which content might be supervenient on lower-level psychological or behavioral properties in something like the way aesthetic features are on simpler perceptual ones. (Even here, though, I would be skeptical of the degree of resemblance between the cases.)

8 *Titles*

"What's in a name? That which we call a rose, by any other name would smell as sweet." This thought of Shakespeare's points up a difference between roses and, say, paintings. Natural objects, such as roses, are not interpreted. They are not taken as vehicles of meanings and messages. They belong to no tradition, strictly speaking have no style, and are not understood within a framework of culture and convention. Rather, they are sensed and savored relatively directly, without intellectual mediation, and so what they are called, either individually or collectively, has little bearing on our experience of them. What a work of art is titled, on the other hand, has a significant effect on the aesthetic face it presents and on the qualities we correctly perceive in it. A painting of a rose, by a name other than the one it has, might very well smell different, aesthetically speaking. The painting titled *Rose of Summer* and an indiscernible painting titled *Vermillion Womanhood* are physically, but also semantically and aesthetically, distinct objects of art. The viewpoint I advance in this essay is that the title of an artwork is an invariably significant part of that work, which helps determine its character, and not just an incidental frill devoid of import, or a mere label whose only purpose is to allow us to refer to the work and distinguish it from its fellows.[1]

[1] Another paper on our topic is John Fisher's "Entitling," *Critical Inquiry,* 11 (1984): 286–98, which I became aware of only after completing the present essay. Its virtues

I have organized my remarks into four sections—headed by four theses—each of which I defend, with qualifications or restrictions for some that emerge in the course of discussion. The four theses are as follows:

I. Titles of artworks are often *integral parts* of them, constitutive of what such works are.

II. Titles of artworks are plausibly *essential properties* of them in many cases.

III. The *title slot* for a work of art is never devoid of *aesthetic potential*; *how* it is filled, or that it is *not* filled, is always aesthetically relevant. A work differently titled will invariably be aesthetically different.

IV. There is significant disanalogy between titles of artworks and *names of persons*, particularly in regard to their roles in the understanding and interpretation of the objects they denote.

The central thesis is thesis III, and it is this I will explore and illustrate at greatest length. But first I will attend to the more purely metaphysical issues raised by theses I and II.

I

One way to show that titles are integral constituents of works of art is to adapt a form of argument I employed in an earlier essay,[2] where my object was to demonstrate that musical compositions were not pure structures but, rather, *indicated structures*—i.e., structures-as-indicated-in-a-given-cultural-setting or by-a-given-historically-located-individual. The upshot of that argument was that composer, time, and/or artistic context be recognized as integrally involved in what the work is. Only under such an assumption can such works intelligibly bear the range of properties—aesthetic and artistic ones—that we determinately ascribe to them. And exactly the same things can be said of literary compositions, as well.

Now, the extended argument, directed at titles, would go roughly

---

are, I think, complementary, particularly as it concentrates on the criteria and conditions of titlehood more than my own effort does. There is substantial agreement between us as to the central interpretive role of artwork titles. Fisher errs, however, in my opinion, in not recognizing the special status of artist-given names as titles.

[2] See Chapter 4, above.

like this. If musical works were even just, say, context-qualified indicated structures, then if two distinct composers were to determine the
same such indicated structure, that is, in virtue of occupying the same
musico-historical position exactly, or one composer were to determine
simultaneously two instances of the same such structure, necessarily
only *one* musical work would be composed. However, it is clear that in
such cases *two* musical works *might indeed* result—if the indicated
musical structures were differently titled. Thus, musical works cannot
strictly be identified even with indicated musical structures, but must
rather be thought of as indicated structures-so-titled (or structures-as-
indicated-and-titled).

Why is it that two musical works may result in such circumstances?
Because not only are the aesthetic and artistic attributes of a musical
work a function of musical structure and musico-historical context,
but they also depend somewhat on how it is titled. Thus, if these
attributes belong to the work in fairly straightforward fashion, they
cannot be ascribed to the mere indicated structure since there could be
at the same time a distinct work comprising the very same such structure, which diverged from the first aesthetically and/or artistically.

How can titling affect the aesthetic/artistic properties of a piece of
music? Since I will have occasion to discuss specific examples of this
phenomenon later in this essay, I here confine myself to a generalized
demonstration of it. I take it that representational properties, on some
plausible analysis thereof, can sometimes be correctly ascribed to
musical works, and thus that it is appropriate, in some sense, to *hear*
certain passages in such works *as* such and such worldly objects or
events. Now, presumably the appropriateness or inappropriateness of
hearing-as, or the degree of appropriateness, is something over which a
composer-given title exerts a justified influence. Titles in such circumstances serve as presumptive guides to perception of a certain sort. This
is particularly clear in cases where a passage could be imaginatively
taken to be *two* rather different happenings in the world; surely in such
cases the title usually settles which is to be heard in the music, and
which is thus represented by it. And since representational properties
are aesthetic—or, at any rate, critically relevant—properties, the case
is made. We thus see that the contextually indicated musical structure
is not yet a *fine enough* type to properly possess the work's representational properties, and that we must recognize the structure-as-
indicated-and-so-titled as the legitimate bearer. For such a work must

be distinguishable from a representationally different work involving the same indicated structure (penned by our composer's doppelgänger) but carrying a different title, or none at all.

Let me cast this amplification of how I would identify musical and literary works in a somewhat different light. Under this illumination, what I have noted here about the constitutivity of titles is not so much a modification of my earlier proposal as a making explicit of something implicitly covered under it before. For the title of an artwork is reasonably regarded as simply a *special part* of its artistic structure— one out of the totality of structural elements which a creator assembles in making a work and projecting an aesthetic content. It is the capstone of an arch, foremost among the myriad components that the artist has determined as constituting the perceivable face of his or her work. With a literary work, such as a poem, a title is of course very readily seen as of a piece with the rest of the work, since title and text share a medium—i.e., words. The verbal structure central to what the poem is can naturally be thought to include the title, if there is one.

But even with musical works, if we recognize structure in the broader sense—as comprising all perceivable, appreciatively relevant components of a work, whether qualitatively homogeneous or not—there seems no reason why a musical work's structure should not be said to include a certain verbal content as well as specified sounds and means of performance. On this understanding, the refinement needed is simply a recognition that the structure indicated when a musical work is composed is one that may involve verbal *as well as* musical elements. (Of course, this should not be surprising at all if we momentarily shift the frame of reference and think of *vocal* music!) Put otherwise, we can conceive musical work types as indicated title/sound/performance means structures, instead of as indicated-and-titled sound/performance means structures (hereafter S/PMs). It would appear that these conceptions are effectively equivalent. That said, I nevertheless tend to invoke the second conception in what follows, thus preserving the nominal distinction between titles and work structures proper.

II

My position here is that titles are plausibly essential to works insofar as they are ineliminably involved in individuating them. And this, it seems, will be so when they are metaphysically integral to what such works are.

Recently, James Anderson has pointed out some putatively undesirable essentialist consequences of the identifications I have proposed for musical works.[3] If a musical work is a structure as-indicated-by-*P*-at-time-*t*, then composer and time appear to be essential properties of the work, and if a musical work is a structure as indicated in a given context, then context of origination and resultant aesthetic character appear to be essential. My response to this is that such implications are not all that unpalatable, and that if we want to locate types to identify with musical works that are both intelligibly determinate *and* logically capable of bearing the work's important attributes, then I believe we may have to accept some such implications. And so if titles are constitutively part of the indicated structures that are musical (and literary) works, we may have to regard them as essential as well.

This is not to deny that there are problems about the extent to which constitutivity implies essentiality. The question of the essential properties of indicated types is, I suppose, the question of what if any alterations they may admit while recognizably persisting in possible worlds other than this. I admit to some weakness of will faced with this query. One approach would be to hold simply that whereas concrete objects have many accidental determinations, all the constitutive properties of abstract objects like initiated types are essential to them. Perhaps so. But if we put aside momentarily the titular, personal, and contextual components of these types, and focus just on the structures they contain, are we even certain what need be preserved here in order to speak of the *same structure*? Must every element of the structure carry over for *the structure* to find itself in another possible world? Beethoven's *Tempest* Sonata involves a musical structure that has a B-flat major chord with tripled root at the opening of the adagio movement. Would it not be the same structure if that chord had lacked one of the doubled B-flats? Couldn't Beethoven's *Tempest* have had one more or less B-flat at that juncture and still have been the same sonata? Another way of putting what I am getting at here is this: If a musical work is identified as comprising an S/PM structure-as-titled-and-indicated-in-context-*C*,

---

[3]See his paper "Musical Identity," *Journal of Aesthetics and Art Criticism*, 40 (1982): 285–91. David Carrier raises related questions for a view such as mine in "Art without Its Artists?" *British Journal of Aesthetics*, 22 (1982): 233–44. (For further discussion, see Chapter 10, below.)

are its constituents as such essential to it? If we ask, musing on some possible world, "Is this the same S/PM/as-titled/as-indicated as before?" there may be no sharp answer unless we know, for one, when to say a *structure* remains the same despite certain envisageable minor alterations in properties.

If structures can suffer accidental alterations, then perhaps analogous things could occur to other constituents of indicated structures. If we are willing to admit some characteristics of a structure as not being essential to it, then we might conceivably admit something similar concerning titles and contexts of creation. Could *For Whom the Bells Toll* possibly count as the same title as *For Whom the Bell Tolls*? What about *The Mayor of Casterbridge*? Could that (very) title have been rather *The Mayor of Casturbridge*? The musical context of creation of Beethoven's *Tempest* Sonata included the sixty-two or so efforts of Haydn at the piano sonata. Would it not have been the same context if Haydn had never written the brief G Major Sonata, L. 54?

The upshot of these queries and reflections, I think, is that given a musical or literary work is identified as a structure-indicated-in-a-given-context-and-titled-so-and-so, the most appealing view is probably to regard the constituents of the type as indeed essential to it—structure, context, title—while recognizing a measure of looseness in what counts as the *same* structure, *same* context, *same* title. In any event, if titles are constituents of type artworks, then it seems fair to say they are as essential to them—at least broadly construed—as any of the other constituents that make the work what it is. This is all I have to say here regarding the essentiality of titles to works. It is their constitutive and interpretive role that is of greatest moment, and that I try to illuminate in the rest of this essay.

It is now necessary to note, however, that the mode of argument which has led us to the conclusion that titles are ontologically integral to abstract *type* works such as symphonies and sonnets does not, I think, go through for *particular* artworks, consisting of unique physical objects (e.g., paintings) or even for type works *essentially tied* to physical particulars (e.g., etchings, cast sculptures, films). The reason is that even though titles of, say, paintings, can influence aesthetic content and meaning as much as or more than titles of symphonies and sonnets, there is no difficulty in ascribing that content to the physical object as such, which as it were happens to have a certain title. There is no need to invoke a more qualified object along the lines of painting-as-titled-so-and-so. The linchpin of the argument used earlier was that aesthetic contents arise which cannot be ascribed to only moderately specific types, since there could simultaneously exist works embodying the same such moderately specific type which were yet aesthetically divergent. And so in order to insure distinctness of works, one must appeal to a more specific type, thus making internal certain relations that usually remain external (to creator and time, or to creative context).

In the case of a painting, though, distinctness of work and sole ownership of its aesthetic properties are insured *by the uniqueness of the particular involved.* There cannot be a possible world in which there is a *given* painted object with title A, *and then the same* painted object (at that very time) but with title B. That is not a conceivable situation, and can only be thought to be so by conflating it with the readily imaginable supposition that the painted object titled A *might have been* titled B. Of course it might, and then the painting—that physical object—might have had a somewhat different meaning.[4] But no specific content or meaning is generated which cannot intelligibly be ascribed to the plain particular in question without fear of logical competition. There is no pure structure or other type from which the painting would fail to be distinguished unless the properties in question were attributed to the as-titled object. Similar reflections show that etchings, cast sculptures, films will not require—at least on these grounds—conception as entities that include their titles in an essential way, because connection to particular physical exemplars or templates performs all the logical individuation called for. This leaves it *open*, of course, that for other reasons (e.g., theoretical uniformity) one might still propose conceiving them in that fashion, that is, as title-qualified entities. Unless we do so, it seems, we are left with the divided conclu-

---

[4] To perhaps make this point clearer: Are paintings, metaphysically speaking, painted-objects-as-titled? They *could* be so understood, but one is not *forced* to do so for reasons of individuation. For example, a given painted canvas can have title A at t_1, and title B at t_2 granted, but we *needn't* say there are *two* paintings (artworks) in this story—we can just say it is the *same* painting, now altered (titularly), and with correspondingly different aesthetic properties. Assuming a painted object has only one title at a time, there cannot arise the sort of problem of logical individuation generated by the role of abstract structures in the identities of works of music and literature, and thus one is not *compelled* to treat the titles of paintings as essential to them.

sion that, in contrast to wholly abstract type works, works consisting of or involving concrete particulars neither possess their titles in an ontologically integral way, nor, as a result, have them as essential determinations.

It may help crystallize some of what I have said so far if I end this section by discussing the notion of a *part* of an artwork, and the connection of that status with others I have invoked in passing. Let me characterize an artwork *part* in roughly this way: a part of an artwork is any element fixed, determined, or generated by the artist which is to be perceived or apprehended in the process of appreciating the work in question. The idea is thus that a part is something belonging—or more neutrally, pertaining—to a work that is *both* a consequence of intentional artistic activity *and* is directly attended to by perceivers. On this construal the parts of a standard painting are, I think, exhausted by regions of painted canvas plus title, if present. Let me next characterize a *component* as an element attaching to a work in an ontologically integral way, one that *enters into* or *qualifies* the sort of entity the work is. Now, something can be a part without being in this sense a component, and something can be a component without being a part. Given what I have said above, titles of paintings are parts without being components, whereas artistic contexts of creation are components of literary and musical works without being parts of them. Let me call something that is *both* a part *and* a component of a work a *constituent* of it. The distinguishable regions of a painting, the sound structure of a sonata, the title of a poem are all obviously constituents of them in this sense. Last, and pushing us in the direction of our third thesis, if we consider the broad status of *aesthetically or appreciatively relevant factor* (arf for short), it seems clear that anything which is *either* a part *or* a component will be an arf, and that certain things that are *neither* parts nor components—e.g., context of creation for a painting—will be arfs nevertheless. Of course there are some things pertaining to artworks which are not even arfs: the artists' purely personal lives, the backs of paintings, the insides of sculpted busts, the ink color of a play's or opera's original manuscript. *But never titles.* Regardless of whether it is strictly constitutive or not, the title of an artwork, from the most flamboyant to the most numbingly literal, *cannot help* being an arf, or aesthetically relevant factor. I will now try to convince you of this.

III

In discussing the role of titles in generating aesthetic content one thing has to be cleared up at the outset. The only titles I am concerned with are *true* titles—those given by the *artist* at roughly the time of creation or constitution of the work. Thus I will not be interested in titles one might categorize as adventitious, shorthand, traditional, or colloquial, nor those attaching to a work due to some critic's honorary or defamatory intentions. Labels that become affixed to a work *through an agency other than the artist's* may occasionally be amusing, or enlightening, or suggestive of ways of approach, but they have no claim to determining artistic meaning as do bona fide titles. The nicknames of many of Beethoven's compositions are not true titles—e.g., the *Emperor,* the *Harp,* the *Archduke,* the *Moonlight,* even the *Tempest* mentioned earlier. (*Les Adieux*—or rather, *Das Lebewohl*—on the other hand, seems to be a true title of the Piano Sonata in A-flat, op. 81a.) "Whistler's Mother" is not the title of that famous canvas, and in fact militates against the interpretive slant given by the true title, *Arrangement in Grey and Black.* "Garp" is not the title of John Irving's recent (and distastefully toned) best-seller, but only *The World According to.* "Explosion in a Shingle Factory" is very apt in a belittling vein, but it does not displace *Nude Descending a Staircase* as the unique title of Duchamp's revolutionary painting. Titian's *Sacred and Profane Love,* however charming, was added later by other hands, and thus has no inviolable right to interpretive consideration.

To come to thesis III directly now, I confess that it strikes me as virtually self-evident, and that I hardly know how to argue for it. I can offer, at least, this simple demonstration: Titles are parts of artworks; artwork parts, as I have defined them, are always arfs; therefore titles are arfs—that is, aesthetically relevant features of works of art. Perhaps there is some residual skepticism as to whether titles (*true* titles, of course) *are* parts of artworks. But how can they not be? They are purposely positioned on works, and they are to be attended to by appreciators in relation to the structured object or event they accompany. A title can in fact be thought of not only as part of a *work,* but as part of a *work's structure,* as suggested earlier. Titles are elements in what is artistically fashioned, and however inconsequential a title may be in a given case, there can never be a justification for excluding it in assessing the total and exact import of a work of art. Would it be acceptable to discount or ignore a certain corner of a mural (by masking, say, or squinting) in taking its measure artistically? Of course not. Then how could it be critically permissible to discount or ignore its creator-given title? (I leave aside what might be *appreciatively advisable*, which is a somewhat different, and more pragmatic, matter.) We cannot as objective critics pick and choose among the fixed ingredients of an artwork, just acknowledging those we wish—even if for the sake, in some sense, of the work itself. Artistic paternalism is no more justified here than is ethical paternalism in most interpersonal situations.

Further, it does not, it seems to me, matter that an artist, having given his work a title, might subsequently say that it has no significance, or that he had to title it something, or the like. This is bootless. A title has a certain force, and contributes to the reading of the work, because of the artistic conventions governing them. An artist cannot negate this by ancillary declarations while still making use of titling as an artistic prerogative. Of course an artist can withdraw a title, after second thoughts, but that merely corroborates my point. There are ways an artist can keep track of and enable discourse about a work without actually titling it. The artist can use a pet description, derived from some key feature of the work, or maintain a completely neutral numerical or alphabetical catalog. But a catalog designation is not a title in my sense. It is not part of the aesthetic package assembled and proffered by the artist.

Perhaps the best thing I can do to further support thesis III is to distinguish a number of different functions or forces that titles can have vis-à-vis artistic meaning. Once I have done that it should seem plausible that any given title will either fall under one of the categories I sketch, or else have some other effectiveness, similar to those already categorized. Let me define the *core* content (or meaning) of work as the content (or meaning) the work would have *if untitled*—or perhaps better, *apart from* its title. Then we can probably express different functions or forces of titles in terms of what effect they have on core content—i.e., in terms of the difference between work content and core content, if any.

Let us start with the simplest and most boring mode of titling, as there is an important point to be made even here. I will call these *neutral* titles—which is not quite to say they are of no consequence. I have in mind titles whose selection seems almost automatic and whose application to the work in question is obvious in the extreme. Often such titles are merely the names of characters, objects, or places that figure prominently in the body of the work and are insusceptible to any additional spotlighting. Thus, the following are neutral titles, I suppose, if any are: *Moby Dick* (Melville), *Cypresses at Arles* (Van Gogh), *Macbeth* (Shakespeare), *Hungarian Rhapsody* No. 2 (Liszt), *David Copperfield* (Dickens), *The Bells* (Poe), *Madame Bovary* (Flaubert), *Portrait of Louis-François Bertin* (Ingres). Another category of neutral titles might be poem titles that are simply reprises of the first lines of the poems. For all such works, work content may be identical to core content; titling seems to alter nothing. If we ask why such works are titled at all, the answer is probably just that it is customary in the genre in question, and that it is useful in discourse to have names for artworks as much as for other things we are interested in.

Does this mean that thesis III must be qualified to exclude neutral titles, if there are any? No, for two reasons. First is the minor point that what I have called neutral titles—those that seem almost redundant—will only *strictly* be without effect on core content if the genre or form in question is one in which titling is something of an *option*, sometimes taken and sometimes declined. In other words, if titling is either de rigueur or virtually unprecedented in a given context, then any title, however "neutral," will make the work artistically different from what it would be without its title. This is because titling or not titling per se in such contexts is a significant act, and thereby makes a work more or less unusual. (A work of architecture with a real title—not a hypostasized definite description, e.g., "The Chrysler Building"—would diverge artistically from its unchristened counterpart merely because this is so rare.)

The second and principal reason neutral titles do not upset my third thesis is that it is not a claim about the class of *actual* titles, but about the enduring semantic potential of the title *slot* in any given work of art, however neutrally filled in actuality. This potential can *always* be evidenced by the thought experiment of imagining the work with *other* titles, and noting a range of changes in content, even if it is not always clearly evidenced (as in neutral cases) by imagining the work with *no* title. What if *Moby Dick* had been called "The White and the Black"?

Consider Flaubert's novel with the title "The Bovarys." Or Van Gogh's canvas entitled "Sinister Trees." Imagine Ingres's portrait having been called "A Gentle Soul." Convert Liszt's unspectacular "Rhapsody" appellation into "Gypsy Night on Bald Mountain." And so on. Obviously something happens to work meaning in each of these instances, though I will not try to articulate what. Even a neutral title might have been otherwise, and this is where its significance, however uncolorful, lies.

I move on to a class of titles only one step removed from purely neutral ones. These I call *underlining* (or *reinforcing*) titles. What such titles do is add additional weight or stress to some theme or subject that is clearly part of core content, but not so overwhelmingly or unquestionably that titular spotlighting is otiose. The title in such cases is something of a coup de grâce that certifies the importance of what it denominates and confirms what the body of the work would be independently saying. A good example of this is Munch's painting *The Scream*. Screaming content is fairly evident in the canvas itself, but the titular stress seems not completely redundant, and makes for a stronger statement by the work as a whole. Underlining titles, in contrast to neutral titles, are typically general or qualitative, rather than denominative of people or places.

The next sort of title, which I call a *focusing* title, begins to do more noticeable artistic work. What a focusing title does is select from among the main elements of core content one theme to stand as the leading one of the work. In order for a title to count as focusing rather than merely underlining, there has to be a certain richness of core content so that two or more elements within could plausibly be regarded as of major importance. What a focusing title does, then, is suggest which of the contending themes should be given center place in interpreting the work and organizing one's appreciation of it. This isn't to say a focusing title can determine this absolutely; there are, of course, well-intentioned mistitlings, and creators who do not comprehend their creations very adequately at all. But a focusing title accords a potent emphasis to what it picks out, and one that may be prima facie definitive, interpretively, in the absence of strong contraindication from the body of the work. *Ulysses* is, I think, a focusing title for Joyce's novel, since the trials and perspectives of Stephen and Molly, in themselves, are perhaps comparably important to those of Leopold.

Similarly for *Swann's Way*, the first installment of Proust's septology, where Swann's competition includes at least Marcel and Odette. In addition, this title with its quasi pun on "way" draws attention to contrasting modes of life as a central concern of Proust's fictional endeavor. *Great Expectations* engenders primary reflection on the twists and turns of fate, and the odd ways in which hopes are sometimes realized rather than on, say, the evils of the criminal justice system in nineteenth-century England. In Fritz Lang's film *Fury*, the title invites us to focus on the causes and effects of that mob emotion, rather than on any particular individual, or any number of other human failings displayed in the course of the story. The title *10* of Blake Edwards's 1982 film similarly spotlights the perfectionist mania bedeviling the protagonist Dudley Moore's pursuit of romantic involvement. Manet's title *Déjeuner sur l'herbe* draws our attention to the event and its social implications, as opposed to, say, the beauties of nature or the personalities of the sitters as depicted in the painting. One could say something similar of Kirchner's expressionist painting *The Street*. Focusing titles thus transform core content into work content in fairly subtle fashion, by raising the profile of some feature in the core physiognomy. Focusing titles are perhaps more common than underlining titles, though possibly less so than neutral ones. I would not claim that the lines separating these three are very sharp, but I think the rough distinction is useful nevertheless.

A fourth and very significant category of titles I call *undermining* (or *opposing*) titles. These are titles whose ostensible drift is counter to that which they crown, and which oppose the work's provisional statement with a statement tending in a contrary direction. In the case of complex and lengthy works, such as novels and films, when this occurs we generally take such a title to be *ironic*—i.e., to *really* mean the opposite of what it flatfootedly says, and thus to really be in line with the body of the work. The following are, I suppose, ironic titles whose undercutting of their hosts is thus only skin-deep. Faulkner's story "A Rose for Emily" or Flannery O'Connor's "A Good Man Is Hard to Find," Bertrand Blier's film *Going Places,* or Eric Rohmer's *Le Beau Mariage*, or Peter Blume's painting *The Eternal City*.[5] Even

---

[5] Of the same nature is Rossini's "Petite Messe Solenelle," for quartet of singers and two harmoniums, which is neither solemn nor, except in respect of performing forces, small.

so, the ironic sort of title, while in effect bending to the will of the work, is hardly artistically nugatory. It always serves to underscore some aspect of core content, and imparts a special flavor—often bitter or mocking—to the work as a whole.

Some opposing titles, however, are not conquered and absorbed as ironic by their bearers, but instead persist in their contrariness, yielding effects of humor, shock, or anxiety. A jagged, flame-toned canvas titled "Lake Annecy" or "Sleep" is not an example of ironic titling. Rather, what we have most likely is a piece of black humor, one whose funniness is founded, as so often, on incongruity. A piano prelude of a placid, Mendelssohnian cast entitled "Buchenwald" will be chillingly unnerving in the contrast it presents, pitting tone against thought and thought against tone. Nonironic undermining titles thus generate work contents quite different from the core contents they subsume, if not quite the reverse of them.

A fifth sort of title, which one might call *mystifying* (or disorienting), resembles the opposing sort in some of its effects. What I have in mind are titles that instead of either *corroborating* or *confounding* something in the body of the work, seem completely *tangential* or orthogonal to it. (In terms of geometrical analogy, we might label these the coincident, the 180-degree and the 90-degree cases, respectively.) This is, of course, a favorite device of Dadaists, Surrealists, and other purveyors of the absurd. An interesting case in this regard is Ionesco's *Bald Soprano*, the idea of which has nothing materially to do with the play, though the phrase itself does occur once *en passant*.[6] A purer example would be Boris Vian's *Autumn in Peking*, which concerns neither Peking nor autumn. The titles of some Surrealist paintings— e.g., Yves Tanguy's *Mama, Papa Is Wounded!* or De Chirico's *Jewish Angel*—have no obvious connection with what is shown in them, and prod us into discovering or perhaps inventing some connection. A typical effect of mystifying titles is conceptual dislocation. Another is the whimsical expression of brute contingency. The element of pure fantasy is also in many cases both a motivation and a result.

My sixth category of title I call *disambiguating* (or *specifying*) and is

---

[6]Ionesco's play was originally more transparently titled *English without Pain* but was subsequently changed to *The Bald Soprano* by Ionesco on a whim, after a forgetful actor, in the course of a rehearsal, substituted the phrase *cantatrice chauve* for *institutrice blonde*.

particularly important where representational identity is involved. If the body of a work is representationally ambiguous, it is obvious that a title can serve to fix or endorse one perceptual reading rather than another, thus giving the work a more determinate content than it would otherwise have had. Many visual works of art, and virtually all musical compositions, are subject to seeing-as and hearing-as, respectively, in a variety of ways. Albers's *Homage to a Square* represents just a square and not, say, a house or window, in virtue of its title. Similarly, De Kooning's *Woman III* represents some sort of woman and not the prehistoric cow it more closely resembles. Brancusi's *Bird in Space* has ornithological, rather than ichthyological content, in virtue of its title, not its specific shape or internal constitution. The same goes for the nautical content of Calder's *Big Sail,* a venerable landmark on the campus of MIT. *Broadway Boogie-Woogie* helps fix the mode of perception appropriate to Mondrian's animated canvas, licensing a framework of urban imagery. And the religious dimensions of Barnett Newman's monolithically abstract canvases have much to do with titles such as *Onement* or *Abraham and Isaac.* Rameau's harpsichord piece *La Poule* is a vivid representation of a *hen* pecking and clucking and not of a *boy* drumming nervously on a tabletop—nor of a *turkey* doing anything! Finally, if Strauss's *Death and Transfiguration* represents those momentous occurrences, it is not because the music could not be heard as other than that.[7]

But disambiguating titles are not confined to visual and musical contexts. In this category would also be included titles so critical to the understanding of literary works that core content is indecipherable without the clue the title provides. (Such works are *oeuvres à clef,* the title serving as the key that unlocks the work's meaning.) In lieu of an actual example, I ask you to imagine a short poem that speaks obliquely and archly of something you cannot quite grasp, but when reviewed in light of the title becomes all transparency. (Some of Emily Dickinson's more abstruse lyrics *would* have fallen into this category *if* they had been given certain helpful titles.) Perhaps *Ulysses* approaches

[7]Another, celebrated example of disambiguating titles is provided by Danto's imaginary paintings, *Newton's First Law* and *Newton's Third Law,* which first saw light in his 1965 paper "The Artworld." There are other illuminating examples of the power of titles, I might note, in Danto's recent *Transfiguration of the Commonplace* (Cambridge: Harvard University Press, 1982).

being a *titre-clef* for Joyce's novel, since it at one stroke reveals and justifies the identification of a day in the life of Bloom with the wanderings of the Greek hero. The divergence of core content and work content in all the examples of our sixth category should be obvious enough. Disambiguating titles change an indeterminate core content into one with relatively definite outlines. Assuming opacity is an aesthetic attribute—though not necessarily an aesthetic virtue—then obviously, how opaque certain works of art are will depend on whether they include or exclude disambiguating titles, and this will thus be of aesthetic moment.

The last classification of titles I suggest is different from the others in that it makes no claim to be disjoint from them, but blithely cuts across their territories. This is the category of *allusive* titles, titles that refer indirectly to other works, other artists, historical events, and so on. An allusive title serves to connect a work to certain things outside it— things the artist wishes to resonate with the work as it is experienced. Clearly, a title that is allusive may also function vis-à-vis core content in most of the six ways I have identified above. Allusive titles may underline, focus, oppose, or specify core contents in given cases. (I don't think allusive titles can be purely neutral, however, and very bizarre, in any case, used in a mystifying vein.) Some of the titles mentioned earlier are allusive ones: *For Whom the Bell Tolls, Ulysses, Abraham and Isaac*. Here are some others: *Measure for Measure, The Way of All Flesh, The Sound and the Fury, The Sun Also Rises,* Matisse's *Luxe, Calme et Volupté*. The connection to realms and sources outside the work that an allusive title effects is not aesthetically negligible—it is always something appreciative understanding must keep in view, and is thus of aesthetic importance to the work.

I have detailed six specific categories of title, though the lines of demarcation among them are, admittedly, a bit hazy. At this point we can perhaps profit by ascending a level in generality. I suggest, now, a tripartite division of titles, into *referential, interpretive,* and *additive* ones. Referential titles are simply those that serve to label their bearers and facilitate intercourse with them, and which do not introduce any perturbations into the arena of meaning. Interpretive titles, as one might imagine, serve to announce or support an interpretation of the work as a whole, in a fairly sharp and central way. Additive titles are those that contribute to meaning in virtue of being elements that a comprehensive assessment of the work cannot ignore, but without declaring interpretations themselves or providing the keynotes of such.

In terms of our earlier taxonomy, then, neutral titles are virtually coincident with referential ones; interpretive titles comprise roughly all underlining, focusing, disambiguating, and allusive ones, plus the ironic variety of undermining title; while the additive titles include the mystifying ones and the remaining incongruous variety of undermining title. Thus, to illustrate from among our earlier examples, *David Copperfield* (neutral) is largely just a tag; *The Scream* (underlining), *Swann's Way* (focusing), *La Poule* (disambiguating), *The Way of All Flesh* (allusive), *Going Places* (ironic) all point to an interpretation in strong fashion; while *The Bald Soprano* (mystifying) and *Lake Annecy* (incongruous) are pieces in the semantic puzzle without directly illuminating themselves, or the works to which they belong. That most titles are interpretive is perhaps sufficiently evident on mild reflection, but I think we are now in a better position to realize the range and importance of this truth.

As coda to our taxonomic discussion, I propose that we consider a certain kind of title which, though at first glance seems the height of dispassionate objectivity, is not really neutral at all, in my sense. Imagine some contemporary abstract paintings titled, respectively, *Untitled, Red Circle on Blue Ground,* and *No. 65.* It might seem that the first of these titles is entirely empty, the second purely descriptive and *de trop,* the third simply a denotational convenience. Nevertheless, such titles do artistically qualify the paintings they are attached to, which would be somewhat changed without them. What all three titles typically do, in subtly different ways, is insist on the abstractness of what is presented on the canvas.[8] They signify a stance opposed to readings, symbolism, emotional appropriation—they are, in Susan Sontag's phrase, "against interpretation."[9] Depending on the specific natures of the paintings and their specific positionings in artistic space (which of course I have not sketched), such pseudo-neutral titles will function to underline (most likely), or else to focus or disambiguate. One can find real aesthetic neutrality, perhaps, but it is not found in all the obvious places.

[8] Or perhaps, in the first case, on the nonexclusive claim of any particular representational seeing.

[9] Though, of course, they are still *interpretive* in the sense I have invoked.

IV

Titles of artworks have in common with names of persons the fact that they are a species of *names*, and thus denote their bearers and facilitate reference to them in thought and discourse. But the differences between the two species are for our purposes of greater interest. First there is the fact that facilitating reference is really the central function of personal names, whereas with titles that function is typically on a par with, if not subservient to, others. Second, and centrally, there is the matter of the semantic weight of titles. At the beginning of this essay I remarked on some dissimilarities between artworks and natural objects, such as flowers. The same can be said for persons as well. Persons are not essentially vehicles of meaning; they do not primarily convey content or make statements, as a whole. The title of an artwork properly influences the statement it embodies or the qualities if projects. But persons are not props in a meaning scheme; thus, their labels do not carry that sort of significance. That a person is named so and so does not thereby affect or modify any of his perceivable properties; but precisely this can occur in virtue of a work having a certain title. I am not denying that personal names have connotations, nor that someone's name may come to seem particularly apt, or ironically inappropriate, as the person matures. But this is not the same as forming part of an intentionally designed cultural entity whose every apprehendable feature, according to the conventions of the practice of art, is potentially relevant to the artistic content of the work. That some parents, in baptizing, grooming, and otherwise orchestrating their children, seem to lose sight of this difference between people and works of art does not, of course, undermine it. Unfortunately, it sometimes undermines such children.

A third point that underscores the difference between titles and personal names is that the former are naturally thought of as parts of artworks, and, as we have seen, as sometimes constitutive of them in the narrow sense—i.e., as ontologically integral to what such works are. Names are, of course, never essential to *persons*. But furthermore, they are not, I think, even *parts* of persons, on any plausible reading of "part." Names do not make up persons, even partially. Persons do not include their names, rather, they possess them. Personal names are more like *properties* than parts.

Last, a few remarks about name change, where persons and art-works are concerned. An individual, or the individual's guardian, can change his or her name without in any sense changing the person. That a new "lease on life" may causally issue from such a renaming does not affect the claim I am making. The case seems otherwise with artist-initiated changes of title. If I am right about musical and literary works, such changes result strictly in new artworks, however slight the aesthetic difference may be. Yet even in other cases, as when the title of a painting or sculpture is revised, though we may not have a meta-physically distinct artwork, we unmistakeably have one that is impor-tantly different from what it was before, in a way that matters from a critical point of view. This cannot be said for changes in ownership, gallery location, marketprice, or catalog designation.

So what's in a name? When that name is a title, probably more than in any other kind of name there is.

Additional Notes

1. There have been a few essays on the nature of titles subsequent to my own of which I am aware, and to which I am pleased to draw attention: S. J. Wilsmore, "The Role of Titles in Identifying Literary Works," *Journal of Aesthetics and Art Criticism*, 45 (1987): 403–8; Hazard Adams, "Titles, Titling, and Entitlement To," *Journal of Aesthetics and Art Criticism*, 46 (1987): 7–21; Gérard Genette, "Structure and Functions of the Title in Literature," *Critical Inquiry*, 14 (1988): 692–720.

   In looking over my specific examples illustrating the species of title, a few of them strike me as a bit hasty or inapt. In particular, I would now say that *Moby Dick* is more of a focusing title than a neutral one, since Captain Ahab is at least as plausible competition for the whale—in terms of unaided prominence in the text—as Molly or Stephen in *Ulysses* are for Leopold Bloom.

2. Further of my reflections on the nature of the art object in the fine arts, a question that is only broached in the present paper, can be found in the following three short essays: "Zemach on Paintings," *British Journal of Aesthetics*, 27 (1987): 278–83; "A Note on Categorical Properties and Contingent Identity," *Journal of Philosophy*, 85 (1988): 718–22; and "The Work of Art," in *The Dictionary of Art* (London: Mac-millan, forthcoming). What I maintain in those essays about the objects of the fine arts is roughly this. Some such artworks—e.g., paintings—are unavoidably physical (or material) objects, but of a complicated sort, whose identities are tied to condi-tions of configuration, function, and intendedness. These are *particular* artworks. Others (e.g., etchings) are not physical objects themselves, though their identities are grounded in specific physical objects (e.g., certain copper plates). Such artworks are instead visual/material patterns-as-bound-by-and-derived-from-particular-archforms/templates. Thus, they are *type* artworks, and so partly akin to works of music and literature, but ones whose instances are always physical objects and whose genuineness resides in a relation to a specific generative object (or objects).

Some, such as Eddy Zemach, have argued that all works of fine art, including paintings, are types. (See his "No Identification without Evaluation," *British Journal of Aesthetics*, 26 [1986]: 239–51, and "How Paintings Are," *British Journal of Aesthetics*, 29 [1989]: 65–71, which is his reply to my critique cited above.) But I cannot see that Zemach has an intelligible conception of types which does not make every physical or material object (e.g., ordinary tables) into a type, in which case his claim loses all content. In addition, I regard Zemach's proposed fundamental linking of identification and evaluation to be a valid insight on the level of art forms or categories, but not on the level of individual assessment of individual paintings. It is fairly invariant, practice-entrenched criteria for the persistence of a given kind of object (a *painting*, or a *painting of a recognized subclass*), and not varying, case-by-case judgments of what "counts" in a given painting, which effectively determine when a painting leaves off and an ex-painting begins.

9   *Artworks and the Future*

"The fundamental things apply, as time goes by."
—Dooley Wilson, in *Casablanca*

I

Consider these rather oft-heard sorts of remarks:

1. "This novel means more, and different things, to us today than it meant to its original readers."
2. "The such and such framework for interpreting drama gives this play a dimension it hadn't previously had."
3. "These poems have acquired this depth and clarity of meaning only recently, in virtue of experiences we have absorbed in the past ten years."
4. "The qualities of this symphony seem now to be entirely different in view of later developments in music."
5. "This film has now become prophetic of a number of subsequent events."
6. "This painter's early work is now not so original or fresh as it used to be."
7. "These compositions have lately acquired an unparalleled influence, which they didn't initially possess."

I want to deny that these sorts of statements, examined critically, are true. I want to deny that artworks change over time, in the implicated and crucial sense. That is to say, I want to deny that the meanings, the aesthetic qualities, the artistic attributes, the proper effects of artworks are subject to evolution, expansion, even revision, as time goes by and as subsequent culture develops. I will not be denying that artworks undergo change, like all other objects, in ordinary *relational* respects—e.g., where they are located, who owns them, how many people are perceiving them at a given time, whether people are recognizing their true features, and the like. Further, I leave aside in this essay the question of change in an artwork's content due to *physical* deterioration or alteration in its material basis where, as in the case of painting, sculpture, drawing, it has such. I also leave aside cases where an artist has altered the composition of a work in later stages, or in a period of afterthought. The issue with which I am primarily concerned is rather this: Do artworks undergo changes in content merely in virtue of the march of time, merely in virtue of their succession by new phases of history, new movements in art, new perspectives undreamt of when they came into existence? Or more simply put, does the content of an artwork inevitably change over time even while the artwork, in some ordinary sense, remains the same?

As the schematic remarks above recall, we often talk as if this was so. We often think of the future as casting light on the artistic past, as transforming it in its very nature. We acknowledge a model of artworks as incomplete, as requiring experience, critics, interpreters to fill out and realize them, in the course of time. We have a tendency, admittedly, to regard an artwork as an organic thing, with a life and a development, which evolves progressively with its surrounding environment until it becomes what it initially was not.[1]

Still, I believe the answer to our question is no. The sentiments I have just reviewed, which are reflective of what I am inclined to call "the myth of the living artwork," are understandable, but ultimately misguided. In this essay I attempt to show that nothing about our central descriptions of artworks, about our appreciation of them, or about their role in human culture gives any support to the affirmative answer to our question, gives any reason to maintain the myth just labeled. My position is roughly this. It is not *artworks* that, in the crucial sense, change over time, it is rather *us*. We think more, experience more,

[1] See R. Wellek and A. Warren, *Theory of Literature* (New York: Harvest Books, 1949), for a prominent expression of the idea that literary text has "a life of its own."

create more—and as a result, are able to find more in artworks than we could previously. But these works are what they are, and remain, from the art-content point of view, what they always were. It is not their content that changes over time, but only our access to the full extent of that content, in virtue of our and the world's subsequent evolution. The latent and unnoted must not be confused with the newly acquired and superadded; later history may *bring out* what *was* in earlier art, but it does not progressively *bring about* that there is *now* more in it.

II

In some previous essays I have focused on the way in which an art-work's content is finely dependent on the specific art-historical context in which it is created, as well as on the perceivable properties that constitute the work's ostensible structure.[2] That is to say, the import of a work of art depends heavily on the complex situation at point of origin—the intentions of the maker, the categories available for perception, the preceding works in that style, the givens of the tradition in which the artist was working, the presence of contemporary events to which to allude, the plausibly known activity in other arts, the existence of much previous civilization. Such import is in large part a product of the past into which the work is inserted, much as a gem-stone placed into its setting acquires a certain determinate allure as a result. What I am now out to explore is, in one sense, the reverse side of this issue: whether cultural and historical developments *subsequent* to a work's creation can be said to determine or modify the aesthetic or artistic properties attributable to it.

The answer to this is more complicated, and depends on whether the emphasis is put on *determining* or *modifying* in the above formulation. Understood in the latter way, I believe the answer is *clearly* no. An art-work's content, though dependent on its historical position, does not fluctuate or pullulate indefinitely as its future unfolds. Understood in the former way, as concerning determination rather than modification, I believe the answer is a *qualified* no, that is to say, a work's art-content

---

[2] See Chapters 4, 5, and 8, above.

is, in its *basic or most important* component, a function exclusively of what precedes,[3] as opposed to what follows, the work's coming into existence. (This component is later dubbed "art-character.") I deal with the substance of this qualification in the penultimate sections of this essay.[4] What should be emphasized now, though, is that my central target is the issue of whether content *alters* with time—whether subsequent historical process can really *induce* modification in it. And I argue that it *cannot*.[5]

III

First, a few words are in order to delimit the realm of attributions with which we are concerned. I understand the *art-content* (or sometimes just *content*) of a work of art to comprise all the following: aesthetic properties (higher-order, typically gestaltlike perceivable properties), artistic properties (appreciatively relevant ones that are not directly perceivable but are inherently relations to other artworks), representational properties, and meaning properties. All of these, I take it, are obviously relevant to the proper understanding of works of art; arguably they comprise everything that is so relevant.

Some examples will help, I think, to pin down the range of these classes sufficiently for our purposes. *Aesthetic* properties divide largely into what we might call *ur*-aesthetic ones, and expressive ones; thus, gracefulness, balance, coherence, flamboyance, and unity, but also sadness, despair, exuberance, nobility, and steeliness.[6] *Artistic* properties differ from aesthetic properties in that they do not merely *depend*

---

[3] 'Precedes' should here and subsequently be understood to mean 'precedes or is contemporaneous with,' in this context.

[4] It concerns future-oriented (e.g., influence) properties: artistic properties that are directly expressive of a work's relation to its future.

[5] That the *determination* of content by future states is, as I make it out, a relatively *minor* affair, fits comfortably with the temporal unalterability of content, but is logically independent of it.

[6] The distinction is roughly one of original employment vs. employment by metaphorical extension. A useful operational test is to ask, for a given aesthetic attribute, whether it makes sense to say a work *expresses* it, as opposed to just *having* it. Still, even with this test, some clearly aesthetic properties are difficult to sort into the two bins— e.g., tension, dynamism, chaoticness—and possibly even daintiness and fragility. Nothing here depends on the sharpness of this sorting.

on the artwork's relation to other artworks and the surrounding artistic background—they are not merely the perceivable upshot of that contextual placement—but are inherently *a matter of* that relationality. The aesthetic properties of, say, a painting are those tied up with how, on a more than merely sensory level, it *looks*—with the impressions it affords, the effects it produces, on a properly backgrounded perceiver. The artistic properties of a painting are those that, while strictly relevant to its appreciation and evaluation as art, *embody* relations to the surrounding cultural context as a whole (including, conceivably, relations to the creative history of that very work), and are thus not, strictly speaking, perceivable in the painting itself.[7] Examples of what I mean by artistic properties are originality,[8] derivativeness, skillfulness, revolutionariness, typicality, influentiality, syntheticness, distinctiveness of vision.[9] Representational properties are

[7] On aesthetic vs. artistic, see P. Kivy, *The Corded Shell* (Princeton: Princeton University Press, 1980), pp. 115–16; T. Kulka, "The Artistic and the Aesthetic Value of Art," *British Journal of Aesthetics*, 21 (1981): 336–50; G. Hermerén, *Aspects of Aesthetics* (Lund: Gleerups, 1983), pp. 53–75. I should caution, though, that none of these writers makes this distinction precisely as I do.

[8] See F. N. Sibley, "Originality and Value," *British Journal of Aesthetics*, 25 (1985), 169–84, for a worthwhile discussion of various senses of "original" in art criticism.

[9] To contrast exuberance, an aesthetic property, with originality, an artistic property, we may note that a painting's exuberance attaches to it *in virtue of* its being properly seen in a certain stylistic framework to which it belongs, but its exuberance is ultimately apprehendable in the painting, and is not *itself* that relationality on which it depends. But a painting's originality *is*, strictly speaking, an extrinsic relational *matter*—its having structures, features, or effects significantly different from those of relevant predecessors—and hence is not clearly apprehendable in the painting in the same way. I would prefer to say that one sees *that* a painting is original, and *reflects* on its originality while registering its structural and aesthetic properties, rather than that one sees the originality *in* the painting.

Similarly, the distinctiveness of vision in a painting would appear to be a feature, like originality, that explicitly involves comparison, in this case to the vision incorporated in other paintings—it is being related to those other ways of painterly seeing by the relation of *distinct difference from*. You can apprehend a painting's mode of vision directly, but you can only grasp the distinctiveness of that by external correlation. Thus, distinctiveness of vision is an artistic attribute, whereas cold harmoniousness (Tanguy) or sexual anxiousness (Munch), which might be qualities in virtue of which a painting's vision was distinctive, would be aesthetic ones.

Finally, consider skillfulness, a rather difficult case. What I have in mind is skillfulness or facility of handling. I sort this as artistic because it seems to be an inherently comparative affair, involving a relation between the rendering in a given painting and a scale of difficulty of tasks in a given medium or material. You can, with suitable priming, see in a painting how the medium has been handled in a certain manner to

such as the following: representing a man, depicting a locomotive in motion, portraying the Duke of Windsor, representing the annunciation of Christ. And finally, meaning properties would include such as these: symbolizing the soul's progress through life, satirizing the foibles of philosophers, criticizing the cruelty of the English to the Irish, exhibiting the inexorability of fate, portraying humankind's deepgrained stupidity and greed, manifesting the warmth and solidity of the bourgeois home, conveying a sense of release from earthly concerns, suggesting the emptiness and precariousness of worldly ambition.[10] It is artistic and meaning properties that will prove most crucial to the argument of this essay.

IV

The view that a work's art-content, whether it has been grasped or not, is effectively fixed at the work's coming into being, is clearly not a view that holds total sway over our art-critical impulses. The schematic remarks at the beginning of this essay are reminders of that. My hope is to show that the intuitions behind them, though fairly strong and widespread, do not survive reflective examination, and thus that such remarks are not to be accepted at face value. It is helpful, before proceeding, to replace those skeletal attributions with some concrete cases.

    1. We sometimes speak of works acquiring new meanings merely as time and history progresses; we can take as an example of this Bosch's paintings depicting Hell, given Hiroshima and the Holocaust.

    2. We often regard subsequent interpretation as capable of injecting old works with new imports they did not previously possess; our example here can be Freudian readings of *Hamlet*, à la Ernest Jones.

---

achieve a certain result, but you cannot, in the same way, see the *relative difficulty* of this in the painting. Of course, you might properly receive an *impression* of skillfulness or facility, and this would signify the presence of aesthetic *analogs* of what are per se artistic attributes. But for a painting, being skillfully done—like being original, being expressively unique, and so on—is rather like being expensive: you can only "see" such in the painting in an extended, inferential sense.

    [10]These are properties that belong, respectively, to Bunyan's *Pilgrim's Progress*, Molière's *Le Mariage Forcé*, Swift's *A Modest Proposal*, Sophocles' *Oedipus Rex*, many of Goya's etchings, many of Chardin's still lifes, the finale of Mahler's Ninth Symphony, Shelley's *Ozymandias*.

3. We sometimes maintain that the meaning or feeling in a previously opaque or obscure work crystallizes for us at a given time, only after we have had and digested certain experiences that were necessary to understanding the work; in this vein it might be said that Rimbaud's most chaotic imagery means something now, given our acquaintance (courtesy of the 1960s) with psychedelic states of mind, that it couldn't have earlier.

4. We occasionally say that the qualities or nature of a given work can be retroactively transformed by succeeding activity in the same art form. Examples here are legion, and particularly intriguing: Bach's *Brandenburg* Concerti heard against Stravinsky's homage-parody, the *Dumbarton Oaks* Concerto, Caravaggio's intense chiaroscuro in light of (or perhaps in dark of!) Ad Reinhart's all-black canvases, Mondrian's spiritually conceived rectilinear formations in the wake of modern commercial Scandinavian design.

5. We say that certain initially self-contained works at some point become prophetic augurs, given the course of events after their creation, within and without the realm of art. Examples are again numerous: Eisenstein's *Alexander Nevsky* (1938), with its vividly evoked struggle of noble Russian against barbaric Teutons (circa 1240) now appears to foretell World War II; the opening of Haydn's Symphony no. 80 seems to prefigure the opening of Wagner's *Die Walküre*, as does, even more intriguingly, the third variation of the arietta in Beethoven's last piano sonata the swinging feeling of mainstream 1930s jazz; the crucifixion in Grünewald's *Isenheim Altarpiece* (1515) now seems a clear forerunner of the Expressionism of Ludwig Kirchner, or even that of Francis Bacon; Blake's religious image of "Satanic Mills" in *Milton* cannot appear but fatidic in relation to nineteenth-century industrial Britain.

6. We remark that works can lose in originality, freshness, revolutionariness, shockingness as time habituates us to their effects, and subsequent developments assimilate and/or overshadow them. Such reflection applies itself to almost any stylistic advance thought noble in its day: Stravinsky's metric freedom and polytonality in *The Rite of Spring*, Constable's use of 'local color' in his landscapes, Virginia Woolf's development of interior monologue in *To the Lighthouse*, Jasper John's stark employment of conventionalized signs and symbols (flags, numerals, block letters) in his paintings of the 1960s.

7. We tend to think of artworks gaining (or losing) in importance, pivotalness, or ꜱᴇᴍɪɴᴀlity in virtue of their emerging degree of influence on subsequent art and culture; for example, the artistic stock of Picasso's *Demoiselles d'Avignon,* or that of Kafka's *Metamorphosis,* appears to have increased immeasurably since those works were created, in view of the breadth and depth of their impact on later painting and writing, respectively, though neither was much appreciated at the time of birth.

The basic intuition or thought underlying these judgments seem to be this: artistic, cultural, or social developments *subsequent* to a work's creation invariably affect the way artworks are approached, perceived, understood, assessed—in short, *viewed*—and thus, if the content of an artwork is a function of how we are inclined to view it, then such content will appear to change with time.

Since I am disposed to defend the relative stability and permanence of an artwork's content, my task is to show how the above-noted tendency to view works retrospectively from the ever-advancing vantage point of what follows them does not, if properly understood, undermine that stability and permanence. Now, in one sense, my response can be rather short: the intuition expressed above is just plain defective, or confused. Although the passage of time *as a matter of fact* beguiles us into seeing a work against the future that spreads out after it, this does not mean that it *is to be seen* that way—at least insofar as grasping its *content* is concerned. And although the *apparent* content of an artwork is clearly a function of how it is being viewed, its *true* content is not a function of that but rather of how it is *appropriately* or *justifiably* viewed.

V

Clearly, it would be desirable to have more of an answer to the intuition represented by the above examples than just this summary reply. What I do now, then, is offer some distinctions and principles that I believe serve, singly and collectively, to defuse much of the intuitive force of such examples. Although I will be recalling only certain of the examples in connection with any individual distinction or principle, I believe all the latter are more or less relevant to all of the former, with varying degrees of directness. My overarching intent is to defend a form of *traditionalism* on these matters, where this is understood not as stylistic conservatism, but as acknowledgment of the special relevance of the *preexisting* traditions in which artworks arise. Along the way I will engage in debate with some prominent revisionist (antitraditionalist) thinkers, Arthur Danto and Graham McFee, on our topic.

The first, and simplest, distinction worth stressing in this context is that between properties possessed by a given work *simpliciter* and properties *known* to be possessed at any given time—between the art-content of a work *tout court* and that part of its art-content that has been *uncovered* at a given point. So, for example, it may seem that *Alexander Nevsky,* when first filmed, has a number of virtues, but that propheticness of the eastern front of 1942 is not among them. Yet if the film truly is prophetic, why is it not so from the outset? (Nostradamus's prophecies presumably did not wait until the nineteenth century to become *prophetic,* but only to become *confirmed.*) There seems to be confusion here over what is true, and what is or can be *known* to be true, at time of creation. There is a straightforward sense in which the propheticness of *Alexander Nevsky* is complete, its prophecy in place, when the film is done.[11] The full impact of Rimbaud's most abandoned outpourings[12] is perhaps more deeply plumbable to us today, through the spectacles of mind-altering drugs, than it was for readers of the 1890s, but the expressiveness of those images has not changed; nor has the spiritual condition they express. What has changed is our ability to encompass, to grasp from within; we know better now, in general, "what it is like" to be in such states of mind. Later pharmacology allows us to better fathom experiences onto which Rimbaud naturally, or perhaps with the aid of wine and opium, ventured.

---

[11] The truth of this prophecy (i.e., part of its being 'prophetic' in the normal sense) depends on future states of affairs, but its *prophesying truly* can still be said to attach to it from the beginning, if not *knowably* so.

[12] From *Delirium* (*Alchemy of the Word*): "I invented the color of vowels!—A black, E white, I red, O blue, U green—I regulated the form and movement of every consonant and with instinctive rhythms I prided myself on inventing a poetic language accessible some day to all the senses. . . . I became an adept at simple hallucination: in place of a factory I really saw a mosque, a school of dreamers composed of angels, carriages on the highway of the sky, a drawing room at the bottom of a lake. . . . Finally I came to regard as sacred the disorder of my mind. I was idle, full of sluggish fever: I envied the felicity of beasts, caterpillars that represent the innocence of limbo, moles, the sleep of virginity!" (trans. Louise Varese).

Beethoven's startling third variation in the arietta of op. 111 achieves an undeniably jazzy *quality* through its diminuitions, cascading dotted rhythms, and chordal syncopations, and may even be said to prefigure boogie-woogie piano style.[13] But this quality, which is particularly striking in the context of a late classical sonata, was always there, though it could not have been designated in that way. What is *not* true is that the passage in question at some point (say, 1910) *becomes* an *example* of jazz. It never was and never will be such, though the subsequent emergence of jazz perhaps enables us to bring its jazzy quality into relief. To go farther than this, and actually hear the passage *as jazz,* would be to *mishear* it.

The import of the distinction I have been discussing—that between art properties *simpliciter* and ones *known* to be possessed at a given time—could be alternatively captured by the following: the appearance of time's passage *producing* (new) content can often be construed rather as the *revealing* of (already present) content.

VI

A similarly obvious distinction, but one whose nonobservance is the root of a certain class of problematic cases, is that between *permanent* and *time-relative* ways of taking certain art attributes, among them originality, provocativeness, revolutionarity. Originality as a property of an artwork is a matter of its exhibiting structural or aesthetic characteristics differing significantly from those of its relevant predecessors. So, though this is obviously a thoroughly contextual property, the appropriate context is fixed—given once and for all. It no more admits of drift or fluctuation than does the year in which a work comes into existence. It is in this sense that the corresponding attribution is a permanent one. On the other hand, when we say of such a work that it is now *no longer* original—that it's not original *today*— we are not really withdrawing our earlier ascription of artistic content—we're not really talking about its art content per se at all. Instead, we are in effect observing that were a new work produced

---

[13] There is little reason, however, to think there was any *influence* of Beethoven's variations on the jazz tradition.

today to exhibit such features, it would not be considered—and in fact would not be—original. But our first work, if every truly original, remains now original, and will always be original—in the art content-relevant sense—even if our sense of its originality is weakened through overfamiliarity.

Thus Stravinsky's changing meters, Constable's bright green grass patches, Woolf's streams of inner thought, and Johns's perky numerals do not become diminished in originality either because we are by now used to them, or because we have been inundated subsequently by their growing artistic progeny. If anything, it is such progeny that become increasingly unoriginal, or we who become appreciatively dulled. Much the same can be said, of course, for provocativeness and revolutionarity. The fact that some earlier artistic object does not provoke us today, or not to the same degree, and has no power at present to initiate a revolution in its art form, obviously takes away nothing from the (permanent) provocativeness or revolutionarity it has in virtue of its unchanged position in the art context out of which it arose and in which it displays its proper effect and character.

VII

My third distinction is one to which literary theorist E. D. Hirsch has devoted a large part of several tomes, that between *meaning* and *significance*. I am happy to enlist its aid in the name of keeping the future from transmogrifying the past, where art is concerned.[14] Here are some of Hirsch's characterizations of this opposition:

> *Meaning* is that which is presented by a text; it is what the author meant by his use of a particular sign sequence, it is what the signs represent. *Significance,* on the other hand, names a relationship between that meaning and a person, or a conception, or a situation, or indeed anything imaginable.[15]

---

[14] I would distance myself, however, from his well-known equation of work meaning and author meaning. That thesis is unacceptable, though closer to the truth than some of its competitors. (See sec. x, below. See also P. D. Juhl, *Interpretation* [Princeton: Princeton University Press, 1980].)

[15] *Validity in Interpretation* (New Haven: Yale University Press, 1966), p. 8.

But significance is the proper object of criticism, not of interpretation, whose exclusive object is verbal meaning. It is a charter of freedom to the critic, not an inhibition, to insist on this distinction, for the liberty of the critic to describe the countless dimensions of a text's significance is closely dependent on his not being constricted by a confusion between significance and meaning. No responsible critic wants to pervert and falsify the meaning of a text, yet at the same time he does not want to be inhibited from pursuing whatever seems most valuable and useful.[16]

What is primarily meant by the nostrum (that everyone must reinterpret the works of the past) is that each new critic or age finds new sorts of significance, new strands of relevance to particular cultural or intellectual contexts. . . . As critics we should remind ourselves that we are not perceiving a new work or a new meaning, but a new significance of the work, which often could not exist except in our own cultural milieu.[17]

Apart from the fact that Hirsch's concern is literature and mine the arts as a whole, the distinction he enunciates can be taken over, mutatis mutandis, and turned to my purposes. Hirsch's idea of *meaning* is parallel to, though narrower than, my notion of *artwork content,* while his idea of *significance* can be readily broadened to comprise all intelligible *relatings of an artwork's content* to matters outside the sphere of proper understanding for that work.

There is, if you will, a sort of loose function that takes as arguments any given artwork with its determinate art-content and any object or situation outside the cultural and temporal context that determines that content, and gives as a value the salient similarities, echoes, or parallelisms discernible between the given work and the external matter with which it is brought into comparative relation. This quasi function has value, no doubt, but it is important to observe two things about it. First, that the first argument of the function can only be the work already grasped and understood—and not the work shorn of any reading or prior to all construal. It would seem bootless, after all, to try to meaningfully connect a meaningless structure or artifact to something outside of it. We must presuppose an artwork-with-content, or that content itself, as the first term of such relating. Second, the upshot

[16]Ibid., p. 57.
[17]Ibid., p. 137.

of this relating of constituted meaning (content) to some other term is not helpfully considered an extension of meaning (content) itself, but rather something different, and 'significance' seems a good label for that.

Let's consider some examples. When we look at some of the more bizarre and horrific portions of Bosch's *Last Judgment* (e.g., a man skewered on a harp, a person half devoured by a giant hag), we may find ourselves connecting those images with ones we have seen or imagined from the Nazi Holocaust, and we may become sensible of certain resemblances and achieve a heightened awareness in both directions. Shall we say that Bosch's painting has now changed or expanded its *meaning,* beyond what it had in the sixteenth century? Shall we say that it is now *about* Nazi inhumanity, as well as the torments of Hell? Shall we say that it has come to *reflect* the degradation of soul in the twentieth century as well as the sadistic side of the medieval imagination? Shall we say that it has turned out to *represent,* or perhaps just *symbolize,* the realm of Buchenwald as well as that of Bosch's Netherlands? We need say none of this, but can instead readily acknowledge the emergence of an extrinsic significance, illuminating of content if not transforming of it. Similarly, the phrase "dark Satanic Mills," which occurs in a poem of Blake's, does not come to refer to the textile factories of nineteenth-century England, though they would seem to be tailor-made for such allusion; instead, a rich significance, exterior to Blake's poem, emerges from the triangulation of the poem's meaning and economic developments a century down the road.[18] Again, a certain significance arises in juxtaposing Caravaggio's deep chiaroscuro explorations with Reinhardt's canvases in shades of black—perhaps we can begin to see the latter as the limiting case of the former—but only in the case of the Reinhardt can this interactive significance properly be elevated to the level of constitutive meaning.[19]

[18] A less rich, though more timely, significance emerges when we read the twelfth line of the poem, "Bring me my chariots of fire," and are made to recall the recent popular British film of that name.

[19] One of the more flagrant attempts to dissolve the distinction between meaning and significance is contained in this passage from a recent essay from Graham McFee, which I discuss further later on ("The Historicity of Art," *Journal of Aesthetics and Art Criticism,* 38 [1980], 307–24): "Not merely conventional changes but also historical developments may be relevant to the meaning of a work of art. Consider the following simple example. In the film *Sleeper,* the awakened Woody Allen is shown by his

Two analogies are helpful here. The contrast between meaning and significance is a little like that between the *qualities* and *propensities* of a material and the *uses* or *applications* to which it is put. The former, the properties in virtue of which the material has uses and applications, do not generally change, but the uses and applications do—they come into being in response to specific needs and demands of the developing situation. Similarly, the content of an artwork, though of course dependent on more than inherent structure, is arguably fixed in its originating context, whereas its possibilities of interesting relatability to anything else—its applications—only grow as history unfolds. Hirsch and others have emphasized, in this light, how distinguishing significance from meaning does not bar one from accounting for the continuing appeal and practical inexhaustibility of the great classics of the past—it's generally a matter of finding new applications of a rich though stable artistic content to our unstable and ever-changing human situation.[20]

Another analogy is this. A work of art is like a *statement* made by employing a verbal vehicle in a specific context. Words change their meanings, and indexical terms their references, over time, but dateable statements made with words in a given situation do not. If I now say, "I'm going to sit here all night until I finish this," then this registers J. L.'s intention to remain in a room on Capitol Hill on February 15,

---

futuristic friends a film of Richard Nixon. They tell him this is a man they believe to have been a president of the U.S.A. but to have done something so terrible that all records of his existence have been destroyed, with the exception of this one film clip. Assuming the film *Sleeper* to have been made in Nixon's halcyon pre-Watergate days, does the Watergate affair and his subsequent resignation give it a new (social) poignancy? Does the reference to Nixon change, as it were, from fictional to actual? Do the inventions of submarine and helicopter not add a similar new poignancy to the novels of Jules Verne? Certainly these facts might provide a critic with a basis for new interpretation. It is surely clear that *these facts do affect the meanings of these works of art*" (p. 310; my italics). It is *not at all* clear.

McFee's essay explores and defends, without delineating them all that clearly, a number of theses about art that can well be called 'historicist.' A main purpose of the present essay is to show that one can buy part of the historicist package without buying the lot; in particular, that one can embrace the historically conditioned nature of artworks and their art-contents without allowing that such contents evolve indefinitely as time marches on.

[20]See Juhl, *Interpretation*, for more discussion of the meaning/significance distinction and its importance to defending stability of literary content.

1987, and work on the essay you are now reading. This meaning is unaffected by subsequent uses of "I" and "this," by other "tonights" across the globe, and by the fact that, let us suppose, the word "finish" will mean only "ingest" beginning around 2000. Such statements, it is true, may acquire ironic overtones, or humorous resonances, in virtue of changes of meaning in the words with which they are expressed. Two examples that come to mind are in fact literary: Matthew Arnold's "vast edges drear and naked shingles of the world" in "Dover Beach," and Shakespeare's "honor pricks me on," from *Henry V*. But surely certain later connotations of "shingles" and "pricks" make these lines sound different to our ears—a kind of significance—without in any way altering the meaning of the literary statements those phrases form a part of. I am suggesting that the 'statements' made by works of art, literary or not, are, like literal statements made by sentences on a given occasion of utterance, unaffected by subsequent drift in the sense of the elements, verbal or not, of which they are composed. In either case, though, one could speak of later significances—those peculiar ones formed by the triangulation of meaningful artistic or literal statements with vehicle components that have undergone meaning change in the intervening years. But again, vicissitudes of significance have no more to do with artistic content than, say, variations in the popularity of various regular polygons have to do with their geometrical characteristics.

Finally, a brief return look at *Alexander Nevsky* from our present vantage point. Recall that Eisenstein's film might be regarded as having limned the bitter confrontation of Russians and Germans four years later. It seems we have two options. One is to say that the film always had a certain theme (Russian-Teutonic mistrust and conflict), and that in virtue of that it can be retrospectively seen as "prophetic" (and as always having been so), in the sense that its embodied sense *turned out to be* instanced by later, unenvisaged and unimplied, events. (This is more or less the way I treated this example above.) The other is to allow a sense in which the film is now prophetic of World War II, although it wasn't at the time of its creation, but to insist that such "propheticness" is not reasonably reckoned part of the film's meaning, but only of its growing pool of *significances*. Either way, there is no threat to the thesis I have been defending.

VIII

One of the most vivid and influential expressions of the opposing view on the problem I am wrestling with was offered, almost parenthetically, by Arthur Danto at the end of his celebrated essay "The Artworld."[21] I will now examine what he says there. This will serve ultimately to introduce a fourth principle, that of not confounding two different kinds of retroactive art-critical assessment.

According to Danto, as new artworks come into existence they often bring with them new properties—i.e., ones not previously instantiated in the art world. Let F-ness be such a recently emerged property. Then while the predicate F is applicable to certain recent works, the predicate non-F is applicable to all *other* works. In this manner, the non-F-ness of all earlier artwork is now marked, and becomes artistically relevant, whereas before it was unmarked, and artistically of no account. Thus, for example, when Cubist representation first arose, this had the effect of rendering all earlier representation non-Cubist, in a significant sense. The non-Cubist mode of depiction of, say, Holbein's *Ambassadors* suddenly appears as an artistically relevant attribute of that painting. This is what Danto means by the "retroactive enrichment of the entities of the art world" that is brought about by the advance of art.

There are a number of things to say about Danto's intriguing art-metaphysical conceit, from my point of view. First, it should be noted that Danto does *not* claim that it is only when F-ness is first exemplified that all earlier works become non-F; he admits that earlier work was non-F *all along*, just that this went unremarked. The supposed changes induced are thus more second-order, not from *not* being non-F to *being* non-F, but from non-F-ness's being an artistically *irrelevant* property to its being an artistically *relevant* property. But, second, it's simply *false* that non-F-ness now becomes an art-relevant property of earlier work. Of course, non-F now becomes an available predicate for marking an all-along possessed property of a given earlier work, but that itself doesn't mean that the property (non-F-ness) is now relevant to the *appreciation* or *understanding* of that work, which is presumably what Danto intends by 'relevance'.

[21] *Journal of Philosophy*, 61 (1964): 571–84.

What happens is rather this: the new property, *F*-ness, is, naturally, relevant to appreciating the new work, and it is *relevant that we recognize* the complementary property, non-*F*-ness, as belonging to earlier work, *as part of our appreciation of the new work*. It plays no appropriate part, however, in the appreciation *of such earlier work itself*—no more than it has ever done. It thus has not, contrary to Danto, crossed into the category of art-relevant properties for such work.

It is important to see the first Cubist portaits as Cubist, and as arising in opposition to a long tradition of staunchly non-Cubist (whether naturalist, Impressionist, Fauvist, or Expressionist) portraiture, but the non-Cubisticity of such portraiture, though we can now explicitly recognize and label it, is of no relevance to understanding those earlier portraits. An Impressionist painter of the 1870s is in no way reacting to Cubist modes of depiction; he is not cognizant of the Cubist way of doing things; he is not choosing among options for portraying, one of which is Cubist style; he is not eschewing Cubist fragmentation for Pointillist decomposition—Cubist vs. non-Cubist is simply not part of the matrix of that painter's artistic activity, not part of the framework of meaning for what results from it. There is an asymmetry here that Danto's analysis overlooks: new work may restructure the artistic past in making us view that past with refocused eyes, so as to grasp such new work aright, but it does not therefore make the artistic future of earlier work a necessary part of the understanding of such earlier work. The artistic lines of the past may well be redrawn with every new development, *but only from the appreciative point of view of each new phase.* The artistic past is not left alone, it is true, with respect to understanding what is future to it, but the future, I suggest, is rightly left aside in understanding the artistic past.

Another example may help. Consider the phenomenon of *shaped canvases*, associated with artists such as Frank Stella. These are paintings that gesture toward sculpture, in that their outer boundaries are explicitly molded into some conspicuous, nonordinary shape, consciously avoiding the canonical rectangle, and the circle and oval as well. Well, it appears now that Holbein's paintings fit squarely (pun intended) into the category of non-(shaped canvas)es.[22] They always

---

[22]Note that this is to be parsed *non-(shaped canvas)*, and not *non-shaped (canvas)*.

were such, of course, but this feature of them had not been an object of attention. Now that we have attended to it, is it relevant to our grasp of those Holbeins, to their meaning as artworks? I suggest not. Stella's canvases derive their meaning partly from their contrast with all the preceding Holbeins, Titians, Monets, Picassos, for which rectangular outer shape comfortably is, à la Walton, a standard property of paintings. But nothing in the artistic import of the Holbeins derives from their contrast with Stella's canvases of four hundred years later. Consider Corot's landscapes. They are, and always were, representational, non-Expressionist, non-Minimalist, and non-Conceptualist. Until relatively recently, however, there was just no way of noting that. What's more, there was no point in doing so. But what point is there now? Only to enable the proper appreciation of *subsequent* artwork that is pointedly nonrepresentational, Expressionist, Minimalist, and Conceptual. There is nothing, as it were, in it for the *Corot*. Nothing involving such categories or distinctions is relevantly brought to bear in perceiving and appreciating those serene, occasionally sentimental landscapes.

In short, what accrues for existing artworks with time are not additional aspects of art-content, but at best new concepts or terms for labeling and making manifest this content, tools of anachronistic description that serve, admittedly, to throw light on the old in the name of the new, without properly illuminating the old on its own account or inducing change in its artistic character. Just because we can apply newly emerged distinctions to older art, and can *now* understand what they mean so applied, does not entail that they are or have become artistically *relevant* to such art—to its understanding and interpretation. I conclude that Danto's observations provide no real problem for the thesis I have been urging.

IX

The root error involved in Danto's analysis is plausibly the equating of what may be labeled *backward* and *forward* retroactivism. The former is, perhaps, legitimate, but it does not legitimate the latter. If we have two works, W_1 and W_2, created in 1887 and 1987, respectively, then adopting the perspective of *backward* retroactivism to them now, in 1987, involves first reconstruing W_1 in light of W_2, and then reflecting that new illumination forward, as it were, onto W_2. Here the present permits us to see the past more clearly, as it could not have seen itself, which in turn clarifies the present understood in relation to, and as a development out of, that past. Adapting to these works the perspective of *forward* retroactivism, on the other hand, involves first construing W_2 in light of W_1, which is just traditional historicism, and then projecting this understanding backward onto W_1.

On the first scenario the movement of thought is from 1987 to 1887, and then back to 1987, where the aim is to understand 1987 in terms of 1887-as-we-now-understand-it-from-the-vantage-point-of-1987. Retroactive reconstruction (of W_1 through W_2) is the *initial* (and *instrumental*) step, and the whole procedure is in effect a swipe backward whose purpose is the understanding of the present in terms of a clarified and reconstituted past. On the second scenario the movement of thought is from 1887 to 1987, and then back to 1887, where the aim is to understand 1887 in terms of 1987-as-we-now-understand-it-in-relation-to-1887. Retroactive reconstruction (of W_1 through W_2) is the *second* (and *ultimate*) step, and the whole procedure is in effect a swipe forward whose purpose is the understanding of the past in terms of a subsequently emerged present.

Backward retroactivism is fair game because its after-the-fact reconceivings do not flout the principle that the basic content of artistic acts—i.e., roughly, what is said or conveyed in them—cannot be a product of what succeeds them. It simply makes use of the idea that what *succeeds* may allow one to discern and delineate more effectively and perspicuously the *preceding* context in which such content emerges. Forward retroactivism, however, does flout this principle, and I suspect that it is the failure to distinguish the one kind of retroactive critical maneuver from the other that gives the forward-aiming variety an air of legitimacy it doesn't deserve.

A nice endorsement of backward retroactivism, coupled with an awareness of the dangers of the forward variety, seems implicit in this excerpt from a recent critical discussion of two paintings by Correggio: "In other respects both pictures look forward rather than back. The impression which his [Correggio's] mature work makes of 'anticipating' the baroque is better explained by assuming that baroque artists looked back to Correggio. In the case of these two paintings, the connection is with the quintessential baroque artist, Bernini himself."[23] We understand Bernini best by seeing him as a successor to Correggio, whose *own* late work we can now see, from a Berninian and post-Berninian perspective, as proto-baroque. But we are not invited to view (we are mildly warned against viewing) Correggio's canvases as essentially anticipators of Bernini—insofar as it is *Correggio's* canvases we are to appreciatively understand.[24]

Describing one of the same paintings, the *Lamentation* of 1524, Benjamin Forgey has this to say: "Correggio, working just a few years after the peak of the High Renaissance in Rome, manages incomparably to look backward and forward at the same time. The painting clearly draws on the idealism and self-confidence of Raphael while comprising a catalogue of profound motifs—emotionalism, realism, illusionism and the dramatic movement of the diagonal and the spiral—that would become the basis of baroque painting a century after his death.[25] These are very astute observations, which I can only endorse. The point to emphasize, though, is that, despite what the phrase "backward *and* forward" might suggest, there is nothing here that implicates what I am calling forward retroactivism. The following is, I think, wholly consistent with the sense of Forgey's remarks, though of course going beyond them: we necessarily appreciate the *potential* and *significance* of the *Lamentation* in virtue of what it spawns and prefigures, while we appreciate its *content* and *meaning* in virtue, partly, of what it presents itself against the backdrop of. We understand Caravaggio, a central Baroque artist, by looking to Correggio, but we don't quite understand

[23] Cecil Gould, in *The Age of Correggio and the Carracci* (exhibition catalog), National Gallery of Art, 1986, p. 104.

[24] The question of legitimate vs. illegitimate searches for and uses of anticipations of one artwork by another is a difficult one, and I don't mean to imply that a work's anticipations of later work can *never* be appreciatively relevant to it.

A connected issue, I think, is that of our justifiable desire to understand a given work with respect to its place in a *completed* corpus or oeuvre, which necessarily entails seeing an artist's earlier work in light of his or her later efforts (anticipations can certainly figure here). Seeing the earlier in relation to the later, as well as vice versa, is part of what's involved in seeing the oeuvre as a whole. We want to see, in later works, what in earlier works was developed further; we want to see, perhaps, what the artist was after in earlier work without completely achieving it. So we consult the future output to see what the artist was *trying* to do or say—though not what the artist has *succeeded* in doing or saying. In any event, what the artist was saying, or even was trying to say, in earlier work does not *change* when later work emerges, it just becomes, in many cases, more clearly *evident*.

[25] *Washington Post*, December 21, 1986.

Correggio in terms of Caravaggio. Rather, what Caravaggio does vis-à-vis Correggio is serve to bring out more clearly ways Correggio diverged from and reacted to his (Correggio's) predecessors, by drawing our attention to what was only nascent in Correggio (Forgey's list of motifs). But the relation to Caravaggio is not an essential link in grasping Correggio's art—whereas it is so in the reverse direction.

A good illustration of the *conflation* of forward with backward retroactivism is an argument advanced recently by Graham McFee:

> A similar line of argument can be used to show that the meanings of works of art are not immune to what happens at some later time. For here too new reasons may become available to us, or the character of the extant reasons become altered. Consider the "meaning" of Velazquez' *Las Meninas*, for example. That Picasso based a whole series of works of his on that masterpiece cannot leave *it* untouched. Putting the point perhaps over-crudely, we might say that a critic writing on the Velazquez now would be able to say, as Velazquez' contemporaries could not, that it sparked off such-and-such in the fertile mind of Picasso. But does this really contribute to, or constitute, a change of meaning? Surely it does. For we will need to refer to the Velazquez in describing the Picasso. If we fail to see the "quotation" as such we will have missed something crucial. Yet if it is crucial to the Picasso, can it be irrelevant to the Velazquez? Doesn't the Picasso in a sense *tell us* something about the Velazquez, something from which a line of criticism might develop?[26]

McFee observes rightly that one can't understand the Picassos without taking into account the Velazquez. And in fact we may, to some extent, even see the Velazquez differently in light of the Picassos *in the context of the project of fully understanding the Picassos in relation to their model*. In such a context we might focus, perhaps for the first time, on the potential for Cubist fragmentation in *Las Meninas*, rather than on its enigmatic baroque recessions. This is just backward retroactivism. But forward retroactivism is another matter. If our project is understanding the Velazquez, then this is simply not to be done *in terms of or with essential reference to* the later Picassos. Surely there is an asymmetry here. What is "crucial to the Picasso" is, indeed, "irrelevant to the Velazquez" in that the quotation relation partly *determines* the former's meaning but not the latter's. And the fact that the Picassos

[26]"The Historicity of Art," p. 310.

may serve to "tell us something about" the Velazquez does not mean
they have succeeded in inducing any changes in the work's original
content. If anything, they have drawn our attention to it from a
different angle, perhaps even given that content a new "face"—but one
that it relevantly wears *only* for the purpose of rounding out our grasp
of Picasso's variations, and not on its own accord, or in its own right as
an artistic expression.

We can now see that certain of our opening examples reflective of
revisionist intuitions pose no real problem for traditionalism, as long as
one does not grant forward rectroactivism immunity from prosecution
on the grounds of passing similarity to the backward variety. The
discovery of Grünewald, somewhat anomalous among his Northern
early sixteenth-century contemporaries, helps put Kirchner's and Bacon's Expressionism in historical perspective—the art-content of their
canvases would be subtly different without their Grünewaldean prece-
dents. And in connection to the enterprise of understanding the development of Expressionism in later centuries, our view on those
Grünewalds is somewhat modified by the availability of the backward
glance. But the art content of the Grünewalds themselves—aesthetic,
artistic, representational, and meaning properties—is not transformed
by the advent of Kirchner and Bacon. Grünewald's paintings are not
now, and never were, appropriately seen as operating in the same artistic space as Kirchner and Bacon, as having been done, say, in a preliminary version of their style(s), or even as inherently looking forward
to their mode of Expressionistic rendering. This is pernicious—i.e.,
forward-aiming retroactivism.

Similar remarks would apply to thinking that Wagner's *Walküre* had
really affected the artwork content of Haydn's Eightieth Symphony,
instead of just casting Haydn's opening in a new light the sole justification for which is the reflexive illumination cast back on Wagner's
strangely similar opening. Again, similarly, it would be a mistake to
think that the efficiency, blandness, and homogeneity of Modern Scandinavian design, which undoubtedly owes some debt to Mondrian,
have somehow in turn managed to rob the Dutchman's canvases of
their proper adventurousness and spirituality. We understand *contemporary rectilinear design* in relation to a Mondrianesque oeuvre itself
now seen as a progenitor of the former; but in understanding *Mondrian's oeuvre* we only *mis*comprehend it if our terms of reference are
purchased on the cheap from the SCANdinavian outlets of its future.

I will close this section by commenting on a well-known essay on our theme, one on its surface supportive of revisionism, Borges's "Kafka and His Precursors." Borges notes various prefigurings of the Kafka of "somber myths and atrocious institutions" in earlier work by Zeno, Bloy, Kierkegaard, Browning, and Lord Dunsany. For example, Zeno's moving object that never completes its traversal, Achilles, and the arrow are "the first Kafkian characters in literature," while Dunsany's "Carcassonne," about an invincible army that sets out in futile quest of a once-glimpsed city, echoes the basic plot of many a Kafka parable. Here is Borges's conclusion: "If I am not mistaken, the heterogeneous pieces I have enumerated resemble Kafka; if I am not mistaken, not all of them resemble each other. The second fact is the more significant. In each of these texts we find Kafka's idiosyncrasy to a greater or lesser degree, but if Kafka had never written a line, we would not perceive this quality; in other words, it would not exist. . . . The fact is that every writer *creates* his own precursors. His work modifies our conception of the past, as it will modify the future."[27] The superficial suggestion, admittedly, is that Kafka's work somehow changes the content of his kindred predecessor's works, because they now become bound together and reborn as pre-Kafkian texts. But I prefer to take Borges's reflections as mainly an endorsement of backward retroactivism, with the more radical (i.e., forwardist) implications shorn off as whimsical aberration. There is certainly a sense in which each writer creates his or her own precursors, in that the writer's work provides a guiding principle for organizing and sorting out the preceding literary field within which that work originates. But this all occurs from the point of view of the later work, with the object of setting that off most clearly in relation to its background; it need not entail reconstruction of the content and affiliations of such earlier work on its own account. Kafka's work does indeed "modify our conception of the past," but only with respect to the project of understanding Kafka. The principle that an artwork's basic content can only be a function of what precedes or is coeval with it, and thus that such content does not suffer continual revision after creation, is not in conflict with the "retroactive creation of precursors" idea *so understood*. Such post hoc conceptual realignment affects not the artistic meaning of what is realigned, but only the

[27] J. L. Borges, *Labyrinths*, trans. J. E. Irby (New York: New Directions, 1962), p. 201.

way it contributes to the artistic meaning of the work that induces such realignment, by forming part of the interpretive background for that work.

Finally, a few words on the "Kafkian quality" in the writings of Kafka's precursors. Surely, though it is *salient* to us in a way it would not have been without Kafka's writings, and though earlier audiences could not have *denominated* it meaningfully in such a way, this quality, in any sense in which it is here legitimately ascribed, inheres in the structure and substance of those earlier efforts, read in their proper context, and is not conjured up ex nihilo. On the other hand, if 'Kafkian quality' is given a weightier reading, on the order of *resonating with Kafka's universe* or *reflecting essential Kafkian preoccupations,* we may well agree, with Borges, that such a quality requires Kafka for its existence. But then it is not a quality that is, or ever was, defensibly included in the literary content of those earlier efforts, involving, as it seems to, an internal relation to a not yet existent writer.[28] As such, it is and remains a quality foreign to them, and not one the passage of time can legitimately bestow.[29]

X

The last principle I will invoke that is of help in blunting the appeal of revisionist thinking is this. There is a difference between perspectives on a work *justified with respect to a time*—in particular, that of the work's origin—and perspectives on a work *available or accessible at a time.* Something that falls under the former description, and which

---

[28] What, then, *does* change in, say, Dunsany's story when Kafka later pens his parables? Well, Dunsany is then *seeable* in a new light, as the precursor to Kafka he (always) was. So seen, he properly forms part of the background to Kafka's particular literary accomplishment. So something—roughly, being seeable in a certain way with regard to the appreciation of Kafka's parables—becomes true of Dunsany's story in 1920 (or so) which wasn't true of it in 1910. But this property, as should be evident, does *not* count as an artistic property of *Dunsany's* tale—it's not a relationality to some work, object, or circumstances that is appreciatively relevant to *it.*

[29] It is worth observing here that what T. S. Eliot proposes in "Tradition and the Individual Talent" (1919)—that each new literary work effects a rearrangement of the tradition into which it enters, e.g., Shakespeare's *Troilus* subtly shifting Chaucer's—is similarly only valid, if I am right, in the form of backward, as opposed to forward, retroactivism.

thus testifies to or indicates something properly belonging to a work's content, need not fall under the latter description. That is to say, a perspective on a work appropriate to, cognizant of, and grounded in its context of origin may not, in all cases, be a perspective that can be attained and wielded by even the most willing of contemporary appreciators. Instead, such a legitimate, historically rooted perspective might, for various reasons, only become *available* later, for use by later appreciators. Since, however, the justifiability of the perspective in question in relation to the given work has not changed, there is no question of change of content but only of postponed revelation of it.

An example of what I mean by a perspective justified with respect to a time but not necessarily accessible at that time is provided by a recent analysis of literary meaning by William Tolhurst. Tolhurst attempts to sketch a position mediating between the textual autonomist extremes of Beardsley and the "New Critics," who hold that a text's meaning is inherent in its self-contained sequence of words (word sequence meaning), and the intentionalist extremes of Hirsch, who equates the meaning of a text with the author's intended sense (utterer's meaning). Tolhurst suggests that the meaning of a literary text is neither of these, but rather the meaning of an *utterance* in context, and that that is to be glossed as "the intention [of meaning such and such] which a member of the intended audience would be most justified in attributing to the author based on the knowledge and attitudes which he possesses in virtue of being a member of the intended audience."[30] That is to say, the meaning of a text is the best hypothesis of what the author meant that is formulatable by the sort of appropriately background reader projected by the author.

Now, the relevance of this to my distinction is as follows. If we accept something like Tolhurst's analysis, then clearly the meaning of a literary text is firmly grounded in the circumstances of its origins and, though not so concrete as what an author meant or some reader understood, is not subject to change over time. On the other hand, such meaning may *not* be immediately accessible from the outset, for several reasons. One is that it may simply take a certain amount of time for the most reasonable conjecture of authorial intent, in the light of all

---

[30] "On What a Text Is and How It Means," *British Journal of Aesthetics*, 29 (1979): 11.

pertinent presupposed background information, to emerge; first readers may simply be in no position to approach this. Two is that some works seem clearly to project, on the part of their author, the demand for an ideal reader, in the strict sense—one who does not or could not yet exist but whom the author is aiming his or her verbal structure at.[31] Three is that there might be special social or cultural conditions operating generally at the time of the work's appearance that temporarily prevent even willing and informed (intended) readers from making a judicious hypothetical construal of the author's meaning. In short, this perspective, which is in fact *definitive* (if Tolhurst is right) of what a literary work means, may just not be occupied, or even capable of being reasonably occupied, at the moment when the work is created and its meaning set. The fact that it is occupied (one hopes) at some future point does not entail change of meaning, but only closer approach to it.

What a literary work means when it is created (i.e., what it means *period*) is not the same as what it did mean, and in some cases, even what it could have meant, to those who were its original audience. The latter approximates the former, often, but is not identical to it. Furthermore, the meaning of a work may even outstrip what may be discerned in it from any point of view that could have been intended by its author. This is because there may be perspectives *justified* with respect to a certain temporally situated work that are, in an even stronger sense than ones already canvassed, not *available* to the author or his intended audience because not yet devised or invented. Usually such perspectives are irrelevant to a work on precisely such grounds, and not justifiably connectable to it. But there may be exceptions. Consider the Freudian interpretation of Hamlet's vacillation, as owing to the unresolved tensions of an Oedipal complex, activated by his father's untimely murder and the subsequent treacherous remarriage of his mother. It seems there is something right in this hypothesis, something that partly explains the peculiarities of Hamlet's behavior. Yet the Freudian identification of the Oedipus complex and its role in adult behavior were not in place until three hundred years after the play was written, so Shakespeare could not have directly intended any such explanatory perspective to be adopted. Still, there *may* be a sense in

---

[31] Of course, this means that even the author might not qualify as such a reader.

which that perspective is justifiable *with respect to* the play's originating context, even though clearly not *available* within it.

The story would go something like this. The play, written in 1580, was intended as an exploration of human nature. We can assume that human nature was roughly the same then as now, and that Shakespeare would have assumed this as well. So it's not unreasonable to take *Hamlet* as inviting reflection on the "springs of human behavior," whatever they might be. Now it turns out that the Oedipal complex *is* one of those springs, and it is now evident that it was operating in Hamlet's case. It is not, then, too farfetched to suggest that we have Shakespeare's implicit endorsement for so discerning it in *Hamlet*, now that we *can*. But on this story, Hamlet's Oedipal motivation was then *always* a part of *Hamlet*'s content—just a *latent* part.

It's clear that the plausibility of this tale relies, in some fashion, on the premise that Freudian theory in this respect *does* form part of a correct account of human behavior. If that is not the case, and so nothing like this tale is acceptable, I think this means the Freudian view of *Hamlet* must be totally rejected as well. The alternative is to allow that a perspective can contribute to a work's content even though it not only could not have been *adopted* in the work's context of origin, but cannot even be *anchored* in that context in some fashion. And that is too high a price to pay.

I now turn to music for another illustration of the difference between modes of approach *grounded* in the historical situation of an artwork and modes of approach actually *implementable* at time of creation. Schoenberg's first twelve-tone works—e.g., the piano pieces op. 23, constructed on a revolutionary principle and a radical departure from his earlier atonal compositions—are certainly to be heard as dodecaphonic works, and yet that category of perception[32] was not and could not have been accessible to audiences of the time, however cooperative, because a corpus of similar works sufficient to enable and hone the requisite perceptual capacity simply did not exist. Still, the aesthetic qualities of op. 23 are those it appears to have when heard "dodecaphonically"; that this perceptual category eventually became inhabitable thus indicates not a change of musical content, but merely the attainment of it by listeners.

[32]See K. Walton, "Categories of Art," *Philosophical Review* (1970).

Staying with music, it is instructive to examine another argument of
McFee's.[33]

> It might be thought that there is some absolute way in which, say,
> Bach and Handel are the culmination of the high baroque, such that
> this fact could have been clear to their contemporaries if only they had
> a little more vision. Such an idea must be rejected. The resources of the
> language, the form of representation, of the contemporaries of Bach
> and Handel may not have contained the categories and concepts for
> that judgment. To simplify, let us assume that they did not and also
> that we wish to press the judgment. We are able to remark these things
> in the works of Bach and Handel on the basis of which we make our
> judgment.
>   Yet surely, the line might run, if "these things" are there to be seen by
> us, they are there to be seen by the contemporaries of Bach and
> Handel. But this is inaccurate. *That we, with our form of representa-*
> *tion, can describe some possibility does not mean that it could be*
> *described in some other form of representation. . . .*
>   To begin deciding the issue of the resources of the form of represen-
> tation of the contemporaries of Bach and Handel we must inquire
> whether or not the possibilities embodied in "these things" were in-
> deed possibilities for Bach and Handel. We must ask whether or not
> Bach, for example, could have *intended* "these things." In part, this is
> surely a question about what concepts he *can* have, what range of
> descriptions are open to him; which in turn depend on his theoretical
> perspective.

One response to this argument would be to directly challenge its
idealist (the author calls them 'constructivist') presuppositions. The
issue is whether it is a fact that Bach and Handel are the culmination of
the musical high baroque even though their contemporaries couldn't
have grasped that in such terms. McFee says no. Is this not just
conflating *grasping* an artistic fact (or its *graspability*) with its *being*
so? That the concepts and categories were not possessed in 1750 for
making this judgment does not entail that there was no such constella-
tional fact coming into being. It's not a question of Bach's intentions or
descriptive possibilities, or those of his contemporaries, but of his
place in music history. And we can *now* see (have seen roughly since
the middle of the nineteenth century) what that (categorically) *is*.

A better response, though, would be to suggest that what is clouding

33"The Historicity of Art," pp. 313–14.

McFee's vision here is the failure to observe the distinction between perspectives and assessments *possible at* a time vs. perspectives and assessments *justified with respect to* a time—i.e., ones not foreign to its self-image and artistic concerns, if not self-consciously explicit within them. Though Bach could not have reasonably said to himself, "I am culminating the high baroque!" he was knowingly working in a broad style inherited from certain of his predecessors (e.g., Schutz and Buxtehude), extending and deepening various of its characteristics. As it happened, nobody extended and deepened them any further; so Bach got to culminate his period. This is an assessment that would have been true beginning with Bach's death even if it was impossible to reach it at that point, both because the relevant style category was then as yet unformed and because events subsequent to Bach's demise could not have been discerned. It would only be slightly parodying McFee's argument to put it thus: "Because Bach and Handel could not have formulated or defended the proposition 'Bach and Handel are the culmination of baroque style' it is therefore not the case that their musical output so culminated the baroque as they were penning it." A characterization can be rooted in and conformable to an artistic situation, not a mere imposition on it, and yet not be reasonably affirmable from a standpoint strictly within that situation; the characterization needn't, however, be thought to only magically acquire truth value once that limited standpoint is transcended.[34] It should be noted, finally, that much the same can be said about the application of any valid period style category (e.g., High Renaissance, Mannerism, Romanticism) before such a period draws to a close, and becomes evident in outline. Beethoven does not become the most important initiator of Romanticism in music only when the nineteenth century, and thus Romanticism, concludes; he is plausibly that as early as the C Minor Piano Trio of 1795. Yet this is compatible with its being impossible for such a judgment to have been intelligibly made at that time.[35]

---

[34] It is worth adding, after all this, that it's doubtful *how much* seeing Bach's music as the "culmination of the high baroque" helps us to understand *his* music per se. It does, though, help us to understand *J. C. Bach*; we see clearly why Johann Christian was driven to do something quite different musically from his father.

[35] Consider one last, rather schematic, argument on these matters: "Suppose a new perspective *P* becomes available at a time for construing a work *W*, created at an earlier time. Now, either *P* is appropriate to construing *W* or not. If the latter, then it is irrelevant to *W*'s meaning. If the former, then we have to ask *why* it is so—what does its

XI

Let me take stock. In the course of these explanations I have proposed
five distinctions, observation of which does much, I claim, to undercut
our undeniably lively inclination to think of works of art as under-
going change in content as time goes by. These were the distinctions
between: (a) properties *possessed* and properties *known to be possessed* at a given time; (b) *time-relative* and *permanent* senses of
certain artistic attributes; (c) *meaning* and *significance*; (d) *backward*
and *forward* retroactivism, and, finally; (e) interpretive perspectives
justified with respect to a time and interpretive perspectives *available
at a time*. What I have left for last is a class of attributions—*influence*
attributions—which are perhaps the most obvious of those that provide an ostensible challenge to the view I have been doggedly defending. It is possible that the distinctions already mustered are enough to
show that these attributions are no insuperable problem for my brand
of traditional historicism. However, they are prominent enough to
warrant direct examination, during which considerations peculiar to
them as a group can be brought into focus.

By influence attributes I understand such as influentiality (in general,
or in respect of a particular work or artist), seminality, importance,
pivotalness, revolutionariness, fecundity.[36] These are attributes involving the effect that a given artwork has on later artistic activity (or
culture as a whole), and as such cannot easily either (1) be seen to
belong to them at the moment of creation, or (2) be explicated or
analyzed wholly in terms of a preceding artistic context.[37] Now, (2)

---

appropriateness come to or rest on? Presumably, something like this: It is apt for,
capable of, *getting at* something in the work—i.e., some meaning (or content) W
possesses. But if it possesses it, then it was there for the perspective to reveal or exhibit.
Thus, such meaning must have been present from creation. In other words, any new
perspective that purports to afford a construal of a work's *meaning* cannot introduce or
impose that meaning, but only disclose or evince it. Valid interpretations from a
perspective *show* us what works mean, rather than *making* works mean what they
previously didn't; they don't create meaning out of whole cloth." Obviously this is a
contentious argument; I offer it in the hope not so much of convincing my opponents as
of making my own view of the issue plain.

[36] The most extensive categorization and analysis of these attributes is to be found in
Göran Hermerén, *Influence in Art and Literature* (Princeton: Princeton University
Press, 1975).

[37] This is also true of an attribute such as *culminating the high baroque*, discussed in
the preceding section, as well as ones such as *foreshadowing such and such* or *precurs-
ing so and so*, considered earlier.

poses no problem for my main thesis—*stability* of art-content—but only for the generally valid principle that art-content cannot be a *function of* later developments, a principle I return to in the next section. As for (1), may this not just be a case, of which we have already encountered examples, where an artistic attribute attaches to a work at a time without it being then *knowable* that it does? The issue, then, is precisely whether attributes such as these can plausibly be said to belong to a work from the beginning.

A contrast between influentiality and propheticness, discussed earlier, is here enlightening. For a work of art to be (correctly) prophetic is for it to contain or imply predictions (or more weakly, propositions that can be regarded as if predictions) which *will* turn out to be true— which *will* be confirmed or fulfilled. Propheticness is thus clearly a property of a work when created, though usually not one that can be justifiably ascribed. For a work of art to be influential, though, seems more strongly to presuppose *actual* achievement, accomplishment, or fulfillment. It seems appropriate to withhold the ascription of influentiality until such influence, as it were, *occurs*.

I don't wish to deny the force of such an intuition. However, I do think it can be counterbalanced. Instead of regarding the future as *making*, in progressive steps, the influentiality, seminality, or importance of a work of art, we might equally well think of it as *revealing* or *disclosing* what is already present, though in covert fashion. We can regard the influentiality of a work as given with the work in its historical setting—for surely it is the work's structure and character, appearing in just that setting, that make it influential if it is—and as something that only becomes *evident* with the passage of time.[38] Perhaps, by analogy with what was said earlier about originality and the like, there is an atemporal, not time-relative, way of construing properties such as *leading to a whole new style of painting* or *inspiring composers one hundred years later,* according to which—given the universe turns out a certain way—they adhere to works from the outset. If so, then we are not absolutely constrained to see the influence of a work as incrementally increasing, rather than progressively un-

---

[38]This viewpoint is, admittedly, more difficult to maintain when it is a question of *undeserved*, freak kinds of influence—as opposed to *deserved*, intelligible influences (presumably the more usual kind). But then there are, perhaps, some grounds for *excluding* the former kind of influentiality from even a *broad* notion of a work's art-content.

folding, as the years pass. To the question "Is this an influential work?" or even "Is this influential now?" asked of a piece created last month, we are not bound to give the answer "Not yet; it may become so." We can just be agnostic: "Influential?—i.e., affecting in a significant way future development in the arts?—I don't know; we'll have to wait and see if it is."

A comparison of influence with its parent concept, *causation*, can be used to strengthen this counterintuition. Can we ever fairly say X causes Y if Y has not yet occurred? Yes, if we have *knowledge* of Y. Usually we don't, so we can't say this, but not *merely* because the effect is future to the time of utterance. For example, if I inhale a lot of asbestos fibers at t_1, we can say that that *causes* my cancer at t_{30}, if we can see the future, or we can say in any case that there is a *good probability* that the ingestion causes cancer at t_{30}, thirty years away. And certainly, looking back from t_{30}, we can clearly affirm that the ingestion caused the cancer, and that it was such a cause, though as yet without its effect, at t_0.

Similarly, since influence is just a special kind of causal relation, we can say that W at t_0 *influences* the creation of W' at t', even though W' is not evident at t_0. We could not say this at t_0, since W' is not known, but if it *could have been* known (through a futurescope, or an infallible art-trend predictor), then it *could have been* truly said then. Thus, even influence properties, viewed in this way, need not be held to be acquired only latterly, by degrees, but may rather be ascribable to works in principle (that is to say, epistemic limitations aside) at creation.[39] So by these lights we could say, for example, that Picasso's *Demoiselles*

[39] Even if this construal is accepted for "solid" influence attributes such as seminality, pivotality, and revolutionariness, it's clear there are other influence-type attributions that unmistakably reflect shifting temporal standing, and which thus cannot be understood on the temporal model just sketched. This would include such as *trendiness, datedness, relevance to a given situation, importance to a particular era*. There is obviously little hope of showing such "attributes" to be rooted in an artwork's created nature, and thus of regarding them as not subject to change. But note that these attributions are similar to the purely external relations I put aside at the beginning of this essay: how many people are interested in W at t (trendiness), how much connection there is between W's content and events at t (relevance), how much of W's interest has effectively faded by t (datedness) are very much like facts such as who owns, or is currently appreciating, W. By contrast, the "solid" influence properties mentioned above reflect assessments of W's place in a historical scheme or progression, viewed atemporally, or from a point sufficiently posterior to W.

and Kafka's *Metamorphosis* are works of immense influence *as of* their creations, in 1907 and 1915, respectively—rather than that they just *were* to be so.[40]

XII

The foregoing is one way to deal with influence properties consistent with the point of view of traditional historicism. I hope it carries some conviction. But there is another move that could be made, and I will sketch that as a kind of insurance. This will also enable me to circumscribe clearly a principle of determination of art-content invoked at turns throughout this essay.

What I propose at this juncture is that we distinguish a proper subset of art-content—call it *art-character*—which is roughly art-content minus influence attributes, or more generally, *future-oriented* artistic attributes.[41] What can now plausibly be claimed is that art-character in fact comprises *all* of what an artwork means or conveys, and that the residue, though admittedly ascribable to a work of art in an art-critical context, is not part of what it is *saying* as art. Future developments, we may suggest, help us to *discern* what is in a given work W, but they don't help to *constitute* its art-character, what it means or conveys, in the way prior developments—through their influence on W, absorption into W, and provision of background for W—do. Influence properties, though in a certain respect analogous to ones such as originality, derivativeness, allusiveness—where these connect a work to its past and predecessors, the former connect a work to its future and successors—stand as something more external to a work: *effects*, rather than *meanings*.

With that brief motivation for the shearing off of future-oriented

---

[40] At this point it is convenient to emphasize that the thesis that artworks have virtually all their art properties at creation is more than the triviality that for any property P that an object will have at a future time t_2, it is *true* at t_1 that it will have P at t_2. Rather it implies that such things as influence, seminality, prefiguration, foreshadowing, and culmination are attributes that artworks can be meaningfully said to possess or share in as soon as they exist as configured wholes or artistic entities.

[41] The following can serve as a definition of "future-oriented property": A property P that, if possessed by a work W, is such that, were the universe to have ceased to exist after W's creation, it would not have been the case that W had P when created.

properties from art-content, I can now restate a restricted determination principle as follows: The art-*character* (if not the full art-*content*) of a work of art is exclusively a function, apart from intrinsic structure, of what precedes as opposed to what follows it. Clearly, then, events subsequent to a work's birth will have no power to alter its art-character. The relevance to my main theme is this. If one has *not* been convinced (by section XI) that influence properties can be understood so as not to alter over time, there is, alternatively, good reason for seeing these as rather *apart* from the rest of art-content. One could then maintain that what I have labeled *art-character,* at any rate, is not something that changes or develops over time.

I believe, however, that the case made earlier (in section XI)—that even the more comprehensive art-content is not subject to temporal alteration—is at least a sustainable one. The non-art-character portion of art-content (e.g., influence properties) is, granted, such that it is *determined* by, necessarily *involves,* circumstances posterior to a work—its having such and such future. But given it *has* (or *will have*) that future, then such properties *can* be attributed to it at its birth and do not change as time unfolds.

In illustration of my preferred position, then, I will take one of my old examples further. Bach's last compositions being the crowning culmination of the baroque and influencing the Romanticism of the early nineteenth century are, surely, states of affairs that *depend* on events subsequent to those compositions. But it was already *true* in 1750, in a sense, that Bach's output culminates the one and influences the other, though naturally this could not be known at that date. Still, neither attribute strictly forms part of the art-*character* of Bach's compositions—what they *say* as music. And that seems as it should be.

XIII

A final disclaimer is in order in the present intellectual climate. Certain radical perspectives on the products of culture, such as deconstructivism, would not even recognize the issue I am addressing as a legitimate or even intelligible one. I willingly leave them aside. I have to an extent framed my argument internally for those who acknowledge *some* kind of distinction between works, artists, audiences, styles, the meaning of a work, interpretations of a work, particular experiences of a work, and so on, and who can profitably discuss the degree of fixity or solidity of these boundaries. I have been arguing for the relative fixity of one such boundary, that between a work's content as art and the vicissitudes of its history after creation.

It is possible I have overstated the case for the position, *traditional historicism*, I have been here defending. But if so, then in presenting it strongly and clearly I will have aided others to see where, if at all, the thesis needs correction. It's worth noting, on the other hand, that if *revisionist* historicism were to turn out to be substantially correct, then one could never feel even reasonably confident of having understood any artwork, of having grasped its content. Instead of what is now our basic task, getting adequate *background* on a given work before attempting to perceive or read it, we would be faced with an impossibility—acquiring an, in principle, unlimited *foreground*. In that event we could, in effect, only stand around and wait. This seems to argue, once more, against such revisionism.[42]

[42] I should note, finally, that I have in this essay been taking for granted certain large-scale metaphysical positions that in other contexts have been the subject of contention. One is that of the logical determinacy of the future—i.e., it being true now that certain things will occur in the course of time. (That is, I am putting aside Aristotelian worries about the status of future contingents.) Two is that there is no upshot of the possible quantum indeterminacy of microevents at the level of the events with which I am concerned—e.g., the influence of one artist's work on another's. (Else it would become even more problematic to think of influence properties as inhering in a work at creation.)

Additional Notes

1. I have been helped by certain readers, Jenefer Robinson and Lydia Goehr in particular, to see that my argument in this essay might be more convincing if its explicit aim were made less ambitious. By these lights, the real strategy of the argument is not so much to *prove* revisionist historicism *wrong*—though its wrongness is of course suggested—but primarily to *demonstrate,* by displaying the depth of its resources, that traditional historicism is *eminently sustainable.* Alternatively put, if one is inclined to believe, on grounds that could not be fully rehearsed in this essay, that a work's art-content is determined by the specific art-historical context in which it is created, then the paper provides a number of ways of exorcising the appearance of the content of works changing over time.

   One thing, incidentally, which should be evident from this essay, and from Chapter 4, above, is that *intertextuality*—the dependence of any given work's meaning on the meanings of many other works and cultural items generally—a condition I fully embrace, does not, in my view, have the skeptical and self-

immolatory consequences that those of deconstructivist bent tend to perceive in it.
2. A recent book by Richard Shusterman, *T. S. Eliot and the Philosophy of Criticism* (New York: Columbia University Press, 1988), offers a reconstruction of Eliot's notion of a tradition which presents a challenge to what I have called traditional historicism perhaps subtler than those (Danto, McFee) discussed in my essay. I cannot, however, consider it here. I also make mention of a subsequent paper by Stan Godlovitch, "Aesthetic Judgment and Hindsight," *Journal of Aesthetics and Art Criticism*, 46 (1987): 75–83, which relates interestingly to my own, as it too is concerned with the propriety or impropriety of retroactive assessments in the aesthetic realm; however, Godlovitch's focus is on evaluative, rather than descriptive, judgments.
3. As I write this, a film that was made twenty years ago but not distributed commercially at that time has just been released, to enthusiastic reception. The film is Michael Roemer's *The Plot against Harry,* and the reason it was shelved in 1969 is that a screening by the director for seventy of his friends and associates elicited not a single laugh. Today they are apparently rolling in the aisles. This certainly looks like a prima facie case of a film that wasn't funny in 1969, but is decidedly funny in 1989, as audiences at the New York Film Festival last summer were the first to confirm.

There are three ways that suggest themselves for accommodating such a case to the thesis defended in "Artworks and the Future."

One, the film *was* funny in 1969, but its original audience was just unprepared, or overstressed, or else somehow lacking in the cognitive and attitudinal mindset the director presupposed in his target audience. This does seem unlikely given the circumstances, though after all it is possible that humor drawn from one's own life is not always best appreciated by one's nearest and dearest.

Two, the film *wasn't* funny in 1969, and *isn't* properly funny in 1989—that is to say, viewed in its *original* context by viewers with the mindset presupposed in the intended audience by its director. Rather, it has now acquired a certain *significance* (rather than *content*)—a borrowed funniness which arises in virtue of the relating of the film's original content to a later, and unintended, context of reception.

Three—and this is the response I favor—the film as released in 1989 is in effect a *different* film from that conceived, made, and projected, though not released, in 1969. Roemer is today presenting it (the same footage, that is) as a manifestly nostalgic and distanced documentary-comedy of an earlier era—which is how it is being received, and unavoidably so. We can laugh at, and admire the incisive depictions in, Roemer's 1989 re-presentation, with viewers as we are now as intended audience, given all we have digested in the way of social and also cinematic evolution since the sixties, whereas our surrogates were unable, apparently, to appreciate the film that was presented to, and aimed at, viewers of 1969. The second "avatar" can accomplish what the first could not, because it is really a different entity artistically, and calls forth a different "cult." So *The Plot against Harry/1989,* viewed in its complex, two-stage historical context of creation, is a success, whereas *The Plot against Harry/1969,* viewed in its simpler such context, is not. This doesn't assume, however, that *The Plot against Harry/1969* is really *accessible* to us at this point, i.e., that we could view it any more in its pure, intended 1969ish context, given its effective supersession by *The Plot against Harry/1989.*

10 *What a Musical Work Is, Again*

In the ten years since my original reflections on what Beethoven's Quintet in E-flat, op. 16—and the other musical works of our standard concert life—precisely were,[1] I have had time to consider whether everything I had to say was completely just. In that I have been aided by the flattering attention of a number of able commentators.[2] The purpose of this essay is to try to respond to some of the more pressing criticisms that have been advanced. I should admit at the outset that I

[1] See Chapter 5, above.

[2] See James Anderson, "Musical Identity," *Journal of Aesthetics and Art Criticism*, 40 (1982): 285–91, and "Musical Kinds," *British Journal of Aesthetics*, 25 (1985): 43–49; David Pearce, "Intensionality and the Nature of a Musical Work," *British Journal of Aesthetics*, 28 (1988): 105–18, and "Musical Expression: Some Remarks on Goodman's Theory," in *Essays on the Philosophy of Music*, ed. V. Rantala et al. (Helsinki: Acta Philosophica Fennica, 1988), pp. 228–43; Peter Kivy, "Platonism in Music: A Kind of Defence," *Grazer Philosophische Studien*, 19 (1983): 109–29, and "Platonism in Music: Another Kind of Defense," *American Philosophical Quarterly*, 24 (1987): 245–52, and "Orchestrating Platonism," in *Aesthetic Distinction*, ed. T. Anderberg et al. (Lund: Lund University Press, 1988), pp. 42–55; David Carrier, "Interpreting Musical Performances," *Monist*, 66 (1983): 202–12, and "Art without Its Artists," *British Journal of Aesthetics*, 22 (1982): 233–44; Renée Cox, "Are Musical Works Discovered?" *Journal of Aesthetics and Art Criticism*, 43 (1985): 367–74; Veikko Rantala, "Musical Works and Possible Events," in *Essays on the Philosophy of Music*. See also Lydia Goehr, *The Work of Music* (London: Oxford University Press, forthcoming), and Gregory Currie, *An Ontology of Art* (London: Macmillan, 1989), both of which deal critically with my 1980 essay. In the present essay I will be responding only to Kivy, Carrier, Pearce, and Anderson.

do not recant much; however, I take the opportunity here and there to offer clarifications and to acknowledge friendly amplifications that have been suggested.

I

I begin with the attacks brought in various places by Peter Kivy, who has been my most persistent critic, and in fact the bulk of this essay spends itself in rejoinders to him. My view, recall,[3] is that a musical work is not a pure structure of sounds—a Platonic universal, as Kivy styles it[4]—but instead a sort of universal brought down to earth: a contextually qualified, person-and-time-tethered abstract object, what I call an *initiated type*. The first of Kivy's charges, offered in the earliest of three related essays on musical metaphysics,[5] concerns the *creatability* (Cre) requirement set down in my essay. It is one of three requirements that lead almost inevitably, I claimed, to the view of musical works I end up proposing.

Kivy submits that the reasons I offered for insisting on this requirement are somewhat weak;[6] there is some truth in what he says, as we shall see. But the thing to stress, which Kivy in his piecemeal broadsides seems to lose sight of, is that the requirements of adequacy I laid down were intended to be seen *as a set,* with no decisive burden placed on any one. As it turns out, the creatability requirement is perhaps the least firmly grounded of the three (the others being *fine individuation*

[3] See Chapters 5 and 6, above.

[4] There is a problem as to what to label my view in terms harking back to the elders of Western metaphysics. Although Kivy has appropriated the label "Platonism" for his position that a musical work is a pure, eternally existing sound structure, there is, of course, something broadly Platonic about my view as well, in that a musical work is regarded as an *abstract* and *independent* entity, and not as existing only *in* things, which was how Aristotle regarded the Forms. On the other hand, I evidently hold musical works to be *creatable* and not eternal, as coming into existence *through* the offices and actions of concrete individuals, and this has an Aristotelian ring. In addition, I take the completed work to have some significant *relational,* and not just *internal-structural,* properties. Thus, I could equally well call my view a qualified Platonist, or a qualified Aristotelian one. I'll adopt the former for this essay.

[5] "Platonism in Music: A Kind of Defence"; see especially pp. 114–19.

[6] This sentiment is echoed in Cox, "Are Musical Works Discovered?" p. 368. Her article, however, is in general sympathetic to my approach, and ends up arguing for the creatability of musical works, though on somewhat different grounds.

[Ind] and *inclusion of performing means* [Per]), but if it be admitted to be *more* firmly grounded than its opposite—if creatability, that is, rather than noncreatability, is at least a positive desideratum for a view of musical works—then where creatability points reinforces, and is reinforced by, the direction in which the other two requirements point. As I see it, of course, they all point in the same direction: toward a conception of a musical work as something more complex than a pure structure of sounds. So in short, if (Ind) and (Per) incline us strongly in that way and are solidly grounded, then even if (Cre) is perhaps less firmly anchored, as long as it has some legs of its own, it will both strengthen the implications of (Ind) and (Pre) toward a more complex conception and, in turn, be vindicated by them as a desideratum we are at least right in *trying* to meet.[7]

Now to those reasons. Kivy denies that a belief in strict creation, in artists literally bringing artworks into being, is "one of the most firmly entrenched" in the Western tradition of art; he also denies what I went on to affirm, that some of the "status, significance, and value we attach to musical composition derives from our belief in this."[8] As to the first, I think he succeeds in reminding us that this belief may not have been so entrenched in artistic reflection before, say, the mid-eighteenth century and is perhaps a quintessentially Romantic idea; as to the second, he succeeds as well in reminding us of the great status, significance, and value that can attach to acts of discovery, and not just invention, if the former do, nonetheless, display creativity, the field of science in particular being rife with examples.

This tempers the force of the considerations I offered, but it doesn't nullify them. To start with the second, even if discoveries are often esteemed as highly as creations, it doesn't *follow* that part of the special way we value works of music—and I would claim, all works of art—does *not* depend on our regarding them as things created, in the strict sense—i.e., brought into being. For it is *only* when we so regard them that they acquire a Faustian aura, that they stand as symbols of our ability to "rival the gods." Of course musicians, like their peers in the sciences, have always striven to discover and reveal as well, but it

[7]I sketched this strategic warning in note 11 of the original essay (see Chapter 5, above), but Kivy seems to have overlooked it.

[8]Kivy, "Platonism in Music: A Kind of Defence," p. 114. The phrases are quotes from my essay.

was, as Kivy himself notes, the discovery and revelation of *truths*, often ones it was held art was particularly suited to convey, at which they were aiming. This is perfectly compatible with the aim to *create* works of art, and *thereby* convey such truths to waiting listeners. Disclosing to our attention aspects of the macrocosm is admirable, and composers are to be praised as much as scientists when they do so, but making microcosms exist is one of the distinctive prerogatives of the former; to strip them of it, especially needlessly, *is* to diminish them.

One point is worth adding here. Part of what we value about art is the essential *intimacy*, if I may call it that, involved in art making. What I have in mind is the kind of "I-Thou" relation we take to exist between artist and work, a relation of unique possession. If works are to *belong* to artists in the full sense—to be theirs in no uncertain terms—then creation rather than discovery seems to be called for. Of course, the *discovery* is theirs—their act—if that is all that is going on, but *what is discovered* is not in the same way theirs. Columbus's America wasn't in this sense logically his in virtue of his discovering it. But Ives's symphonic essay *The Fourth of July* is irrevocably and exclusively his, precisely in virtue of his composing it.

Composers create musical works by putting things together—notes, chords, progressions, motives, instruments, styles—in a particular context. They don't create the sound (or other abstract) patterns involved in their activities, but they do nevertheless create the works—patterns-in-contexts—and so invest those works with meanings not possessed by the abstract patterns *tout court*. One could say that selecting and assembling sound and other patterns to create specific musical meanings (formal, expressive, representational, allusive), using the structures and materials, abstractly conceived, available in one's musical system or tradition, *is* creating musical works. But the putting together against a preexistent background of musical history does yield something new, something not previously in the world.

Now let me return to the first of my original reasons, the entrenchment of the notion of created works in our musical practice. As already admitted, Kivy may be correct that such a notion has relatively shallow roots, reaching down perhaps only 250 years or so. But Kivy is certainly inclined to underestimate the *strength* of these roots, even if not extending uncontroversially to the dawn of Western music. We need only consider the centrality that "creation" locutions have in our current musical thought and practice. Musicians "make" music, they don't "find" it; pieces are "written" or "composed," not "described" or "registered"; we have biographical titles such as "Beethoven the Creator" but not "Beethoven the Discoverer"; musical works, like other artworks, are "commissioned" on the understanding that something will be brought into existence as fulfilling the commission, and not merely unearthed in answer to it; and so on. It is hard to avoid the impression that composers are invariably viewed as actually *adding* something to culture—namely, their compositions—and not just uncovering preexisting possibilities of musical combination.

Kivy gives one argument to the effect that not only is it not *precluded* that musical works might be discovered, this conception in fact *recommends* itself to us upon reflection:

> Think of the *Tristan* chord. It seems to me quite plausible to regard it as a discovery of Wagner's rather than his invention, although, of course, the discovery of that chord required the labor of more than one lifetime. Nor does it stagger the metaphysical imagination to picture the *Tristan* chord—that particular relationship of four pitches—as pre-existing its discovery, in the manner of a Platonic object. But, after all, the *Tristan* chord is part of a larger relationship of pitches called *Tristan und Isolde*. And if you grant that that small but vital part pre-existed its composition, it seems to me you are on the slippery slope that must propel you into granting that the large composition of which it is a part also pre-existed its compositional discovery by Wagner. (118–19)

The correctly observed and the misjudged are so intertwined in this passage that it is hard to sort them out. But we must try. First, if the *Tristan* chord is held to be just those four notes in that combination, and I am agreed to so regard it, is it *really* plausible to think of this as a discovery of Wagner's? Do we really doubt that Bach, Beethoven, or Brahms were capable of noting—actually, just of acknowledging— that F, G-sharp, B, and D-sharp could be sounded together at one time, that such an arrangement existed in the tonal system common to them all? At most Wagner can be said to have discovered the musical *use* of such a chord, its syntactic and expressive *potential*.

Second, when Kivy says that this chord is part of "a larger relationship of pitches called *Tristan und Isolde*," such a description is plainly question begging, since it just *assumes* the Platonic object—purely sound (or here, tone)[9] structural—view of what that thing, *Tristan und Isolde*, is. By my lights, this is exactly where Kivy goes wrong, in assimilating an achieved and constituted musical *work*, which takes its place in a developing culture and tradition, and a simple *chord*—an ordered quadruple—belonging to a completely defined preexistent tonal framework. If we wish to stress the sense in which this chord seems anything but simple, then we are shifting, once again, to Wagner's compositional appropriation of this already-available chord, and to its artistic functioning and significance in its passage, in the composition as a whole, and in the context of music history at that time. And this, of course, does *not* predate Wagner's composing, but is instead coeval with it. Third, we may agree, and in fact insist, that the large object that consists of the notes of *Tristan und Isolde* in sequence, and which contains the famous chord a number of times, *does* preexist Wagner's compositional activity. But such an object is not yet the *work*, and Kivy cannot just *assume* that it is.

There is, finally, another reason for trying to satisfy (Cre) if we can, one only briefly noted in my original essay,[10] namely the demands of *theoretical unity*. Since it seems incontestable that works in the fine arts and in a number of other arts as well are, as either physical objects or events (or else items logically anchored in these), literally created, it seems perverse, if we can avoid it, to stick to a conception of musical (and perhaps literary) works that separates them from their fellows in the other realms of art. And all the more perverse where they are, when all is said and done, positive reasons to embrace the creatability condi-

---

[9]The *tonal* structure of a traditional piece, on my usage, is its *sound* structure *minus* its timbral specifications. (Sound structure, though, still excludes performance-means specifications.) Kivy generally means by "sound structure" what I am calling "tonal structure"; where the difference is important, as in the upcoming discussion of Kivy's third essay, I have tended to insist on "tonal structure" in contrast to "sound structure."

The discrepancy arises because Kivy unfortunately declines to observe clearly the distinction between *timbral* properties per se, and *performance-means* properties, which as the synthesizer makes manifest, are physically and logically separable from them. (Cf. Wolterstorff's distinction between *acoustic* properties and *instrumental* properties, in *Works and Worlds of Art* [London: Oxford University Press, 1980], p. 69.) Timbral properties are generally both specified and secured via performance-means properties, but it is theoretically and practically possible for this relation to be dissolved. As we shall see more closely in Chapter 16, below, *both* kinds of property are aesthetically important.

[10]See Chapter 5, above.

tion. Shall paintings, drawings, etchings, sculptures, palaces, dances, films, and so on all be truly creatable, in the full sense of the word, and only symphonies and novels denied this possibility? There would be little profit, and false economy, in that.

II

I turn now to the more substantial case Kivy has mounted for my view in the second of his essays on our subject.[11] Here the primary target is, rightfully, the fine individuation condition and the consequences I draw from that: that musical works must be construed more narrowly, and counted more discriminatingly, than sound structures per se if we are to make sense of a significant range of critical descriptions of pieces of music, of attributions to them of artistic and aesthetic properties. Kivy begins his objections with a misunderstanding to which he is not the only party:[12] to wit, that it is a premise of my argument that musical works have their aesthetic properties *essentially*: "it is, he goes on to point out, a consequence of identifying work with sound structure that 'if two distinct composers determine the same sound structure, they necessarily compose the same musical work.' This, Levinson argues, cannot be the case, because musical works possess essential aesthetic properties by virtue of being composed by particular composers at particular times in musical history."[13]

But this is just not so. The *essentiality* of these properties—their being borne by such works in any conceivable possible world—is not what's at issue, but something more basic: rather, their *being possessed at all*, with anything like the specificity that our understanding of

[11] "Platonism in Music: Another Kind of Defense." I acknowledge moral support in composing this section from Kendall Walton's response to Kivy's paper on the occasion of its delivery at the 1987 Pacific Division Meeting of the American Philosophical Association; some echo of the defenses that he formulated in our joint behalf will be found here. A fuller account of Walton's own second thoughts on the ontology of music can be had in the revised version of his "Presentation and Portrayal of Sound Patterns," reprinted in *Human Agency: Language, Duty, and Value*, ed. J. Dancy et al. (Stanford: Stanford University Press, 1988), pp. 237–57.

[12] It is also reflected in Carrier's "Art without Its Artists." I anticipated this rather natural confusion, and tried to forestall it, by an extensive footnote on the matter in my original essay (see Chapter 5, note 29). But the issue is a difficult one.

[13] "Platonism in Music: Another Kind of Defense," p. 245.

music seems to underwrite. The point is that a musical work, stripped of its contextual coordinates in musico-historical space—thus yielding, roughly, a pure sound sequence—is incapable of bearing many of the determinate aesthetic properties that we ascribe to it (leaving aside whether those properties are essential or not). And the way to show this is to observe that for all we know there *are*, and at any rate easily *could be*, works containing (incorporating) *identical sound sequences* and yet presenting nontrivial aesthetic differences; the conclusion is inescapable that such works, if they truly differ aesthetically, *cannot* be identified with the lone sound sequence itself. By implication, the same goes for all musical works in our tradition. A sonic doppelgänger, residing in another aesthetic-complexion generating musical matrix, can clearly be posited for any given, concretely situated musical work, thus demonstrating that the work is not the sound sequence: There are two works, but only one such sequence.[14]

A key element in this demonstration, of course, is a harmless principle known as Leibniz's law, which for present purposes we can just gloss as the rule that if A and B differ in any respects, then A and B are simply not identical.[15] Kivy finds this rule "very scary," and claims that

> it lays down a requirement for identity far too stringent in the present context. . . . For Leibniz' law, notoriously, makes no distinction between essential and accidental properties. . . . On Leibniz' principle, *Don Giovanni* is a different work in a possible world in which Mozart was poisoned by Salieri from what it would be in one in which he was not, since there would be something true of it in the former case, not in the latter, namely, "*Don Giovanni* was written by the composer Salieri poisoned."[16]

Now, I agree that Leibniz's law applies to all properties, whether essential or not, but this does not yield the unsettling consequences to

[14] The proof given in the second paragraph of Chapter 5, note 16, is in effect a careful statement of this doppelgänger argument. Kivy gives little sign of having attended to this.

[15] Logically equivalent is that if A and B are identical, they must share all their properties. The converse of this, that things sharing all their properties are identical, is a distinct principle, known as the Identity of Indiscernibles, and is not the same, on my usage, as Leibniz's law.

[16] Kivy, "Platonism: Another Kind of Defense," p. 245.

which Kivy alludes. Leibniz's law doesn't say anything about what *would* be different from what in counterfactual circumstances; it speaks to what *is* different from what. Leibniz's law does not concern the identity of objects—e.g., operas—*across possible worlds*, which is what Kivy's example invokes, but is confined in operation to a *given* world. What Kivy's example does, however, show is that *being composed by someone who was poisoned by Salieri* is not an *essential* property of *Don Giovanni*, whatever essential properties it might have. Of course *Don Giovanni*, like any other contingent entity, has *some* different properties in different possible worlds;[17] that's just another way of saying that some of its actual properties are *accidental* ones. But that hardly prevents it from being identical with itself, and without violating Leibniz's law! If Kivy's worry about an unbridled Leibniz's law and Mozart's opera were sound, we would also have to be concerned with whether my newly mauve-painted workshed really was itself, since I might very well have painted it maroon, and in another possible world, no doubt, I happily do. The behavior of *Don Giovanni* in other possible worlds is not the issue, but rather its character in *this* one; the properties it *does* have, not those it *would* have in other circumstances, are enough to distinguish it from any *actual* pretenders lacking those properties, or any *potential* rivals that, were they to exist, would lack those properties.

David Carrier airs worries similar to Kivy's in the following amusing passage:

> Doesn't [Levinson's] argument prove too much? Surely some features of the artwork [a sonata of Beethoven] are contingent. The sonata Beethoven wrote in Vienna in March in black ink might have been composed by him in Salzburg in April. He might have had to use red ink to finish writing it out. The descriptions "written in Vienna," "written in March," "written in black ink" would not then apply. But surely such a possible sonata is not a different art work.
>
> Suppose during the composition Beethoven sneezed 866 times and the tallest man in Peking ate 69 dumplings. Had Beethoven sneezed 867 times, or that man eaten 70 dumplings, then the descriptions, "composed while Beethoven . . ." and "composed while the tallest . . ." would no longer apply to the sonata. This is puzzling. Surely the

[17] This is the only sense one can give to a phrase such as "*Don Giovanni* is a different work in a possible world in which. . . ."

number of Beethoven's sneezes or dumplings eaten by the man in
Peking during the composition are irrelevant to the sonata's identity.[18]

Not surprisingly, I want to agree with what Carrier is here urging
regarding the irrelevance of sneezes, dumplings, ink colors, and loca-
tions of writing desks.[19] But despite Carrier's suspicion to the contrary, my argument does not prevent me from doing so. There is no
problem in affirming that the sonata—the person-and-time-qualified
performed-sound structure, if I am right—was composed while Beethoven was stopping in Vienna, underwent an access of sternutation,
and had a good supply of black ink, and while scores of dumplings
downed the hatch in Deng's domain, and yet declining to integrate
properties such as these into the kind of entity proposed as the musical work. Of course the sonata might have seen day in Salzburg,
without those sneezes, partially in red ink, and while appetites in
Peking were held in closer check; these are accidental properties of it, if
any are. The point is that the performed-sound structure-as-indicated-
by-Beethoven-in-March-1806, unlike the mere note sequence, is a
specific enough entity to intelligibly possess, whether essentially or
not, the aesthetic and artistic properties we ascribe to the sonata, and
yet also capable of sporting, as accidents, the incidental relational ones
that Carrier has brought to our attention.

III

Kivy's next move, in his second outing, is to attempt to discredit two of
the central illustrations I offered in order to make the inadequacy of
the sound structure view plain. These concern pairs of works with
identical sound structures, in the one case composed respectively by
Strauss in 1897 and Schoenberg in 1912, in the other, by Johann
Stamitz in the eighteenth century and a modern epigone of Stamitz
(whom Kivy usefully labels "Damitz") in the twentieth century. The
musical works in each pair are clearly distinct because they have

[18]"Art without Its Artists," p. 233.
[19]I leave aside the issue of March vs. April, since that is an extreme instance of
something that, in general terms, I hold may be highly relevant, namely, dating of a
work relative to others of the composer and to others in his musical tradition.

different aesthetic or artistic properties; Strauss's (postulated) song cycle is more bizarre, unprecedented than Schoenberg's (actual) one, and Stamitz's symphony is exciting, exhilarating while Damitz's is funny or silly.[20]

With respect to the Strauss/Schoenberg case, Kivy says only that it is "flat out impossible."[21] It is hard to know what to make of this assertion. Of course the case is *extremely unlikely*; it is also *invented* (or suppositional). But that hardly makes it *impossible,* in causal terms. Couldn't Strauss have written out that sequence of notes and those instrumental specifications, all of which (notes and instruments) were manifestly familiar to him from earlier composing?[22] Yes, if he had thought to do so, you say, but he couldn't have so thought, it wasn't in his stylistic ambit. But couldn't he have had a sudden inspiration? Mightn't the gods, or just some errant brain chemicals, have vouchsafed him a special, visionary afflatus? Don't radical changes of style in fact sometimes occur? Kivy's "flat out" would appear to have more than a few hills and bumps in it.

Kivy has more to say about Stamitz/Damitz. In discussing the *excitement* in Stamitz's opening allegro, Kivy first tries to substitute for this the patently nonequivalent property of *being exciting to its auditors*, which, of course, varies from audience to audience. But then Kivy admits, after this red herring, that there is, after all, an enduring

---

[20] As Kivy notes, although Damitz could be either a self-conscious copier-appropriator, or an oblivious-to-music-history accidental-arriver-at of the same sound structure, my description of the piece fits better with the latter construal. Still, I must thank Kivy for adding, however unintendedly, another work distinct from Stamitz's symphony to the roll call of this example, a work with the sound structure of that symphony but deriving from a post-modernist sensibility, and so calling for an entirely different way of hearing and taking, thus generating a third, noncoincident, set of aesthetic and artistic properties.

[21] Kivy, "Platonism: Another Kind of Defense," p. 246.

[22] As it turns out, my choice of *Pierrot Lunaire*, a song cycle to texts by Albert Giraud (rendered into German by Otto Hartleben), brings unnecessary complexity into the issue, owing to its literary component, and would also have been impossible, in a *strong* sense, for Strauss to have composed a double of in 1897, because Giraud's poems were not written until after that date. Since this is clearly not the sort of impossibility with which Kivy is concerned, let me here retroactively substitute in the example Schoenberg's *Five Pieces for Orchestra,* op. 16, of 1909, an atonal masterpiece of the same period as *Pierrot,* and imagine Strauss having preceded this with his own note-identical *Five Pieces for Orchestra,* op. 35a, of 1897, coming between *Zarathustra* and *Heldenleben.*

property there which can be grasped, and with which musicology and criticism are intimately concerned.[22] "Now, to be sure, the 'genuine' Stamitz symphony does possess, in a timeless sense, a property of excitement that its clone does not, bestowed upon it by its peculiar history: its particular place in the history of music. It was exciting to its first auditors, and its clone was not; and we consider that musico-historical property a very important one."[23]

Of course, Kivy here still distorts the allegro's *excitement* into something less than it is, by equating it with its excitingness to its *original* auditors, rather than with its excitingness to auditors who hear it *correctly*, in a way that reflects its provenance and musico-historical position. (These are not necessarily identical, since original audiences are sometimes not appropriately prepared or attuned ones; consider those at the premiere of Stravinsky's *Rite*.) However, this admission is sufficient, one would think, to settle the issue against the sound structure criterion of work identity. But no; Kivy just declares, unaccountably, that this is not enough reason to deny the identity of a work exhibiting such with its nonexciting "sound-alike" *semblables*, offering in support only some animadversions against considering too seriously cases well out of the ordinary ("science fiction examples"). One suspects it is the specter of Leibniz's law that is still operating here, and Kivy's sense that its unrestrictedness is an affront to the person in the street. But those are just the facts of life—or perhaps logic—and it makes no difference whether the distinguishing property is essential or accidental, relational or nonrelational, important or unimportant: if one piece has got it and the other not, then they ain't the same piece!

Before proceeding, it is worth noting that Kivy has chosen to ignore my other examples on this wavelength, ones not easily tarred with his "virtually impossible" brush, and which also avoid invoking fac-titious composers. These confine themselves to considering the work-profile consequences of imagined changes in authorship or other relations (e.g., temporal) among various nineteenth- and twentieth-century works. In Kivy's screed against the distinctness of Damitz's and Sta-mitz's symphonies, there is little indication of how he would deal with the *influence* or *satirical* properties of the Brahms and Bartok examples,

[23] Kivy, "Platonism: Another Kind of Defense," p. 247.

respectively, and even less hope of making them out to be doubtful or passing.

But let us, finally, consider an example fully rooted in actuality, which Kivy himself provides to exercise his intuitions:

> There is a little prelude and chromatic fugue in E♭, long thought to be an early work of J. S. Bach, which we now know, through the discovery of the autograph, to be a mature work of [his older cousin] Johann Christoph Bach. Do we want to say we have discovered it to be a different work? Certainly we hear it differently as the mature work of an earlier, and lesser composer, than we used to as an example of the great Johann Sebastian's juvenilia. . . . It somehow seems a more daring, more powerful, and of course a more mature piece. . . . It has "lost" certain sonic features, "gained" others. But are these features essential enough for us to say that it has lost its "identity" and gained another? Do we think of it as a different work or as the same work with a different history?[24]

Is it now a different work? We have no call, nor any need, to say that. It isn't a different work, depending on who the actual composer turns out to be, than *before*, but only a different work, in a sense, than previously *thought*. Does it, then, have different *features* than it did previously? No, it is only *we* who have changed, by improving our epistemic relation to the music. What happened is that we have discovered more fully what the work was that we were, all along, dealing with, and have gotten clearer as to some of its more subtle, contextually dependent properties. In terms of *identification*, there is no question which piece we are talking about, either now or in the past. What has changed for us is our acquaintance with and comprehension of the selfsame piece. Just as with persons, we can come to know pieces more adequately the longer our exposure and the more extensive our grasp of their *backgrounds*—"where they're coming from," in modern parlance.

IV

The last part of Kivy's second essay returns to the issue of creation vs. discovery. Kivy first tries to render the "discoverist" perspective more attractive by suggesting, in a way that complements his effort in the

[24] Ibid., p. 246.

earlier essay, that discovery and creation are perhaps not so far apart;[25] his main idea is to once again emphasize the creativity inherent in much discovering. This, however, is not strictly relevant: The issue is cre-at*ability*, not creat*ivity*, and the difference between bringing a thing into existence and doing something with (e.g., making use of) a thing already in existence simply cannot be fudged, as long as we take care not to switch what things we are referring to in midstream.

But then Kivy gets down to new business and attempts to meet what he takes to be a pressing problem for a "discoverist":

> Even if the initial implausibility of construing musical works as discoveries rather than creations is removed, a further difficulty seems to follow hard by. For the same discovery, clearly, can be made by more than one person: [e.g.] the independent discovery of the calculus by Leibniz and Newton. . . . Whereas it seems wildly implausible, indeed impossible, that both Haydn and Mozart (say) should both have "discovered"—which is to say composed—the sound structure of Mozart's 40th Symphony.[26]

Now, I am surprised to see Kivy trying to offer, from a Platonic vantage point, an explanation of this putative impossibility; much easier, it seems, would have been to allow that such dual discovery was in fact possible but, owing to the complexity of sound structures in typical symphonies, highly improbable. However, since he has decided to eschew the simpler path, we can hardly forebear observing the brambles he encounters in his effort to explain the unexplainable. Relying on a strained comparison between musical works and such things as quarks, viewed in instrumentalist fashion as "theoretical constructs," and which physicists working independently might de-velop at roughly the same time, Kivy argues that

> [α] *merely* being a creation, as opposed to a discovery, does not, *of itself*, imply that it cannot be the outcome of the independent efforts of separate individuals, scientific "creations" being, on the instrumental-ist's view, cases in point . . . by parity of reasoning, it may well show that [β] merely being a discovery, rather than a creation, does not imply the possibility of shared accomplishment . . . it becomes quite plausible . . . to suggest that there might be a reason, other than their

25 Ibid., pp. 248–49.
26 Ibid., p. 249.

being creations, that makes musical structures unshareable outcomes of human endeavor.[27]

The easy response to this would be to observe that the scare quotes give the example away: "creating" quarks is not really creating *them* (i.e., those particles), but rather creating a new theoretical *category*: *the quark*. As it turns out, this category was created largely by one man, Murray Gell-Mann, in 1963, *might* have been co-created by some independent theorist simultaneously, but could *not* have been created by others at any later time, though of course they might have come up with it again. If Gell-Mann had truly created *quarks*—and not just the quark-notion—by his postulating and theorizing, then all the millions of dollars of linear accelerator research money subsequently spent to verify whether quarks really did exist would appear to have been misspent.

But suppose we grant Kivy's intermediate conclusion—α—for cases of simultaneous creation. How does this, by "parity" or any other route, give support to β? Why would the possible *shareability* of certain unusual *creations* (things created) give any reason to think that certain unusual *discoveries* (things discovered) might be *unshareable*? If something is there, in logical space, to be discovered by one person, how could it not be there to be discovered, at the same time, by another?[28] That there is no adequate answer to this, from within Kivy's Platonism, becomes evident when he inadvisably pushes on and tries to supply the reason that, as he says, there might be, which would illuminate how "there are kinds of discoveries that can be shared and kinds that cannot, discoveries of musical structure . . . being one of the latter kinds."[29] This is what we are offered: "why couldn't it be the case that some 'objects' are so unique as to be discoverable only by people uniquely constituted to notice them. . . . A different personality from Beethoven's could no more give forth with Beethoven's 7th Symphony than could two different people have the same handwriting. . . .

[27] Ibid., p. 250.
[28] Note that complications having to do with being the *first* person to find or arrive at something, and the existence of a narrow use of "discover" whereby only the first person to find or arrive is said to have *discovered* such and such, are not germane to the present discussion, which concerns multiple *simultaneous* uncoverings. Nor does Kivy appeal to this narrow construal anywhere in his brief.
[29] Kivy, "Platonism: Another Kind of Defense," p. 250.

we do not know why, but we are intuitively certain . . . that only
Beethoven could have been responsible for the sound structure we
know as [*sic*] the 7th Symphony."[30]

Now, it is *true* that some musical objects are "so unique" that they
are only able to be connected up with a unique individual. But these
objects, as I have argued, are *works,* and individuals connect with
them by *creating* them—by mixing their labor and identity in with
them, so to speak, and thus assuring their uniqueness—they are not,
and can't intelligibly be made out to be, sound structures *tout court.*
For it is perfectly possible for a different individual (think of identical
twins), even one with a different personality and background (think of
Pierre Menard), to have "given forth" the sound structure involved. So
Kivy's claim regarding the patterns (whether verbal or musical) which
might conceivably issue from persons is either rhetorical exaggeration,
or strictly irrelevant. It's exaggeration if taken to allege logical, physical, or even behavioral impossibility, and it's irrelevant if meant only to
remark that certain occurrences would be very, very unlikely. (What is
highly unlikely cannot simply be ruled out where claims of in principle
unshareability are at stake.)

As the final flourish in this attempt to make uniquely discoverable
items acceptable to common sense, Kivy decides to bring in one of
Picasso's most sublime and seemingly effortless creations, the *Head of
a Bull* (Paris, 1943). Kivy's account of this work is that Picasso just
" 'discovered' the form of a bull's head in a bicycle saddle and handle
bars—that, you will recall, is all that the *Head of a Bull* is. There was
nothing, really, to 'create': the saddle and handle bars were already
there" (p. 251).

Surely, this is going too far. That is *not* all that Picasso did. If
Picasso, in making *Head of a Bull,* did not strictly *create* a unique
object, then who does or ever has? This is not to deny, however, that in
the course of doing so he might make cognitive discoveries, or might
embody a discovery made earlier, perhaps only minutes before. But
until he takes the step of assembling those "already there" parts in
precise fashion, titling and artistically projecting them as well, there is
no artwork to speak of—and it is that artwork, remember, and not just
the ideas or observations that went into it, to which Kivy hopes to

[30]Ibid., pp. 250–51.

assimilate Beethoven's Seventh Symphony. Standing behind Picasso on that fateful morning may very well have been his archrival and compatriot, Bigasso, who noticed the same things but then took a siesta; Picasso and Bigasso made the same discovery, but only Picasso expanded his oeuvre that day. I daresay that on a good day I discover a number of comparable, if not quite so brilliant, things about the visual resemblances, resonances, and possibilities of the ordinary manufactured goods that surround me, but I have never, to my knowledge, made a sculpture of any kind.[31]

V

In Kivy's third essay[32] his target of attack is what I called the *inclusion of performance means* condition (Per).[33] Since Kivy upholds the view that a musical work is just a pure tonal structure,[34] he must deny that instrumentation is essential to musical works in the Western tradition. And he offers a number of stratagems to make this stick, most of which I will try to address.

Let me begin by confronting a nonissue to which Kivy devotes a good portion of his third essay, and which he raises by indirection in the other two: the time period with which my analysis was concerned. I should think it was fairly explicit in my essay that I was aiming only at capturing the elements of the most typical works in the current repertoire, and that I had no pretension to arrive at an analysis general enough to accommodate music before, say, 1750. My running example of Beethoven's Quintet op. 16 (composed in 1797) should have at least suggested some lower bound for the scope of my proposal, historically speaking. Besides, if you ask the ordinary music lover to name some musical works, the answers will rarely be items before the eighteenth century. If my analysis is adequate to composing from

[31]There are lessons concerning certain assumptions of the practice of fine art in Wollheim's "Minimal Art," *Artforum* (1965), which Kivy's treatment of the Picasso suggests he has not absorbed.

[32]"Orchestrating Platonism." (Page references for some quotations appear in parentheses.)

[33]"Musical works must be such that specific means of performance or sound production are integral to them" (Chapter 5, p. 78).

[34]See note 9, above.

roughly J. C. Bach to John Cage, that was all I was seeking.[35] So on this topic I am willing to cede to Kivy most music before 1750, certainly any score that merely says "for three treble instruments and bass"; I wasn't talking about them.[36] But I will briefly comment anyway on Kivy's remarks on the bearing of this early repertoire on the question.

Concerning his opening putative counterexample, the numerous pieces by Giovanni Gabrieli (1554–1612) titled *Canzona per sonar,* Kivy at one point asks rhetorically: "Would any musician or concert-goer think that when the New York Brass Ensemble 'performs' a Gabrieli *canzona per sonar* on modern brass instruments it has not presented an instance of *that* work but of a different one?" (43). I object that this is not an exhaustive disjunction; they may have "performed" that piece without instancing it, and yet without instancing any *other* piece either. It is also curious that toward the end of his dilation on early music Kivy affirms the following: "If the era of instrumental music goes from the last quarter of the sixteenth century to 1986, at least half is clearly dominated by a completely *ad libitum,* non-essentialist attitude towards what instruments any given piece is to be realized on" (44). This seems to presuppose, or at least strongly suggest, the truth or plausibility of the essentialist position for the other two hundred years. Finally, Kivy throws up some problems for my having ventured, cautiously, that although J. S. Bach's *Well-Tempered Clavier* may not be a work belonging solely to the harpsichord, it is certainly a work for *keyboard*. The most germane of these, that a lute

[35] In fact, it seems pretty clear that a theory that was adequate to the nature of musical composition in the West from 1300 to the present day, or in musical cultures anywhere in the world, would likely be *less* illuminating than the one I offered, because of the range of what it would have to comprehend.

[36] Another reason one could give for regarding compositions from roughly the late eighteenth century on as the paradigm musical works of the classical tradition, and for focusing on them exclusively, is that the very *concept* of a musical work does not jell, does not exist completely in recognizable fashion, until around 1800, and that our discerning musical works per se in the period before 1750, or in music of other traditions (e.g., jazz or Javanese), is a kind of back projection or extension of a concept that is only *fully* exemplified in Western classical music from the Classical period on. This thesis is persuasively set out by Lydia Goehr in an important recent article, "Being True to the Work," *Journal of Aesthetics and Art Criticism,* 47 (1989): 55–67. If something like it can be accepted, then my focus on examples of the past two hundred years in my attempt to analyze the essential parameters of a musical work has a certain historical-conceptual justification, as well as the pragmatic one foremost in mind in writing my original essay.

performance could be "tonally [that is, timbrally] indistinguishable from a performance on the harpsichord with the buffer stop" (45), and so means of production apart from tone color could not be held to be definitive, is a good example of his detaching timbral from instrumental (or performance-means) properties only where convenient, endorsing timbral properties as a means of attacking instrumental properties, while elsewhere repudiating timbral properties themselves.

Coming eventually to the music with which I was concerned, Kivy observes that many musical works from the late eighteenth century to the present exist in forms other than those they had when originally composed, and that it is often the composer who is responsible for them. These are called *transcriptions* (or *arrangements*) and involve rethinking and rewriting a work for a different set of performing forces. Kivy feels confident in declaring that, as far as musicians are concerned, these always count as "the same work." But can they be so easily satisfied with that casual judgment, assuming Kivy is right about the frequency with which they make it? Note that full-scale transcriptions are generally assigned distinct opus numbers ("opus" in Latin, of course, is "work"). One can certainly prefer a work to its transcription or vice versa: If these are the same thing, logical absurdity—preferring a thing to itself—appears to result. Furthermore, transcriptions can demonstrably "ruin" musical works, in a familiar sense, but without those works ruining themselves.[37] If one knows only a transcription, and later encounters the original or vice versa, one is likely to say it's the same *music*, granted, but unlikely to say it's the very same *composition*.[38] Finally, and relatedly, those reluctant to buy recordings of alternate *performances* of a piece are often eager to buy recordings of successful *transcriptions* of originals they already possess: for example, Mozart's String Quintet, K. 406 (adapted from the Wind Serenade, K. 388), or Ravel's orchestral *Valses nobles et sentimentales*

---

[37] Good examples of this are, in my opinion, Schoenberg's orchestral transcription of Brahms's G Minor Piano Quartet, and Bernstein's orchestral transcription of Beethoven's *Grosse Fuge*.

[38] For example, if you hear the *Fantasia Cromatica*, for solo viola, of Zoltan Kodaly, you will probably say, "I know that music," since it is effectively that of the *Chromatic Fantasy* for keyboard, BWV 903, of J. S. Bach; you will recognize the music as "the same." But you are unlikely to consider it the same *piece*, especially since it basically preserves the top line, with some double and triple stopping for the rest.

of 1912 (adapted from the *Valses nobles et sentimentales* for piano of 1911)—an example Kivy himself mentions.

This is no place to develop a full account of transcriptions and versions,[39] but I will venture a few remarks to indicate how my take on them differs from Kivy's. A transcription is, I think, best thought of as a *distinct* musical work, but it is not a *primary* musical work—it stands in a subsidiary, derivative relation to its original, a relation that is always properly recalled when perceiving and assessing it. A transcription and its original, though, might be said to be the same work, *loosely* speaking, by which would be meant that they belong to the same *broader* type—that of the tonal structure forming the core of the original work. We might usefully reserve the term *version* for a minor variant of a work, one that is not, like a transcription, a wholesale reformulation of it for different forces and means.[40] The relation between different *versions,* in this sense (e.g., plus or minus a doubled bass line, with English horn added to oboes in a given passage or not), is distinct from the relation between pieces related as *transcription and original*: The former are refinements within *one* basic conception, whereas a transcription is an importantly *different* conception, necessitated by a new confrontation with the capacities and liabilities of some performing means, but which relates to its original by sharing, as far as possible, its complete tonal structure.

An alternate way to think about transcriptions would be this. Transcription is an *expansion* or *extension* of the original, initiating an option of performing means as between the original instrumentation and the new instrumentation. The work, thus, has *changed*; whereas before, instrumentation i_1 was required for its (correct) performance, now *either* instrumentation i_1 *or* instrumentation i_2 is possible–but not, of course, just *any* instrumentation. So it would remain true that specific instrumentation is integral to the work, it would now just be an explicitly *disjunctive* instrumentation.[41] The work as now broadened

[39] One has been offered recently, by Stephen Davies ("Transcription, Authenticity, and Performance," *British Journal of Aesthetics,* 28 [1988]: 216–27), but I am unable to take account of it here.

[40] Obviously, the boundary between *transcriptions* and *versions* would be a fluid one.

[41] There is one well-known nineteenth-century example that Kivy cites in his own connection which was constituted with a disjunctive instrumentation from the first, Brahms's two Sonatas for Clarinet *or* Viola and Piano, op. 120. But note that Brahms's alternation specifies two instruments that, their family differences apart, are quite

would, however, as a result have somewhat broader—less specific—aesthetic properties, and that could ultimately prove problematic with respect to critical description.

If, though, we rest with the view that transcriptions are distinct works, it remains true that they are relatively slight ones from an artistic point of view; they usually possess much less creativity, originality, import than their originals, and the composer's procedure is obviously not comparable in the two instances. But that needn't mean, once again, that instrumentation is only an incidental part of the *original*'s creativity/originality/import.

Kivy next raises an interesting question concerning the identity of works throughout their process of creation: "Mendelssohn continually tinkered, over the years, with the orchestration of the *Schöne Melusina* overture. Was he composing a new work each time he altered the orchestration?"[42] I have no general theory to offer here as to which are the vicissitudes a work may suffer during composition and remain the same work as was begun at some earlier time. I will only observe that any problems such indeterminacy makes for the role instrumentation plays in work identity threaten just as strongly the elements of Kivy's beloved tonal structure: melody, rhythm, harmony, phrasing. Was Mendelssohn composing a new work each time he fiddled with the voicing of the opening arpeggios, threw in some chromatic passing notes in a secondary theme, or adjusted the length of some transition passage? Obviously not; whether it was tone structure or orchestration that received touching up of this magnitude, what Mendelssohn was evidently doing was changing what was to *be* that work, in full specificity.

VI

That there just might be "performances" of Beethoven's String Trio op. 9, a work composed around the same time as the op. 16 Quintet, on three variously sized tin whistles—and if so, they would be at the very border of reasonable attempts at instantiation that were reasonably

---

similar in tone color—"mellow" being one of the usual terms for it. Kivy can hardly regard this as without significance for the point at issue.

[42] Kivy, "Orchestrating Platonism," p. 46.

successful—doesn't prove string instrumentation is not crucial to the op. 9. For the notion of what the work is is tied to what a *correct* performance requires or would be like.[43] After all, there just might be a "performance" of the op. 9, detectable as such, played on violin, viola, and cello, but with a third of the notes missing; this would hardly show those thousand or so notes were inessential. They, as well as the proper instruments, are needed if a performance is to be an *instance* of a work.[44] In many of his remarks in his third essay Kivy seems to be on the verge of confusing the issue of recognitional criteria with that of artistic identity. That you can more readily *recognize* something to be a performance of a piece, on the liberal standard I've been allowing, with significant instrumental change than with significant tone structural change, does not show that its musical essence is purely tone-structural. What might, on *loosest* reckoning, be accounted a performance of a work does not so much illuminate what is definitive of the work as show what its most hardy or indestructible features are.

Kivy's occasional claims that one could *tell* what work one of his irregular instances—e.g., a Bach fugue performed by "a choir of kazoos"[45]—belonged to (what it was a performance of) is not much more convincing than noting that if I gave you good full-sized reproductions of Rembrandt's *Portrait of Saskia* and Ingres's *Portrait of Mme. d'Haussonville,* you would have no doubt which was which— which belonged to the Rembrandt, which to the Ingres. But you would not say that they really were those paintings, that they were authentic instances of them. So the fact that we would *refer* the kazoo rendering to Bach's work hardly means we implicitly accept it as an adequate *presentation* of the work, one that shows us that intended instrumentation was always dispensable.[46]

It is clear that tonal structure is generally the most important, most readily recognized, most reusable, most transferable part of a musical

---

[43] Here I am in agreement with Wolterstorff, *Works and Worlds of Art,* part two.

[44] If instrumentation in the relevant (i.e., post-Bach) class of works is definitive of what a *correct* performance amounts to, this means that requiring proper instrumentation *is* essential to the kind, and constitutive of it. It is thus on a level with prescriptions of melodies, rhythms, harmonies, dynamics, and tempi. (Cf. Wolterstorff, *Works and Worlds of Art.*)

[45] Kivy, "Orchestrating Platonism," p. 55.

[46] Nor need we, as Kivy gibes, be regarding the performance as "a performance of something else" (55).

work—but that doesn't make it the *whole* of such. Even if we allow that transcriptions preserve that part of a musical work, this doesn't mean they transmit all the work really, constitutively, is. Writers such as Kivy are in effect drawing attention to the fact that musical works, viewed from certain perspectives, have "cores": *compositional* cores, what figures generally as the chief object of compositional activity and intent;[47] *recognitional* cores, sets of aspects that most firmly anchor recognition of "the music" through alterations in other respects; and, so to speak, *practical* cores, what survives in any performable transcription. Now, the tonal structure of a piece[48] very likely often fulfills all three roles—is the compositional, recognitional, and practical core of a piece. But this scarcely proves it to be the musical work in its *entirety*, the complete artistic entity arranged by the composer, the composition aimed at a particular category of performers possessing appropriate stylistic habits and techniques, and the proper object of musical criticism and appreciation.

To be played on a piano, by my lights, is as much a constitutive feature of the *Waldstein* Sonata as its *opening on a chord of the tonic in root position*. The fact that it would be *recognized* as the *Waldstein* if the first chord were altered by the performer to that of the tonic in second inversion, if the left hand's first eight measures were omitted, or—probably less readily—if the whole thing were played on two guitars, is hardly the relevant point. No one need deny that something one might be willing to call a 'performance' of a work might result from flouting a good number of a work's constitutive features. Performing a work, as I suggested in my earlier essay, might be construed as seriously attempting to instantiate a musical work, and succeeding to a reasonable degree—the attempt can count as serious, and the

[47] Kivy's comment on the Ravel example is pertinent here: "The Ravel example is a particularly relevant one for our purposes, because it belongs to an era, and to a style of composition which we tend to think was intimately connected with tone color as an 'essential property'. . . . Yet it is clear that even here, the composer thought in terms of sound structure, and only later in terms of instrumentation" (46). It is true that orchestration tends to occupy the later stages in the genesis of a composition, and perhaps this was true as well for Ravel's *Valses*. But what is thought of *first*, or even as having pride of place, by a composer—the compositional "core" if you will—is hardly adequate to settle by itself what is *definitive* of the work ultimately produced.

[48] Recall, again, that this is more abstract than *sound* structure, since the latter, on my usage, *includes* timbre.

success as reasonable, if most of a work's structure is observed and comes across.[49] The features flouted in such cases are still fundamental to the work in the sense that they constitute the work as necessarily distinct from other musical works lacking such features, and are such that any proper example of the work exhibits them.

VII

In some of his remarks, Kivy seeks to exploit to his advantage the difficulty of giving clear content to the idea of "same instrument" (or "instrumentation"), on which the integrality of performance means thesis must at some level rely. I would not suggest that it is essential to musical works that they be played on *precisely* the instruments available to their composers and original performers—down to specific maker, exact dimensions, year of manufacture, and color of wood stain. We must naturally understand "same instrument" in a way that allows some logical room in application. But the looseness of "same instrument" is arguably not much greater than that which affects sameness of sound structure. Is it the same sound structure (the one prescribed), with an *f* instead of an *fff* at one bar, an octave doubling at another, a smoothed-out rhythm at yet a third, and allegro assai tempo rather than presto throughout? In many contexts we would probably allow it was.[50] But clearly no uncertainties of this sort show that either sound structure or instrumentation are completely negotiable.[51]

Kivy points out that a Handel concerto conceived as virtuosic when performed on the sort of oboe for which it was intended will not be

[49]So I am happy to allow, for example, that I *perform* oboe solos on the alto recorder, but that doesn't mean I am producing *instances* of the pieces I am playing—only certain performances count as instances. An instance must exemplify all that is constitutively *in* a piece (cf. Chapter 8, above), and clearly not every performance fulfills this condition. Many performances are near instances; perhaps this includes performances with a number of wrong notes, and performances on makeshift or substitute instruments. These seem much on a par to me. We would not say the dropped A-flat was inessential to a piece became some (incorrect) performances—and thus noninstances—lacked it; why, then, should we say this for an oboe dropped in favor of a recorder?

[50]See Chapter 8, sec. III, above.

[51]It is significant that in all the cases Kivy defends of pieces being correctly performed, even if not on the precise instruments entertained by the composer, it is always a later version of structurally the same instrument that is involved.

perceived as virtuosic, by either performer or audience, if performed on the modern many-keyed oboe.[52] On this kind of case I am inclined to dig in my heels and say, right, perform it that way if you like, or if practical necessity dictates, but virtuosity is still a property of the work that Handel wrote, and one that is regrettably lost or—to be accurate, diminished—in a modern rendition. As already allowed, this may be a *performance* of the original work, but its counting as a performance doesn't make it an *instance*, doesn't mean it's a bona fide presentation of the work—i.e., doesn't thus imply that any properties *it* fails to convey fail to belong to the *work*.

In the same vein, Kivy argues that Mozart's Clarinet Concerto loses its originality when clarinets come to be widely employed in the following period, and when in the course of time we become habituated to woodwind concerti of expanded dimensions.[53] This, it should be clear, is just a misunderstanding of what artistic orginality means. Originality is a historically contextual property; roughly speaking, if a structural or aesthetic feature of a work is significantly different from those displayed by its relevant predecessors, then it's an original feature.[54] Since the historical context is fixed, this property is fixed along with it and doesn't change.[55] Mozart's Clarinet Concerto always was and always will be original in the noted respect—even if by mishearing it in relation to works that follow it, it may not always *appear* so.[56] It should be evident that in both this example and the preceding one we have to do with the same tactic of substituting apparent properties for actual (albeit time-bound) properties as surfaced earlier in regard to the excitingness of Stamitz's allegro.

---

[52] Kivy, "Orchestrating Platonism," p. 53.

[53] Ibid.

[54] For the distinction of structural vs. aesthetic properties, see Chapter 6, above.

[55] For further discussion, see Chapter 9, above.

[56] By the way, originality is *not*, strictly speaking, a sonic attribute, in the sense of one directly aurally perceptible. This is part of what I meant by calling it *artistic* as opposed to *aesthetic*. The difference between artistic and aesthetic attributes, as I use these terms, is this. *Artistic* attributes are attributes of artworks *directly descriptive or reflective of* their place in art history, their situation in the field of artworks as a whole; this includes the influences they undergo or exert and their various relations—referential, imitative, allusive, parodistic, denunciatory—to other works of art. *Aesthetic* attributes are a species of perceptual attribute, which although complexly *dependent* on a work's art-historical context, do not have as their *content* (some aspect of) that contextual embeddedness. For illustrations of this distinction, see Chapter 9, note 9.

Let's move to my *Hammerklavier* example. Kivy claims that the cragginess, sublimity, and awesomeness of Beethoven's sonata (I had in mind particularly the first and last movements) will come through in some measure played on any instrument capable of giving forth the notes, and to listeners who have no knowledge either of what is actually producing the sounds or of how keyboard instruments produce sounds in general.[57] Now, as to the first point, I maintain there is a fairly specific cragginess and sublimity that belongs to, is truly ascribed to, parts of that sonata and which evaporates, in favor of something more generalized, if it is not rendered on a piano of some sort, with the particular sense of limitations that that involves. And *this* quality, which is proper to Beethoven's work and is noted by any competent critic, does *not* come through in just any note-preserving rendition. We may argue whether the specific cragginess we recognize is conveyed *only* on a circa 1830 broken-register hammerklavier, but there can be no doubt it departs the sonata if the sonata is not conceived to require performance on *some* variety of the wood-metal-fabric contraption we call a piano. Does Kivy really think it survives in good measure, as he says, on any performing means capable of rendering the sound structure? What about a flute quartet?[58] As to the second point, I believe Kivy is just wrong; if musical background knowledge about instruments, their capabilities and manners of employment, falls below a certain threshold, grasp of a work's specific aesthetic complexion— and it is after all that, and not only rough-and-ready character, with which criticism must concern itself—is seriously endangered.[59] To throw in another example of the same sort, double-stop passages on the violin (e.g., in Bach's unaccompanied sonatas, or Tchaikovsky's Violin Concerto) often display a quality of strained intensity that would be largely dissipated, its specificity lost, if such passages were

---

[57] Kivy, "Orchestrating Platonism," pp. 51–52.

[58] Of course, I am not sure, once instrumental forces are set adrift, what Kivy would count as fully conveying the sound structure (*sans* timbres, naturally) of the *Hammerklavier*. If relative dynamic levels is part of this, then a flute quartet could, I think, manage to render the gamut *ppp* to *ff on its own terms*. If absolute dynamic level, comparable to that of the piano, is demanded, then obviously flutes cannot oblige; but it would not be in the spirit of Kivy's view to insist on the latter.

[59] For a fuller defense of this claim, the reader is referred to Chapter 16, below.

rendered even on a pair of violins—much less a multiband synthe-sizer.[60]

To repeat the central moral of my original essay, works of music must be specific enough to bear the aesthetic and artistic attributes we importantly ascribe to them. We have to conceive them so that they are what such attributions are *of*. And the tonal structure per se simply does not fill the bill. We don't find critics—or knowledgeable listeners—saying of, for instance, the first movement of Mahler's Second Symphony, "It's earth-shaking, brooding, pessimistic *in that guise*" (i.e., with that instrumentation), but rather just, "It's earth-shaking, brooding, pessimistic" *period* (i.e., as it is constituted, in all respects). Certainly it would *not* be those things, in the same (or perhaps any) degree, if orchestration were considered a completely free variable. A very slippery slope, down which a work's aesthetic and artistic character is poised to tumble, beckons at any decision to consider as "just optional" any significant specification of a piece as originally conceived—whether tone-structural, timbral, or simply in-strumental.

Kivy has tried to argue that certain properties of musical works, such as virtuosity and originality on the one hand, and cragginess and sublimity on the other, are either naturally *evanescent* (first sort) or else sufficiently *durable* (second sort) that in neither case must instru-mentation be brought in as partly constituting works that can have such properties. But I hope to show that these properties are, respec-tively, neither so evanescent nor so durable as a Platonist would like to believe. They will not disappear just by misconstruing them, yet they won't stay around if you take their toys—i.e., instruments—away. As such, they're all that's necessary, I submit, to bring Kivy's Platonism to grief.

VIII

There is, finally, one more issue that needs to be addressed, and this concerns the legitimacy of viewing specific instrumentation as con-

---

[60]The concerns broached in this paragraph are likewise given fuller discussion, and a more explicit basis, in Chapter 16, below.

stitutive of works *on the grounds of the appearance in scores* of more
and more specific designations of performing forces. Of course not
everything figuring in a score is a firm prescription, as opposed to a
recommendation to the performer on achieving the best sort of performance. Naturally, it is not always easy to tell whether the former
characterization applies.[61] But I don't think that in specific cases, in
light of performance and notational practices, the question of whether
a designation is of one sort or the other is generally unanswerable. And
such answers, when obtainable, do not seem to lend support to the
thesis of instrumental dispensability.

But Kivy disagrees, and for rather deep reasons, which we shall get
to. He claims that the fact that scores after, say, 1780 seem to call for
instruments in no uncertain terms is actually something of an illusion,
not to be taken at face value. It is worth examining this part of his
demurral from instrumentalism carefully since he takes it to be "the
one most crucial to [his] case."[62]

Kivy begins with a caricature of what he takes to be my argument
"from scores": "Scores are definitive of works. Instrumentation instructions appear in scores. Therefore, instrumentation instructions
are (in part) definitive of works."[63] As he himself soon allows, my
second premise *must* be understood as stronger than that. It is not just
that instrumentation instructions appear in scores, but that they appear in a certain *way,* are construable as expressing *demands* rather
than wishes, are acknowledged to have a certain obligating *status.* But
I will agree with Kivy that it is best to leave the argument "from scores"
per se and see if we can get at the truth of the understandings and
practices that stand *behind* the scores in the music with which we are
concerned.

---

[61] Cf. Wolterstorff, *Works and Worlds of Art*, p. 64: "a composer may have views as
to what an aesthetically excellent occurrence of his work would be like, and views as to
how best to achieve such an occurrence. He may think a certain tempo would give the
best performance, or a certain registration on the organ. But if he does not lay these
down as requirements for correctness they remain as matters of opinion or judgment on
his part. . . . Of course it's not always clear, at every point [in a score], whether the
composer selected a set of criteria for correctness of occurrence or whether he expressed his views as to how correct occurrences of the work composed can be made
aesthetically excellent."

[62] Kivy, "Orchestrating Platonism," p. 51.

[63] Ibid., p. 48.

Here is where Kivy makes what I feel are his most telling observations in his various attacks on my position. Acknowledging that instrumental instructions in the post-1780 period are clearly *more* than mere *suggestions*, he maintains that they need not yet be regarded as *definitive* of works in which they are required, because there is a way of viewing such requiredness as being only provisional (or "instrumental") not something prescribed in and of itself. Required instrumentation can be seen as required in the service of, and only insofar as necessary for, adequate rendering of the increasingly complex and ambitious tonal structures that composers, toward the end of the eighteenth century, were beginning to devise:

> The musical structures became more and more complicated and expansive in ways that made greater demands upon instruments. The range, for example, that was demanded in a violin sonata or concerto, or the double-stopping, made it impossible anymore to play such pieces on the flute or oboe. Thus it ceased to be possible to advertise a sonata or concerto as "for violin or . . . other melody instrument," as had been the custom, simply because no other melody instrument could realize the structure of the work. In *that* respect, certain instruments became *essential*, but only temporarily, and, if you will pardon the pun, *instrumentally*. That is to say, they were essential to the realization of the work because they were the only instruments capable, at the time, of realizing it, so were essential as a *means*. . . . I say "temporarily," of course, because the development of new instruments, the technical development of old ones, and the development of instrumental technique, can make a sound structure realizable in ways other than those envisaged by the composer. . . .
>
> The point I am making here is that a good deal of interest in instrumentation in the period in which it emerged from the "ad lib" stage had to do not so much with "color" as "construction"; not so much with the timbre of instruments as with their capabilities of realizing sound structures; with, that is, their ranges, and the varieties of musically complex figurations they could, with advancing technique, produce.[64]

What Kivy is adducing here is highly interesting, worth emphasizing, and to a large extent true. But does this point—that the driving force behind instrumental choice, starting in the late eighteenth century, was often technical—show that instrumentation is not truly

[64] Ibid., pp. 48–49.

integral to musical works conceived in the last two hundred years? I
think not. First of all, the fact remains that timbral qualities per se, and
expressive effects dependent on the presupposed gestural repertoires of
instruments envisaged (see Chapter 16, below), become progressively
more and more considerations in their own right guiding such choices.
(We will return to this shortly, when we consider Kivy's most direct
confrontation of this fact, in discussing examples from Brahms and
Berlioz.) Second, in some cases it is not even clearly intelligible to think
of sound structure as preceding, and independent of, instrumental
designation. Double-stopping is a good example of this. If taken, as
Kivy does, as part of the envisaged sound structure needing realization, it already implicates a certain kind of instrument and performing
action. (Double-stopping is not just sounding two notes simultaneously on one instrument: pianos cannot double-stop.) A similar point
could be made about pizzicato; ideas for pizzicato passages do not first
occur to composers and then, only later, what will serve, for the nonce,
to realize them.[65] Third, when instruments are chosen for passages
whose notes are, let us say, already set, there will in the grand majority
of cases remain alternatives—e.g., xylophone vs. flute, bassoon vs.
cello—which could have *equally* well sounded the note sequences in
question. Are the composer's choices between these alternatives to be
regarded as completely arbitrary, as reassignable at will so long as the
notes are clearly sounded?[66] This is incredible.

But this still leaves the central force of Kivy's observation, which is
that instrumentation was in many cases determined not by coloristic
or expressive objectives but by structural needs and technical constraints. What shall we say to this? I think the best response, beyond
what we have already essayed, is this. The fact that such may have been
the decisive *reasons* for these choices, even in a great many cases, does
not mean that, the choices having been *made,* the instrumental/timbral
aspects of those choices did not in fact *become* integral generators of
the aesthetic and artistic content of those works. To ascertain whether

---

[65] I might cite, in illustration, a delicious, irreplaceable pizzicato passage toward the
end of the andante of Beethoven's very early Piano Quartet in D (1785).

[66] To carry this a step further, consider a sequence in which a theme within the range
and figurative capacity of both flute and xylophone is carried first by flute, and then by
xylophone. Would it do no violence to the work to give the second occurrence to the
flute as well?

this indeed happened we must consult critical reaction, the subsequent course of musical composition, and our own considered experience of what counts in such music. I think when we do this, we see that as soon as composers began to call unequivocally for specific instruments, for whatever reasons, their works began to be taken up into history, criticism, and practice the way they were made, inclusive of performing means. Of course it was always *open* to a composer to indicate explicitly that his (or her) rationale for choosing an instrument was, as Kivy puts it, *entirely* "instrumental"—thus licensing future performance by any means that gets the bare notes out—but I daresay I know of no such case in the history of music, and no grounds for ascribing such a rationale hypothetically in any case after 1780 or so. Even if specificity of instrumentation was initially justified, during the eighteenth century, as a means for realizing desired structures, the burden seems to be on the Platonist to show that it did *not*, after all, very soon become more than just an ignorable artifact of the exigencies of sounding tonal sequences. A case in point: The charm and gaiety of the phrases exchanged among woodwinds in the first movement of Beethoven's First Symphony, whether assigned to winds for technical reasons or not, would not have such gaiety and charm—like that of breezes passing from one tree branch to another—if not for the timbral and gestural upshot of having so assigned them. Nor, one might add even more obviously, would the piquancy of Beethoven's writing for winds generally ever have attracted any attention to itself if the only credit it could legitimately claim was that of having gotten the notes across.

But what, then, of those expressive effects in much nineteenth-century music which are directly *aimed at* on the basis of instrumentation, and whose explanation does not reside in any technical or structural constraint? Kivy believes such effects have already been "written in" to the musical structure, orchestration "being employed to enhance effects already musically there." He cites measures 30–38 of the final movement of Brahms's First Symphony as a passage in which "noble quality is achieved by the melodic and harmonic structure . . . the horn merely adds to an already accomplished effect."[67] But it is all a question of how *specific* an effect one is talking about. The effect

[67] Kivy, "Orchestrating Platonism," p. 50.

I hear at those measures, and the peculiar nobility, is gone when one subtracts the color and underlying gesture that the horn contributes; far from being already accomplished, it is accomplished *in and through* the orchestration, melody and harmony being given.[68]

Similarly, Kivy tries to dismiss Berlioz's ineliminable use of oboe and English horn to suggest shepherds' pipes in the third movement of the *Symphonie fantastique* as not germane, given the dispute is about the nature of "pure" (that is, nonrepresentational) instrumental works. But this is a dangerous compartmentalization. Many acknowledged "pure" pieces of music have some representational import—e.g., certain of Haydn's quartets—and those representational touches can furthermore tie up with expressiveness in subtle ways.[69] So if some representationality depends essentially on instrumental identification, the consequences of that cannot be cordoned off as easily as Kivy thinks.

But there is no reason at this point to let Kivy's selected examples control our picture of the field involved. The position he espouses seems to be beyond redemption for music of the past 150 years—leaving even the most avant-garde (e.g., aleatory) developments aside. How is it possible to defend "aninstrumentalism" after Rimsky-Korsakov's treatise on orchestration and the many brilliant illustrations of it found throughout his works? After Chopin's writing piano music, even when he ostensibly wasn't, as in his small amount of chamber music? After Strauss's tone poems, with their explicit sound effects added in some cases to the most carefully judged instrumental combinations? After Mahler's symphonies with their very particular scoring for odd members of the horn family? After Debussy's *Prelude to the Afternoon of a Faun*? After Schoenberg's and Webern's *Klangfarbenmelodie*, or "mel-

[68]Kivy also says, apropos of the Brahms, that "timbre per se is pretty hard to imagine as being involved in compositional choices very often. Composers tend to think in structure, not color" (50). I don't find this very hard to imagine; a composer might very well first decide he wants something "high and brassy" at a given point, before committing himself to anything in the way of melodic shape or rhythmic pulse. Anyway, whatever the truth of Kivy's generalization, it is belied by at least one composer's admission, that color and structure were for him inseparable: "I never compose in the abstract, the musical thought never appears otherwise than in a suitable external form. In this way I invent the musical idea and the instrumentation simultaneously" (letter from Tchaikovsky to his friend and benefactor Mme. von Meck, June 25, 1878).

[69]See on this Jenefer Robinson, "Music as a Representational Art," in *What Is Music?* ed. P. Alperson (New York: Haven Publications, 1987), pp. 167–92.

ody of tone colors"? After Varèse's *Ionisation*? After Cage's *Pieces for Prepared Piano*? After Conlon Nancarrow's *Studies for Player Piano*? After George Crumb's *Night Musics I, II, and III*? Can performance means or timbre be thought of as inessential in any of the above cases? As any less constitutive of what the composition is than other specified features? Can you imagine, finally, the opening of Janáček's *Sinfonietta*, with its richly overtoned, overlapping fanfares, performed not by brass but by a consort of oboes—even very loud ones? The music would be totally transformed, and not for the better.

Perhaps the reductio ad absurdum of Kivy's position is provided by another piece of Ravel's, the justly famous (though for doubtful reasons) *Bolero*. Consisting essentially of nine repetitions of the same sinuous melody and countermelody, varied almost exclusively through changes in instrumentation, the piece would make no sense if rendered on, say, two pianos, which could handle all of the notes, give or take a few. Nor would it make the sense Ravel gave it if comparable instrumental variety was retained, but not the particular sequence of changes that Ravel prescribed. For example, nothing can substitute for the heightening of sultriness and sassiness Ravel achieves by introducing the tenor, soprano, and sopranino saxes as carriers of his countermelody about halfway through, after all the more reserved and conventional woodwinds have had their say. The *Bolero* is a singular case, *pace* Kivy, only in its extremeness: the instrumental indispensability on which it is founded and which it displays throughout is just displayed more subtly, and less foundationally, in most other musical works of the past two hundred years.

IX

It's useful here to bring in a point about evaluation. It seems plain that one can't evaluate works of music unless one hears them properly. One can't evaluate the musical worth of Beethoven's op. 9, say, if it is played by tin whistles, or even by an assortment of proper orchestral winds, if only because part of what we evaluate is how well composers write *for* the instruments they choose. One is not even entitled to say, from the point of view of judgment, that one has *heard* a work unless one has heard a *substantially correct* performance of it—i.e., at least a near instance. And gross violations of performing means certainly disqualify a performance from that status. Now, can aspects of musical compositions that absolutely *must* be considered in fairly evaluating them be reasonably *excluded* from a notion of their essential makeups—of what is integral to them as compositions? It seems perverse to so maintain.

Let me expand on this a bit. "I heard a performance of Beethoven's op. 9 String Trio on tin whistles" is more like "I saw a reproduction of Van Gogh's *Sunflowers* in a magazine" (which, of course, does *not* entail "I saw Van Gogh's *Sunflowers*") than it is like "I talked to Jack on the telephone" or "I saw Jack on closed-circuit TV" (which perhaps do, respectively, entail "I talked to Jack" and "I saw Jack"). Hearing a performance of Beethoven's op. 9 with five wrong notes amounts to having heard Beethoven's op. 9, but hearing a "performance" of the op. 9 on three tin whistles cannot plausibly amount to achieving such acquaintance. Such an auditor could not reasonably claim exposure to the op. 9, and could no more legitimately essay an opinion as to its merit than the skimmer of the magazine above could legitimately assess the quality of the paint handling in Van Gogh's canvas. Not all performances of a work, and not even all near instances of same, give an auditor aural acquaintance with a work. And this is often because they obscure or delete timbral and instrumental features essential to considered evaluation of a work—features essential to the work as music.

Before we have done, finally, with Kivy's sustained attack, one point needs reemphasis. There are three factors pushing us toward a more complicated ("qualified Platonic") view of the paradigm musical work of the last two hundred years, and away from the purity of extreme Platonism. In my assessment, Kivy has failed to impugn the most central of these—fine individuation of works as bearers of distinct sets of artistic and aesthetic properties, beyond what can be ascribed to pure tonal (*or* sound) structures—and has succeeded only at inducing some qualifications in the force of the other two: personal creatability and instrumental involvement. But taken *together,* as noted earlier, these considerations are more compelling than taken individually, since they all point in the same direction, a synergy it suits Kivy to ignore in his piecemeal assaults.[70]

[70]This is especially damaging since Kivy is willing to grant that the creation/discovery debate is more or less a toss-up, leaving Platonism and qualified Platonism on an

Platonism about standard musical works of the past two centuries or so is a view that suits, perhaps, Schenkerian music analysts unconcerned with a work's origin, individual expression, aesthetic effects, or performing aspect, and who believe our familiar tonal system to be eternal. But what is eternally surprising to me is that a philosopher of Peter Kivy's sophistication and musical sensitivity should so cling to it.

X

The challenge of David Pearce's articles for my view is quite different from that posed by Kivy's, and comes from closer quarters. Pearce agrees with me in rejecting an extensionalism that strict Platonism, with its embrace of works as pure sound (or tonal) structures, is committed to, and is instead sympathetic to regarding musical works as intensionally individuated by their more fine-grained aesthetic meanings and artistic significances. Where he parts company with me fundamentally is in my meeting, or accounting for, the intensionality of musical works via the occasion-bound intentionality of the composer who creates them. Instead, Pearce proposes in effection an intensionality *without* intentionality.

What are the problems he sees for my view? One seems to concern the implications of my account for how performances are to be assigned to works. I hold that performances of works (W_1, W_2) with identical sound/performance means (S/PM) structures would not be performances of the other; this is because even if sonically indistinguishable, the first would be, in virtue of an appropriate intentional-causal relation[71] holding between the performers and W_1 (and mediately, the composer of W_1), a performance (only) of W_1, whereas the second would be, for parallel reasons, a performance (only) of W_2. Pearce objects to this on the grounds that it entails "the rather implausible thesis that the total of all perceivable qualities of a performance as a sound event do not suffice to determine which of two different musical works is being realised." He then goes on to observe that "this

---

equal footing, and since he grants as well that recognizing instrumental involvement is unavoidable for some (he thinks few) works in the Western tradition ("Orchestrating Platonism," p. 51). These admissions, when coupled with a rout on the individuation question, leave little holding the fort.

[71] For more discussion of this relation, see Chapter 5, above.

incidentally seems to have the effect of making performance depend on the history of production and thus, in one sense at least, to restore the analogy between music and printmaking."[72]

My response to these points, I'm afraid, is not very elaborate. What Pearce regards as an "implausible thesis" I hold to be manifestly *true*, and take my various illustrations of the distinctness of identically scored musical works to be *pro tanto* illustrations of the distinctness of their actual or potential performances; furthermore, this "implausible thesis" has, I think, been conclusively established by others.[73] Yes, even the total sonic aspect of a performance is not enough to make it belong to a work—make it be *of* a work. Here is an analogy: Each of my utterances of the lone sound {kee}—which are, after all, mini-performances of a sort—conforms both to the French word for "who" and the English word for that which opens locks, but does not belong to either *automatically* just because it fits it phonetically.[74] As for the other charge, to partly restore the "analogy between music and print-making," to show that they are both—by Goodman's yardstick (irrelevance of history of production), though not by that which I would recommend (absence of notational determination)—autographic arts, was the express purpose of my follow-up essay on the subject.[75] So I embrace this supposedly untoward consequence.

Pearce actually lodges a stronger objection than these in a footnote. He claims that my argument for work-distinctness of identically scored works of distinct composers based on the one possibly having performances that the other would not[76] requires the further premise that "no two works could have any performances in common," and this, he thinks, rests too circularly for comfort on "the requirement that authorship be a necessary ingredient in the specification of the work,

---

[72]"Musical Expression: Some Remarks on Goodman's Theory," p. 238. That my view has the "failing" of making music Goodman-autographic is a charge reiterated in Pearce's second essay, "Intensionality and the Nature of a Musical Work," p. 111.

[73]Notably Walton, in "Presentation and Portrayal of Sound Patterns." Danto's demonstrations of work-distinct though visually-indistinguishable instantiations of a kind of red canvas, in *Transfiguration of the Commonplace* (New York: Columbia University Press, 1981), though obviously not concerned with music, are in the same spirit.

[74]As it turns out, some of them belong to English, some to French, and I daresay it's what I have in mind when I so utter that makes the difference.

[75]See Chapter 5, above. (Pearce seems to have been unaware of this essay.)

[76]See Chapter 4, pp. 85–86, above.

i.e. . . . just what the argument is supposed to show."[77] But I would reply first that the aforementioned premise which Pearce rightly notes is presupposed in the argument he is addressing, seems eminently reasonable on its own merits: We *do*, I submit, take for granted that there is a unique answer to "What is this a performance of?" where there is any answer at all. And so, second, it's not the case that such a premise rests *directly* on taking authorship to be necessary to a work; there are grounds, it seems, rooted in our partly unreflective practices of sorting performances into bins, for positing *some* identifying relation (intentional or causal or whatever) linking a given performance to a single work of which it is purported to be a performance, which grounds do not themselves *presume* that authorship is logically integral to the work performed.[78]

Pearce develops his thoughts further on what is problematic for my view in his second essay. Observing once again that on my account what is a performance of what depends on contextual (including intentional or causal) factors, so that wholly sonically identical performances are not thereby automatically of the same works, Pearce thinks this regrettable because then one could never *accidentally* perform a work of music.[79] But I confess this seems to me as it should be. Could one *accidentally* recite the opening of the Gettysburg Address, meaning, without bearing any intentional-causal relation to it, at any point?[80] The most one in that position—e.g., a recently immigrant Pole of high accomplishment in English but no knowledge of U.S. history—could do, it seems, is come up with that sentence, that string of words, by happenstance in the course of linguistic exercise aloud. But this person would not be reciting the Gettysburg Address. One can

---

[77] Pearce, "Musical Expression: Some Remarks on Goodman's Theory," p. 242, note 10.

[78] Of course, it is a point of the argument to show that although not explicitly *presumed* by the practice itself, the postulate of authorship integrality is a good *explanation* for—and perhaps *vindication* of—the practice.

[79] "Intensionality and the Nature of a Musical Work," p. 111.

[80] One might emit it unknowingly, from memory, in a dreamlike or semiconscious state, but this would not be completely *accidentally*, in the sense under consideration. By invoking a strict sense of "accidental," I sidestep the issue, raised in both Chapter 4 and Chapter 5, of whether it is intentional or causal relatedness between work and performer which is ultimately crucial; the issue is complicated further by the fact that if something like a causal theory of reference is correct, then intentional relations to individuals are also partly causal as well.

no more perform a musical work wholly accidentally than that prover-
bial monkey can be voicing Shakespeare's sonnets by its antics at the
keyboard—though of course it may, if we wait long enough, type out
the bare sequence of symbols that constitute, in Elizabethan English,
the sentences thereof.[81]

We come now to Pearce's most substantial worry about my view. He
begins by noting that cases in which musical and historical context
qualify our understanding of a musical work, and even "make a
difference to our categorizing a performance as a genuine instance of
it,"[82] are not all of them hypothetical. He cites the instructive case of
the *Serenade* Quartet, formerly attributed to Haydn (as op. 3, no. 5),
now correctly (let us assume) ascribed to the obscure Hofstetter, as a
work of 1775. As Pearce astutely observes, if attributed to the Haydn
of 1775 it would appear as the oddly retrograde effort of a composer
who was well on his way to revolutionizing the string quartet as a
medium of serious musical discourse, rather than as akin to a diverti-
mento. As a work of Hofstetter's at that date, it is simply a pleasant
effort of one who, as far as we know, had no innovative ambitions in
the sphere of music. The musical properties of performances will even
be affected by which work one takes it to be.[83] This looks, so far, like a
good brief for counting the composer's identity as integral to the
identity of a musical work. What, then, is Pearce's reservation? It is
this:

> It is important here that, at least in principle, *perceptible* musical
> differences should affect our classification of a given rendition as a
> performance of the 'Serenade-quartet-as-attributed-to-Haydn' or as a

---

[81] Another difficulty Pearce offers at this juncture is hard to take seriously. He
remarks that the "S/PM structure indicated by the author at the time of composition
may differ markedly from the S/PM structure accepted by performance practice a
century or so later" ("Intensionality," p. 111). So what! Casual misunderstandings and
willful distortions invariably befall works as temporal distance from them increases;
poems in Sanskrit become unreadable, sculpted figures meant as votive are taken as
erotica, paintings are painted over or rudely "improved," and in the year 2500 Mahler's
Ninth Symphony may be played without the final movement, or else treated as
Muzak—and even regarded as having always been so intended. This is just the issue of
authenticity, and there can be little need to argue basic adherence to it in any discussion
of musical ontology.

[82] Ibid., p. 111.

[83] Ibid., p. 110.

performance of the 'Serenade-quartet-as-attributed-to-Hofstetter'. If no perceptible differences of interpretation were to arise, the real authorship of the piece would remain, as in the case of mathematics, largely a matter of historical, rather than musical or aesthetic, concern.[84]

So according to Pearce, only if performances project hearably different interpretations is there any ground to ascribe them to different works. But it is hard to see what the grounds of this sort of operationalism are. First of all, that performances of what is unequivocally a single work—e.g., Schubert's *Death and the Maiden* Quartet—differ dramatically in the interpretations *they* embody provides us with no inclination to assign *them* to separate works. Second, a performance of Hofstetter's quartet, embodying interpretation A, and a performance of Haydn's identically scored quartet—assuming there was such a thing, which there isn't—embodying interpretation B, could quite easily end up *sounding the same,* and yet we would have no reason to want to assign them to the same work, if only because there *are* different interpretations involved, interpretations that have to be understood as interpretations of different works.[85] Third, Pearce's principle for assigning performances to works puts things back-to-front. Once performers know what work they are dealing with—who wrote it and when—and not just what score they are to execute, then this may rightly *affect* how they decide to play it, for various reasons. But it seems perverse to invert this and claim that our *criterion* for what works given performances will be held to be of—especially when there are, as in the cases we have been considering, close competitors—will be audibly manifested interpretive differences between them. For as I have tried to suggest, on the one hand, hearable interpretive differences between performances may not be grounds for assigning them to different works, and on the other hand, interpretive differences be-

---

[84] Ibid., p. 111.

[85] To make this more concrete, a forward-looking reading of the Hofstetter and a backward-looking reading of the "Haydn" might be cashed out by musical choices on the part of performers that would just *converge,* as far as the sonic result was concerned. Put the other way around, a reading construed *as of the Hofstetter* might seem to be making that piece out to be on the verge of Haydnesque, whereas construed *as of the "Haydn"* it might seem to be emphasizing its distance from the core of Haydn's oeuvre.

tween performances of different works may not be hearable, regarded just as sound events.

Pearce formulates a variant of his preferred principle somewhat later: "any features of the work that are determinant for correctly assigning a performance to the work must be *manifest in use,* i.e. must contribute to the perceptible properties of the performance as a sound event, whether they be strictly musical or more broadly aesthetic properties."[86] Now, I maintain, of course, that features definitive of a musical work—by my lights, musico-historical situation as well as S/PM structure—will have a bearing on *its* aesthetic complexion, but this does not mean that these features must manifest themselves in the direct manner that Pearce requires, that is, by necessarily *modulating* in some way the purely sonic aspect of any performance that counts as a presentation of the work. For what this overlooks is that the primary job of a performance is to project the aesthetic properties *of the work* (and not its own aesthetic properties, whatever they might be), but that (1) it can *only* do that intelligibly against a background conception of what the work *is* musico-historically; and (2) as a sound event it could project *different* aesthetic properties without any sonic alteration if simply *referred* to different works musico-historically speaking.

A final aspect of what Pearce objects to in my intentionally-histori-cally rooted intensionalism is reflected in the following observation, the essentialist consequences of which he, like some others,[87] finds curious: "Levinson's characterization of the musical work as a 'sound/ performance means structure as-indicated-by-[composer]-X-at-[time]-t' makes authorship and date of composition fully integral to the work, not merely to reflect current musical theory or practice in the case of *some* works but as a matter of logical *necessity* for all works."[88] What this remark fails to appreciate is that my overriding objective in "What a Musical Work Is" was to offer a *general* answer, for a certain class of musical works, to that eponymous question. I was accordingly looking for a characterization that would be adequate to dealing with all problems of identification and individuation which could be thought *foreseeably* to arise, not just ones that have *actually* arisen. A proposal

---

[86] Pearce, "Intensionality," p. 113.

[87] For example, James Anderson, in "Musical Identity." I tried to dull the sting of such curiousness a bit in section III of Chapter 8, above.

[88] Pearce, "Intensionality," p. 111.

that told you what Beethoven's op. 16 Quintet was, but only on the condition that there was not actually any similarly scored work by some throwback composer a hundred years later, or any obscure closeted-away pupils of Albrechtsberger poised to confuse our grasp of the details of Beethoven's development or the extent of his corpus, would not seem to be a satisfactory philosophical solution to the problem of musical work identity.

XI

Pearce does not confine himself to indicating dissatisfaction with my view, of course; he has one of his own to propose. In this section I briefly consider his positive proposal and what strike me as some problems it brings in its train. Though Pearce's is the most interesting alternative to my view that I know of, I don't think it ultimately emerges as the more recommendable.

What Pearce suggests, at base, is that by adopting an intuitionist or constructivist view of mathematical objects, and by extension other abstract structures, one can show them to be both objective and creatable.

> The most common, naive view of the ontology of mathematics is undoubtedly the realist or Platonist one: mathematics studies independently existing objects and structures and seeks to discover their properties. The realist position emerges most sharply when mathematicians regard certain undecided, and perhaps even undecidable, statements [e.g., Goldbach's conjecture] as possessing objective truth-values. . . . The intuitionist position is the one most directly opposed to Platonism. It adopts a conceptualist view, according to which all mathematical objects are free creations of the human mind . . . [all] varieties of conceptualism have in common the idea that mathematical objects exist only in so far as they can be explicitly *constructed*. . . . If constructivist principles are sound we can therefore reconcile the 'abstract' and objective character of musical works with their being free creations of the human mind.[89]

This is all well and good. Unfortunately, I do not find intuitionism/constructivism an independently plausible view of the mathemati-

[89] Ibid., pp. 106–8.

cal realm, especially in its most familiar and basic territories. I do not think that the square root of 2 (an example Pearce mentions) was created by anyone, though of course the idea that there was such a number (or quantity) had to be hit on, and the formalism for indicating such numbers developed. But there has always been such a number— assuming, for the moment, the givenness of the natural numbers— namely, the number such that when multiplied by itself yields 2. And few things seem as clear to me as that Goldbach's conjecture, that every even integer can be expressed as the sum of two primes, is (right now) *either* true or false, whether or not a proof is ever arrived at.[90]

What, then, is a musical work, from an intuitionist point of view? "*A musical work is a (certain kind of) mental construction, created by the activity of the composer.* Once created, however, the work has an 'objective' character in that it can be referred to, studied, performed . . . *a musical work is explicitly presented by a performance of it.* A performance, even a single performance, characterizes the work in much the same way that [a specific construction characterizes a given mathematical object]."[91]

Now I willingly grant, of course, that musical works derive from the activities, mental and nonmental, of composers, but I see little gain in qualifying the *result* of such activity as itself something mental. Though Pearce says that such an object remains or becomes public and accessible, he no better than Croce or Collingwood, or more recently Renée Cox,[92] shows how this is possible.[93] One suspects this is the old error of confusing an object thought about with the process of thinking it. Nor is it any clearer how the musical work, a mental entity, can be "explicitly presented" by a performance of it.

The sort of intensionalism involved in Pearce's view, while adumbrated in his suggestion that musical works can be presented differently in different performances, just as mathematical objects can be "constructed" by different routes, comes out most centrally in his remarks on understanding a piece of music:

[90] I must confess that I am confident it *is* true, on a combination of aesthetic and inductive grounds.

[91] Pearce, "Intensionality," pp. 107–8.

[92] "A Defence of Musical Idealism," *British Journal of Aesthetics*, 26 (1986): 133–42.

[93] Roman Ingarden, who takes a musical work to be an *intentional* object, is perhaps more successful in this vein. See *The Work of Music and the Problem of Its Identity*, ed. J. G. Harrell (Berkeley: University of California Press, 1986).

Our understanding of a piece of music depends on our background knowledge, such as authorship and musico-historical context, but it especially depends on our perception of the piece as presented through the medium of a performance. Aesthetic qualities are then encapsulated in the performance as a sound event, even though we may attribute those qualities to something "beyond" the performance, namely the work itself.

... to understand or "know the meaning of" a musical work is to be able to recognize something as a genuine performance of it. By "genuine" here I do not of course mean simply "faithful to the score." As a layman I might learn easily enough to distinguish note-perfect renderings of a piece from those unfaithful to the score. But, without musical training of a certain sort, and the requisite background knowledge, I would certainly be unable to pick out those renderings that count as genuine performances, those which truly express the qualities of the work.[94]

It is evident that Pearce's view and my own are quite close at this juncture. He agrees with me, contra Goodman, that a work's aesthetic meaning is too fine-grained to inhere in an extensionally defined sound structure, and that whether a performance counts as of a work outstrips its conforming to the mere patterns of a score. The only difference, one might say, is his declining to go with an integrally musico-historical and personalized way of identifying and individuating works, and his reliance instead on a criterion based on audible recognizability of genuine performances.[95] But the problem with this, as I tried to indicate in the preceding section, is that there is *no* reliable set of audible characteristics, even for those with the proper musical training and full background knowledge regarding a work,[96] which will infallibly pick out what would count, intuitively, as all and only the work's genuine performances. A musically acceptable, even sensitive, performance of work W_1 might conceivably by aurally indistinguishable from one of W_2, a distinct musical work, even to the most comprehending listeners. To accomplish such picking out we must, I maintain, have recourse to a

---

[94]"Musical Expression: Some Remarks on Goodman's Theory," p. 239.

[95]This is made explicit in the other essay: "[this view of understanding] allows us to obtain a very simple solution to the problem of identification and individuation of musical works. Works are characterized by their classes of possible performances." "Intensionality," p. 113.

[96]It is important that this is only background knowledge regarding a *work* that Pearce can allow himself; to admit background knowledge regarding the *performance* in question would in effect be conceding to the position (mine) he is opposing.

historical, occasion-bound conception of the work itself, and to historical (intentional, causal) relations between the work and its occasions of performance.[97]

I return now to one last remark Pearce makes apropos of my view, for responding to it will allow me to clarify something in my original exposition. Intuitionism/constructivism, Pearce claims,[98] would reject the distinction I elaborated as central to my theory between *implicit* and *initiated* types.[99] But I would reverse the logic of this observation. Since there *is* good basis for that distinction, there is, on the contrary, reason to *doubt* constructivism, at least as applied to the current issue. The basis is this. Given a framework of elements or properties, involving rules or ways of combining such as well, there exists automatically a range of possibilities and configurations of such things, which does not rely on anyone's explicitly and individually noting or demonstrating them. These are what I called implicit types. They are akin to pure universals, except that the elements or properties out of which they are composed may themselves have the status of entities initiated, rather than ones preexisting absolutely. But when attention *is* drawn to one such possibility/configuration—when such a one is selected, demonstrated, discovered, chosen, indicated—we also recognize, in certain cultural contexts, that something further comes into existence, not identifiable with any of those preexisting possibilities or configurations, because possessing properties of a sort and a specificity that those do not. These are what I called initiated types, of which the structures-as-indicated (indicated structures) of music and literature were examples.

I see now that I did not perhaps sufficiently stress in my original essay that implicit types are implicit *relative to a system or framework of elements and rules*—a system or framework that is often, at least in part, a product of human invention. Still, the point is that, given such a system or framework—e.g., the scales, pitches, and durations of tonal music, or the board, pieces, and moves of chess—individual patterns or configurations within it do not need to be explicitly constructed in

[97] Or, as Walton, might put it, to the contextual factors determining which of various sound-structural patterns it is the *function* of the performance to present (see "Presentation and Portrayal of Sound Patterns").

[98] "Intensionality," p. 117, note 3.

[99] See Chapter 4, pp. 80–82, above.

order to exist; their existence is in effect a consequence of the ground rules or defining parameters of the system. On the other hand, an initiated type, again relative to such a system/framework as background, is one that *does* require explicit, individual "construction," involving what I called *indication*, before it can be said to exist.

I will follow Pearce and give a mathematical illustration of what I have just affirmed. If the natural numbers are given, and the operation of addition as well, then surely we can say that all sums of pairs of such numbers exist as well, as *implicit* in this system or domain. But we will not say this of such things as: *273 and 372 as summed by Smith*, or *69 proposed as the most admirable of numbers by Adams*. If we did, for some reason, find ourselves led to recognize entities such as these, they could only be viewed as abstracta of a different sort, *initiated* in terms of the system, rather than implicit in it. And that is how I propose to regard musical works, though not the elements and patterns from which they are constructed.

XII

James Anderson has been the friendliest of my critics, and it is to a suggestion offered in the second of his two essays on our subject that I now happily turn. Though sympathetic to my account, Anderson feels, rightly, that there is something missing in it:

> In his explanation of the creation of musical works, Jerrold Levinson has proposed a definition that incorporates the pre-existing kind [an S/PM structure] associated with the work while *not* identifying the work with that pre-existing kind. . . . This definition can be seen as identifying the musical work not with its associated kind but rather with, to use Wolterstorff's terms, the kind-as-made-*his*-by-a-composer at t.
>
> A definition along the lines suggested by Levinson does, indeed bring us closer to a correct ontology of musical works. However, both [Levinson's] definition and a version of it which I have offered are, at the central point, unsatisfying. For what is it for a kind to be "indicated-by-P-at-t"? While we all understand, with Levinson, that typically this is done by creating a score, no general account of "kind-indication" is to be found in Levinson's paper.[100]

[100]"Musical Kinds," pp. 43–44.

The key to filling out the notion of "indication," Anderson suggests, is to bring my notion of musical works as creatable, historically conditioned artifacts into conjunction with Wolterstorff's conception of musical works as norm-kinds (i.e., as having incorrect as well as correct instances). Anderson proposes that the norm-kinds involved in music be identified as preexistent, descriptive kinds that have been "normativized" by composers: "Some norm-kinds are created by human beings from descriptive-kinds by the activity of stipulating that the properties of some descriptive-kind be treated as normative properties. . . . Perhaps the best way to understand the activity of creating a norm-kind is as an intentional operation on a previously existing descriptive-kind."[101] When this is done, the missing content noted earlier is handily supplied: "How does composition as indication differ from, say, describing a musical piece in all its detail? Or merely entertaining a certain sound structure? The answers to these questions are found in our view of the musical work as a norm-kind. To compose, or to 'indicate-a-kind' is to select certain properties and render them normative."[102]

While I remain unconvinced of the usefulness of the *general* notion of norm-kind that Anderson adopts from Wolterstorff,[103] my vagueness on the relation of "indication" is usefully redeemed by this discussion of making normative—i.e., laying some feature down as required in order for a properly formed performance (what I call an instance) to have occurred. What this highlights is that, in composing a musical work by writing notes on score paper—in contrast to just doodling or copying or demonstrating—the composer is in effect saying, with each mark, not just "note *N* here and so," but rather "note *N* *is to be played* here and so." Making-normative certainly at least helps explain what

---

[101] Ibid., p. 47.

[102] Ibid., p. 48.

[103] See Chapter 1, note 34, above. In addition, I have doubts that the notion of norm-kind (e.g., *the lion*), rooted in the biological sphere and connected to an idea of inner constitution and natural function, properly applies to musical and literary works, which are *basically* structures, and nonnatural ones, with no hidden "internal" (e.g., genetic) principles of identity. It's not clear that *structures* (as opposed to organisms) have proper and improper instances. It seems, rather, that they are either *instanced* or *not*—near instances often being set apart, pragmatically, as important cases of the latter. If something is basically a pattern or structure, then it seems right that an instance of it is something that *actually* has or fits that pattern or structure, not something that just approximates it.

indicating consists in, and differentiates it from other activities of an intentional nature directed on abstract structures. At any rate, it is more illumination than I had provided, and I am grateful for it.

XIII

In concluding, I revert to one issue on which I was divided in my original essay, though I opted for one side rather than the other,[104] and offer some thoughts on a second issue, which my original essay passed over in silence. On the first issue, that of how to conceive of the structure at the core of a musical work, my inclinations have shifted. I now definitely favor thinking of a musical work unitarily, as an indicated *performed-sound* structure (PSS), rather than dually, as an indicated *sound/performing-means* structure (SPMS). For one, the former conception fits in better with and is reinforced by the kind of argument offered in Chapter 16, below. But in addition, my original notion of a conjunction or combination (SPMS) of a sound structure (SS) and a performing-means structure (PMS) suggests both (i) that a musical work is actually *produced* by joining an (antecedently determined) SS and an (antecedently determined) PMS, and, relatedly, (ii) that the PMS has a *reality* and *importance* in itself comparable to that of the SS.

But neither of these is true. In many cases, works are integrally composed, through directly envisaging phrases-on-particular-instruments, or in at least a back-and-forth interplay between desired notes and performing means. But even where performing means are standardly a later addition (the case of "orchestration," emphasized by Kivy), this is not happily conceived as joining a fully determined *structure* to the one already represented by the notes.[105] On the other hand, the omnipresence of transcription, theme borrowing, plagiarism, whistling, and so on testifies to the obvious greater worth, interest, and hardiness of the sound structure itself (as we noted in section III), in comparison to what might be abstracted as the performing-means structure, detached from its sonic companion.

The second issue concerns the *destructibility* of musical works and,

---

[104] See Chapter 4, note 25, above.
[105] It is unclear what would even *count* as a PMS by itself. A list of instruments? In a certain sequence? A set of ordered pairs of measures and associated instrument groups?

by implication, abstract objects of culture generally. If musical works can be created, and by human agency, it stands to reason—or at least recommends itself on grounds of symmetry—that they could be destroyed, possibly in the same way. So let us reflect, for a moment, on what it would take to destroy Beethoven's Quintet op. 16—for it to henceforth, from a certain point, not *exist*.

There is a range of possible responses to this query, and I survey them in order of strength, beginning with the most defiant, as it were. (1) Nothing can destroy it, once created; the most that can occur is its becoming permanently "lost"—i.e., never again entering anyone's consciousness. (2) Little short of the destruction of the human species, leaving no successors, would suffice to destroy it. (3) The permanent elimination of all records and memories of it would suffice to destroy it (this is equivalent to "no one knows of the work, or ever will again"). (4) Disintegration of the musical practice in which recognizable performance of the work is possible—including instruments, techniques, capacities, stylistic knowledge—would suffice to destroy it (this is equivalent to "no one can play the work, or ever will be able to again"). (5) Loss of the musical tradition and background knowledge necessary for the work to be adequately understood—i.e., for its kinetic, aesthetic, artistic and other features to be properly experienced and gauged—would suffice to destroy it (this is equivalent to "no one understands what the work means, conveys, expresses, or ever will again"). (6) Absence of all material embodiments of the work—scores, original manuscripts, recordings, live performances—though not of conceptions and memories and reproductive capacities in individual minds, would yet mean that the work had (at least temporarily?) ceased to exist. (7) Irreversible large-scale neglect of, or disrespect for, the work would be enough to destroy it (this is equivalent to "hardly anyone cares about this work anymore, or ever will").

Having sketched this range of responses, I won't attempt to settle at which point, exactly, the work can be most justifiably thought to have ceased to exist.[106] I'd guess the most defensible answer is to be found in the middle of this range, somewhere around (3), but I'm not sure what would be the rationale for it.

---

[106] There is some question, for one, about how to interpret the *permanence* or *irreversibility* conditions built into some of these criteria.

On the other hand, the residual pull of (1) is hard for me to deny. Once a PSS is indicated, in a coherent musical context, it *might* just inhabit the abstract realms of the universe, it seems, forever. Why should it lapse into nonexistence, one might ask, just because we do? It is perhaps a comforting thought that the nonmaterial products of culture, once given their start, may be logically destined to outlast us— at least in the rarefied sense here in question.

PART THREE

MUSICAL MATTERS

11 *The Concept of Music*

Music, in its most common signification, designates a familiar art form, or the activities associated with it, or else the products of such activities. But what is this art form or sphere of culture, exactly? How shall we describe true instances of these activities, or characterize their products? This is the task faced by a philosophically adequate elucidation of the concept of music. Not having come across such, I shall attempt to provide one in this essay.

A number of years ago I offered a general characterization of what it can now mean to call something *art,* in the most inclusive modern sense.[1] The definition I arrive at is notable for withholding from the general notion of art, in its current sense, virtually all intrinsic lineaments traditionally accorded it. A few words on the relation between that endeavor and the present one are thus in order. This essay aims to

---

[1]See Chapter 1 and its sequel, Chapter 3, above. The definition proposed there, recall, went like this: "*X* is an artwork *iff* it is an object seriously intended for regarding-as-a-work-of-art, i.e., regarding (treating, taking) in any *way or ways earlier (prior, preexisting) artworks were correctly regarded (treated, taken),*" where the phrase in italics is to be understood in both a referentially transparent sense (picking out intrinsically conceived ways of regard that happen to be among the correct ones for some past artworks) and a referentially opaque sense (satisfiable thus by such as: ways that *these* artworks were correctly regarded, for some indicated works).

characterize a *particular* art form, whose general profile goes back to antiquity, whose exemplars have certain ineliminable intrinsic features (e.g., audibility), and whose practice will be assumed, at least provisionally, to exhibit a certain degree of unity of purpose—more, at any rate, than seems exhibited by the current practice of art, comprising any and all arts, *tout court*. In other words, "music" will be here presumed to have not only a *narrower extension* than "art" in the broad sense, but also a more *specific intension*. The convincingness or usefulness of the characterization I arrive at can serve as a measure, retrospectively, of the validity of that presumption.

What I propose to do, then, is give a working answer to what is in one sense the most basic philosophical question about music, namely, *what is it?* What makes something an instance of music? What is the distinction between music and nonmusic?

II

The object is to give a set of conditions that are necessary and sufficient for musichood. We will have succeeded if *all and only* those things that, on reflection and after consulting our intuitions, we are willing to count as music—in the primary (i.e., artistic) sense—satisfy the proposed conditions. These conditions would then comprise a definition of music taken neutrally and would serve as an answer to the straightforward question "What is music?" My aim is to capture the widest, most inclusive central usage of "music" current at the present time, though stopping short of what are clearly metaphorical extensions. The concept to be explicated will, predictably, be that possessed by twentieth-century Westerners, but it is one intended to have application to phenomena all over the world. We want our analysis of "music" to be adequate not only to Beethoven symphonies and Bob Dylan songs, but to whatever ethnomusicologists, say, would agree is music in cultures other than our own.[2]

---

[2]However, the suggestion that we should take account not only of non-Western *musics* but of non-Western *concepts of music* seems to be fundamentally misguided. If "their" concept of music is significantly different from "ours," then very likely they do not have a concept of *music* at all, but a concept of *something else*—which of course may be similar to the phenomenon we call music, with many overlapping instances.

We should at the outset distinguish the question "What is music?" from some others with which it might be confused. One of these is the question of what *kind* of thing a piece of music is—that is to say, what ontological or metaphysical category (e.g., particular, universal, mental, physical) it belongs to and what its identity conditions are. This question, addressed in essays elsewhere in this book (Chapters 4, 5, and 10), can to a large extent be dealt with independently of the distinction between music and nonmusic, and vice versa. We can determine what it is to count something as an instance or occasion of music without deciding precisely what ontological characterization pieces of music should receive.

A second question is how we generally *recognize* something to be music—what criteria we employ in making judgments of that sort, by ear, in ordinary situations. It should be apparent that this is more a psychological question than a conceptual one. It asks, in effect, for *typical* features of music which are aurally accessible and prominently noted—e.g., regular meter, definite rhythm, melody, harmony. But something might be a piece of music that lacked almost all typical musical features, and might possess many such features without being a piece of music. There are, furthermore, conditions essential to being a piece of music which are not even directly hearable, and which thus cannot figure as criteria of *recognition*. Nor, since our criteria for recognition are fallible, will everything that satisfies them in fact be an instance of music. A third question asks what it is that makes a piece of music *good*, or *great*, or just *better* than some other piece of music. This question is clearly an evaluative one and should be kept separate from the fundamentally descriptive inquiry into the bounds of music per se, as contrasted with nonmusic.

It has often been suggested that music be defined as *organized sound*. But this is patently inadequate. While sonic organization has some plausibility as a necessary feature of music, it is hardly a sufficient

Since "music" is *our* concept, we will get scant illumination as to what it is by inquiring into concepts, only resembling that of music, which are prevalent in other cultures. Some cultures may simply lack both music and the broad concept of music, or they might just possibly have music without having the concept of it, at least reflectively. But if a phenomenon in another culture with some resemblance to music simply *cannot* be encompassed in the broadest notion of music we can discover in our own conceptual scheme, then it is a confusion to say, for instance, out of misplaced liberality, that it is at least music "to them."

one. The output of a jackhammer, the ticking of a metronome, the shouts of a drill sergeant during a march, the chirping of a sparrow, the roar of a lion, the whine of a police siren, a presidential campaign speech—all are organized sounds but not instances of music.[3]

We can prevent the roar of the lion and the chirping of the sparrow from being counted as music if we amend the initial proposal so as to require that the organized sound be *humanly* produced—or at least produced by intelligent creatures to whom we might accord the status of *persons*. For it seems that one would not strictly consider anything music which was not the outcome of intentional activity on the part of an intelligent being. On the other hand, this may just be indicative of a deeper reason for excluding roars and chirps—that they do not exhibit the appropriate aim or purpose for qualifying as music. I will return to this point later.

Even if we introduce "humanly" as a qualification to "organized sound," we are still left with various sonic items mentioned above which conform to this conception but are not indeed instances of music. We might seek to exclude many of these (e.g., the jackhammer output, the presidential speech) by insisting on those features of music which an elementary textbook of music considers definitive (e.g., *melody, rhythm, harmony*). But that this will not do is brought home to us by early music, contemporary music, and music of non-Western cultures. Gregorian chant and shakuhachi[4] solos are music but lack harmony. Takemitsu's *Water Music* (derived from taped raindrop sounds), African drumming, and Webern's pointillistic *Five Pieces*, op. 5, lack melody but are nonetheless music. Certain kinds of atmospheric modern

---

[3] Since I will ultimately retain "organized sound" as a *necessary* condition of music, a few clarifications are in order regarding my understanding of the phrase. First, I certainly understand it to comprise the organization of sound *and silence*, or sounds and silences taken together; there are very few imaginable musics, and no actual musics, for which silence—the space between sounds—would not be a structural principle. Thus, to spare a word for Cage's notorious 4′33″, we can include it in music if we like, as a limiting case of the organization of sound-and-silence; and this is made easier, of course, if we recognize that Cage has in effect organized for listening, at a very abstract level, the anticipated but unpredictable sounds that will occur at any performance of his piece. Second—and a piece such as Cage's, where organization takes the form of *framing*, illustrates this as well—the notion of "organizing" should be understood widely as covering what might be more idiomatically put in some cases as "designing" or "arranging."

[4] A low-pitched wooden end-blown flute used in Japanese traditional music.

jazz and synthesizer compositions have virtually no rhythms, yet they are music also. Melody, rhythm, and harmony are important features of a lot of music, but they nonetheless remain only typical features for music in general, not necessary ones. In fact, it should be apparent that there are no longer any intrinsic properties of sound that are required for something possibly to be music, and none that absolutely excludes a sonic phenomenon from that category.

It might be thought that what makes African drumming, modern jazz, and Mozart piano concertos music is that they are all organizations of sound which stir the soul or, more soberly, affect the *emotions*. Or perhaps ones that express the emotions of their *creators*. But although emotional evocation and emotional expression are central aspects of most music, they are not definitive ones. The roar of the lion and the whine of the police siren induce emotion in the auditor perhaps more surely than most music does. The orator's speech and the poet's lyric (possibly also the lion's roar) may express their creators' emotions as much as does the *Pathétique* Sonata. On the other hand, some music seems neither the embodiment of a creator's inner state nor a stimulus to emotional response in hearers, but rather an abstract configuration of sounds in motion and/or a reflection of some nonindividual—or even nonhuman—aspect of things. Examples of this might be some Javanese gamelan music, Bach's *Art of the Fugue,* George Crumb's *Makrokosmos,* Conlon Nancarrow's *Studies for Player Piano,* and Tibetan ritual music. So it is clear that music cannot be defined by some special relation to emotional life; no such relation holds for *all* music and *only* for music. Nor can music be understood as humanly organized sound that transmits or communicates *ideas* or the like. For this net is far too wide. Though it may include much music, it also includes sirens, shouts, and messages in Morse code.

It should be fairly obvious that what our preliminary definition lacks, and what is needed to get close to the concept of music, is some sufficiently general notion of the *aim* or *purpose* for which the humanly organized sound in question is produced. Music is such sounds produced (or determined) with a certain *intent*. But what intent is this? Since music in the primary sense is an art (or artistic activity), and the arts are doubtless the foremost arena for aesthetic appreciation, it might seem that music could be defined as "humanly organized sound for the purpose of *aesthetic appreciation*." Indeed, this is an advance over "organized sound," but there are significant flaws in this formulation which prevent us from resting with it as an acceptable definition.

One flaw is that there are musics in the world which do not seem aimed at what we can comfortably call "aesthetic appreciation." Music for the accompaniment of ritual, music for the intensification of warlike spirit, and music for dancing are all examples of musics whose proper appreciation does not involve contemplative and distanced apprehension of pure patterns of sound, or put otherwise, does not call for specific attention to its beauty or other aesthetic qualities. Another, perhaps more serious, flaw is the failure of the definition to exclude verbal arts such as drama and (especially) poetry. For poetry, at least in its spoken guise, consists of humanly organized sounds for aesthetic appreciation; it so happens that in that case the sounds are words meaningfully arranged.

We can deal with the poetry problem by requiring that the organized sounds in music be intended for listening to primarily *as sounds,* and not primarily as symbols of discursive thought. This is not to say that music cannot contain words—clearly songs, opera, *musique concrète,* and collage musics do—only that to constitute music the verbal component must either be combined with more purely sonorous material or, if not so accompanied, be such that one is to attend to it primarily for its sonic qualities and whatever is supervenient on them.

The other difficulty is that regarding the ultimate *end* of attending to organized sound as sound. We need to find a replacement for "aesthetic appreciation," since this is too narrow an end to comprise all activity that we would count as the making of music. One suggestion would be this: that music, whether absorbed reflectively in a concert hall or reacted to frenetically during a village rite, is engaged in so that a certain *heightening* of life, or of consciousness, is attained. In other words, all sound phenomena that are categorizable as music seem aimed at the *enrichment or intensification of experience* via engagement with organized sounds as such. I claim that this is indeed the central core of the music-making intention. It is this that enables us to construe examples from any number of times and places as examples of the artistic-cultural activity we conceive of as music, despite the absence of any limiting intrinsic sonic characteristics beyond that of mere audibility.

An instructive hypothetical example that we would not count as music, and which our definition in its present state just manages to exclude, is the following. Imagine a sequence of sounds devised by a team of psychological researchers which are such that when subjects are in a semiconscious condition and are exposed to these sounds, the subjects enter psychedelic states of marked pleasurability. Such a sequence is not a piece of music; yet it is humanly organized sound for the purpose (arguably) of enriching experience. It does not, however, seek this enrichment through requiring a person's *attention* to the sounds as such. Sound organized for our own good but which does not ask us to listen to or otherwise actively engage with it is not music.

Now that our definition is approaching adequacy we must add one minor qualification, making explicit something only implicit until now: namely, that the organization of sound must be *temporal* organization if the product is to count as musical. What other sort of organization could there be? Well, one can imagine an art in which the point was to produce colorful instantaneous combinations of sounds—i.e., chords of vanishingly brief duration—which were to be savored independently, each in splendid isolation from the next. My intuition is that we would not regard this art as a type of music (though existing musical knowledge and technique would be relevant to its successful practice). It would be the auditory equivalent of jam tasting or rose smelling—the receiving of a sensory impression, sometimes complex, but one for which temporal development was not an issue. Music as we conceive it seems as essentially an art of time as it is an art of sound.

Our complete definition of music would then go roughly like this:

> *Music* = df sounds temporally organized by a person for the purpose of enriching or intensifying experience through active engagement (e.g., listening, dancing, performing) with the sounds regarded primarily, or in significant measure,[5] as sounds.

I believe this formulation covers all that it should—e.g., classical music, folk music, party music, avant-garde music, opera, the varied

[5] The point of this last qualification is to allow for cases, such as that presented by rap music, where conceptual concept verbally conveyed may be of an importance at least equal to what is offered in the way of sound organization for its own sake. Perhaps rap music is not *primarily* intended to be listened to for its distinctive sonic (e.g., rhythmic, dynamic, timbral) features, but these still constitute a *significant*, if not the *most significant*, focus of attention.

phenomena studied my ethnomusicologists—and nothing it should not (including Muzak).[6]

Some brief observations on the analysis, highlighting its salient features: (1) The analysis accords to music certain intrinsic characteristics, albeit limited ones—to wit, soundingness or audibility, and temporal structure. (2) The analysis is intentionalistic and human-centered; it is people (or the near like) who make music in a purposive way, and not unthinking Nature. (3) The analysis purports to be adequate in application cross-culturally, though of course it is not intended as an analysis of any other culture's concept. (4) The analysis explicitly ascribes a normative attitude to the makers or offerers of music: they necessarily conceive or intend their efforts as worth interacting with.[7] (5) The analysis is creator-oriented or creator-driven: producers make their production music, through their intentional orientation in bringing it forth, and not the receivers or consumers of such production through anything they might do.[8]

[6] An interesting challenge to my proposal as it stands was offered by Jenefer Robinson (in correspondence). Are kids, she asks, banging on pots and pans for fun thereby making music? Well, we need to know more about these particular urchins. Are they aiming to have fun—i.e., heighten their experience—through attention to the collection of sounds produced, engaging, say, bodily or otherwise, with the rhythms that, helter-skelter, emerge? Or are they mainly just blowing off nervous energy, exercising their arms, and above all enjoying the disrupting effect likely produced on others, adults in particular? If the latter, then there is no question of their being involved in music. If the former, then we may just have to allow music is being made, albeit of an unsophisticated, all-but-oblivious-to-tradition sort. But this seems all right to me.

[7] By contrast, the definition offered of art in general in Chapter 1, above, ascribes normative ends to art makers only implicitly. This feature, however, is in the end explicitly acknowledged in the revised formulations of Chapter 3.

[8] Having proposed an analysis of music with a certain amount of specific content, we may now acknowledge that certain tendencies in recent music (or would-be music), especially those beholden to performance art, conceptual art, and the most extreme laboratory serialism, might reasonably engender skepticism as to whether *any* circumscribable intent, any core beyond the sonic, can still be said to attach to all that goes under the name of music. In this skeptical vein there is something to be said, it seems, for a definition of music modeled rather on that I have offered for art in general, to wit: "X is music *iff* it is humanly and temporally organized sounds intended for overall taking as any prior music is or was properly taken." Adopting this would in effect be allowing that music's essence, like that of art generally, had become almost purely historical, all traces of traditionally musical intent having been finally extruded. By marginalizing this reflection in the depths of a footnote, however, I am suggesting that we are not *quite* at that stage yet.

III

I now raise some further points about the concept of music. The first is that there is a distinction between what *is* music, and what can be *treated* or *regarded* as music. One way to ignore this distinction is to claim, in the spirit of John Cage's Zen-inspired reflections, that any and all sounds are music. This is simply false, and the most cogent of Cage's reflections fails to establish it. What Cage shows perhaps is that any sounds can be listened to *as if* they were music (i.e., attentively, with regard to form, with emotional sensitivity), that one can transform (just about) any sonic environment into an occasion for receptive awareness. It does not follow that all sound events are at present music. The whirr of my blender and the whistling of the wind are not instances of music. They could only be such if they were produced, or proffered, for a certain purpose, as indicated above. But one can *adopt* attitudes toward them which are appropriate for music, with varying degrees of reward.

This Cagean view of music connects to a use of "music" with some currency, in which the word serves as in effect a predicate of experience. The rule of usage is roughly this. If there is a musical experience going on—characterized in some phenomenological fashion or other—then there is music; if not, then the situation is devoid of music. The auditor, through having the right kind of experience, determines whether music is present or is occurring; the source of the sounds experienced in the appropriate way, their raison d'être—or even whether they actually exist—is regarded as irrelevant.[9] It should be clear that from my perspective this is a degenerate notion of music, which obscures more than it illuminates, and denies to music several features that I have argued are central to it, namely, sentient origin, artistic intent, and public character. Furthermore, it is a hopelessly relativistic notion, making the status of anything as music (even Mozart piano concertos) relative to each individual listener and occasion. The concepts of a distinctive musical *experience,* or of the hearing of something *as* music, are useful ones, to be sure, but there is little to be gained by collapsing them into the cultural and objective category of music itself.

[9]A characterization of music along such lines is offered by Thomas Clifton in the opening chapter of his *Music as Heard* (New Haven: Yale University Press, 1983).

A second point is this. The concept of music we have captured in our definition is the concept of a kind of *artistic* (or expressive) *activity* and the *products* thereof. And this is properly thought of as the central use of the term "music." But it must also be admitted that there is a use of "music" in which it means simply a type of *sonic phenomenon*.[10] Whereas "music" in the central sense is defined by a characteristic intention or aim and contains no limits on audible features of sounds involved, "music" in this secondary sense insists on certain audible features and makes intention or aim irrelevant. In this sense, anything that aurally resembles paradigms of music or exhibits enough of the typical features of music can be called "music."[11] Thus, although birdsong, the sound of the Aeolian harp, the rhythmic gurgling of a stream, chant for the sole purpose of pacifying the gods, and so on would not count as music in the central sense, they could qualify on this looser usage. And such "musical" phenomena might merit analytic study (with regard to meter, rhythm, tessitura, and so on) as much as some, and more than other, examples of music in the "artistic activity" sense.[12]

[10]Unlike the "phenomenological" (or "experientialist") use of *music* just discussed, this "sonic phenomenon" use at least operates "music" as a public, observable, and objective category.

[11]Correlatively, we have the term "musical," which is often applied to anything audible that exhibits a number of the typical features of music—e.g., melody, rhythm, flow, continuity, teleology—independently of whether the phenomenon in question is a genuine instance of music.

[12]The musical semiotician Jean Molino has introduced a tripartite distinction concerning music, according to which it may be viewed from the neutral, purely acoustic perspective (i.e., as a "sonic phenomenon"), the creational, productive perspective, or the esthesic, receptive perspective. (See Molino, *Musique en jeu* [Paris: Editions du Seuil, 1975]. Molino's division has been taken up and extended, in an approving vein, by another musical semiotician, J. J. Nattiez.) Molino suggests that these perspectives or levels are in some way distinct from and irreducible to one another, and thus that there can be no integral definition of music, but only three different definitions, corresponding to the three possible perspectives or levels. If I have succeeded in what I set out to do in this essay, of course, then Molino is wrong. My proposed definition comprises and synthesizes all three aspects, though under the guiding hand of the second—the creational—which, I have suggested, is natural to the characterization of something that is first and foremost an artistic or expressive activity.

With regard to attempts to characterize the essence of music semiotically, I offer the following brief caveats: (a) Music does *not* straightforwardly constitute a *language* or *code,* though it, like many other cultural manifestations, can be *used* to *communicate* something in a given context. (b) Music makers need not *intend* to signify anything,

My third, and last, point: At the beginning of this essay I stressed the descriptive or classificatory nature of the beast being stalked, to wit, the basic and broad concept of music. I did not, however, mean to deny the force of the impulse or tendency to use "music" in a strongly normative or evaluative way. We can at this point even fruitfully acknowledge it, by invoking yet another distinction, that between the *concept* of music and what we might call individual *conceptions* of music. If this essay has succeeded in limning a general concept of music that most reflective speakers of our language would allow conforms with its current employment in a neutral sense, still many speakers would be inclined to insist that such an analysis does not capture how *they* "conceive of music." And of course they would be right; different people *do* conceive of music differently. That is to say, they have varying *conceptions* of music.

What do I mean by "conceptions"? Roughly, a way of organizing the entire musical field, recognized at some neutral level, in terms of *ideals, norms,* and *paradigms.* Different individuals regard different genres or types of music as more *central* than others to their idea of music, of what music can or should do, of what music is best as music. This normative idea—what I am calling a conception—is sometimes expressed as a judgment of what is "really" music and what is not (e.g., "Now *that's* what I call music!"). Our varying conceptions of music express our divergent values in regard to music, our sense of what is most worthy and/or representative in the field of music. For some, symphonic music occupies center place in their conceptions, for others progressive rock, for others bebop jazz, for others bluegrass, for others only the severest efforts of Minimalist composition, and for still others, the music of India, Indonesia, or Japan. But presumably all such individuals would acknowledge, in a sober moment, the existence of genres as incontrovertibly music which do not occupy a very central place, or even any at all, in their own personal pantheons. Even to say something like "That stuff doesn't loom very large in *my* notion of

---

though such signification may emerge out of the musical material and the cultural matrix in which it appears. (c) Music is not always and necessarily *symbolic,* or even meaningful; meaning is a widespread potential of most musical systems, and a resulting feature of almost any instance of music, but it is clearly not a *defining* condition of music on the conception I have defended.

music" is implicitly to acknowledge a broad classificatory concept of music against which a personally tailored normative conception is operating in contrast.

Finally, suppose we now allow ourselves to ask, given our analysis of the basic concept of music, why music is *important* to us. Well, it seems that to answer this would be to explore the manners and means by which actively engaging with organized sounds, intentionally produced for such purpose, can enrich experience. And doing that most fruitfully would involve considering specific kinds of music, and particular examples within kinds. For different musics are important to us for different reasons. Some music enriches primarily through conveying emotional content, some more through stimulating the ordering faculties of the mind. Some music exercises the imagination in virtue of its representational aspects, some music satisfies particularly by giving a sense of tradition and shared community. Listening to some music seems to provide insights into the mysteries of the psyche; listening to other music seems to illuminate the underlying pattern of the universe at large. Some music makes one pleasurably aware of one's body; other music makes one feel bodiless. And some music seems capable of effecting real and relatively permanent alterations in the outlooks and attitudes of listeners. But if it is *music* at all, whether good or bad or indifferent, it must, I suggest, display the combination of intrinsic and intentional features sketched earlier.

12 *Truth in Music*

"What, after all, could we literally mean by
characterizing a sonata as true?"[1]

I

The notion of truth clearly has some application to representational
works of art. Representational works provide a content that can be
held up and compared to the world or parts thereof. A representational artwork presents its subject in a certain way, which may or may
not accord with the way the subject actually is. A painting shows
Lackawanna Depot in 1860 as the terminus of ten tracks. But how
many were there actually? A sculpture represents Napoleon as of
noble mien. But was he? A novel portrays New York society in the
1890s as a cruel place. But was it so? Since representational artworks
can have real subjects, they can be true or false to those subjects; they
can represent them as they are, or as they are not.

The concept of the fictional provides another way of getting a
handle on the truth potential of representational art. Representational
works, correctly interpreted, generate fictional worlds—i.e., make
certain propositions fictionally true (or fictional).[2] Thus, the aforementioned painting generates a fictional world in which Lackawanna

---

[1] Douglas N. Morgan, "Must Art Tell the Truth?" *Journal of Aesthetics and Art Criticism*, 26 (1967): 23.

[2] See Kendall Walton, "Pictures and Make-Believe," *Philosophical Review*, 82 (1973): 283–319.

Depot exists and possesses ten tracks, or alternatively, makes it fictional that Lackawanna Depot exists and possesses ten tracks. Such works can then be considered true insofar as their fictional worlds mirror the actual world—i.e., insofar as their fictional truths are also actual truths.

Thus what we mean when we call a representational artwork "true" can usually be captured by one or the other of these formulations:

(R) If an artwork represents the world in such and such a way, or as having such and such properties, then the artwork is "true" *iff* the world in fact is such and such a way, or has such and such properties.

(F) If an artwork makes it fictionally true (or fictional) that *P* (where *P* is some proposition), then the artwork is "true" *iff* it is actually the case that *P*.[3]

Note that when we call a painting or novel "true" on either of these grounds, we do not presuppose that the painting actually *asserts* anything about the Lackawanna Depot, or that the novel literally *claims* anything about New York society. However, the connection with statemental truth is not very remote: a representational work is "true" if its representings-as or its fictional propositions, respectively, would be true *if* taken as statements, claims, or assertions.

When we turn to nonrepresentational art, however—and I will take absolute music as my primary point of reference in this essay—it is not clear that the idea of truth has any foothold. Since absolute music does not represent anything, it cannot represent it in any particular manner. A piece of absolute music, furthermore, does not generate a fictional world; there are no conventions of music listening which enjoin us to regard a certain sequence of sounds as making any proposition fictionally true. So how can works of absolute music be in any way true or false?

Granted, musical works typically lack a representational content that can be assessed for correctness vis-à-vis the world. However, musical works have other sorts of content, in particular *expressive* content. All we need, then, is that such contents be appropriately held

[3] I leave aside here obvious complications having to do with truth *in a respect* as opposed to truth *simpliciter*.

up to related aspects of the world, and the degree of match noted. To the extent that the content of the music and the aspect of the world agree we might speak of the work as "true," much as we do when representational content accords with the actual condition of objects represented. Correspondence between something in the music and something related to it in the world can be seen as weakly analogous to the matching between representation and represented object that is at the base of one notion of truth in representational art.

Again, musical works as we ordinarily understand them do not generate fictional worlds, or make propositions fictionally true. However, it might be the case that musical works, on reflective listening, tend to bring certain propositions to mind, particularly ones concerning the work's expressive content, which it may sometimes be appropriate to interpret the work as putting forward in a mild degree. Let us say that such propositions are *suggested* by the work—as opposed to being asserted by, or being made fictional by, the work. Actual truth of suggested propositions of musical works can be seen as weakly analogous to actual truth of fictional propositions of representational works.

So two general notions of truth for nonrepresentational artworks would be these:

(CT) A nonrepresentational artwork is "true" *iff* some aspect or feature of the work *corresponds to or matches* some aspects or feature of the world to which it is appropriately or standardly referred. (Call this "correspondent truth.")

(PT) A nonrepresentational artwork is "true" *iff* some *proposition* about the world which is *suggested* by the work is actually true. (Call this "propositional truth.")

My objective in this essay is to propose and explore some specific senses of "truth in music" which conform to one or the other of the above general conceptions.[4] Whether there *is* any such truth in musical works

---

[4] In this essay I am interested primarily in ways musical works might be "true" which are analogous to the ways representational artworks are characteristically "true"— that is to say, in virtue of mirroring or reflecting the *extra*musical world. Thus, I will not be concerned with notions—such as Wilson Coker's notion of "congeneric truth"— wherein musical works possess truth in virtue of certain intramusical relations between various parts of the work. Similarly, I will not be entertaining the idea of quasi-fictional truths arising within the autonomous, self-referential microcosms of absolute music, as intimated, for example, in the writings of DeWitt Parker.

is an open question, of course. It depends on whether one can defend the claim, with respect to a particular species of musical truth and in a particular case, that a musical work *is* appropriately or standardly referred to or compared with something outside itself, or that a musical work *does* suggest some particular extramusical proposition. I will attempt to defend such claims in a few instances. But my primary aim will be served, however, if I can succeed in showing that there are interesting senses of "musical truth" whose application would not entirely lack point.

II Correspondent Truth

In this section I consider some possible uses of "true" in regard to music that conform to the correspondence model, CT. In the following section I consider uses that fall under the propositional model, PT.

Although a work of absolute music lacks a representational aspect that can be true to the world, it has sometimes been claimed that there can be something true about such a work's *expression*. One way to interpret this claim is in terms of a Langerian hypothesis about musical expression. According to this hypothesis, a passage of music P expresses emotions[5] that are isomorphic to P—i.e., which share with P a certain form or shape.[6] A musical passage exhibits a complicated melodic, harmonic, rhythmic, dynamic, and textural pattern over time, which pattern may be analogous in various respects to the patterns

[5] In this essay I use the term "emotion" to cover a wide range of psychological properties and states, including emotions proper, but also feelings, moods, attitudes, character traits, and so on.

[6] See Susanne Langer, *Philosophy in a New Key* (Cambridge: Harvard University Press, 1942), chap. 8. By calling this hypothesis "Langerian" I mean to sidestep the issue of whether this hypothesis could strictly be attributed to Langer. Langer's discussion in chap. 8 is intriguingly obscure. My view of what she is proposing is roughly this: "Music is not symbolic/expressive of specific, commonly recognized emotions such as fear, love, hope, sorrow, but it is more than just generally symbolic/expressive of emotional life as a whole. Rather, a particular passage symbolizes all those emotional conditions (or the class of emotional conditions) which share its specific morphology or shape. These emotional experience classes cut across usual lines of distinction for emotions. They are characterized not so much in terms of quality of inner feeling, or in terms of thought content, but rather in terms of pattern of progression and development, of tension and release." Thus, Langer probably held what I am calling the "Langerian" hypothesis for classes of emotions, though not for specific emotions.

traced over time by dimensions of emotional states—quality, intensity, complexity, rate, and so on. The idea is that a musical passage expresses an emotion whose structure in the foregoing sense closely mirrors or resembles the structure of the passage. Langer believed that music had the ability to articulate and draw attention to the structure of human emotions by so expressing, or as she would say, symbolizing them.

There are many difficulties with the Langerian hypothesis, of course. One is the question of exactly what the structure or form of an emotion consists in. Another is the assumption that all instances of a given emotion in fact exhibit a common form or structure. A third is the assumption that the particular manner in which an emotion progresses is reasonably distinctive of it. But I will set aside these difficulties here. I wish simply to consider what notion of truth for musical passages this picture of expression might underwrite. Clearly, on the correspondent model, it would go something like this: A musical passage's structure is a feature of it. The emotion expressed by that passage, or more particularly, the structure of that emotion, is a feature of the world, and moreover one to which the passage's structure is appropriately and standardly referred. It is common for a passage P expressing E to be assessed for what it is internally about P and E that makes the one express the other. Thus, one might propose that a musical passage P is true (L) *iff* its structure matches or corresponds to the structure of the emotion expressed by P.

There is a grave defect in this formula, however, given the Langerian hypothesis. For what emotion is it that is expressed by P? Why, it is just that emotion whose structure matches that of P! But if so, then *every* musical passage that expresses some emotion will be true (L), because its structure will mirror the structure of the emotion it expresses just as any expressive passage does. Truth (L) would thus appear to be a fairly worthless commodity.

We can improve its market value, though, if we accept the idea of music/emotion isomorphism but reject the Langerian hypothesis concerning expression. That is to say, we can reject the claim that expression is *entirely* a function of structural mirroring. In that case, treating "true (L)" as a comparative term, musical passages will differ in the degree to which they are true (L).

It clearly is unreasonable to think that music/emotion isomorphism is the sole determinant of what a passage expresses. In fact, this should be obvious if one simply reflects that very small units of music (e.g., three measures) can already convey fairly definite emotional content, but they can hardly be thought to do so by limning the essential development pattern of some emotion. If we take expression to be a matter of what emotional predicate provides the *best metaphor* for the emergent regional quality of the passage and is drawn attention to by the music[7]—or just what emotion we are inclined to say the music most *sounds like* on the whole—then there are plausibly several other factors that contribute to the resulting expression in music. Among them are these: what emotion the passage typically evokes in a receptive listener, what emotion seems likely to have been felt by the composer of such a passage, what emotion the passage resembles the characteristic verbal manifestations of,[8] what emotion the passage resembles the characteristic nonverbal behavioral manifestations of,[9] what emotion is conventionally or traditionally associated with music of a type to which the passage belongs. Since there are these other grounds of expression the Langerian hypothesis is clearly false; thus some passages will fail to be true (L) to any appreciable degree.

But what, after all, does truth (L) come to? It amounts to a measure of the extent to which a passage's expression depends on internal structural mirroring—as opposed to anything else. But is truth in this sense something we are likely to be interested in? Is expression based primarily on structural mirroring particularly noteworthy or admirable? Two observations are germane here. First, it does not seem *entirely* inapt to say that a musical passage is truer if its expressiveness is based on natural connections, as opposed to purely conventional or arbitrary ones. Thus a loud, rising chromatic passage for strings which expresses mounting anger seems reasonably called truer than a passage consisting of the pianissimo tinkling of a triangle which expresses

---

[7]Cf. Nelson Goodman, *Languages of Art* (Indianapolis: Bobbs-Merrill, 1968), chap. 2. (For a later proposal regarding expressiveness, see Chapter 14, below.)

[8]For example, a characteristic verbal manifestation of grief is speech that is slow, halting, punctuated by gasps and sighs, falling in tone. It is clear how a musical passage might resemble such a manifestation.

[9]For example, a characteristic nonverbal behavioral manifestation of elation is hopping up and down and waving one's hands. Again it is clear how a musical passage might resemble such to some extent.

mounting anger in virtue of a longstanding association, on some story we could tell, between passages of that kind and angry situations.[10] Second, since Langerian expression involves structural mirroring, a passage that is significantly Langerianly expressive may remind us, via its own structure, of the inner movement and flow of the emotion expressed—i.e., of its "true nature" on a familiar identification of the internal and the true.[11] A passage whose expression is based on accidental associations, or even on resemblance to behavioral manifestations, will not do this. So there is some reason to think of a Langerianly expressive passage as truer to its object than a passage with primarily non-Langerian expression. I conclude that "true (L)" could have some use, and captures something intuitively truthlike. Of course, truth (L) is only as coherent as Langerian expression itself, and there remains fundamental skepticism about that.

I turn now to another way in which we might recognize something as true in a musical work in virtue of its expression. This depends on the notion of expression-as, which I develop by analogy with representation-as. It is a familiar observation that a painting cannot just represent S simpliciter; it must rather always represent S as X, for some X. Unlike a name, a painting denotes its referent in such a way that its formal features properly read are taken to furnish that referent with a representational identity or character. Thus, John Doe may be represented as John Doe, but also as a general, as a seducer, as a man with a harelip, as a cassowary, and perhaps even as a piece of cheese. It goes without saying that some of these manners of representation may be true to him, and some false. On Goodman's well-known analysis, if a painting represents S, and is (as a whole) an X-representing picture, then the painting represents S as an X.[12]

---

[10]Less hypothetically, one can think of the association tying organ music in lower registers to solemnity or sacredness, or the association of trumpet tone and military spirit. An actual judgment of differential truth (L) would be this: the opening of Beethoven's Sixth Symphony is truer (L) vis-à-vis the expression of pastoral feelings than is the clarinet's quail imitation in the second movement.

[11]I am not claiming that we can *come to know* the structure of emotions just from listening. The scenario I have in mind is rather like this. One listens to passage P; one notes that it expresses E; one compares the form of P with the known form of E; one surmises that expression here is primarily Langerian; one has one's attention drawn to the structure of E by the music.

[12]*Languages of Art*, pp. 28–29.

Consider a musical passage that expresses melancholy. Might it further express melancholy *as* something or other? By analogy with representation-as, it seems that the passage would have to be an E-expressing passage, for some E, as well as expressing melancholy. However, there is a problem with this right off. It is not clear what a passage's being E-expressing can amount to as distinct from its just expressing E. What grounds the distinction in the representational case, namely, that when a painting represents S as opposed to being S-representing it denotes a particular individual, does not operate in the case of expression. A passage that expresses E does not denote a particular instance of E.

But if being E-expressing does not differ from just expressing E, then how can a passage expressing melancholy and also E express melancholy *as* E? Suppose the passage expresses both melancholy and agitation. Since the passage is both melancholy-expressing and agitation-expressing, what ground can there be for taking it to express melancholy *as* agitated? Why that rather than agitation *as* melancholic? Putting the problem generally, when, if ever, would it be appropriate to hold that a passage expressing emotions θ and ϕ expressed either θ *as* ϕ or ϕ *as* θ? How is a passage expressing θ *as* ϕ different from a passage merely expressing θ *and* ϕ? The asymmetry present in the case of representation-as, where subject (what the picture denotes) and characterizer (what kind of picture it is) are clearly distinguishable, seems missing in the sphere of compound expression. What I will attempt to do, however, is recover this in a different guise.

What we should note is that if a passage P expresses, say, melancholy and agitation, it does not necessarily express *both* melancholic agitation and agitated melancholy. Why? Because although "melancholic" and "agitated" are sufficiently apt metaphors for the sound quality of P, "melancholic agitation" and "agitated melancholy" may not be equally apt metaphorical descriptions of that quality, and may not be drawn attention to equally by the music. The two descriptions, certainly, are not equivalent in connotation. They contain different emphases, putting different emotions in center place. One makes *agitation* the primary condition and *melancholy* the modification, while the other reverses this. Depending on the passage in question, one description or the other will seem more fitting.

However, such fittingness will not be entirely a matter of which individual emotion is more strongly displayed by the passage. For we appear to have an inclination to treat some emotions or states as more eligible objects of primary expression than others. For example, imagine a passage that we find both resigned and lighthearted, and perhaps more strongly the latter than the former. It is still more likely we will find the passage expressive of lighthearted resignation than of resigned lightheartedness. Some psychological states naturally seem to be modifications of others, and some expressive aspects as secondary to and amplificatory of others. Furthermore, expression can also be of nonpsychological properties. In cases where there is nonpsychological as well as psychological expression it seems that as a general rule the psychological property will be regarded as primary. For example, a passage expressing both ethereality and desire will if anything express ethereal desire and not desirous ethereality.

Let us grant, then, that when a passage expresses θ and ϕ it may sometimes further express ϕish θ though not θish ϕ. This restores the asymmetry to cases of compound expression that at first appeared to be lacking. What I propose now is that when a passage P expresses ϕish θ it is possible to understand this as P's expressing θ *as* ϕ. In other words, in a case of *asymmetric* compound expression one fairly natural reading is to regard the primary expression (θ) as the expressive subject of the passage—as what it is about expressively—and the secondary expression (ϕ) as a comment, angle, or perspective on what is primarily expressed. Thus, a passage expressing lighthearted resignation can be construed as presenting a picture or image of resignation, as showing resignation a certain way, namely, as lighthearted. And a passage expressing corrosive despair can be taken as a view of despair, can be taken as showing despair in a corrosive light. So construed, such instances begin to resemble instances of representation-as. A sculpture that represents Napoleon in a particular pose presents a subject, Napoleon, and a view on that subject; it presents Napoleon in a certain way, as being, say, of noble mien.

Of course, passages with compound expression need not be regarded in this manner. A more straightforward and obvious attitude toward passages expressing lighthearted resignation or corrosive despair is that they are just about particular species or kinds of resignation or despair, and not about resignation or despair more generally. Thus, a passage expressing corrosive despair is readily understood as simply expressing a variety of despair *which is* corrosive, as opposed to expressing despair *as being* corrosive. My point is not that one *must* understand such passages in the latter way, but only that one fittingly *can*. It seems that in reflecting on music with asymmetric compound expression we are in fact likely to alternate between these two ways of regarding it.

If we thus grant the propriety of regarding passages with asymmetric compound expression as presenting one expressed state as *characterized* by the other, then we have given adequate content to the notion of expression-as. A passage P can be said to express θ as ϕ— i.e., can be said to present θ as having character ϕ—just in case it expresses ϕish θ but not θish ϕ. In short, we may treat any case of asymmetric compound expression as a case of expression-as.

We are now finally in position to formulate a second notion of musical truth on the correspondent model. A musical passage P is true (A) *iff* (i) P expresses ϕish θ (and so, θ *as* ϕ) and (ii) θ is in fact ϕ. Put otherwise, a passage will have truth (A) if it embodies a true characterization (ϕ) of some emotional state (θ).

But *are there* facts about emotions of the sort that a passage's expression-as can be true or false to? Do emotions have characterizations that are just plain true? Consider the last movement of Brahms's Sonata in D Minor, op. 108, for Violin and Piano. Let us take it that some passages (e.g., the opening one—cf. fig. 3) in this movement express violent passion, and thus that they express passion as violent.[13] Now, we ask, *is* passion violent? Well, that is hard to say; *violent* passion is violent, at least. But what about passion in general? Is it violent? Perhaps there isn't any answer to this question. And if not, then the passages in question will be neither true (A) nor false (A).

We should not, however, conclude too quickly that "true (A)" is without application. For even though there does not quite seem to be a fact of the matter concerning the violence of passion, we do seem inclined to ascribe characteristics to emotions, or to maintain generalizations regarding them, some of which must be considered true. These truths may be grounded in how most people regard certain emotions,

---

[13] If readers disagree with this assessment, they may feel free to substitute a compound assessment of expression which they believe is either more nearly correct or more likely to be that of a consensus of informed listeners.

FIGURE 3. Johannes Brahms, Sonata in D Minor, op. 108, for Violin and Piano (fourth movement), measures 1–16.

or how most people experience them, or something else similarly statistical. But they seem to be truths of a sort, nevertheless. They are well entrenched characterizations of emotional states. Thus, for example, it appears true to say that love is mysterious, that anger is destructive, that exhilaration is short-lived, that joy is contagious.[14] If such things are true, then a passage's expression-as could reflect this, and thus be true (A).

[14] Remembering that to say—e.g., that love is mysterious—is not to say that each and every instance of love is mysterious.

Are there, or could there be, passages that express love as mysterious, anger as destructive, exhilaration as short-lived, and joy as
contagious? I believe so. Passages that are amorous and also mysterious occur in Rimsky-Korsakov's *Scheherazade* (e.g., the first violin
solo with harp accompaniment at measures 14–17). Passages that are
angry and also destructive can be found in the fourth movement
("Sturm") of Beethoven's *Pastoral* Symphony, or in the scherzo of
Mahler's Ninth Symphony. The other cases are somewhat more difficult. But expressing exhilaration as evanescent does not seem an impossible achievement for music. Perhaps some of Scriabin's etudes are
candidates for this (e.g., the Etude op. 8, no. 10). I will leave it to an
astute reader or enterprising composer to come up with a passage
expressing contagious joy.

Thus, it appears that musical passages can have truth (A). But then
they can also have falsity (A). If a passage expresses exhilaration and
also eternality, then it may well express eternal exhilaration, and thus,
exhilaration as eternal. But if what we have said above is correct, this
passage is false (A). Since eternal exhilaration strikes one as at least an
interesting thing to express, it becomes apparent that falsity (A) does
not necessarily militate against aesthetic worth. Truth (A) is actually
fairly common coin. It is probable that most expressive passages are
true (A) with respect to some expressed emotion and characteristic
thereof.

The third notion of truth I will explore here in connection with a
work's expression does not strictly conform to the correspondent
model as initially set out. On that model there must be an implied
comparison between an aspect or feature of the music and an aspect or
feature of the extramusical world. In the case of L-truth, the comparison is between the structure or form of a passage or work and the
structure or form of the emotion it expresses. In the case of A-truth, the
comparison is between how a passage characterizes an emotion it
expresses and how the emotion is actually characterized. In the present
case, the relevant comparison is between the *actual* expression achieved
by a passage or work and the *apparently intended* or *aimed* at expression. Now, the latter is not strictly a feature of the extramusical world
but rather a feature of the work. Still, it is a *quasi*-external feature in
that it relates to—though it is not to be identified with—the expression
that the composer in fact intended or aimed at. And the latter feature is
clearly external to the work. But let us go back a few paces.

We certainly have an inclination to refer the emotion expressed in a work to the emotional state of its creator. We are interested in what Schubert might have been feeling while he composed the *Death and the Maiden* Quartet, and whether Mendelssohn was jubilant when he penned the opening of the *Italian* Symphony. When there is a match between the expressed emotion and the creator's emotional state we speak of *sincerity*. Sincere music (in this sense) does not mislead; what it wears on its sleeve is or was in the composer's heart. Clearly we sometimes consider this a kind of truth—correspondence to the composer's psychological condition. Truth of this stripe has been praised to the exclusion of all else by some theoreticians, notably Tolstoy, and dismissed as without aesthetic relevance by others. However, I am not interested here in this kind of artistic "truth," especially since it has been amply discussed elsewhere. Nor am I interested in the correspondence between a work's expression and the expression its creator in fact *intended* it to have. The correspondence I am interested in is really internal to a work—though close enough to the just mentioned external correspondence to warrant truthlike status. This is correspondence between a work's expression and what the *work itself* conveys that it is out to express. When these match, as is usually the case, we can speak of *internal sincerity*. This is independent, moreover, of whether ordinary (external) sincerity is present.

Are all expressive works at least internally sincere? I think the answer is no. With some pieces of music we are aware that the expression actually achieved falls short of or otherwise misses the expression after which the work is striving. How do we tell what a work is striving to express? First note that this is always a metaphorical attribution, since musical works do not literally strive for anything. How do I know, say, that "*P* is striving to express φ" or "*P* is trying to express φ" is an apt metaphorical description of *P*? There is no general answer to this, any more than for any other metaphorical attribution. What I can say is that *P* sounds *like that*, and perhaps point out some specific features that particularly contribute to the impression. There is a literal equivalent of this attribution, but how we manage to make it is no easier to explain. To say a work is (metaphorically) trying to express φ is roughly to say (literally) that the work is *apparently* an attempt at expressing φ. It is a fact that these appearances are sometimes present to us. Of course, familiarity with the particular genre and style involved, familiarity with musical conventions of the period, knowledge of human nature, knowledge of typical expressive aims of the period, and so on are probably essential to receiving such impressions and assessing their objectivity. But this doesn't make them any less real.

To amplify somewhat on the way in which such impressions are generated, two factors might be mentioned which are regularly involved when a piece P expresses θ, while suggesting that it aims to express ϕ. One factor is ϕ's being a commonly aimed at and desirable sort of expression, when θ is not. A second is P's musical resemblance to pieces successful in expressing ϕ, or P's being recognizably of a musical type that is often expressive of ϕ. To give an example in which both factors are operative, certain passages of inferior film music convey nothing more than cheap bathos, while clearly aiming at a sort of rhapsodic passionateness. We register the latter impression in part because composers rarely set out to convey cheap bathos, and in part because of the music's rough resemblance to certain heady pages of Rachmaninoff and company, which are indeed filled with rhapsodic passion.

A musical work is internally insincere, then, or false (I), if it is trying to express ϕ but failing to do so, if there is a discrepancy between expression projected and expression attained. It is not too hard to find examples of such works within the classical repertoire. Liszt's orchestral music is a good source. Consider the tone poem *Tasso*. Even apart from its program, much of the piece conveys the impression of aiming at noble heroism. However, what is achieved, particularly in the concluding section ("moderato pomposo"), is something closer to blustery bravado. Or recall some of Franck's orchestral music—e.g., *Psyche* or the Symphony in D Minor—parts of which project an intention toward piety or religious fervor, but end up expressing sensuality of a somewhat mawkish sort.[15] And in much of the music of the early classical composer Dittersdorf one readily discerns something like cloddishness, although it is equally obvious that the music is straining to be sweetly elegant. It is not simply that these pieces fail to be heroic, pious, or elegant—after all, so does the first movement of Beethoven's Ninth Symphony. It is that they are (metaphorically) *trying* to be, and we are aware of this.

[15] I personally like most of Liszt's and Franck's orchestral music despite this feature, which I do not regard as in itself rendering the music bad. But this feature may help to explain why many critics have had little good to say about these corpuses.

I would suggest that the idea of internal sincerity as I have explained it is the usual root of a judgment that a work is *pretentious*. Such a work purports to offer one thing, but regrettably delivers another. The high-class goods we are primed to expect turn out to be rather shoddy merchandise. Pretentious musical passages are probably always examples of falsity (I), that is to say, lack of accord between what a work achieves and what it gives indication of striving after.

Looking backward now, we have uncovered three sorts of "truth," or three truth*like* properties, which can be understood as involving correspondence, and which have some application to musical works or passages. These are truth (L), or structural correspondence between a passage and the emotion it expresses; truth (A), or correspondence between how an emotion is expressed by a passage and how it actually is; and truth (I), or correspondence between a passage's actual expression and the expression it apparently aims at.

III PROPOSITIONAL TRUTH

I will now explore some possible uses of "true" in music conforming to the propositional model, PT. Once again I will concentrate on the expressive dimension of music.

Are there any propositions that a musical work or passage might be taken to *suggest* in virtue of its expressing E? We will require of a candidate for a suggested proposition that the music have at least some tendency to bring the proposition to mind in a receptive listener, and that there is some prima facie propriety in regarding the music as advancing this proposition, however weakly.

The most minimal proposition one might take a passage expressing emotion E as conveying is that E is a *possible* psychological state for us. But this is too minimal to be of much interest. How could an emotion expressed by a passage be impossible for us to have? If we cannot conceive of experiencing it, how could it be available to us for metaphorical description of the passage? If we could not conceive of experiencing what a passage expressed, could what it expressed even count as an emotion? It thus seems that if a passage P expresses emotion E it would be absurd to regard it as conveying that E is a possible state for us—for unless that were true, P probably could not express E at all. The absurdity of the proposed suggestion is further brought out by noting that if there were such suggestion, absolutely *every* expressive passage would be "true" on this count.

A somewhat less minimal suggestion would be that E is an *actually occurring*, and not just a merely possible, human psychological condition. That is to say, perhaps a passage expressing E (where E is a psychological state) suggests that at least *someone* has experienced E. Another alternative one could entertain is that a passage expressing E (where E is a psychological state) suggests that E is *commonly* or *widely* experienced.

How reasonable are either of these alternatives? Well, it has long been held that music speaks to us of human emotions, and that it is a reflection of happenings in that realm. If so, then when it expresses a given emotion E, perhaps it is at least imparting that E occurs—i.e., is instantiated in someone? If music shows us, among other things, what our emotional life is like, then isn't it appropriate to take a passage expressing E as weakly implying that E is an actual part of that life?

The short answer to this, I suppose, is that music is *not* reasonably taken as showing what in the way of human emotional conditions as a matter of fact occurs, but as displaying the *possible* range and variety of such conditions. Music stands to emotional life not as a literal record or report but more as a general map of the region, some of it unvisited. So even if music reveals emotional life to us, it need not be taken to reveal actual occurrences in any individual's personal history.

The second of the remaining suggestions is no more plausible than the first. If we are not inclined to read a musical passage as even suggesting that what it expresses is instantiated, we will hardly be inclined to read it as suggesting that what it expresses is *widely* instantiated. Surely neither of these propositions is likely to be brought to mind in an experienced listener.[16]

But there is another problem with these proposals which goes be-

---

[16] Of course, expressive music does in fact regularly bring to mind in many listeners the proposition that a *particular* person—the composer—experiences or has experienced the emotions expressed. And perhaps it is to some degree (or in some circumstances) acceptable to regard music as conveying this proposition. If so, then the music can be said to be "true" if the composer is in fact subject to the emotions in question. This is just "truth" in the familiar sense of external sincerity, which was mentioned in section II.

yond simple implausibility. It is that application of musical "falsity" in the senses generated would probably be vacuous. Suppose we grant in the abstract that a piece expressing *E just might* reasonably be regarded as "saying" that some people, or many people, have felt *E*. This suggested proposition would then be either true or false and so, accordingly, would the piece. But the point is that we are *at most* disposed to take a piece of music as suggesting propositions of this kind on which it comes out *true*. Put otherwise, if the candidate proposition of this type is going to turn out to be *false,* we generally will *not* allow that it is suggested by the piece. Consider the opening adagio of Beethoven's Quartet in C-sharp Minor, op. 131. Let us make the reasonable supposition that it expresses a psychological state (which I will not attempt to describe) unencountered in human life. Call this *Q*. Now, if the adagio suggests the proposition that *Q* occurs in human experience, then it is a false piece of music. But this is all the reason we would need to deny that that proposition is suggested. ("The op. 131 adagio false? That's preposterous!") Consider the opening of Mahler's Second Symphony. It certainly expresses an emotion (bitter, pessimistic despair) which, if not unknown, is rarely encountered. If that opening be taken to suggest that bitter pessimistic despair is widespread, then it is a false bit of music. However, we will resist considering the music false; instead we will consider the suggestion absent. In sum, if we take music to suggest propositions like these, and to have the resulting propositional truth capacity, then either this capacity will never be exercised in the negative direction, or else typically works that we value very highly are going to be "false," and valued often in virtue of what in part makes them "false." So this species of musical "truth" is either otiose or decidedly counterintuitive.

So far we have considered the idea that a passage expressing *E* might be true or false in virtue of suggesting that *E* is possibly experienced, that *E* is actually experienced, or that *E* is widely experienced. This has all come to nought. Let us consider one more alternative of this stripe: the suggestion that *E* is a *significant* or *important* emotional experience. Is there any reason to take this suggestion as present? Well, one might say, when we are presented with a piece of music by a composer, we naturally assume it will be worth listening to and thinking about. And thus that its expression will probably be worth our attention. Do we then regularly take music to be "claiming" that what it expresses is significant or important? No, because there is a difference between being worth attention and having a significant emotional import. Mozart's wind divertimenti, Offenbach's *Gaité Parisienne*, Stravinsky's *Circus Polka* are certainly worth our attention as music, but what they express is hardly profound. Thus, even were we to take music presented to us as saying implicitly that it is worth a hearing, we can hardly regard it as a standing suggestion of musical works that what they *express* is of notable importance. So there is not much ground for a notion of truth with respect to which works that express the non-earthshaking, such as Mozart's divertimenti, would be false.

Instead of looking for musical truth in what *single* passages might suggest about the occurrence, frequency, or profundity of what they express, I focus now on propositions works might suggest in virtue of what is expressed by the *different* passages or sections that comprise them. That is to say, can we justifiably ascribe any import to the multiplicity of what a work expresses in its various parts? One form of suggestion would be this: a work expressing ϕ and θ in neighboring passages suggests that ϕ and θ are *often* or *regularly* experienced together. Thus, a piece would be true, given this suggestion, if its expression reflected some common emotional grouping in human experience. The problem with this candidate suggestion is the same as with the suggestion by a passage expressing E that E is commonly experienced, which was discussed in the previous section. The associated sense of "true" would be one we would be little inclined to invoke—it would make some of our most interesting and admired music false. We can hardly agree to stigmatize in this way all compositions that present us with unusual emotional mixtures.

A more promising suggestion schema, I think, would be this:

(J) A work that expresses emotions ϕ and θ in neighboring passages suggests that a single individual *could naturally* experience ϕ and θ in juxtaposition.

To say that it is possible for a pair of emotions to be experienced *naturally* by a single individual in a given period is to say something of this sort: The transition from one of the emotions to the other is understandable or conceivable, given our knowledge of human nature, without supposing extrinsic perturbation of one sort or another. Another way to put it would be this: emotions that cannot naturally occur together in immediate proximity are ones whose proximate occurrence lacks even a minimum psychological plausibility on the face of it—that is to say, without appeal to a background story invoking external influences or sudden changes in thought or belief. A pair of emotions do not form a natural complex if their joint experience within a short span is not prima facie psychologically credible. Although this notion of what can naturally occur is not terribly precise, it should at any rate be clear that the possibility at issue is not logical possibility, but something narrower, reflecting our perspective on the limits of human psychology. However, it is not as narrow as the idea of emotional groupings that *often* or *regularly* occur.

There are certain pairs of emotions which are such that—at least as far as our common knowledge of human psychology leads us to believe—a person's experience in a given period cannot naturally consist of just that pair. For example, within the space of five minutes, extreme grief and extreme merriment, anger and contentment, flaming jealousy and blithe abandon. There is no plausible path from one of these to the other in terms of internal psychological progression—there are no such "natural courses of events." This is not to deny that extrinsic perturbations are usually imaginable, which could account for such transitions—e.g., receiving a telegram announcing a parent's death while in the midst of birthday celebrations.

Now, one likely feels, at first glance, that we are not much inclined to read expressive multiplicity as (J) would have it. Rather, we generally regard such multiplicity as having no import for the world outside the work, but as simply a complex of emotional contents motivated and justified on purely musical grounds. However, although this is our attitude *generally*, I am not sure it is so *invariably*. I think we may sometimes regard musical works as purporting to offer a compressed slice of at least possible emotional life—in some cases, doing so with credibility, in other cases, without.

Consider a sonata movement in which unrelated, diametrically opposed emotions are expressed in close proximity with little or no mediation. Suppose also that neither the musical context nor the context of composition offer any indication that the movement is not to be taken "straight," so that any assumption of humorous or satirical intent is undercut. Suppose further that norms of formal balance, key relationships, textural continuity, and the like are more or less observed, so that our narrowly musical sense is not notably offended. I submit that such a movement would probably still make us uncomfortable. It would strike us as wrong in some way.

How can we explain this? One explanation would be that we do understand some pieces of music to carry at least weakly the implicit suggestion that the various states they express in a given musical unit go together in human experience—i.e., could constitute the internally developing experience of an individual in a given period. The sensation of wrongness occasioned by a piece with psychologically antithetical expressions brushing up against one another does not seem to be sufficiently accounted for by appeal to "purely aesthetic" criteria—e.g., unity in variety, continuity, moderation of contrast. It can be explained, however, if we both note that such juxtapositions do not correspond to possible natural complexes of emotional states, and also recognize that to some extent we do take some multiply expressive works as suggesting that there are such natural complexes corresponding to them. This suggestion would thus be false for a sonata movement such as the above; the requisite intermediate states, the states that in our experience link highly disparate states, are missing from the expressive picture. A piece that presents us with an assortment of emotions within a given movement which could not occur together naturally in the course of experience seems not unreasonably thought of as false. I conclude that (J) generates a sense of "truth"—viz., a work is true (J) insofar as its associated J suggestions are true—which has some application.

There is another suggestion that might be taken from a work's expressive multiplicity which is somewhat stronger than (J). It is also, I suspect, a more likely one. Instead of taking expression of ϕ and then θ to indicate just the possibility of instantiation of ϕ and θ in close proximity, we might rather take it to indicate the possibility of definite emotional *sequence*, ϕ followed by θ. Thus, we would have this suggestion schema:

(S) A work that expresses emotions ϕ and θ in successive passages suggests that in the experience of a single individual θ *could naturally* succeed ϕ.

According to (S), sequential expression in a work is to be read as possible emotional sequence in human experience. Whereas (J) registers only juxtaposition, (S) registers direction as well. If an S suggestion proves correct, so does the corresponding J suggestion, though not vice versa.[17]

I now turn to some actual examples of musical works which occasion a certain species of discomfort. I maintain that this discomfort is plausibly explained as an awareness of "falsity" in senses which either J or S suggestions would ground. In the rondo of Mozart's Violin Concerto in A, K. 219, the innocuous and graciously relaxed main theme is followed at one point by a somewhat hysterical "Turkish"-sounding episode of pugnacious cast, which gives way to the main theme once again. In the first movement of Tchaikovsky's *Pathétique* Symphony, a passage at the close of the exposition which can be characterized as subdued and reflective, perhaps nostalgic, is immediately succeeded, at the opening of the development, by a passage of startling anger and resolve. Prokofiev's First Piano Concerto consists of a series of sections of widely differing moods, strung together in what appears to be almost arbitrary fashion.[18] A rough stab at the succession of expressions in the First Concerto would be this: tense grandeur, rollicking abandon, mild lugubriousness, sober sprightliness, sensuous languor, quizzical gaiety, fearful hesitancy, joyous affirmation.[19]

[17] In addition to emotional successions that are naturally precluded, in the sense that such successions are psychologically incredible in themselves, there *may* be some that are conceptually precluded as well. There may be pairs of emotions which on "logical" grounds cannot occur in a certain order. That is to say, for some θ and φ, there may be essential features of θ and φ which make it conceptually impossible for φ to directly follow θ. A likely strategy for showing this would involve appeal to essential build-up and fade-away times, essential follow-up states, resistance to reversal of essential belief components. Perhaps on such grounds it can be demonstrated, say, that going from grief to insouciance is a conceptually impossible sequence. If there are any conceptually impossible sequences, then they are a fortiori also naturally impossible ones. If not, there are still naturally impossible ones, in the sense explained, and that is all we need for some pieces to have the potential for falsity (S) in virtue of their expression as a whole.

[18] This is not to deny that the piece is well organized from a purely musical point of view; for instance, the opening theme is transformed and brought back very effectively in the closing statement of the work.

[19] These are, respectively, the passages at rehearsal numbers 0, 3, 12, 15, 21, 27, 31, and 34.

Can a state of hysterical pugnacity naturally follow directly on one of gracious relaxation? Can a state of resolute anger naturally immediately succeed one of subdued reflection? Could any one person's unperturbed experience in a given period contain all and only these states: tense grandeur, rollicking abandon, mild lugubriousness?[20] If the answers to these or similar questions is no, then the compositions just mentioned, given they carry suggestions of form (J) or (S), indeed have something false about them. And so perhaps they make us uneasy because they are somewhat false in those ways. Just as we expect and assume that a unitary piece of music will have a reasonable degree of textual, harmonic—or more generally—stylistic consistency, so we often expect and assume, it seems, that such a piece will display a certain measure of emotional consistency as well. The compositions above feel false insofar as, given the sort of pieces they are, the emotional changes involved are too abrupt, too disconnected, too inexplicable.

The force of the above assumption, or the strength of the associated J and S suggestions, depends in part on how *unitary* the genre is to which the piece in questions belongs. Thus we are more likely to hold a piano prelude, a fugue, or a sonata movement to this sort of standard than a set of variations or a minuet and trio, which are movements composed of independent subunits. In those latter forms, a wider span of emotional coloring is tolerable before anything like a feeling of falsity rears its unpleasant head. Perhaps the greatest emotional freedom attaches to the genre of the Classical keyboard fantasy, as evidenced by C. P. E. Bach, Mozart, and others. C. P. E. Bach's fantasies, comprising several discrete sections, are veritable gallimaufries of affects, and are accepted as just that. There is no presumption of coherent psychological development. But in other forms there is, and the occasional violation of such is characteristically registered by us in our experience of the music.[21]

[20]The composer Hindemith, in discussing the evocation of feelings by music, is clearly inclined to answer such questions in the negative: "If we experience a real feeling of grief—that is, grief not caused or released by music—it is not possible to replace it at a moment's notice and without any plausible reason with a feeling of wild gaiety; and gaiety, in turn, cannot be replaced by complacency after a fraction of a second. Real feelings need a certain interval of time to develop, to reach a climax, and to fade out again" (*A Composer's World* [New York: Doubleday, 1961], pp. 44–45).

[21]I have proposed that if one views the set of emotions expressed in the course of a sonata movement as putatively naturally experienceable in succession by a *single*

It is important to remember that I am not pressing the thesis that *all* musical works in *all* contexts carry suggestions (J) and/or (S). What I have tried to show is just that in *some* cases it seems plausible that such suggestions are present—that assumptions of emotional coherence serve as background to our perception and assessment of a piece. If so, then the associated notions of truth (J) and truth (S) have some employment in regard to music.[22]

I want, further, to caution readers who sense a threat to some favored piece of music that I do not mean to imply that if a piece admits of J or S falsity it is *necessarily*, or even *probably*, a bad piece of music. Consider, as another example, Beethoven's Sonata for Violin and Piano in C Minor, op. 30, no. 2. The first movement could be considered false in the above ways. The opening subject, which is agitated and tragic, is followed after only a few bars of declamatory transition by a blithely skipping second subject which is the soul of naiveté. A greater antithesis can hardly be imagined. However, these two subjects are so skillfully developed and brought together in the course of the movement—for one, the second subject is later stated more aggressively and in minor—that the shock of their contrast is more than made up for. The slow movement is, to my mind, psychologically false in a less resolvable way. Twice toward the end of a set of variations on a lyrical and stately theme the piano erupts in rocketing scale figures of brusque character for which there has been no psychological preparation nor any subsequent justification. But this is a small

individual in a given period, then one may well find some such sonatas "false." But most such sonatas would likely not seem "false" if they were viewed, not as reflections of a single individual's possible experience, but instead as emotional dialogues (or multilogues) between two (or more) individuals. What would then be a naturally impossible emotional juxtaposition or sequence for one person becomes a perfectly acceptable transition from one person's emotional stream to another's. Having acknowledged this, I will say here only that the "individualistic" construal of most sonatas of the eighteenth and nineteenth centuries seems to me at least as appropriate and historically defensible as the "multiple persona" construal, and thus that J or S suggestions can justifiably be taken to be in effect in many cases.

[22] It is worth observing that truth (J) and truth (S), which we have explained in terms of suggested propositions, can alternatively be conceived on the correspondence model. For example, we could say that a work is true (S) insofar as its sequence of expression *corresponds to* some possible natural sequence of emotions. To legitimize truth (S) on this conception one would argue that referring expressive sequence in music to the sphere of psychological possibility is an appropriate thing to do—instead of arguing, as we did above, that musical works can plausibly be regarded as carrying weak suggestions of type S.

FIGURE 4. Ludwig van Beethoven, Sonata for Violin and Piano in C Minor, op. 30, no. 2 (second movement), measures 82–97.

blemish in an otherwise admirable movement. Instead of the uniformly noble utterance it might have been it is one with a touch of
unexplained quirkiness. Even so, none of this prevents the C Minor
Violin Sonata from being overall probably the finest of Beethoven's
efforts in that medium.

IV

I have not, in all, said much about the relevance that musical truth, in
the various senses we have managed to uncover, has for the evaluation
of music. What, briefly, are the evaluative vectors of the various sorts
of musical truth? Truth (L), the property of resembling the structure of
the emotion expressed, might count as a mildly good-making feature
(though far from a good-guaranteeing one), in that true (L) compositions, if there are any, have the capacity of displaying for contemplation the shapes of emotional life. Truth (A), or conformity to some
generalization concerning an emotion, seems evaluatively neutral; its
presence betokens only that what compound expression is involved is
of a familiar, rather than an unusual, sort. Truth (I), or match between
projected and achieved expressiveness, strikes one as clearly a good-
making feature; for a piece to be false (I) is for it to be in that respect disunified, awkward, and unsuccessful. Finally, to the extent that
one believes music in its expressive dimension should stay within the
bounds of the possibilities of feeling, truth (J) and truth (S) will be
good-making in some degree.

If one may generalize on the basis of this, it appears that any notion
of truth in music acceptable to us will be such that its possession by a
work is *at worst neutral* with respect to aesthetic value. If truth is not
equivalent to beauty, we hardly want it to be inimical to it.

I have also said little about the bearing of musical truth on the
possibility of acquiring extramusical knowledge—for example, about
emotional life—from a musical composition. I fear that what can be
said here is mainly negative. In order to come to know something from
listening to a composition that was true in one of our senses one would
have to know *that* the composition was true in that sense. But in general, one will *not* know that the composition is true unless one *already*
knows precisely that which hearing the composition and knowing it

was true would have illuminated one about.[23] So music's potential for yielding knowledge in virtue of its "truth" is rather limited. It is more likely to perform the function of activating what we dispositionally know, or dramatizing what we usually overlook, by virtue of the respect in which it is true.

So what, after all, could it mean to say that a sonata was true? Well, with some point, it might mean that its structure mirrors that of the emotions it expresses, or that it expresses emotions as they are, or that its achieved expression accords with its apparently intended expression, or perhaps that on the basis of a sequence of expressive passages it contains it suggests truly that a parallel sequence of emotions, or just that set of emotions within a given span, is, in a narrow sense, psychologically possible. Surely, this is a long way from meaninglessness.

I will refrain, however, from investigating here what it might mean to say that one was justified in *believing* a sonata!

[23]For example, if a musical composition is false (J) because in a short space it expresses bitter rage and pie-eyed geniality, we will only come away with the knowledge that those emotions do not naturally occur together *if* we know that a particular part of the composition is false (J)—and we would only know *that* because of our prior psychological knowledge.

Additional Notes

1. In light of the interesting, but partly misplaced, critique of my ideas on truth in music by Göran Hermerén ("Representation, Truth and the Languages of the Arts," in *Essays in the Philosophy of Music*, ed. V. Rantala et al. [Helsinki: Acta Philosophica Fennica, 1988], pp. 179–209), I will take this opportunity to clarify what I am, and am not, affirming in this essay. Hermerén charges, in essence, that I confuse truth with sincerity, coherence, or other critically noteworthy but not really "truth-equivalent" characteristics. But I do not say in the essay (nor do I believe) that passages of music are *literally* true—i.e., that an assertion such as "this passage is a true one" has a standard employment, or would elicit agreement from a set of knowledgeable listeners or musicologues. The thrust of "Truth in Music," rather, was exploratory and hypothetical, and might be captured in the following query: "If we were to review the range of critical and appreciative judgments we are inclined to make about instrumental music, which among them could be *most plausibly viewed* as ascribing a kind of truth to the music involved?" All that I am really claiming about, for instance, Truth (S) is that it denominates an evaluatively significant property of some musical works, one that is both experienced as a kind of truthfulness, and that a critic is even likely to think of in terms of truth—truth, as it turns out, to emotional life.

   It should be noted, also, that I don't even insist (in section 1) that the "truth" of a portrait or a historical novel vis-à-vis its model, from which I take off to explore the possibilities of "truth" in a nonrepresentational realm, is truth in the strict sense;

that is to say, I don't claim that such a painting or novel *is* literally a statement, or even literally *makes* a statement. I do, however, differ with Hermerén as to how *far* "truthfulness" in such cases is from the literal notion—not very far, by my lights. And that is because the proviso included in my characterization of "truth" in representational contexts—namely, "if its representings were to be *taken* as statements or assertions"—is *sometimes,* though of course not always, *legitimately* invoked with respect to such paintings or novels.

Finally, since Hermerén's discussion of my paper occurs in the cadre of an inquiry into whether the arts are or contain *languages,* I want to be explicit that it was never my intent to argue that tonal music was a language, merely because some music might with some justification be called true or false to certain facts of human psychology if referred to them.

2. Recently on rehearing the passage from Beethoven's C Minor Sonata for Violin and Piano discussed in section III of "Truth in Music," I was struck by the fact that the "rocketing scale figures" I refer to could reasonably be heard as an *allusion* to the soloist's first entrance in Beethoven's C Minor Piano Concerto. [Despite its lower opus number, the sonata was composed in 1802, two years after Beethoven's initial sketches for the concerto.] This would not, I think, remove the falseness (S) I attributed to the passage, but it might provide some other ground for justifying the interruption involved.

13 *Music and Negative Emotion*

A grown man, of sound mind and body, manipulates the controls of an electronic apparatus. He settles into an easy chair, full of expectancy. Then it begins. For the next hour or so this man is subjected to an unyielding bombardment of stimuli, producing in him a number of states which prima facie are extremely unpleasant, and which one would normally go to some lengths to avoid. He appears upset, pained, and at turns a small sigh or a shudder passes through his body. Yet at the end of this ordeal our subject seems pleased. He avers that the past hour and a half has been a highly rewarding one. He declares his intention to repeat this sort of experience in the near future.

What has our man been doing, and more interestingly, why has he been doing it? He has been listening to music—just that. It turns out that his fare on this occasion was the *Marcia Funebre* of Beethoven's *Eroica* Symphony, the Scriabin Etude op. 42, no. 5, the third movement of Brahms's Third Symphony, Mozart's Adagio and Fugue in C Minor, K. 546, and the opening of Mahler's Second Symphony, all neatly assembled, with suitable pauses, on a reel of recording tape. What he experienced can be described—at least *provisionally*—as intense grief, unrequited passion, sobbing melancholy, tragic resolve, and angry despair. But why would anyone in effect torture himself in this manner? What could induce a sane person to purposely arrange for himself occasions of ostensibly painful experience?

306

My object in this essay is to give a comprehensive answer to this query. The general question can be formulated thus: Why do many sensitive people find the experience of negative emotion through music a rewarding or valuable one, and, what is especially paradoxical, rewarding or valuable partly in itself? Not only do appreciators of music appear to regard such experiences as instrumentally good or worthwhile—which itself needs much explaining—but they standardly seek them out and relish them for their own sakes, enjoying them or pleasuring in them, if truth be told.

At this point many readers will have ready some favorite wand for dissolving this paradox with a wave of the hand. But I do not intend to encourage them. While admitting that my initial description of the phenomenon will need to be modified somewhat, I maintain that even when all niceties on the aesthetic and psychological fronts have been attended to, the phenomenon, in essence, remains.

II

In its general form, of course, the problem of the value and desirability of the negative or unpleasant in art is one of the hoariest in aesthetics. It is the problem Aristotle raises for the appreciation of tragedy, evocative of pity and terror, and which he answers with the doctrine of catharsis. It is the problem of the sublime in eighteenth- and nineteenth-century thought, the "delightful horror" analyzed among others by Burke and Schopenhauer, which a spectator feels face to face with some threatening aspect of life as embodied in a work of art. But in the case of music the problem is generated in the absence of any representational content, and so answers to it must be framed accordingly.

We see in the following more recent writers a concern with the specific paradox of enjoyment of emotionally distressing music. It is interesting to note the virtual consensus of these writers that negative emotion is not actually evoked in the attuned listener by even the most intense of musical works.

> If to hear the intense grief of the fugal passages of the *Eroica* required real tears and adrenal secretions, then an anomalous if not impossible psychological state would have to prevail. The gorgeous clash of dissonant minor seconds which brings the tremendous but short fugue to an incomplete close—several measures of almost unbearable anguish—

has been a source of supreme delight to countless lovers of music. How can a listener be at once pleased and pained?[1]

Why should I ever wish to hear . . . (sad music)? Sad experiences, such as suffering personal bereavement or keen disappointment, are not the kind of thing we wish to repeat or prolong. Yet sad music does not affect us in this way; it may bring relief, pleasure, even happiness. Strange kind of sadness that brings pleasure![2]

The most unpleasant emotions imaginable are perceived in music; and if that meant our *feeling* these emotions, it would be utterly inexplicable why anyone would willfully submit himself to the music. *Tristan und Isolde* is full of music expressive of deep anguish. None, I would think, except the masochists among us, would listen to such music if indeed it were anguish-producing.[3]

I agree with these writers, on the bottom line, that full-fledged emotions of the paradigm sort fail to be aroused by music in the course of aesthetically respectable auditionings. But I want to stress that this failure in many cases is only a marginal one, and thus that the paradox of desirable-though-unpleasant experience in music remains despite this admission. Something *very much like* the arousal of negative emotions is accomplished by *some* music, and so there is indeed something to explain in our avidity for such experience.

Before essaying explanations of my own, it will help to review a number of responses to the problem which attempt to solve it, roughly, by dissolving it. This will occupy me for the succeeding six sections. These responses in effect deny the phenomenon while introducing in its stead harmless replacement. Such moves are inadequate, however, to resolve the paradox of musical masochism limned in the opening illustration.

It is best to forestall at the outset a possible misunderstanding. In defending the reality and importance of emotional response to music I imply no position on the proper analysis of emotional expressiveness in music. The three writers quoted above are all concerned to undercut the equation of expression in music with evocation by music. In that

---

[1] Carroll C. Pratt, Introduction to *The Meaning of Music* (New York: McGraw-Hill, 1970), pp. 3–4.
[2] John Hospers, "The Concept of Artistic Expression," in *Introductory Readings in Aesthetics*, ed. J. Hospers (New York: Free Press, 1969), p. 152.
[3] Peter Kivy, *The Corded Shell* (Princeton: Princeton University Press, 1980), p. 23.

they are certainly right. What a passage expresses and what it standardly evokes are, for an assortment of reasons, rarely (if ever) quite
identical. But while I reject an evocation theory of expression, I am unwilling to see emotional response to music—particularly of a "dark"
sort—exorcised so completely in the name of it. One can reject the
evocation theory without regarding every instance of negative emotional response to music—whatever the work and whatever the conditions of listening—as either illusory or aesthetically inapropos. It
seems to me that there are indeed compositions that can, when listened
to in certain appreciatively admissible frames of mind, produce in one
real feelings of both the positive and negative variety.

It is our attitude toward the latter that seems puzzling. One can be
on the musical rack—one can hear the screws turn—and yet like it.
This is what we must explain.

III

One hypothesis concerning the effect of music would, if accepted,
neatly defuse the paradox which concerns us. This hypothesis, less
popular today than at some earlier times, is that of a special "aesthetic
emotion," totally different from the emotions of life and occasioned
only by the perception of works of art. This view is identified with
Clive Bell in its general form, but its foremost exponent with specific
application to music is the English psychologist Edmund Gurney.[4]
According to Gurney, there is a unique, sui generis "musical emotion"
that is raised in listeners by all pieces of "impressive" (i.e., beautiful)
music, and only by such. This unvarying effect of impressive music is
either a kind of pleasure itself, or else something the experience of
which is pleasurable. Clearly, if the chief result of music that was both
impressive and, say, anguished was the arousal of such a "musical
emotion," there would be little difficulty in understanding how such
music could be enjoyable.

There is, however, little else to be said for the view that appreciative
response to music consists of but one type of emotion, a music-specific,
invariably pleasant one. The effects of different sorts of music are too

---

[4] His chief work, *The Power of Sound*, was published in 1880.

different from one another, and too reminiscent of life emotions, for this view to carry much plausibility. Our manifest interest in a multiplicity of musical works and experiences begins to seem puzzling if the primary benefit to be derived from any or all of them is this selfsame "musical emotion." It just is not the case that all good or impressive music induces a single positive emotion in listeners.

This is not to say that there could not be something specifically musical, and perhaps unduplicatable, in the experience of a particular piece of music. The total experience—perceptual, emotional, cognitive—of listening to a given work may indeed be unique to it, and this fact not without aesthetic relevance. But one can maintain that without adopting the hypothesis of an invariant and specifically musical emotional element in each such experience.

IV

Another approach to our paradox is implicit in some reflections on music by the composer Paul Hindemith. Hindemith denies that music has an emotional effect on listeners, properly speaking. One of his main reasons for this denial seems to be the rapidity with which the typical musical composition changes its emotional character, coupled with a reasonable assumption of emotional inertia on the part of human beings. Hindemith believes that since a person cannot change emotional states as quickly as music changes its expression, it is implausible to think the music is evocative of real emotion in him.

> There is not doubt that listeners, performers, and composers alike can be profoundly moved by perceiving, performing, or imagining music, and consequently music must touch on something in their emotional life that brings them into this state of excitation. But if these mental reactions were feelings, they could not change as rapidly as they do, and they would not begin and end with the musical stimulus that aroused them. . . . Real feelings need a certain interval of time to develop, to reach a climax, and to fade out again; but reactions to music may change as fast as musical phrases do, they may spring up in full intensity at any given movement and disappear entirely when the musical pattern that provokes them ends or changes.[5]

[5] Paul Hindemith, *A Composer's World* (New York: Doubleday, 1961), pp. 44–45.

Instead of emotions themselves, Hindemith claims that musical passages evoke in the listener merely memories or images of emotions that the listener has experienced in the past. It follows that there can be no emotional reaction to music which is not strongly rooted in emotional experience in life. On Hindemith's view listening to music becomes an occasion for a selective tour of one's gallery of emotional remembrances, with some sonata or symphony functioning as guide.

The musicologist Deryck Cooke offered two replies to Hindemith's remarks which are worth recalling.[6] The first is that even admitting a certain inertia in the average person's emotional responsiveness, the rapid changes of character from passage to passage in a musical work do not themselves insure that no emotions are raised in the course of it, for we need not assume that such reactions come abruptly to an end when the passages that stimulate them are over. According to Cooke, the response elicited by a passage will often linger and develop after the passage is no longer heard, instead of being entirely obliterated or erased by succeeding passages or completion of the piece.

Second, Cooke very plausibly maintains that our reactions to music cannot all consist of memory images of prior experiences, since it appears that music (some music) has the power to make us feel in ways that we simply have not felt before. The feeling raised in me by certain auditions of the finale of Schumann's piano concerto was distinct from any I had encountered in ordinary life before those hearings. It may have been related in complex ways to particular prior experiences of mine, but it was clearly not equivalent to a memory replay of them either singly or collectively.

Furthermore, if what we can neutrally call a *sadness-reaction* to sad music typically consisted of some memory image of a particular earlier sadness, it seems we would generally be conscious while listening of the particulars of that occasion—the time, place, object and reasons of it. But we are not. Listeners' capacities for feeling sadness from music will be exercised and deepened by their experiences of sadness in life, to be sure, but there is little reason to think either that listeners could not possibly be saddened by music if they had not been saddened outside of music or more important, that their sadness-reactions could

---

[6]Deryck Cooke, *The Language of Music* (London: Oxford University Press, 1959), chap. 1.

only be the recollection of particular experiences of sadness in their pasts.

Two other observations on Hindemith's remarks are in order with respect to the problem of negative emotional response in music. First, if it is doubtful whether the listener's response to varied, swiftly changing musical works can be a coherently emotional one, we can focus attention instead on extended parts or sections thereof which are emotionally relatively homogeneous. There is certainly enough time in the course of the sustained *Eroica* Funeral March to build up a substantial feeling of grief leavened with little else. Our paradox remains even if only a small number of compositions have sufficient continuity and depth to properly elicit these ostensibly undesirable affects.

Second, even were Hindemith right that emotional response to music is simply a matter of the reviving of old emotions in memory, this would not really dispel the paradox of why we should desire to hear music that revives memories that are of negative emotional experiences. If it is puzzling that one should want to be *made* sad, it is only a little less puzzling that one should want to *remember* particular occasions of having been sad. For memories of sad occasions are often sad themselves; that is to say, summoning them up often reawakens the sadness they encode. Memories are not only records, but repositories as well. To revive a memory of sadness often is in part to relive that sadness. Experiential memories standardly preserve and transmit the affective tone of the original experience.[7]

Thus, we will no more find a solution to our puzzle in Hindemith's hypothesis than in Gurney's.

V

In order to discuss certain other approaches to our problem we must pursue the analysis of emotion somewhat further. It is by now orthodoxy among philosophers of mind that emotions are more than simply states of inner feeling.[8] Although there is not absolute accord on what

---

[7]See on this Richard Wollheim, "On Persons and Their Lives," in *Explaining Emotions*, ed. Amelie O. Rorty (Berkeley: University of California Press, 1980), pp. 299–321.

[8]See the discussions in William Alston, "Emotion and Feeling," in *The Encyclopedia of Philosophy*, ed. Paul Edwards (New York: Macmillan, 1967); Georges Rey, "Func-

all the components of an emotion are, and on which, if any, are essential to the emotion, most writers agree at least that emotions contain a *cognitive* component in addition to an *affective* one. This may be expressed in the form of a belief, attitude, desire, or evaluation, focused on and identifying the *object* of the emotion. Thus, if one is afraid, one feels a certain (rather unpleasant) way, and feels that way *toward* some object that one believes to be dangerous and wants to avoid. If one hopes, one feels a certain (rather more pleasant) way, and feels that way *about* some situation that one believes may possibly obtain, and that one desires to obtain. The presence of an intentional object on which thought and feeling are directed, then, is taken as central to the paradigm of an emotion.

In addition to affective and cognitive components, a case can be made that emotions have *behavioral* and *physiological* components as well. Being afraid may typically involve cowering, shaking, or the like, and perhaps necessarily a tendency or disposition to flee in the presence of the feared object. Being afraid may require, in addition to anything one is subjectively experiencing, a certain state of the endocrine or circulatory systems.

Concerning the affective component—that part of an emotion which consists in what one *feels* in a narrow sense—there is some question as to how this should be conceived. On one view, the affective component of emotion consists in a certain overall coloring of consciousness, a certain quality of inner feeling, of which pleasurable/painful is an important, though not the only, dimension. On another view, the affective component is simply a set of internal sensations of bodily changes—e.g., sensations registering lumps in the throat, goosebumps on the skin, churnings in the stomach, and tension across muscles of the head. I am inclined to think that the feeling component of emotion is best understood as involving both sorts of things. I will accordingly refer to these, respectively, as the *phenomenological* and the *sensational* aspects of the affective (or feeling) component of an emotion.

It is time to say clearly that the standard emotional response to a

---

tionalism and the Emotions," in *Explaining Emotions*; Moreland Perkins, "Emotions and Feeling," *Philosophical Review*, 75 (1966); Patricia S. Greenspan, "Ambivalence and the Logic of Emotion," in *Explaining Emotions*; and Malcolm Budd, "The Repudiation of Emotion: Hanslick on Music," *British Journal of Aesthetics*, 20 (1980). The first two essays include rather extended analysis of the concept of an emotion, and I am particularly indebted to them for some distinctions I employ in this essay.

musical work—e.g., what I have called a sadness-reaction—is not in truth a case of *full-fledged* emotion. This is mainly because music neither supplies an appropriate object for an emotion to be directed on, nor generates the associated beliefs, desires, or attitudes regarding an object which are essential to an emotion being what it is. When a symphonic adagio "saddens" me, I am not sad at or about the music, nor do I regard the adagio as something I would wish to be otherwise. Furthermore, this weakening of the cognitive component in emotional response to music generally results in the inhibition of most characteristic behaviors and in the significant lessening of behavioral tendencies.

Yet the purely physiological and, more important, affective components are occasionally, it seems, retained in something like full force. If music inevitably fails to induce by itself a proper, contextually embedded *emotion* of sadness,[9] still, some music appears fully capable of inducing at least the characteristic *feeling* of sadness. This is enough, I take it, for the problem of negative emotional response to music to resist complete solution by any of the proposals shortly to be considered. I shall have occasion to distinguish between *emotions* (including cognitive elements) and associated *feelings* (lacking cognitive elements) in what follows. And when I speak subsequently of "emotional response" to music, this should be understood as an experience produced in a listener which is *at least* the characteristic feeling of some emotion, but which is short of a complete emotion per se.

I am going to assume for the purposes of this essay that the majority of common emotions have affective components (comprising both phenomenological and sensational aspects) which are more or less distinctive of them, apart from the cognitive components that are perhaps the logically distinctive ones. That is to say, I will assume there are introspectible differences between common emotions. Evidence for this is provided by cases in which persons suddenly realize that they are sad, happy, depressed, anxious, or in love without recognizing ex-

---

[9] It is helpful to keep in mind a distinction between the inducing and the reviving of emotions. Music does not by itself normally *induce* full-fledged emotions, but it can sometimes *revive* ones had earlier so that they are reexperienced—beliefs, desires, feelings, and all. (More often it will simply *recall* such emotions—i.e., revive the *memory* of them.) But the objects and cognitive contents of revived emotions will have been supplied on earlier, nonmusical occasions.

plicitly that they hold certain beliefs, desires, or evaluations, and thus apparently on the basis of quality of feeling. There is, granted, some psychological research that appears to suggest that common emotions are not much differentiated in inner feeling or affect, but this research strikes me as inconclusive and as somewhat questionable in its method.[10] In any event, it is undeniable that negative affect is integrally involved in a number of emotional conditions, and that there is at least *some* range of qualitative difference in affect across the spectrum of negative emotions. The persistence of our problem and the viability of certain answers to it that we shall entertain actually require nothing more than that.

VI

Those who are skeptical of the claim that music often induces familiar emotions in listeners sometimes maintain that what is induced is neither one special aesthetic emotion nor memory images of past emotions, but instead musical *analogs* of the familiar emotions of life. There are two questions that arise here. One is the respects in which these music-emotions differ from ordinary emotions. The second is the respects in which they are the same and which presumably justify calling them by a common name.

John Hospers, in a well-known essay on expression in art, suggests that the emotional response to sad music is indeed not real sadness, but only music-sadness. Here is Hospers's explication of this phenomenon:

> Sadness expressed in music is a very different thing from sadness in life; it is only by a kind of analogy that we use the same word for both. . . . Sadness in music is depersonalized; it is taken out of or abstracted from, the particular personal situation in which we ordinarily feel it, such as the death of a loved one or the shattering of one's hopes. In music we get what is sometimes called the "essence" of sadness without all the accompanying accidents, or causal conditions

[10]For example, one might draw this conclusion from S. Schacter and J. E. Singer, "Cognitive, Social and Physiological Determinants of Emotional State," *Psychological Review*, 69 (1962). However, that paper barely recognizes the possibility of an affective component in emotional states distinct from that of purely physiological arousal, and is mainly concerned to establish the *necessity* of cognitive components in emotion.

which usually bring it into being. In view of this, it is said, we can continue to say that music expresses sadness, but we should distinguish the *music-sadness,* which is a happy experience, from *life-sadness,* which is not.[11]

We may interpret Hospers as saying that music-sadness feels (narrow sense) like life-sadness but (1) lacks an object or situational context, and (2) lacks the usual causal conditions of sadness. What it has in common with life-sadness, then, is presumably a certain mode of feeling, possibly lessened in intensity, and certain underlying physiological disturbances.

It is not obvious that the invocation of music-emotions—muted, objectless analogs of life-emotions—is of itself any help in understanding why negative emotional response in music should be so sought after. The prick of a needle hurts less than the stab of a knife, but it is not for that reason to be desired. One would not go out of one's way to have it administered, even if all consciousness of perpetrating agent, physical environment, and lasting effect were eliminated. The appeal to weaker, cognitively impoverished forms of the normal negative emotions faces the following dilemma: If music-φness involves the same mode of inner feeling as life-φness, however muted in strength, then its prima facie unpleasantness would seem to make it something to avoid. On the other hand, if music-φness and life-φness involve different modes of inner feeling, then it becomes unclear what connection there is between them at all, and unconvincing that emotional response in music consists in something so wholly unrelated to the ordinary emotion by which we are disposed to denominate it. In short, if there is such a thing as music-sadness, resembling life-sadness and evoked by sad music, it has not yet been shown how this can be a "happy experience."

Another suggestion worth considering here is that when we are "saddened" by music we are not made really sad, but only make-believedly so.[12] That is to say, music raises certain states of feeling in us, which we then make believe to be emotions in the full sense, by ourselves supplying the requisite cognitive filling out.

[11]Hospers, "Concept of Artistic Expression," p. 152. In this paragraph Hospers is considering evocation theories of expression, and so the assumption that expression equals evocation is in effect.

[12]A suggestion like this might be drawn from Kendall Walton, "Fearing Fictions," *Journal of Philosophy,* 75 (1978): 5–27.

Our response to the previous suggestion would seem to apply here as well. If the feeling component of, say, make-believe anger were the same as that of real anger, then given its unpleasant tone, it is unclear why make-believe anger should be any more pursued than real anger. Why should make believing that I am angry, given an appropriate state of inner agitation, provide me with satisfaction? Furthermore, to the extent that the make-believe is effective, the *more* distressed I would seem to become, imagining not only that I felt (narrowly) a certain unpleasant way, but that all the undesirable life consequences and accompaniments of being truly angry were also in the offing.

In addition, I am skeptical that in the cases we are interested in, those of deep emotional response to music, we in fact standardly make believe that we are truly possessed of various emotions—at least if this requires that we do so in an *explicit and fully determinate* manner. It seems our imaginative responses to music are typically not so definite as that. When we are "saddened" by sad music, or "frightened" by fearful music, we generally are not making believe that there is a particular object, with particular characteristics, for us to be sad about or frightened of. Nor do we make believe that we have certain attitudes or desires toward such determinate intentional objects. Emotional response to music does not have the same degree of cognitive structure as emotional response to well-delineated entities of fictional worlds. To maintain otherwise is to exaggerate the extent to which listeners intellectually augment their basic affective responses to music. On the other hand, this is not to deny that a listener may, in a less concrete way, imaginatively assume an emotional state in virtue of identifying with music that is engaging him. I shall return to this point in section IX.

VII

Another possible way around the question of emotional response to music, and thus around the problem of negative emotion in music, is to claim that the appearance of emotional response is simply a well-buttressed illusion, founded on a confusion between perceiving and feeling. The proper aesthetic response to music, it will be said, is a purely *cognitive* one, consisting in among other things the recognition and appreciation of emotional qualities in music. What occasionally seems to us to be the experiencing of something like sorrow, while listening in anything like a correct manner, is in fact always only the vivid grasping of sorrowfulness in music.

I regard this line as highly implausible. Of course, the exclusively cognitive response to expression in music is a possible mode of aesthetic involvement—the detached, critical mode of the auditory connoisseur. To be sure, one can detect expression without being moved, and one can come to understand a work's moods without necessarily mirroring them. But the detached mode of involvement is just one mode among several which can be adopted, and is hardly the only aesthetically recommendable one. Its aesthetic superiority over a more open and inclusive mode of involvement—in which one both registers *and* reacts to emotion in music—is at least questionable.

Responding emotionally to music is clearly consistent with perceiving emotional qualities in it. But what is more, these activities may be subtly interdependent ones. What we seem to perceive influences what we feel, and what we feel influences what we say we perceive. On the one hand, part of what inclines us to describe a quality of music with a given emotional term is a sense of what emotion the music tends to evoke in us; but on the other hand, part of the reason we have an emotional reaction to music is perception of a corresponding emotional quality in it, provisionally identified on the basis of physiognomic resemblance—analogy to expressive behavior—or conventional associations. We are saddened in part by perception of a quality in a passage which we construe as sadness, but we in part denominate that quality "sadness"—or confirm such denomination of it—in virtue of being saddened by the music or sensing its capacity to sadden us under somewhat different conditions. Recognizing emotion in music and experiencing emotion from music may not be as separable in principle as one might have liked. If this is so, the suggestion that in aesthetic appreciation of music we simply cognize emotional attributes without feeling anything corresponding to them may be conceptually problematic as well as empirically incredible.

VIII

Nelson Goodman, certainly, does not make the error of representing the perception of expression in music as an emotionless undertaking.

On the contrary, he emphasizes the role of feeling as an essential aid in determining what expressive properties a work actually has. In his now familiar words, "In aesthetic experience the emotions function cognitively."[13] Their chief role is to inform us about the character of the works we are involved with.

But can this by itself explain the attraction that negative music has for us? Goodman tells us that "in aesthetic experience, emotion positive or negative is a mode of sensitivity to a work."[14] The value of despairing or sorrowing response to music, then, is that it is requisite to our correctly discerning the emotional qualities of the music. So by this account we let ourselves in for often considerable distress solely in order to learn accurately the characteristics of the object that is tormenting us. What seems puzzling is why we should be so committed to ascertaining the properties of works of art that put us in unpleasant states. Do we have a duty to all artistic objects to discern their characters correctly, whatever the cost? Surely not. Does the cognitive reward we derive from perceiving rightly that a movement is, say, anguished outweigh the anguish we may feel in the course of that perception? It would not seem so. Getting to know a work's dark qualities may be a partial justification for suffering from it, but it cannot be the whole story. Two things in particular seem insufficiently explained. One is the depth to which we often want to feel negative emotion in music, beyond what could plausibly be required as an assist to cognitive assessment; the other is the fact that the Goodmanian observation, as far as it goes, accounts more for the instrumental value than for the peculiar desirability of negative emotion from music.

IX

In this section I describe more fully what I take the typical strong emotional response to music to consist in. Sketching the outline of this experience in greater detail will aid us in determining what value it has that has not been adequately explained on any of the perspectives canvassed above.

I begin by stating the conditions of listening that conduce to a

13 Nelson Goodman, *Languages of Art* (Indianapolis: Bobbs-Merrill, 1968), p. 248.
14 Ibid., p. 250.

response of this kind. For clearly not every audition of an emotionally powerful work will affect a listener in that way, nor would one want it to. The first condition would seem to be that a work be in a familiar style, and that the work itself be rather familiar to the listener, so that its specific flow and character have been registered internally, but not so familiar that there is anything of boredom in hearing it unfold on the given occasion. This occurs when a piece is well known though not tiresome, when expectations are firmly aroused in the course of it but denouements remain uncertain.[15]

The second condition is generally taken to be central to the "aesthetic attitude" on any account of that frame of mind. And that is a mode of attention closely focused on the music, its structure, progression, and emergent character, with a consequent inattention to, or reduced consciousness of, the extramusical world and one's present situation in it.

A third condition is one of emotional openness to the content of music, as opposed to distant contemplation of the same. One must be willing to identify with music, to put oneself in its shoes. One must allow oneself to be moved in a receptive manner by the emotion one hears, as opposed to merely noting or even marveling at it.

Such a listener is not, however, moved straight into a slough of feelings and as a result into oblivion of the music itself. On the contrary, deep emotional response to music typically arises as a product of the most intense musical perception. It is generally in virtue of the *recognition* of emotions expressed in music, or of emotion-laden gestures embodied in musical movement, that an emotional reaction occurs.[16] Usually what happens is of an *empathetic* or *mirroring* nature. When we identify with music that we are perceiving—or perhaps better, with the person whom we imagine owns the emotions or emotional gestures we hear in the music—we share in and adopt those emotions as our own, for the course of the audition.[17] And so we

[15] An interesting account of the point of "optimum appreciation" for a musical work, from an information theoretical perspective, can be found in Leonard Meyer, "On Rehearing Music," in *Music, the Arts, and Ideas* (Chicago: University of Chicago Press, 1967), pp. 42–53.

[16] I leave out of account, for simplicity, the extent to which identification of emotional expression in music and evocation of feeling by music may be mutually dependent (see section VII).

[17] Of course, it is possible to have an emotional response to music that is not *empathetic*, but rather *reactive* in nature. Instead of identifying with music, we may just

end up feeling as, in imagination, the music does. The point to note here about this phenomenon is that cognition is central to it. If I don't perceive what emotions are in the music by attending to it intently, I have nothing to properly identify and empathize with.[18]

Now, what I am maintaining is simply that when the three conditions indicated above are fulfilled, then for certain musical compositions there is often an empathetic emotional response that consists in something very like experience of the emotion expressed in the music. As noted earlier, this experience includes at its core the characteristic physiological disturbances of the emotion and its characteristic inner affect. The crucial falling off from bona fide emotion occurs in the cognitive dimension; music-emotions lack objects and associated thoughts about them.

This is not to say, however, that emotional responses to music have *no* cognitive (or thoughtlike) component. They do, but it is *etiolated* by comparison to that of real-life emotion. Say the emotion expressed in the music is sadness. Then in an empathetic response, in addition to physiological and affective elements, there is, in the first place, the general *idea* (or *concept*) of sadness. Since a listener is standardly made sad by apprehending and then identifying with sadness in the music, naturally the thought of that emotion is present to the mind concurrent with whatever is felt. In the second place, identifying with the music involves initially the cognitive act of imagining that the music is either *itself* a sad individual or else the *audible expression* of

---

react directly to a quality the music is literally possessed of, or we may imaginatively regard music as an other and react to it from the outside, instead of equating ourselves with it emotionally. Examples of the former sort would be amusement at humorous music, indignation at plagiaristic music, annoyance at badly constructed music. In such response the music serves not only as the cause but as the proper object of the emotion aroused. Examples of the latter sort would be a fearful response to a threatening passage imaginatively taken to be a threatening individual, or a pitying response to an agonized passage that one imaginatively regards as a person in agony. To deal further with reactive emotional responses to music would take us too far afield. It should be obvious, however, that some of these responses pose the same problem of negative emotion in music as empathetic ones when they are ostensibly unpleasant in feeling tone.

[18] There is, naturally, much more that could be said to fill in the basic picture of how affective response to music is generated. For a description of the mirroring response to emotion characteristics in music, see S. Davies, "The Expression of Emotion in Music," *Mind*, 89 (1980): 67–86. On the mechanism of identifying with music, see the insightful discussion in R. K. Elliott, "Aesthetic Theory and the Experience of Art," in *Aesthetics*, ed. H. Osborne (London: Oxford University Press, 1972), pp. 145–57.

somebody's sadness. In the third place, such identification involves subsequently a cognitive act of imagining that one, too, is sad—that it is *one's own* sadness the music expresses—and thus, however amorphously, that one has something to be sad about.

Let us look at this last phase more closely. When one hears sad music, begins to feel sad, and imagines that one is actually sad, one must, according to the logic of the concept, be imagining that there is an object for one's sadness and that one holds certain evaluative beliefs (or attitudes) regarding it. The point, though, is that this latter imagining generally remains *indeterminate*. That is to say, one does not actually imagine a *particular* object for one's sadness and does not imaginarily hold beliefs about it. In imagining that I have actually become sad by virtue of hearing some music I allow only that my feeling has *some* focus, but without going on to specify this any further. In other words, the object of an empathetic sadness response to music is a largely formal one. When through identification with music I am saddened by the *poco allegretto* of Brahms's Third Symphony, my "sadness" is not directed on the music, or on any real-life situation of concern to me, but instead on some featureless object posited vaguely by my imagination.[19]

Summing up, then, empathetic emotional responses to music of the sort we are interested in—the sort that our anecdotal hero underwent at the beginning of this essay—typically comprise the following: physiological and affective components of the emotion that is embodied in the music; the thought or idea of this emotion; and the imagination, through identification with the music, of oneself as actually experiencing this emotion, though without the usual determinateness of focus.

X

We are now, I think, in a decent position to offer explanations of the appeal of negative emotional response to music, the nature of which I

---

[19] It might be suggested that the imagined object of my sadness is just whatever is the object of the sadness of the sad person "in the music" with whom I am identifying. I think this may sometimes be so, but it does not really affect the matter of indeterminacy I am addressing since this object, too, remains completely unspecified, only formally indicated.

have been attempting to make clear. I begin by acknowledging two contributions to a complete answer which emerge from views mentioned earlier. The first is the Goodmanian observation that emotional response facilitates our grasp, assessment, and description of the expression in a musical work. This is doubtless true, and even if it can hardly account totally for our willingness to suffer negative emotion from a sonata, neither should it be ignored.

The second is the Aristotelian element of catharsis. Surely in some circumstances the virtue of, say, a grief-response to music is that it allows one to bleed off in a controlled manner a certain amount of harmful emotion with which one is afflicted. One "grieves" while listening, in a pure and limited way, thus purging oneself to some extent of real grief that one has either been consciously yielding to, in typical unruly fashion, or else has been suppressing in the oubliettes of the unconscious. From a cathartic perspective, negative emotional response to music is desirable because it conduces to mental health, improving the listener's future self by administering momentarily painful doses of emotional medicine in the present. There seems no denying that dark music can be therapeutic in this way; the thing to notice, though, is that the cathartic explanation applies strictly to listeners currently in the grip of unhealthy emotions, whether on a conscious or unconscious level. Yet it seems that negative emotional response has appeal for, and offers rewards to, listeners for whom this is not the case. I may seek out and relish grief, longing, and anguish from music when I am neither overwrought by these emotions nor occupied by them in subterranean fashion. Furthermore, just the raising of such emotions seems to provide satisfaction prior to any siphoning off that may ultimately ensue. Cathartic benefits, while occasionally very real, seem too indirect and prudential to be the whole or even the largest part of why we crave the experience of negative emotion from music.

XI

The first point to be noted in arriving at the more comprehensive solution we seek is that emotional response to music and emotion in ordinary life differ in one crucial and obvious respect, connected to the attenuation of cognitive content in the former. Emotional responses to music typically *have no life-implications,* in contrast to their real counterparts. The "sadness" one may be made to feel by sympathetically attending to music has no basis in one's extramusical life, signals no enduring state of negative affect, indicates no problem requiring action, calls forth no persisting pattern of behavior, and in general bodes no ill for one's future. One does not really believe—though one may intermittently imagine—that one's sadness-response is objectively apt, that some situation exists in one's life which is to be bemoaned. On the other hand, if one is truly sad one must believe this, and will, accordingly, both expect one's feeling to persist until objective conditions are changed and be disposed to take action to remedy one's unhappy state. The person having a sadness-response to music is generally free, however, from this expectation and disposition. The experience of sadness from music consists primarily of a feeling under a conception, but bracketed from and unfettered by the demands and involvements of the corresponding emotion in life.

Since negative emotional response to music is devoid of the contextual implications of such as sadness, grief, anger, we are able to focus more fully on just the feeling involved in these emotions. This opens the way for three benefits which we may reap by allowing ourselves to mirror darkly emotional music. These are benefits of enjoyment, of understanding, and of self-assurance.

To make out the first requires a somewhat startling claim, but it is one without which we cannot, I think, wholly resolve the paradox we have been addressing. This claim is that emotive affect itself, divorced from all psychological and behavioral consequences, is in virtually all cases something that we are capable of taking satisfaction in. That is to say, the pure feeling component of just about any emotion—providing it is not too violent or intense—is something we can, on balance, enjoy experiencing.

When feelings are made available to us isolated, backgroundless, and inherently limited in duration—as they are through music—we can approach them as if we were wine tasters, sampling the delights of various vintages, or like Des Esseintes, the hero of Huysmans's *À Rebours*, reveling in the flavors conveyed by a mouth organ fitted with a variety of liqueurs. We become cognoscenti of feeling, savoring the qualitative aspect of emotional life for its own sake.

This is not to say that the pure feeling has nothing unpleasant about it. If in itself it did not possess a negative tone it could hardly count as the feeling of some negative emotion. But in the detached context of musical response, it becomes possible for us to savor the feeling for its special character, since we are for once spared the additional distress that accompanies its occurrence in the context of life. The characteristic feeling at the core of, say, grief or despair has an irreducibly painful aspect, to be sure, but the distastefulness and undesirability of the emotion as a whole springs at least as much from the beliefs involved in it regarding the real existence of an evil and the consequent persistence of negative affect. An uncomfortable state that we know will not last and that testifies to no fault in our world does not pain us as it would if we had no such assurance. It is not so much the resulting feeling that we mind in grief or despair as the *significance* of that feeling, which is carried by the associated beliefs or attitudes. When these are absent, as in emotional response to music, we find ourselves able to a large extent to appreciate feelings—even negatively toned feelings—for themselves. We relish the particular qualities of such feelings to a degree sufficient to compensate us for the element of painfulness they still contain. The undistracted experience of affects of just about any sort, when free of practical consequence, appears to have intrinsic appeal for many of us. I will label this the reward of Savoring Feeling.

The second reward attaching to negative emotional response to music in virtue of its contextual freedom is that of greater understanding of the condition of feeling involved in some recognized emotion. It is notoriously difficult to say what the knowledge of how an emotion feels consists in, but I think it is clear that such knowledge, whatever it amounts to, can be augmented by emotional experiences during or after occasions of music listening. At such times we have an opportunity to introspectively scrutinize and ponder the inner affective dimension of an emotion—say, anguish—whose idea is before the mind, in a manner not open to the individual who is caught in the throes of real anguish. We can attain insight into what the feeling of anguish is *like*, not in the sense that we learn what it resembles, but in the sense that we perceive and register it more clearly. This in turn cashes out in an improved ability to recognize and to recollectively contemplate this feeling in future. One can deepen or reinforce one's image of what it is to feel melancholy by experiencing the *poco allegretto* of Brahms's

Third, or of what it is to feel hopeless passion by responding to Scriabin's C-sharp Minor Etude. Note, finally, that the cognitive reward attested to here, that of Understanding Feeling, is distinct from (though not unrelated to) the Goodmanian one mentioned earlier, that of Apprehending Expression.

The third of the rewards announced above relates directly to a person's self-respect or sense of dignity as a human being. Central to most people's ideal image of themselves is the capacity to feel deeply a range of emotions. We like to think of ourselves as able to be stirred profoundly, and in various ways, by appropriate occurrences. The individual whose emotional faculty is inactive, shallow, or one-dimensional seems to us less of a person. Since music has the power to put us into the feeling state of a negative emotion without its unwanted life consequences, it allows us to partly reassure ourselves in a nondestructive manner of the depth and breadth of our ability to feel. Having a negative emotional response to music is like giving our emotional engines a "dry run." If there is something wrong with the plane it is better to find this out on the runway than in the air. Although one would not opt to try on real grief just to see if one were capable of it, confirmation of this of a sort can perhaps be had less riskily by involvement with music. Whether such confirmation can legitimately be had in this way is not clearly to the point; for even if it is epistemically flawed, its psychological effect is real enough. Furthermore, in exercising our feeling capacities on music we might be said to tone them up, or get them into shape, thus readying ourselves for intenser and more focused reactions to situations in life. It is worth noting that this reward of emotional response to music is more naturally associated with negative than with positive emotions. It is usually not emotions like joy, amusement, or excitement that we have a need of proving ourselves equal to and prepared for feeling, and it is generally not the ability to feel those emotions which has the most weight in the common idea of an emotionally developed individual. Call this the reward of Emotional Assurance.

XII

So far we have reckoned up certain rewards of negative emotional response to music which accrue to it regarded as an experience of pure feeling concurrent with the mere idea of a corresponding emotion. We must now turn to the rewards of imagining, through identification, that one is in the full emotional condition, while knowing throughout that one is not.

These are collectively as important as the rewards already considered. There seem to be at least three of them, which I will address in turn. The first is of special relevance to the paradox we have been concerned with in that it, unlike any of the other rewards mentioned, attaches almost exclusively to negative as opposed to positive emotional response to music.

If I empathetically experience feelings of despair or anguish from a despairing or anguished piece of music and also regard the music as the unfolding expression of someone's despair or anguish, then I may begin to identify with that someone and consequently to imagine, in a fashion described earlier, that I am myself in actual despair or anguish. I may even have the impression that I am generating the music de profundis as an expression of the despair or anguish I imagine I am now experiencing. In any case, since my imagined emotion is one with that of the music's persona, it will partake in the destiny and vicissitudes of that emotion as conveyed by the development of the music.

Since I have identified my emotional state with that expressed in the music, I can feel that what seems to happen to that emotion in the course of the music is happening to me as well. And this, because of the way in which emotional content is carried by musical structure, is often a source of satisfaction, especially where unpleasant or difficult emotions are involved.

Emotions presented in and imaginatively experienced through music, unlike those encountered in real life, have a character of inevitability, purposiveness, and finality about them. This is undoubtedly because they seem so intimately connected with the progress of musical substance itself as to be inseparable from it. Thus what primarily or initially characterizes musical movement or development comes to seem as well an attribute of the emotional content it underpins. Emotion in a musical composition, because of its construction, so often strikes us as having been resolved, transformed, transfigured, or triumphed over when the music is done.

When the first section in C minor of Brahms's *poco allegretto* gives way smoothly to a trio in A-flat major, we can imagine our sobbing melancholy melting into a mood of hesitant gaiety. When the main material of the *Marcia Funebre* breaks at midpoint into a stately fugue on the same themes, we can imagine our bottomless grief as metamorphosed, diffracted into shining fragments of a more easily borne pathos. And when the extended musical logic of the finale of Dvořák's Seventh Symphony in D Minor eventuates in a dissonant though shortly resolved brass-dominated yawp in the final measures, one can share in its experience of stern tragedy culminating in hard-won, reluctant resignation.

By imaginatively identifying our state with that of the music, we derive from a suitably constructed composition a sense of mastery and control over—or at least accommodation with—emotions that in the extramusical setting are thoroughly upsetting, and over which we hope to be victorious when and if the time comes. And emotional response, it should be emphasized, seems necessary to reap this benefit. Unless one actually feels something as the music is heard, and projects oneself into its condition, one will not be entitled to think: "That was my emotion, that is how I dealt with it, that is what became of it." This clearly helps compensate us for whatever additional distress derives from allowing in imagination that we are melancholy, despairing, grieving, or the like. Call this the reward of Emotional Resolution.

The second reward of identifying with music to the point of imagining oneself possessed of real negative emotion is simpler than and in a sense prior to that just discussed. If one begins to regard music as the expression of one's own current emotional state, it will begin to seem as if it issues from oneself, as if it pours forth from one's innermost being.[20] It is then very natural for one to receive an impression of expressive power—of freedom and ease in externalizing and embodying what one feels. The sense one has of the richness and spontaneity with which one's inner life is unfolding itself, even where the feelings involved are of the negative kind, is a source of undeniable joy. The unpleasant aspect of certain emotions we imagine ourselves to experience through music is balanced by the adequacy, grace, and splendor of the exposition we feel ourselves to be according that emotion. Of course we do not really have such expressive ability—that which we seem to ourselves to have while identifying with music is obviously founded in the musical abilities of the composer. But we are not actually deceiving ourselves. We do not literally believe we are creators of music. The composer's musical genius makes possible the imagina-

[20] Cf. Elliott, "Aesthetic Theory," on the experience of hearing music "from within."

tive experience described above, and we can remain aware of that throughout. But this does not take away the resulting satisfaction. The coat may be borrowed, but it is just as warm. Call this the reward of Expressive Potency.

The last reward of imagining negative emotion I will discuss arises most clearly when a listener is willing to entertain what I call the Expressionist assumption concerning the emotional content of what he is hearing. On the Expression theory of music, espoused by Tolstoy and Cooke among others, emotion heard in a sonata is always emotion experienced by the composer on an earlier occasion, which has now been transmuted into music. The sonata is a vehicle for conveying a particular sort of emotional experience from one person to another. Now, it seems that without subscribing to the obviously inadequate Expression theory itself, we may sometimes as listeners adopt the Expressionist assumption—that the emotion expressed in a particular piece belongs to its composer's biography—while imagining ourselves to be possessed of the full emotion whose feeling has been aroused within us. If we do so we are in effect imagining that we are sharing in the precise emotional experience of another human being, the man or woman responsible for the music we hear. This, as Tolstoy so well appreciated, carried with it a decided reward—the reward of intimacy—which accrues whether the emotion is positive or negative in tone. The sense of intimate contact with the mind and soul of another, the sense that one is manifestly not alone in the emotional universe, goes a long way toward counterbalancing the possibly distressing aspect of the grief, sorrow, or anger one imagines onself to have. The emotional separateness and alienation which occur frequently in daily living are here miraculously swept aside in imaginative identification with the composer whose feelings are, on the Expressionist assumption, plainly revealed for any listener to hear and to mirror. Call this the reward of Emotional Communion.

XIII

In this section I address a charge sometimes levied against concern with evocation of emotion by music.[21] It has been said that an interest

[21] This is particularly well formulated in Malcolm Budd, "The Repudiation of Emotion," pp. 39–41.

in music for the emotional experience it can induce cannot be an aesthetic interest. For to have an aesthetic interest in music is to be interested in it for its own sake, in all its concrete and particular detail, and not as an instrument to some further end. One must be interested in a piece of music *itself*, so that no other object, musical or nonmusical, would do equally well even though it induced the very same emotional state. The specific composition must be *integral* to aesthetic appreciation of it, and not in principle replaceable by anything that provided approximately the same effects.

I have some doubt as to whether this position as to the necessary character of aesthetic interest is ultimately defensible. But that aside, I want to consider to what extent an interest in music for the negative emotional response it can occasion can be construed so as to qualify as aesthetic by these lights—so that, in particular, the specific composition involved can be seen to have an ineliminable role in the resulting experience.

If we consider the eight rewards of negative emotional response we have detailed,[22] we may note first that three of them—Apprehending Expression, Emotional Resolution, and Expressive Potency—inherently involve attention to specific musical substance concurrently with any feelings that are aroused. For it is manifest that one cannot categorize the emotion in a passage, hear one's emotion transmuted in the course of a development section, or glory in the power and richness of one's expression of emotion in sound without attending explicitly to the musical matter of what is before one's ears. The music is not just a means to an end which can be understood apart from it, but integrally involved in that end.

But even with respect to the other five rewards it may be possible for appreciation of emotional response to music to be aesthetic in virtue of the way such response is tied to perception of individual musical form. In we review the total experience of emotion in a musical work we typically find something like this: (a) perception of individual musical form; (b) apprehension of embodied expression; (c) empathetic feeling response to embodied expression; (d) imagination of real emotion on

---

[22]To list them together, they are: (1) Apprehending Expression, (2) Emotional Catharsis, (3) Savoring Feeling, (4) Understanding Feeling, (5) Emotional Assurance, (6) Emotional Resolution, (7) Expressive Potency, (8) Emotional Communion.

the basis of (c); and lastly, (e) awareness of how (b), (c), and (d) are rooted in (a). The perceptual part of this experience is irreplaceable; not only is it causally responsible for the affective part, but the relation between them is an object of awareness in its own right. Now, since musical works are perceptually distinct from one another, no other work can have associated with it the same comprehensive experience— the same fusion of evoked emotion with apprehension of musical form and quality, together with awareness of their relation. Thus, if this total experience is what we are after—if what we are primarily seeking is emotion embedded in a particular complicated perceptual activity that generates it—then whatever further rewards attach to such emotion, our appreciation remains recognizably aesthetic, focused on individual compositions and involving them essentially.

In maintaining an aesthetic interest in music, the apparent extrinsicality of certain of the rewards we derive from evoked feeling is modified if our concern is specifically with those feelings *as communicated by a particular musical structure*. Deriving satisfaction from an emotional reaction seems legitimately aesthetic if one attends to the particular musical entity responsible for it and if appreciation is basically directed on an emotional state as founded in and intertwined with an intricate aural perception. In the aesthetic mode we properly value the specific (though not necessarily *unique*)[23] shade of feeling a passage evokes through apprehension of its wholly individual note-to-note form, and not just that shade of feeling *tout court*, however produced.

The question, though, is how plausible it is to maintain, with respect to the remaining five rewards, that the appreciative focus is this complex I will call the *music-qualified* feeling or emotion—i.e., the feeling or (imagined) emotion *as induced by and as experienced with* these particular notes—as opposed to the feeling or emotion by itself, apart from that musical environment. The answer, I think, is that it is more plausible for some of our rewards and less so for others.

If I am savoring a bit of objectless sorrowful feeling aroused in me by Albinoni's famous *adagio*, it may be that I am savoring especially that

---

[23] I do not assume that the emotional content of a musical structure, or the emotional response it induces as a result, must necessarily belong to it alone, for reasons explored in Chapter 6, above.

feeling as emerging from the adagio's unique strains. And if I commune in imagination with Schubert's psyche by way of the stern determination raised in me by some passages of his C Minor op. post. Piano Sonata, it may be that the state I imagine us to share is specifically such determination *as felt in* the sounding of those very measures. So I might, for these rewards [(3) and (8)], be valuing particularly the music-qualified feeling rather than the feeling in the abstract. And if so, then Albinoni's and Schubert's works are essentially involved in the satisfactions I extract from them; the experience I am specifically valuing is not detachable from the music that provides it.

On the other hand, when it comes to appreciating or valuing feeling evoked by music because of the occasion it offers for either deeper understanding of what it is like, or increased conviction of one's emotional range, or eliminative catharsis [rewards (4), (5), and (2)], then it appears unlikely that the focus of appreciation or value would be the music-qualified feeling rather than the feeling *simpliciter*. What I want to know better, assure myself about, or purge myself of is just the ordinary feeling, and not a perceptually qualified relative of it.

Thus we can reclaim most, though not all, of the rewards of negative emotional response to music from the anteroom of the aesthetic. Whether the others could be redeemed or not would depend on re-thinking and broadening what may properly be included in aesthetic intercourse with works of art. But what should not be lost sight of is that even if some of these rewards are ultimately adjudged nonaesthetic, that would not affect their relevance to the basic problem of this essay, namely, to explain how negative emotional response in the course of normal, if not unadulteratedly aesthetic, interaction with musical works can be valued and desired by listeners.

XIV

Have we now succeeded in rescuing the occupant of the musical "electric chair" with which we began? I think so. We have suggested, first, that although this person is actually registering the feelings of some negative emotions this may, in the circumstances, itself afford a certain satisfaction, and second, that there are a number of more indirect rewards deriving from those feelings and the imagined emotions erected upon them, which more than compensate for what disagreeableness we may be inclined to ascribe to the conditons assumed in the course of listening. Those works of Beethoven, Mozart, Brahms, Scriabin, and Mahler do not constitute for aesthetic appreciation a bed of hot coals, to be sure, but neither do they present themselves as merely a display case of mineral specimens, mounted and remote. I hope in this essay to have avoided the errors of both images and to have presented a more balanced picture. Little short of the story I have told, I think, can fully account for why we often seek negative emotion from the art of sound rather than remaining content with mere perception, at arm's length, of its musical embodiment.

Additional Notes

1. Peter Kivy, in the course of a general attack on music's power to engage the ordinary emotions ("How Music Moves," in *What Is Music?* ed. P. Alperson [New York: Haven Publications, 1987], pp. 147–63), holds my essay up at the end to show that he has not been "beating a dead horse." His main target is the claim that music can, in nonpathological individuals, arouse full-fledged *emotions* of the ordinary variety. With this, of course, I agree, and Kivy is good enough to acknowledge it (162). Where we differ, apparently, is on whether anything *like* those emotions—e.g., the *feelings* characteristic of them—might be raised by music, or whether music's emotional effect on us is exclusively of a different and sui generis order. Kivy maintains the latter; he says that music can *move* us—by its beauty, perfection, craftsmanship, or even the excellence of its expressiveness—but that this emotion is unrelated to the ordinary emotions that such music might embody (157–59).

   Now, I am happy to allow that there is a distinctive reaction to the beauty and other artistic virtues of a piece of music, that this kind of reaction is central to aesthetic appreciation of the music, and that, being of the nature of admiration or even exaltation, it can well be qualified as emotional. But I am unwilling to allow that that is *all* there ever is, on the emotional side. Identifying a kind of feeling called "being moved" does nothing to show that *other*, more specific feelings, ones characteristic of the ordinary life emotions, are not sometimes present *as well*. I have tried, in my essay, to show how those might reasonably come about; via the listener's vivid *imagining* of the emotions in question, courtesy of the music embodying them, and not by the listener's actually *having* those emotions, for the music or anything else. And whereas that latter would be irrational, there is nothing irrational about imagining, say, a real sadness belonging to the music's persona—and then, by extension, to oneself—given the rewards one is then, if I am right, in a position to reap.

   [I note that Kivy has subsequently launched a full-scale critique of my essay, in Chapter 16 of his *Sound Sentiment* (Philadelphia: Temple University Press, 1989). I cannot, however, respond to that critique in this space.]

2. Since I have found that "Music and Negative Emotion" has given some readers the impression that I am endorsing an *evocation* or *arousal* account of expression,

despite my explicit disclaimer to this effect in section II, I think it worth restating my position with respect to music's evocative capacity. One is saddened* by sad music if one is made or led to *feel* a certain way—a way I claim is fairly distinctive of sadness, though that is not at issue at present—and to *imagine*, on that basis, that one is sad or is experiencing sadness. This typically occurs, recall, through an act of empathetic emotional identification with the perceived persona of the music. It was, then, a claim of my essay that listeners are *sometimes* saddened* by sad music, and that the state of being saddened* is *somewhat like*, and particularly internally, the state of being sad. But it was not my intent to intimate either (a) that listeners are *always*, or even *usually*, saddened* by sad music, or (b) that music's expressing sadness is *a matter of* its evoking sadness*, or (c) that music's expressing sadness is even a matter of its evocative *power*. (For a recent writer who *does* unabashedly endorse the musical evocation of emotion, and an account of musical expression based on this, see Peter Mew, "The Expression of Emotion in Music," *British Journal of Aesthetics*, 25 [1985]: 33–35, and "The Musical Arousal of Emotions," *British Journal of Aesthetics*, 26 [1986]: 357–61.)

3. I now believe that when I wrote, in section IX, that "since a listener is standardly made sad by apprehending and then identifying with sadness in the music, naturally *the thought of that emotion* is present to the mind concurrent with whatever is felt," I was overstating things a bit. If the apprehending and identifying is done on a *self-conscious, intellectual* level, then the thought of the emotion will indeed be present. If not, then perhaps only some traces of the thoughts, fleetingly glimpsed, which are *characteristic* of such an emotion. (I go into more detail on this sort of point in Chapter 14, below, with *hope* as my prime example.)

4. Much work on emotions relevant to the issues in this essay has appeared since it was written. Note especially two recent papers, by Stephen Leighton, which are sympathetic to and argue for the idea that the standard emotions involve *differing characteristic feelings*: "A New View of Emotion," *American Philosophical Quarterly*, 22 (1985): 133–41, and "On Feeling Angry and Elated," *Journal of Philosophy*, 85 (1988): 253–64.

   It is a matter of contention, and hard to settle introspectively, whether the different *higher* (or more *complex*) emotions—ones such as hope or shame or despair or jealousy, as opposed, say, to sadness, joy, or anger—have distinctive affective (sensational and/or phenomenological) components. But I believe it would be rash to say it is *unlikely* they do. First, we should take care to consider feelings occurring at the most characteristic, or more intense, phases of such emotions, otherwise we may too easily "discover" that all emotions involve, at one time or another, more or less the same feelings. Second, we should remind ourselves that the fact that, in perhaps the vast majority of cases, we logically individuate complex emotions by their cognitive components hardly entails—doesn't even give good reason for thinking—that their noncognitive components are virtually interchangeable.

   Finally, the place of desires or wishes or concerns or carings—what we might call *conative* elements—in a complete account of emotion was insufficiently acknowledged in my essay. It has, however, been well emphasized of late by others. (See, for example, Jenefer Robinson, "Emotion, Judgment and Desire," *Journal of Philosophy*, 80 [1983], 731–41; Robert Roberts, "What an Emotion Is: A Sketch," *Philosophical Review*, 97 [1988]: 183–209; Ronald de Sousa, *The Rationality of Emotion* [Cambridge: MIT Press, 1987]; and Patricia Greenspan, *Emotions and Reasons*

[London: Routledge & Kegan Paul, 1988].) I don't believe my conclusions regarding the rewards of negative emotion in music are materially affected by this oversight, but I will grant that a fuller picture of what one is imagining about oneself when one is empathetically saddened* by sad music would need to recognize more explicitly the conative aspect of emotional states.

5. An interesting paper that appeared at roughly the same time as "Music and Negative Emotion" is Donald Callen's "The Sentiment in Musical Sensibility," *Journal of Aesthetics and Art Criticism*, 40 (1982): 381–93. Callen offers a number of suggestions regarding our experience of music, and our interaction and identification with it, that are congenial to my own, though Callen takes further than I am comfortable with the idea of music as *representational* of emotional life.

6. A much-discussed problem, related to though hardly identical with, that of emotional response to music, is the problem of emotional response to literary fiction. I have offered a few ideas on that topic in "The Place of Real Emotion in Response to Fictions," *Journal of Aesthetics and Art Criticism*, 48 (1990): 78–80.

14   *Hope in* The Hebrides

Many philosophers who accept the general notion that music can be expressive of emotional life, at least in the guise of moods, feelings, and simple emotions, balk at the idea that music might be capable of expressing the higher ranges of emotion per se, the more so the more intellection, reflection, or conceptualization such emotions appear to involve. So, in particular, while it is often readily allowed that music can express joy or sadness, or serenity, or anxiety, or even fear or anger, it is somehow barred (usually on "logical" grounds) from expressing such more complicated states as shame, embarrassment, disappointment, guilt, pride, jealousy—or hope.[1]

But what I maintain in this essay is that a particular passage of music, from Mendelssohn's *Hebrides* Overture, is in fact expressive of one of these higher emotions, namely, *hope*.[2] My broader objective is to show that the considerations that philosophers of music, beginning with Hanslick, have advanced in an attempt to show that music is *in principle* incapable of such expression simply do not have that upshot. I will examine a number of considerations of this sort, beginning with that highlighted by Hanslick, whose discussion is echoed in almost

[1] Most philosophers and psychologists, beginning with Hume, are in agreement in considering *hope* an emotion, but not all; see J. P. Day, "Hope," *American Philosophical Quarterly*, 6 (1969). Without entering that debate I will just say that even if hope turned out not to be an emotion properly speaking but only some relatively complex *quasi*-emotional psychological condition, nothing in the concerns of this essay would be changed.

[2] Of course, it is not just *any* old hope, but a specific kind of hope, with its own qualifying predicates. But more of this later.

every subsequent skeptical treatment of the matter. I will try to show, for each consideration, where reasoning about it has somehow gone astray. I will then turn to my musical "Exhibit A" and endeavor to convince the reader of the particular identification of its emotional character that I propose, showing its plausibility through a contextual analysis of the passage itself, seconded by a contrastive consideration of it in relation to passages in other works of the same composer.

The two parts of my brief—the theoretical and the empirical, as it were—though obviously mutually reinforcing, remain logically independent. Thus, it might turn out that my critique of the arguments against musical expression of higher emotions was somehow faulty, and yet that that passage in *The Hebrides* was in fact expressive of the lofty emotion of hope. Or, that my critique of those arguments in fact both demolished them utterly and established the possibility of such higher expression, while the passage in *The Hebrides* failed to express hope, or any other emotion on that level. The point is that one could thus find the theoretical refutation convincing without buying the specific musical identification advanced or vice versa. Naturally, I regard both components of my case as valid and hope the reader will eventually do so as well. Autographically, however, I confess it was my conviction in the truth of my experience with passages such as that in *The Hebrides* that initially convinced me there must be something wrong with the oft-repeated arguments in question, to the effect that music's capacity to express more elevated psychological states is so inherently and unalterably limited. I can only *trust* that I have adequately diagnosed the ills of those arguments, but I *know* that the *Hebrides* passage expresses, if not hope, then at least some higher emotional condition beyond what those arguments appear to allow.

Part One

I

I will first say how I propose to understand the state of affairs which is a passage P expressing a psychological condition α. I take it that expression (or expressiveness) in music is a mode of meaning, broadly speaking, and one that works fundamentally through analogy between music as heard and the life of human beings, particularly their characteristic expressive behaviors. This is not, however, to say that musical expressiveness is to be *defined* or *analyzed* directly as the holding of such analogy or resemblance. My specific proposal is this:

> P expresses (or is expressive of)[3] α *iff* P is most readily and aptly heard by the appropriate reference class of listeners[4] as (or as if it were) a sui generis personal expression of α by some (imaginatively indeterminate) individual.

By *personal* expression I mean, roughly, behavioral expression, the expression of emotional states by a sentient being through behavior. The idea is that expressive music is heard *as if it were* an alternate, audible but sui generis mode of behaviorally manifesting psychological states, emotional ones in particular. It is a mode imagined or felt as akin to singing, gesturing, posturing, dancing, and so on, but not as equivalent to any of them, presenting itself instead as a novel and distinctive alternative to ordinary modes of personal expression.[5] I will refer to the individual indefinitely imagined as the subject of the state being expressed as the *persona* of the music.[6]

---

[3] See Alan Tormey, *The Concept of Expression* (Princeton: Princeton University Press, 1971), and Peter Kivy, *The Corded Shell* (Princeton: Princeton University Press, 1980), for admonitions regarding this distinction. When I speak of expression in this essay as a property of passages, it is always to be understood as equivalent to expressiveness—i.e., a passage's inherent musical expression, with no implication that there is any occurrent psychological state of any sentient being causally connected to the music.

[4] Roughly, ones versed in the historical position and stylistic matrix of the piece in question, and who have heard the given piece a sufficient number of times to have acquired a basic aural grasp of it, in respect of musical shape and progression.

[5] Another stab at this idea would be the following: Music that expresses α is music that strikes us as how a person experiencing α would behaviorally express his or her α *if* persons naturally behaved "in music"—i.e., if the physical gestures and resulting sounds involved in playing musical instruments were a natural (unlearned, unmediated) manifestation of human emotions.

It is perhaps useful to note that one inevitably arrives at this degree of complexity in an answer to what expression in music amounts to, by refinement on what seem to be promising, but simpler, answers. One might first think 'sad music sounds like a sad person'; but then sad people don't necessarily or even usually make noise. One then offers 'sad music sounds like a sad person expressing his or her sadness'; but, for one, some expressions of sadness by sad persons are not audible, and for another, those that are audible are not, after all, very much like music. Well, then, perhaps sad music is music we have a tendency to construe *as if it were* a sad person expressing sadness.

[6] On the idea of a persona in music, see Chapter 13, above. As for the imagined sui generis mode of expression, this is quite possibly not *wholly* unanalyzable. It might,

The bottom line for the presence of expressiveness of α in music is thus favored *hearability as* (a new sort of) human expression of α. Of course, qualitative similarities and structural resemblances between the sound of a passage and standard behaviors for expressing α will typically play the largest role in *bringing about* such preferential hearability. But it would be a mistake, as I suggested a moment ago, to simply regard such hearability as *equivalent* to the behavior resemblance on which it is usually centrally based, if only for the fact that this simply excludes all other (e.g., conventional) bases for the resultant hearability that is constitutive of expressiveness. For example, certain entrenched associations of timbres with moods, such as that of the oboe with pastorality, or that of the trombone with solemnity, which contribute to the ready hearability of passages employing them as sui generis expressions of emotions related to such moods, without this being founded on any similarities between those timbres and any behaviors standard for expressing those emotions.[7]

I do not undertake to defend this analysis here.[8] Approaches to it can be found in the writings of many recent writers on expression in

---

perhaps, be approximated by the idea of the music's persona somehow being able, through bodily behavior, to produce unassistedly sounds equivalent to those produced by playing on any instrument and on any number of them simultaneously. In other words, when we hear a passage as expressive, we may, first, be imagining a persona for it, and second, be imagining this persona to have the power to achieve in unmediated fashion an outpouring of sound that normally requires—for example, on the part of the actual performers of the music—the intermediary of musical instruments and the possession of musical training. One advantage of this more specific identification of the imagined mode of expression is that it makes directly intelligible the involvement of knowledge of the performing forces inherent in a piece of music in our assessment of its expressive character and aesthetic content more generally. (See Chapter 16, above.)

[7]From another angle, there are likely instances where the basis of expressiveness in a musical passage is not direct resemblance to human expressive behavior, but to certain *natural phenomena* that have long been found expressive—which have, in effect, an antecedent expressiveness. For example, sun beginning to shine (dispersing gloom); waves crashing (angrily) on the shore; earthquakes (inducing terror); birds suddenly taking flight (in anticipation or startlement). Yet music's *being* expressive of α just means, once again, that it is readily and aptly heard as sui generis expression of α by the class of appropriate listeners. Whether it is direct resemblance to human expressive behavior, or conventional associations attaching to certain musical features, or resemblance to expressive natural phenomena or even partial isomorphism between the flow of the music and the inner flow of feelings, which we identify in a particular case as undergirding the expressiveness we take to be present, such factors do not, I maintain, figure in the analytic explication of the concept of musical expressiveness.

[8]I attempt to do so in another essay, "The Concept of Musical Expressiveness" (in preparation).

music, though none of them offers exactly the formulation provided above, and possibly none of them would endorse it.[9] But the particularities of the proposal I offer does not matter, I think, for the defusing of arguments against the expression of higher emotionality by music, which is our principal concern. As long as it is accepted that musical expression is tied to ordinary, extramusical expression in something like the above way—that the former somehow involves supporting or engendering imagination of the latter through music— my argument is not, I think, materially affected.[10]

I now turn to the considerations contra higher expression in music which will chiefly occupy us. They are, in preview, these:

1. Emotions are individuated by the thoughts they involve, and music cannot indicate thoughts.

[9]See R. K. Elliott, "Aesthetic Theory and the Experience of Art," in *Aesthetics*, ed. H. Osborne (London: Oxford University Press, 1972), pp. 145–57; Richard Wollheim, *Art and Its Objects* (New York: Harper & Row, 1971); Stephen Davies, "The Expression of Emotion in Music," *Mind*, 89 (1980): 67–86; Peter Kivy, *Corded Shell*; and Roger Scruton, "Understanding Music," in *The Aesthetic Understanding* (London: Methuen, 1983). Some more recent treatments that are close in spirit, if not in letter, to the view I would specifically defend are found in Ismay Barwell, "How Does Art Express Emotion?" *Journal of Aesthetics and Art Criticism*, 45 (1986): 175–81; Bruce Vermazen, "Expression as Expression," *Pacific Philosophical Quarterly*, 67 (1986): 196–223; and Kendall Walton, "What Is Abstract about the Art of Music?" *Journal of Aesthetics and Art Criticism*, 46 (1988): 351–64. The most pessimistic recent writer in regard to any such analysis of musical expressiveness is Malcolm Budd, who develops his views in his formidable *Music and the Emotions* (London: Routledge & Kegan Paul, 1985). In chap. 7 of his book Budd carefully examines, among others, a suggestion something like the one I propose, but ultimately rejects it on the grounds that listeners do not engage in the sorts of imaginings that would be required. I hope to respond to Budd's reservations at length elsewhere, but here I submit that he is just wrong as to the psychological facts.

[10]Incidentally, I do not mean necessarily to deny the general validity of Goodman's suggestion, in *Languages of Art* (Indianapolis: Bobbs-Merrill, 1968), that the emotional properties expressed by music are those it metaphorically exemplifies—that expression in music is metaphorical exemplification. It may well be. (See, though, Kendall Walton, "Pictures and Make-Believe," *Philosophical Review*, 82 [1973]: 283–319, for a possible problem with this.) Only it seems to me that expression in music— and perhaps in the other arts—has also a more *specific* sense or meaning, and that is what analyses such as mine attempt to illuminate. (In this I agree with Vermazen, "Expression.") To say a passage expresses sadness or anger is to say something more, and more specific, than that it is metaphorically sad or angry and refers to this; it might also metaphorically exemplify its interminability, or its steeliness, while not specifically *expressing* those qualities. Expression in art plausibly has some essential connection to human expression, behaviorally manifested.

2. Higher emotions, at least, necessarily have or take specific objects, and these cannot be indicated by music.
3. Higher emotions have cognitive aspects (conceptual contents) that are simply too specific or complex for music to convey; music is thus ultimately expressively ambiguous between one higher emotion and another.

II

1. Emotions are individuated by the thoughts they involve, and music cannot indicate thoughts.

I begin by reviewing the argument of Hanslick's which is the spiritual source, at least, of most recent opposition to music's claim to being able to express the (as we might say) "finer" emotions. Of course Hanslick's argument is directed against the claim of music to express *any* emotion, properly speaking, and not just the more complex ones with which I am most concerned, but it is plain that it has always been thought to tell doubly against those. Here is a full statement of the argument, from an excellent new translation of *Vom Musikalisch-Schönen*:

> What, then, makes a feeling specific, e.g., longing, hope, love? Is it perhaps the mere strength or weakness, the fluctuations of our inner activity? Certainly not. These can be similar with different feelings, and with the same feeling they can differ from person to person and from time to time. Only on the basis of a number of ideas and judgments (perhaps unconsciously at moments of strong feeling) can our state of mind congeal into this or that specific feeling. The feeling of hope cannot be separated from the representation of a future happy state which we compare with the present; melancholy compares past happiness with the present. These are entirely specific representations or concepts. Without them, without this cognitive apparatus, we cannot call the actual feeling "hope" or "melancholy." . . . If we take this away, all that remains is an unspecific stirring, perhaps the awareness of a general state of well-being or distress. Love cannot be thought without the representation of a beloved person, without desire and striving after felicity, glorification and possession of a particular object. Not some kind of mere mental agitation, but its conceptual core, its real, historical content, specifies this feeling of love. Accordingly, its dynamic can appear as readily gentle as stormy . . . and yet still be love. This consideration by itself suffices to show that music can only ex-

press the various accompanying adjectives and never the substantive, e.g., love itself. A specific feeling . . . never exists as such without an actual historical content, which can only be precisely set forth in concepts. . . . Is the result of all this not psychologically irrefutable? It is that music is incapable of expressing definite feelings.[11]

The essence of this argument is captured in the following perspicuous formulations of two contemporary philosophers, Malcolm Budd and Roger Scruton:

> The conclusion of Hanslick's argument is that it is not possible to represent definite feelings or emotions by purely musical means. His argument may perhaps be rendered this way: (i) Music cannot represent thoughts. (ii) Definite feelings and emotions, hope, sadness, and love, for example, involve or contain thoughts. Therefore, (iii) music cannot represent definite feelings or emotions.[12]

> Every emotion requires an object: fear is fear *of* something, anger is anger *about* something. We can distinguish emotions and classify them only because we can distinguish and classify their (intentional) objects; and we can do *this* only because we can identify the thoughts through which those objects are defined. In this case, it is difficult to see how a nonrepresentational art like music can really have a genuine expressive content. It would be impossible to describe that content, since its [intentional] object could never be identified.[13]

It will be noted that these formulations of the argument differ in only one important respect. And that is whether the differentiae of the various emotions are directly the varying *thought-contents,* or else the varying *sorts of intentional object,* they involve or entail. It is, however, clear that these are effectively equivalent since, as the second

[11]Eduard Hanslick, *On the Musically Beautiful,* trans. G. Payzant (Indianapolis: Hackett, 1986), p. 9. There is an aspect of Hanslick's argument as here rendered which is not usually emphasized by commentators, and indeed is not conveyed in either of the modern encapsulations to be given shortly. This is the idea that every specific instance (case) of emotion has not only a characteristic thought-content or intentional object, but also an actual *historical* content, by which Hanslick might mean either a real-world situation in which the emotion is embedded or else a complex of concrete causal factors underlying the emotion. However, this phrase might just reflect as unresolved shifting in Hanslick's mind between two senses of 'specific feeling', one in which it indicates a narrow *kind* (or *type*) of emotion (e.g., melancholy vs. sadness) and a second in which it indicates a concrete *case* (or *token*) of some emotion. Only in the second sense, it seems, does every specific feeling have an actual historical content.

[12]Budd, *Music and the Emotions,* p. 21.

[13]Roger Scruton, "Analytical Philosophy and the Meaning of Music," *Journal of Aesthetics and Art Criticism,* 46 (1987): 172.

passage affirms, sorts of intentional objects are individuated by the descriptive thoughts constitutive of such objects. So, for example, whereas Budd would say, on Hanslick's behalf, that *love* is characterized as the emotion that centrally involves the *thought* that its object is desirable, admirable, and deserving of happiness, Scruton has Hanslick saying that this emotion is characterized as necessarily involving a desirable, admirable, and happiness-deserving (intentional) *object*. The characteristic thought-content of an emotion and the sort of intentional object the emotion projects are intersecting notions; shifting to the opposite emotion for another example, if *hatred* of my wife's secret lover is what's at issue, my (hateful) thought directed on this paramour is hardly to be separated from my conception of the (hateful) individual himself.

I refer to the thought-content aspect, or the correlative sort-of-intentional-object aspect, of a standard emotion indifferently as the *cognitive aspect* of the emotion. Note that this aspect, as I understand it, is strictly distinct from an emotion's intentionality—i.e., its being object-directed per se. The latter is a general characteristic and does not provide the differentium of any ordinary emotion; I refer to this as the *intentional aspect* of an emotion. Both the cognitive aspect and the intentional aspect of an emotion can be said to attach intelligibly to either the type or the tokens of that type. And there is also a third such "aspect," sometimes confused with the other two, which consists in the *specific object* on which an emotion is directed—or more precisely, the property of being directed on that specific object—and this, obviously, is displayed only by the tokens (or instances) of an emotion; for clarity's sake I refer to this as the *objectual focus* of an emotion.[14] Finally, I use the verb 'signify' as a neutral, overarching term for the meaning of emotions by music, covering what Hanslick usually indicates by 'represent', what most recent writers prefer to label by 'express', and even what others (e.g., Langer) have denominated by 'symbolize'.[15]

[14]Example: Suppose I love my Labrador retriever, Edgar. Then the *intentional aspect* of my emotion is its being directed toward, or being about, something; the *cognitive aspect* of my emotion is the complex of cherishing, admiring, and desiring thoughts or attitudes toward Edgar which it centrally includes; and the *objectual focus* of my emotion is Edgar, that particular dog—at least as individuated and identified in my mental space or epistemic world. (This last qualification is necessary to take account of emotions with no actual, real-world correlates.)

[15]My point in doing this is simply to sidestep here any issue of differences in modes of meaning that these terms might be used to mark.

Here, then, is my own distillation of Hanslick's argument, in harmony with those above, but in a form most useful for the examination I undertake: Hanslick's view is that the cognitive aspects of emotions are (a) the *only* distinctive features of the individual emotions, and thus (b) such that music would *have* to signify them in order to signify any individual emotion, and yet (c) *incapable* of signification by music. The conclusion, then, follows neatly that music *cannot* signify individual emotions.

But we can, in fact, question each of these premises, (a), (b), and (c), though most importantly the first. Even if it is granted that the standard emotions—and even more so, the "higher" emotions that especially concern us—are *defined*, logically *individuated*, and necessarily *conceived* in terms of their respective cognitive components, it does not follow that there is nothing else that is *in fact* distinctive or characteristic of the individual emotions. Emotions comprise, at the least, affective, hedonic, conative, behavioral, and physiological components as well,[16] and there is nothing to show that reliable and cognizable differences in the total constellations of noncognitive components of the various emotions could not exist. On the contrary, it seems more than plausible that with all such factors taken into account—qualitative feels, desires, and impulses, varieties of internal sensation, degrees of pleasure and pain, patterns of nervous tension and release, patterns of behavior (gestural, vocal, postural, kinetic)—each of the emotions standardly distinguished in our extramusical life would have an overall profile that was subtly specific to it, even leaving its cognitive core to one side. So if the possibility remains that something other than the cognitive component is distinctive of, if not logically definitive of, a given individual emotion, then it may be that music can signify such emotion by adequately signifying that something. In other words, music *need not* provide the conceptual content characteristic or even definitive of a given emotion if it can connect to other aspects of the emotional state which are, as a whole, sufficiently peculiar to it to

---

[16]Though most recent writers on emotions are willing to regard the complex states that are emotions as having components, at least one is not, insisting that since emotions are experienced as wholes or unified conditions, philosophical analysis should respect that fact ultimately as well. (See Robert Roberts, "What an Emotion Is: A Sketch," *Philosophical Review*, 97 [1988]: 183–209.) Even if we allow such qualms as to whether emotions have *components* (implying, perhaps, separability in principle?), there can be little argument against their having distinguishable *aspects*, at the least.

effectively guide imaginative projection, in an appreciative context, in that direction rather than another.[17]

Of course, Hanslick intimates here and in his subsequent discussion[18] that the noncognitive aspects of an emotion—e.g., its "dynamic"—are not sufficient to distinguish one from another, but it is clear, with his fixation on only coarse properties of speed or strength, that he is not acknowledging all that this could comprehend. Further, on the signifying side, he focuses almost exclusively on the "motional" resources of music—rhythm, tempo, dynamic change—and hardly at all on "nonmotional" ones—melodic shape, harmonic complexion, timbre, articulation; it seems far from established a priori that music, given both kinds of resource, and all the sorts of analogies those might undergird, would be incapable of indicating such assumedly differentiated noncognitive components.

But this brings us to (b). Is it even true that in order to signify a thing X one must *signify* some thing Y that is a distinctive part, aspect, or component of X?[19] I suggest not. A medium such as music might very well have to connect with—hook into—whatever was distinctive of what it was to signify, but it might not have to independently and literally *signify* that thing as well. This would be to assume that signification (meaning) was a kind of distributively transmitted property—if had by the whole, then had by the parts, or at least those parts that make the global signification effective. But there is no reason to assume this. One scenario that is then not ruled out on purely logical grounds is that a musical passage might sufficiently resonate with some distinctive aspect of an emotion—whether cognitive or noncognitive—so as to end up signifying it (e.g., being rightly hearable as it) without it being the case that it signified that aspect *as well*. To be sure, there must be something that *accounts* for any resultant signification in one direction rather than

[17] Malcolm Budd raises the possibility of this sort of response to Hanslick in his discussion of Hanslick's argument (*Music and the Emotions*, pp. 21–25), and airs the plausible suggestion that the noncognitive aspects of the emotions might very well be naturally mirrored in "the nature of tonality and the phenomena of consonance and dissonance" (25), but it is fair to say that he is at most agnostic as to whether anything in the noncognitive realm is likely to prove distinctive of individual emotions. I aim to project a more positive attitude on this question.

[18] See Hanslick, *On the Musically Beautiful*, p. 11.

[19] As Budd remarks in his discussion of the Hanslick argument, it hardly seems true that in order to represent a thing you must represent *everything* that is included in it—i.e., all its proper parts. What I am concerned about at the moment is whether you must even represent (or signify) *any* distinguishing part.

another, but there is no reason to insist that *what so accounts* must be itself directly signified, or even signified along the way.

Finally, we come to (c). Even here there is some room for doubt, though it is not my intention to put much weight on this objection. Why is it so clear that music cannot manage to signify thought-contents? Well, it's obvious that the rather large dissimilarity between music and language, in terms both of elements and syntax, and the absence of any notable rules or conventions connecting musical sequences with discursive propositions, gives one considerable pause. But that is just to say we cannot expect any *systematic* or *widespread* connections to turn up between musical structures and propositional contents, ones that are there, so to speak, because we put them there. But it is surely not inconceivable that certain forms and shapes of musical progression should have the power—unexpectedly, perhaps— to regularly call to mind in culturally backgrounded listeners certain thoughts, even ones of some complexity. If that were to occur in regard to some of the thoughts definitive of the various emotions, we would at least have *some* grounds, if not conclusive ones, for saying that the music signified those thoughts. Not all that music signifies need be, so to speak, prearranged, nor need even the basis for it be in any way set up by us in advance.

III

2. Higher emotions, at least, necessarily have or take specific objects, and these cannot be indicated by music.

This appears, for example, to be one of the grounds advanced by Daniel Putman, in his recent article "Why Instrumental Music Has No Shame," for the conclusion implicit in his title. The following remarks are at least suggestive of the thesis that a state's necessarily taking an object is per se a bar to its being expressible by music: "Why is there sad and joyous music but no 'shameful' or 'embarrassing' music? . . . Emotions in the passive voice, those which can *only* be produced in the subject by the causal properties of objects or events, are noticeably absent in instrumental music. . . . The point I want to draw is that those same emotions that *require* objects in non-musical contexts are those which pure instrumental music cannot express."[20]

[20] *British Journal of Aesthetics*, 27 (1987): 55–61, 57.

In any event, this second consideration has surely on its own account influenced some philosophers to discount the possibility of music's expressing "higher" emotions.

I begin by examining briefly the meaning of the claim that the standard emotions—or at least the subset of them I have labeled the "higher emotions"—*necessarily have objects.*[21] In the case of something like hope—or shame, or pride, or remorse, or despair, or resentment—what this means can be put, it seems, in two ways. First, that the concept of hope is that of a (type of) state that necessarily involves an (intentional) object on which the state is directed. Second, that, necessarily, each instance (or token) of hope has a specific (intentional) object. (It is important to realize, of course, that on either way of putting it, there is no identifiable object of hope "in general.")[22]

To the objection that music cannot supply the object that any of these higher emotions must possess we may then respond as follows. Specific objects only attach to *instances* of individual emotions, not to the individual emotions themselves; that is, objectual focus[23] is not a property of the individual type emotion, but only object-directedness—i.e., intentionality. So the most that would need supplying by music on this score would be intentionality. Thus, even if music is clearly incapable, without special assistance, of identifying for a listener a specific *object* of an emotion, that wouldn't preclude a sense of a psychological state's *being intentional* (i.e., its intentional aspect) from reliably arising in the minds of listeners confronted with music they perceived as emotive in

[21] Some philosophers have argued, not unconvincingly, that at least not all *instances* of the ordinary emotions are in fact robustly object-directed. (See Julius Moravcsik, "Understanding and the Emotions," *Dialectica*, 36 [1982]: 207–24, and Roger Lamb, "Objectless Emotions," *Philosophy and Phenomenological Research*, 48 [1987]: 107–17.) I will, however, assume that anything deserving the label of 'emotion' must *in general* take an object, must at least be *capable* of having an object—i.e., must be fundamentally an intentional condition. On my view there is then an absolute disjunction between the kind of psychological state that is an *emotion*, and the kind that is a *mood* or a *feeling*, even though some *cases* of emotions might, atypically, lack objects, and so thereby be like moods, and even though most emotions arguably *include* certain feelings characteristically. In any event, the above authors, as well as Putman, agree that what I am calling the "higher" emotions do necessarily take objects.

[22] Though there is, as explained earlier, an intentional-object *sort* distinctive of the emotion of hope.

[23] See note 14, above. By the property of objectual focus I of course mean any property of form *being about or directed on* β, where β is a definite individual (e.g., *being about or directed on Edgar*).

some way. Such a sense might typically register itself, consciously or subconsciously, through some such thought as 'it [the state] seems like it's *about* something'. And this would clearly be a pivotal contribution to the music's expressing of any higher emotion.[24]

In other words, even if higher emotions necessarily take objects, a musical expression of them, being plausibly concerned exclusively with the type, need not indicate any such object; all that need ultimately be conveyed is at most the *idea or impression* of having an object, which is crucial to the state's being a bona fide emotion at all. What remains to be somehow gotten across after that is only the kind of emotion involved, via its cognitive or noncognitive differentiae. What need *not* be conveyed, in the domain of musical expression, is either the specific *object* of the emotion, or the *subject* of the emotion, or the concrete *material context* of the emotion—which is just as well, since these are all literally absent in such situations.[25] To hold otherwise is to fail to appreciate that if some musical passages manage to express some types of higher emotions by appropriately tracing their lineaments, it is not through signifying any *tokens* thereof whatsoever, whether that of the composer or that of a listener—or even that imagined to belong, in the act of hearing what expressiveness the music possesses, to the music's persona.

It might be thought, however, that this dismissal of the relevance of

---

[24] It is important to realize that accepting the above does not constrain us to hold that there is any particular aspect or dimension of a musical passage which acts to separately convey this idea or sense—that of having an object—thus contributing to signifying the emotion as a whole, nor that there is an accretion of such signifiers over time. It may rather be that the passage *as a whole* manages to convey the emotion *as a whole,* and only *thereby* conveys a sense of object-directedness—given the emotion conveyed is understood as one necessarily taking an object. A certain musical passage might, for unspecified reasons, reliably be heard as the expression of pride, or reliably put attuned listeners in mind of that emotion; then a state with cognitive content C—that definitive of pride—would, a fortiori, be before the mind. But it might very well *not* be that anything particular in the music *first* indicates this cognitive content C, which *then* together with other cues of emotionality in the music enables the listener to subsequently grasp that the emotion involved is pride. The perception of a passage as expressive of some higher emotion might be fairly holistic, only later (if at all) yielding awareness of various conceptual implications—as opposed to atomistic and sequential, involving discrete, successive conveyings of emotionality-in-general, behavioral-profile-P, inner-feeling-F, conative aspect A, and cognitive content C, adding up to a positive identification of the emotion and at last sanctioning its entry into musical perception.

[25] This point is nicely emphasized in Tormey, *Concept,* p. 122: "The sadness of the music is not *over* or *about* anything."

emotional instances, and thus the sidelining of the problem of their specific objects, has here gone too far. For is it not the case that on my account of a passage's being expressive of some emotion (see above), the passage is heard as if it were the sui generis personal expression of an emotion by an individual? And does this not mean that in the intentional world of the listener attuned to the passage there will indeed be an emotional particular, that belonging to the imagined persona of the music? And will not this emotional particular—the imagined persona's hope, or shame, or pride—have an object, and a specific one? And so, finally, are we not still left with the problem of undetachable specific objects of higher emotions, and music's inability to identify them?

The answer is no. Even though the emotional particular imagined in the course of perceiving a passage's expressiveness of a bona fide emotion must be imagined to *have* a specific object, and even un-detachably, there is no need for the listener to imagine this object *itself,* to invest *it* with any particular identity. And so the fact that music lacks resources for directing such specific imagining or investment of identity is in no way prejudicial to its possibly being capable of supporting the hearability of such an emotion in it, and of sustaining the degree of less precise imagining that such hearability arguably *does* require. When we hear a passage as expressive of α we in some fashion imagine that α is being expressed, but without imagining in any definite way either the subject or the object of the α involved.[26]

A couple of visual analogs should prove helpful. A painting, even an untitled one, might adequately represent an individual *father,* through appropriate indications, while neither supplying any particular child nor implying a specific identity for such within the frame. And yet, of course, for any individual (even fictional) father there must indeed *be* some particular child of which he is a parent, and in understanding the painting a viewer would have to see the man in the picture as related in a certain way to some (unspecified) person (or persons) outside of what is shown. Another painting might represent a man *as looking at something*—at a very particular something, as evidenced by the fixity or intensity of his gaze—and still neither show that something nor entail anything about its specific character; and yet particular some-things do *have* specific characters, and so a comprehending viewing of

[26]See Chapter 13, above.

the painting would implicitly grant that this was so, though without being compelled to "fill in" that character in any way.[27]

Similarly, then, a musical passage might—by inducing appropriate listeners to imagine the personal expressing of a positive future-oriented state of mind in which "what is wanted may possibly come about"[28]—succeed in being expressive of hope even though failing to provide or delineate in any way the specific object or aspect of the future upon which, of course, any imagined instance of this state of mind would have to be imagined as being directed.[29] There is no reason to think music is necessarily powerless to impart the *crucial* element under discussion—an impression or directedness or aboutness—in order that some emotion of a higher sort be possibly brought into perceptual experience (hearing-as) for a backgrounded listener. It might be that the listener above hears specifically hope in the music, rather than just happiness or joy, partly *because* something about the music manages to suggest this character of *focused aboutness*—yet, once again, without delivering any object appropriate to such a character. I conclude, then, that there is no insuperable obstacle to the expression of higher emotions posed by their necessarily having objects.

Before moving on, though, we should observe that the supposition at the head of the above paragraph arguably concedes too much. For it seems possible to have a particular higher emotion come determinately to mind, at least in the way in which it needs to so as to function in the

---

[27] A third, more remote, analogy: An individual baseball game, played on some particular occasion in the past, certainly had a definite score at the beginning of the ninth inning. But the smell of sizzling hot dog, arriving at your nose today, might very well summon up for you *that very game*, without your mental representation of it necessarily including that late inning score particular from which, among others, it is in some sense inseparable.

[28] This is Budd's paraphrase of Hanslick's characterization of the conceptual essence of hope (*Music and the Emotions*, p. 21).

[29] There is a difference in content, for example, between ⟨imagining someone being in pain⟩ and ⟨imagining someone being in pain for a quite specific reason⟩, even where the latter does not include a filling-in of the reason.

The "logical grammar" of dreaming is similar to that of the sort of imagining involved here, in a way that supports my point. If in reality I am riding in a car, drinking lemonade, and then suddenly dump my drink out the window, there is surely some part of the road it lands on. But if I *dream* I am riding, then drinking, then dumping, it can very well be (logically and not just epistemically) indeterminate on what, if anything, my disdained beverage lands. And yet it may be not at all indeterminate, in my dream, that while riding along I indeed dumped out the window some perfectly good, physically unremarkable lemonade.

expressive construal of music, without *all* of its veritable distinctive features coming formally to mind as well. I might conceivably be dependably put in mind of hope, or made to perceptually construe something as an expression of hope, not only without any specific object being indicated, but also without at least *some* of the state's true distinguishing features—intentionality, future-orientedness, positivity, desiringness, a certain sort of inner feeling, a certain kind of bearing—being conveyed to the mind as a matter of course.[30] Neither thinking of α nor having been directed to think of α presupposes that at any time one is thinking or has been made to think *all* the earmarks of α. I can be thinking of tigers without thinking of their chromosome number, their mammality, or indeed of any other given distinctive characteristic—e.g., diet, running speed, eye type, geographical distribution.[31] We would do well to consider that if a musical passage brings hope to mind and enables us to hear hope in it, this may not require that every element in the concept of hope—or anything near that—is present to mind in the course of this.

IV

3. Higher emotions have cognitive aspects (conceptual contents) that are simply too specific or complex for music to convey; music is thus ultimately expressively ambiguous between one higher emotion and another.

[30]We must be clear not to conflate (a) those aspects of an emotion with which music must necessarily connect in order dependably to bring that particular emotion before the mind and allow it to enter into musical perception, and (b) those aspects of the emotion before the mind which are then necessarily consciously grasped and entertained when music is perceived in terms of the emotion. The sets of aspects (a) and (b) are obviously not coincident, and it is possible they might not even overlap in every case. (For example, it may be that De Gaulle cannot be summoned up in a line drawing without indicating his [stereotypic] nasal profile, but not the case that in understanding the drawing [i.e., seeing what it represents] a viewer unavoidably reflects on the great general's nose—he may only be brought to think explicitly on his nationality, his deeds, his height, things that by hypothesis the drawing does not connect with directly.)

The present discussion is more concerned with (b) than with (a); we touched on (a) in section II, in suggesting that these might be noncognitive ones, and shall have more to say about this soon.

[31]Whether I could have tigers before the mind without thinking on *any* of their distinctive (or "defining") characteristics—e.g., being felines, having stripes—is a more thorny question, which I will not try to settle, since this would take us far afield into contemporary semantics.

Some form of this observation is probably the real mainstay of those who dispute particularly music's pretention to express higher emotions, as opposed to its claim to emotional expression more generally. Thus, it is argued, it is not so much their object-directedness (their having objects) nor their involving thoughts (their having cognitive content) per se which dooms hope, shame, despair, and the rest to being inexpressible by music, but rather the *specificity* or *complexity* of the thought-contents they involve, or equivalently, of the intentional objects they define. It is sometimes additionally suggested that this complexity is rooted in the level of self-reference involved in such emotions.

The flag of conceptual complexity as a bar to musical expression of higher emotions is often waved in an unreflectingly a priori manner. The following is not so great a caricature of this stance: "How can musical passages express higher emotions, with their complex conceptual contents? I just don't see *how* that sort of complexity can be conveyed by music, which is obviously not a linguistic medium. Therefore, musical passages *cannot* express higher emotions."

First, the fact that one may have difficulty seeing how some process occurs is not in itself very good grounds for denying that it occurs, if there is some positive evidence of its occurrence. Let it be granted that music does not generally rise to the level of specific implication required to point to individual higher emotions; that is no reason why it might not occasionally do so. Second, as we have remarked above, a passage expressive of some higher emotion might not be effective in doing so in virtue of reflecting its cognitive aspect, but instead through hooking up with some portion of its noncognitive aspect. Third, as we have also already remarked, such a passage would not necessarily have to summon before the mind the full panoply of such complexities in order for that emotion to nevertheless be said to be cognitively involved in a listener's experience of the passage.

Another contributor, I suspect, to hasty dismissal of the possibility of music's expressing higher emotions, under the present rubric, is the notion that emotions that have a *more specific* cognitive aspect probably have a *less specific* noncognitive aspect. That is to say, that the more precise and differentiated an emotion's cognitive component, the more imprecise and undifferentiated its noncognitive component is likely to be. But is the latter supposed to be a consequence of the former? Clearly it is not, and to reason otherwise is to fall into a kind of arithmetic fallacy. It is to think of the noncognitive component of an emotion as a sort of remainder that is left when the cognitive component is taken away from an emotion with a fixed amount of individuating specificity.

To uncover a more serious source of opposition on this wavelength we will have to begin again. Let me go back to Putman's insistence that it is precisely those emotions that *must* take objects—i.e., roughly those I have denominated "higher" emotions—which cannot be expressed by pure instrumental music. Now, is it really this condition per se which presents the putative problem? If so, then we have adequately seen in the preceding section that it is no problem at all, as long as object-directedness and objectual focus are not conflated. Thus, it would rather seem that necessarily taking objects can be only an earmark of the class of emotions that prove problematic, and that it is really *another* characteristic, associated with this, which directly causes the trouble. And that characteristic is plausibly the relatively high *complexity or specificity* of the conceptions essentially involved in those emotions that, it happens, are inconceivable without objects. An emotion such as shame entails a highly specific conception of the character of the (intentional) object it (necessarily) has—subjects of shame think of themselves as possessing some trait, or having performed some act or undergone some event, which they regard as worthy of blame and as discordant with their ideal selves—and such a conception, it appears, is not communicable by musical sound. Musical passages have an inherent "expressive ambiguity," and can only limn emotions in broad strokes, too coarse to delineate any of the finer inhabitants of the realm.

The idea that artworks (or parts thereof) are likely to be irresolvably expressively ambiguous was advanced prominently not too long ago by Alan Tormey. The following is, for our purposes, his most important statement on the matter:

> There is a further and perhaps more decisive reason for believing the expressive ambiguity of many art works to be essentially uneliminable. The expressive "gestures" of art often occur in an aesthetic space devoid of explicit context and intentional objects. And it is the absence or the elusiveness of intentional objects that impedes our critical attempts to dissolve the ambiguity and disclose an unequivocal expressive quality in the art work. It may be true that we cannot tell from a smile, isolated from its context, whether it is a smile of parental

benevolence directed toward a sleeping child or a smile of sadistic satisfaction directed toward a suffering victim. But these are uncertainties that could theoretically be resolved by uncovering the intentional context. In contrast, many art works [e.g., pieces of pure instrumental music] are intentionally incomplete. There are no further contexts to be uncovered and no intentional objects to be disclosed.[32]

This may seem, on the face of it, to be a form of consideration 2: Emotions must have objects, which pure music fails to indicate or provide. But its real force, as I read it, is as a form of consideration 3: An individual emotion, particularly a "higher" one, can only be determinately identified if its cognitive aspect—characteristic thought-content or intentional-object-sort—is pinned down, and pure music, in not offering any concrete context for the emotion it presents, does not afford any of the cues that in a real-world situation would enable us to project that cognitive aspect with any confidence.[33]

That cognitive specificity, as much as objectual focus, is also central to Putman's opposition to "higher" expression is evident in the following, which occurs soon after an explicit nod to Tormey's just-cited argument: "Emotions . . . such as embarrassment, respect or shame whose experience is *necessarily* linked to the perceived properties of objects or situations, succumb to the high degree of 'expressive ambiguity' inherent in instrumental music. Only with lyrics or clear dra-

[32] *The Concept of Expression*, p. 136. It is worth remarking that one of Tormey's other reasons for postulating universal expressive ambiguity in art is the desire not to run afoul of Frank Sibley's famous thesis of the 'non-condition-governedness' of aesthetic attributions (including expressive ones) upon the nonaesthetic foundation of a work. (Thus: "the relation between sets of nonexpressive properties and the expressive properties of art works is such that a given set of nonexpressive properties may be compatible with, and constitutive of, any one of a *range* of expressive properties" [132]; and see pp. 131–33 generally.) Leaving aside the obscurity of the constitutivity relation postulated by Tormey, the offering he makes to Sibley is a needless one and is based on failure to distinguish *occurrence-conditions* (of aesthetic properties) from *application-conditions* (of aesthetic terms). (On this, see Monroe Beardsley, "The Descriptivist Account of Aesthetic Attributions," *Revue internationale de philosophie*, 28 [1974]: 336–52.) Sibley's thesis really concerns the latter, and is not meant to preclude the possibility of complete constellations of nonaesthetic features giving rise determinately to unambiguous expressive results. Recent work on supervenience has attempted to clarify the relation between high-level and low-level properties of complex structures, with application to the case of art. (See Chapter 7, above.)

[33] Kivy's endorsement of Tormey on this point supports my reading of it: "It is often *what* you are angry *about* that tells me what the *exact nature* of your emotion is; *what* you are depressed *over* that distinguishes depression as melancholy rather than neurotic morbidity, and so on" (*The Corded Shell*, p. 102; my italics).

matic settings can the precision and transitivity of such emotions be expressed."[34]

'Precision', of course, refers to what I call cognitive specificity, whereas 'transitivity' seems to cover both object-directedness (belonging to type and token) and objectual focus (belonging to token only).

We must now assess whether the cognitive specificity of the "higher" emotions, often decipherable outside of music from clues embedded in concrete contexts, really poses any bar *in principle* to their expression by pure music. First, as we pointed out in our discussion of Hanslick's original argument, if the total noncognitive aspects of individual emotions *are* generally distinctive of them, then it may not matter if music is incapable of delineating in any part an emotion's cognitive aspect; a fortiori, it is of no additional moment if the cognitive content involved is especially specific or complex.

Second, suppose their cognitive aspects *are* the only things distinctive of higher emotional states. It is still not obvious that music cannot convey *enough* of that (e.g., a sense of self-awareness, an idea of desire) so that, together with what it conveys of (a) the incompletely distinctive noncognitive profile of the emotion, and (b) the sense of intentionality (aboutness) in general, a determinate signification in context (*musical* context, that is) of one such emotion, rather than another, is achieved. The proof is in the aural pudding, of course, but at this point there is simply insufficient logical ground for declaring apodictically that the pudding can never turn out all right.

Third, the fact that in the extramusical arena we typically use contextual clues to fill out our hypothesis of the cognitive content of the emotion whose expression we are observing, thus enabling us to identify the type of the emotion with some precision, does not, of course, entail that we must operate similarly in the musical sphere. For starters, we are dealing with a token emotional occurrence in the one case but not in the other. Context will have a role to play, perhaps, in discerning higher emotions in music, but it will not be a context of causally interacting individuals and their motivations, but rather one of musical features and their implications. Indeed, at this point we have likely exhausted what can be said on an abstract plane against the arguments contra higher expression in music. We must soon look to our chosen specimen and make our argument in the musical sphere.[35]

[34]Putman, "Why Instrumental Music Has No Shame," p. 59.
[35]I will mention one last matter concerning the internal complexity of emotions

Before doing so, though, I am pleased to note that there is another philosopher, at any rate, who does not regard it as impossible that music might express higher emotions, at least occasionally. As it turns out, it is also *hope* that Stephen Davies takes as his example in the following remarks, which attempt to sketch how such expression might be effected:

> It is arguable that, *as feelings,* emotions have natural progressions; for example, from slightly hysterical gaiety to fearful apprehension, to shock, to horror, to gathering resolution, to confrontation with sorrow, to acceptance, to resignation, to serenity. Such progressions might be used by the composer to articulate in his music emotions other than those which can be worn by appearances without regard to feelings. Thus, by judiciously ordering the emotion-characteristics presented in an extended musical work the composer can express in his music those emotional states which are not susceptible to presentation in mere appearances. . . . In this way hope, for example, may be expressed in music, although hope cannot be presented as the emotion-characteristic in an appearance. Thus, the range of emotions which can be expressed in music, that music can be said 'to be', goes beyond the range of emotion-characteristics that can be worn by appearances. . . . Before hope can be expressed in a musical work that work must have sufficient length and expressive complexity to permit the emotions presented in its 'appearance' to form a progression in which hope occurs naturally.[36]

These are sage observations, and I cannot help but agree with the

---

which could be thought to pose a problem for their musical expression (see Jenefer Robinson, "Emotion, Reason, and Judgement," *Journal of Philosophy,* 80 [1983]: 731–41). It has been argued, with some justice, that particular emotions involve not only characteristic feelings and characteristic perceptions (thoughts, attitudes), but also a *causal relation* between the two, so that if the feeling is not present as a result of the perception, you don't have a case of that emotion. Must, then, a passage expressive of *hope* somehow convey this internal relation between its cognitive and its affective sides? I don't see why, if it conveys other elements that adequately mark the state as hope—i.e., that reliably lead a listener to hear *hope* in it—rather than some odd, unnamed, pseudo-emotional state that is just like hope except for unconnectedness among its components. But when listeners are apprehending a passage as expressing hope, must they not then hear it as if it were the expression of a state *involving* such connection? Possibly so—at some level in any event—but this is no more of a problem than the emotion's object that, as we have discussed, must be (indeterminately) posited as well. Just as I implicitly attribute to the passage's persona such an object—something on which hope is directed—perhaps, if Robinson is correct, I implicitly attribute to the persona's condition causal relatedness between its cognitive and its affective aspects.

[36] Stephen Davies, "The Expression of Emotion in Music," p. 78.

thrust of the passage. There are, however, two exceptions I would want to take. First, Davies is unduly pessimistic as to the existence of subtle behavioral/figural/postural manifestations that might characterize one who is hopeful, particularly at peak moments, and thus contribute to a characteristically hopeful appearance, which music might, in turn, reflect, independent of any light cast by the passage's contextual situation. Yet it is clear, as Davies indicates, that such contextual factors will be relatively more important the more complex, or the less behaviorally straightforward, the emotional condition. My second exception concerns the manner in which context might operate in an extended piece of music. I would not confine the possible contextual determination of emotive character to matters of "natural progression";[37] it seems there are other means by which a passage's relation to other passages, to the piece as a whole, or even to passages outside the piece might bring its specific character into relief or (more accurately) invest it with that character. But it is time to give this all some musical flesh.

Part Two

I

The passage on which I will focus is measures 57–66 of Mendelssohn's *Hebrides* Overture, op. 26, hereafter to be referred to as Q (see fig. 5). This passage comprises the second statement of the second theme of the overture; thus, it is largely the expressiveness of the theme that is operative, though the specific instrumentation, dynamics, and structural position of the passage have some role to play. The overture— also called by the name Fingal's Cave—was composed in 1830 and revised in 1832, and is scored for full orchestra. As is well known, Mendelssohn was inspired to its composition during a tour of Scotland in 1829, following his successful presentation to the English musical public.[38] The *Scottish* Symphony, Mendelssohn's other, more trans-

---

[37]The reader will of course recognize these matters to be those with which Chapter 12, above, was concerned in detail.

[38]Interestingly, Mendelssohn's original title for his overture was "The Lonely Island," a probable allusion to the isle of Mull, on which he had stopped for a night

parently titled tribute to Scotland, was not completed until 1842. Pleasant as it is to dilate on such matters, that is all I plan to recall of the creative aims and circumstances of the work. As a matter of fact, I am going to treat it hereafter as if it were a piece of pure instrumental music, with no representational mission—as on musical grounds alone it very well could have been, being cast, for one thing, in exemplary sonata form.

Let me be perfectly clear here. I by no means wish to *deny* either that *The Hebrides* is a piece of representational music *or* that it is successful as such. It is, as it were, just an accident that I have chosen a passage from a composition that happens to have an implied program; I will make no use of that program in my brief for Q's specific expressiveness.[39] But strictly speaking, since I am abstracting from the true state of affairs, this does mean that I will be arguing for my passage's expressiveness in a mildly hypothetical vein—that is, as the expressiveness the passage *would* have if the piece in which it is embedded was otherwise the same except *not* explicitly projected as representational. However, and ironically, this hypotheticality would very likely be canceled if one *were* to take account of the representational aspect, since that would only strengthen the proposed emotional identification, given the concrete intentional context (à la Tormey) thus made available: sea, ship, waves, fear of capsizing, and so on. I will ignore this element of abstraction in my chosen example for the rest of the essay; clearly, it does not at all prejudice examination of the possibility I am defending since, as is evident, the passage need not have had the programmatic aspect to be effective, and further, resembles closely any number of passages of nineteenth-century symphonic music which have no such aspect.[40]

---

during his Scottish tour. It is known that he disliked the title *Fingal's Cave*, which was in fact supplied by his publisher, and that the overture's initial musical idea was conceived and written down by Mendelssohn before his visit to that famous grotto. The term "overture," of course, used as a designation in ninteenth- and twentieth-century symphonic music, does not entail that there is any dramatic (e.g., operatic) work of which the piece so named is the overture.

[39] In other words, I will treat *The Hebrides* as if it had been designated by Mendelssohn as only, say, "Symphonic Fantasy in B minor."

[40] As testimony to the overture's musical self-sufficiency, I cite the following remarks of British analyst and critic Hans Keller: "all the sea-gulls and salt-fish in the Hebrides did not prevent Mendelssohn from designing a complex sonata structure such as many

360

362

II

My claim, already well heralded, is that passage Q is expressive not generically of positive sentiment, but specifically of hope. I, of course, have my philosophical reasons for spotlighting this bit of music, but the reader will be reassured to know there are musical ones as well; Donald Tovey, the celebrated English critic, describes the passage thusly: "in its first and complete form [it is] quite the greatest melody Mendelssohn ever wrote."[41] Before proceeding to an examination of Q itself, it will be useful to review cursorily the course of the overture from its beginning up to the point at which Q occurs.

The major events of the first part of the exposition are as follows:

ms.   1–12   B minor: opening motive (x), descending figure outlining tonic chord [first theme]

ms. 13–20   variant of opening motive (x')

ms. 21–25   "swelling" tremolo strings, rolling tympani

ms. 26–33   countermelody, somewhat more lyrical, in winds (y)

ms. 34–44   tail of y developed, combined with x, alternating with clarinet and bassoon outlining in unison the dominant of B (F-sharp triad)

ms. 45–46   modulation to D major: trombones intone octave A-naturals, dominant seventh of D [ms. 46],

ms. 47–56   first statement of second theme (z), bassoons and cellos $[= P]$

ms. 57–66   second statement of second theme (z), violins $[= Q]$

ms. 66–69   'dolce' rocking figures

ms. 70–75   return of ominous opening motives in minor in winds, leading back to first real climax [ms. 77] in D

---

a fanatically 'absolute' musician would have been proud of; if the sea-gulls actually helped, so much the better. The structure's art of unforced contrast, developmental transition, development itself, and of creatively modified recapitulation—modified, that is, in view of what has happened in the development—make it one of the 19th century's very few classical sonata build-ups, if I may so call it: classical in the retrospective inevitability of its unexpected events, in its emotional comprehensiveness and balance—its perfection" (*Of German Music*, ed. H. H. Schönzeler [London: Oswald Wolff, 1976], p. 207).

[41] *Essays in Musical Analysis* (London: Oxford University Press, 1937), 4:92.

In addition to the two appearances of the overture's second theme noted above, in the exposition, there is also a third, which occurs in the recapitulation; I will not be much concerned with this latter, which is significantly altered in form and effect in comparison to its predecessors, though I will suggest a possible role for it in my brief later on. As I have said, I stake my claim primarily on the second appearance of our theme, measures 57–66, which I have labeled Q. However, certain contextual points involving the first appearance, which I have labeled P, will come in for discussion below.

Let me now outline the structure of the melody as it occurs in Q: first, an arpeggiolike rising figure in eighths (a), then a quarter-note figure including leap of a fourth (b), then a figure with semidetaché upbeat and fall of a fourth (c), which is then repeated (b') and made to flow seamlessly into a reprise of (a), at a higher pitch level, involving this time a leap of a fifth. This is succeeded by two more occurrences of (c), at lower pitch, and the melody is effectively rounded off with (a). The second violins, we may note next, do not play in unison with the firsts throughout the melody, and offer in the second measure a D-sharp underneath the first violin's leap of a fourth to B.[42] Finally, the accompaniment, mainly in the lower strings, consists of gently agitated legato figuration in sixteenths.

We are now ready for some observations on the expressive import of some of this.[43] (1) The leap of a fourth in (b), with its swell on B, is experienced as a slight strain; the leap in the reprise of (b), now a fifth, occasions even more. We hear these phrases as reaching for something—for something higher. These successive leaps, the second an amplification of the first, go some way to account for the melody's

[42] This seems to be mainly to avoid the reassertion of B minor (B–D–F-sharp) in that measure, by opting for the B major (B–D-sharp–F-sharp) triad instead.

[43] I will not especially remark the most obvious features of all—moderate tempo, major mode—conducing to the expression of a hopeful sentiment, but of course they should be kept in mind. Also, though most of what I draw attention to I will suggest has some natural relationship to hope, echoing in some way its features, I don't mean to deny that there are conventional, and thus stylistically variable, grounds of expression in this music. For example, that major mode conduces to positive mood is partly a conventional matter, due to the history of musical practice and the stock of major mode/positive mood associations contained therein. (I say "partly" because, with Hindemith, Cooke, Bernstein, and others, I think there is something naturally based in the expressive difference between major and minor triads.)

quality of *aspiration*; also, that the first leap goes from F-sharp to B, while the second leap from that B to the F-sharp above, underlines the continuity of the two "reachings" and makes them more like a single movement of the spirit. Of course aspiration—earnest desire for something good or noble—is closely related to hope and might almost be said to be its 'double'. (2) The figure (c), coming after each occurrence of (b), conveys a sense of repose and reassurance; we might see this as arising from the gentle articulated upbeat to the fall of a fourth, a less effortful mirror of the interval in (b), and the reduced dynamic (*p* instead of *mf*). This figure, repeated each time it occurs and set off by rests, seems in context also suggestive of the poised bearing, the restrained carriage of one who calmly hopes in the face of tribulation.

We now move to contextual matters. (3) Consider Q in relation to the first section of the exposition as a whole. The overture's opening is clearly anxious, restless, troubled, even mildly menacing; viewed in this light, Q not only follows but serves to lighten, to alleviate, to dispel—for a time—the gloom that hangs over those first forty measures or so. What might, outside of this particular context, be just bright, happy, or serene is here specifically hearable as in some manner hopeful—the antidote or counterweight to a clouded situation. Of course, an important issue here is the appropriateness of taking a later passage to be a "response" to a preceding one; without offering any general principal on that score, it seems that such is completely intuitive here. If the opening is granted to be troubled and foreboding, then what follows it—given the particular internal structural features noted above, and given its obviously positive tone—is justifiably seen, or heard, under the specific guise of a hopeful counterreaction to such dark humors, rather than as just, say, cheerful or happy or contented. Hope is clearly one of the most appropriate remedial responses to a worried frame of mind.

(4) My next observation concerns a relation between z, the theme of both P and Q, and the almost despairing transitional B minor theme (y) of measures 26–33, underscored by the diminished seventh harmony under the first accented note. There is, I submit, a decided echo or resonance between the one and the other. Compare the upbeat figure in measure 26 and the rising notes of measure 47 or 56, and also the leap of a fifth prominent in both themes. Subconsciously, I suggest, z is experienced as linked to y—as perhaps an answer to it or resolu-

tion of it. Thus, on an emotive plane, the appropriateness and likelihood of hearing Q as in part an affective response to the B minor passages preceding it is even more concretely anchored.[44]

(5) We must now give some attention to P, the first statement of the theme we have been analyzing, and consider its relation to Q. First, P by itself has, naturally, some of the same—that is, hopeful—character as Q, though in a more hesitant or subdued form; since P contrasts sharply with the troubled music that precedes it, the listener is perhaps not as sure how to take it, whereas the heightened repetition in Q gives no doubt that this brightening of mood is really "meant." And second, the temporal relation of P to Q, its in effect serving as a prelude to it, helps define the specific character of Q; P sets the tone, as it were, lays the emotive groundwork for a fuller-blown expression of hope in Q.[45] The main difference between the passages, apart from their relative positions, is of course their instrumentations. In P the theme, on cellos and bassoons, gives off a lambent glow; in Q, on violins, it shines out resplendently.

(6) Finally, a word on our theme z's reappearance in the recapitulation (measure 202). I would not put too much weight on its relevance for our construal of Q, since I believe that *succeeding* events in a piece, especially if remote, are less important than *preceding* ones in fixing emotional character. I regard prospective and retrospective reflections on a piece's overall progression to be much less potent in leading a listener to hear emotively in such and such ways than the actual

[44] Following up this idea of thematic interrelations, and reflecting on the previous point (3), it is possible that z even relevantly relates to the main motive, x, which so dominates the first section of the piece. Alan Walker, in *A Study in Musical Analysis* (London: Barrie & Rockliff, 1982), p. 142, has argued that the first two bars of y are a "free retrogression" of x. If so this probably contributes to the unity of the overture, as is natural, but may also help account specifically for our taking y as responsively linked to the discourse of the overture's opening section. The retrogression, however, is admittedly very "free"; perhaps it is enough to say that the one motive is a downward triadic motion, with fall of a fourth, the other an upward one, with subsequent rise of a fourth. (For a useful discussion of thematic grounds of unity, with particular reference to Walker's procedure, see R. A. Sharpe, "Two Forms of Unity in Music," *Music Review* [August 1983].)

[45] In light of the intimacy with which P and Q are related, one might well have advanced the claim that the larger passage consisting of P and Q *together* (measures 47–66) was *as a whole* expressive of hope, and partly in virtue of the way Q succeeds and builds on P's initial utterance—a swelling, not unlike that of the sea the music in its pictorial side, here undiscussed, evokes.

musical argument addressed to the ear in the fairly *immediate* past. Be that as it may, we may find something at least confirmatory of our way of hearing Q in the quality of that reappearance.

It is often noted how transfigured in character this theme is in its last guise: it seems to come to us as from a distance, consoled and free of urgency.[46] Such a passage, if now seen in relation to Q provisionally construed as *hopeful,* can only seem to reinforce that construal, since its own blissful, distracted air is at least consistent with the construction *hope realized.* To say any more than this is probably unwise, and in any case unnecessary, if (1)–(5) have been well taken.[47]

This completes the direct case for Q as an expression of hope. It is, as I have already said, a particular hope—ardent, steadfast, and with not a little touch of faith as well.[48] Of course, none of what I have drawn attention to can *prove* (*vide* Sibley) that Q expresses hope—it only expresses such if musically prepared listeners will eventually agree that it is most aptly heard that way on an emotional plane. But I trust that what I have said so far can make it seem plausible that it would and should be heard that way.

It is evident at this point that *quasi-narrational* elements, if we may so dub them, have played a significant—though not the principal—part in my case for the expression ascribable to Q. The impression might then arise that I have left behind the behavioral conception of expressiveness sketched at the beginning of this essay, in that my recent appeals to relations between later passages and earlier ones could suggest a narrative model instead, in which successive emotional states are directly ascribed to a narrator, who communicates them to the listener. But this impression is misleading.

The notion of musical expressiveness, I maintain, is still to be cashed

---

[46] "Particularly magical [is] the . . . transformation of the ardent second theme in the recapitulation, sounded *tranquillo assai* on the clarinets" (Richard Wigmore, Liner Notes, DG Cassette 419 477-4).

[47] A sort of "hermeneutic circle" problem beckons here, and in the comparative survey to be undertaken shortly. For we seem inevitably drawn, in spiral fashion, to try to fix the psychological character of part *x* by reference to part *y* or the whole, the character of *x* by reference to *y* and the whole, the whole by reference to *x* and *y*, and so on, without preordained stopping point. To the extent that this is so—and that extent should not be exaggerated—success can still be measured by the attainment of a stable equilibrium in the final assignments or construals, taken all together.

[48] Faith to weather the storm, we might say, if we were to allude to the overture's sidelined marine dimension.

out as given earlier, whether it is a question of passages in situ (such as *Q*) or just passages taken in isolation. What we now see more clearly is just that our sense of a passage's expressiveness where it occurs—i.e., our reading of what sort of emotion its motion is more aptly seen as a sui generis "behavioral" expression of—will be *contextually determined,* will be affected by our grasp of the expressiveness particularly of earlier passages. In some complex way, we refer a given passage's expressiveness to those of other ones, often under the postulate of a *shared persona.* It is this sort of involvement that I have labeled *quasi-narrational;* the "narrative frame" of a given passage—i.e., its place in a sequence of neighboring expressions—influences to some extent our construal of its own expressiveness.

But a *fully* narrational view would be something else again, and probably *not* entirely reconcilable with our original behavior-based notion of expressiveness. I can explain my hearing *Q* as specifically hopeful partly in virtue of having heard the opening (call this *N*) as troubled, without assuming that the states form the content of a story being attributed to an implied speaker. I hear *Q* as the sui generis behavioral expression of hope (rather than just, say, joy) in part because *N* naturally exerts an interpretive pull on *Q* to be experienced in relation to it, and more specifically, because I implicitly hold the persona of *Q* to be the *same* individual as that inherent in *N*, and so construe "his" gestures in *Q* as the expression of something that would be an appropriate reaction or follow-up to what "he" was feeling and expressing just before (i.e., gloom and apprehension). So, *in that musical context,* hope *is* the emotion that I most readily take the musical gestures to be a sui generis expression of, though I would not necessarily (or so determinately) so construe them in another (musical) context.[49] Diachronic contrastive relations can thus be shown to intelligibly influence the expressive interpretation of *Q*'s gestures without our invoking the idea of a narrator who is successively *relating* an emotional saga to us, which would imply, as does not seem the case, that we are only vouchsafed a specific identification of that passage's expression from the perspective of a narrator.

[49]This does suggest, though, that an amplification of the formula offered earlier, where contextuality is made explicit, has something to recommend it: Passage *P, in context C,* expresses α *iff P* is most readily heard, *in that context,* as if it were the sui generis expression of α.

III

Before closing, I turn to a quick series of comparisons between Q and other passages to be found in Mendelssohn's oeuvre, passages also expressive of positive emotions, to be sure, but not, I claim, of *hope*. My purpose in doing this is to highlight, through contrast, the aptness of identifying Q's expression as specifically a hopeful one.

Comparison with the opening of the Octet, op. 20: The latter is exuberant, excited, perhaps anticipatory—but too febrile, too uncontrolled, too unreflective to wear the face of hope. It is also probably too contextless—in being an opening—to pinpoint an emotion as particular as hope, even were its inherent motion more fitting.

Comparison with parts of the *Italian* Symphony: The opening theme, with its leaping thirds and fifths, is the epitome of good spirits, of chest-expanding vitality, but contains no element of straining toward what is to come, no trace of concern as to how things will turn out; similarly, in the minuet's melody we find elegance and gentle solace, but no air of expectation of what is not present.

Comparison with parts of the Violin Concerto: The G major theme of the first movement (measure 131) is soothing, caressing, infinitely tender; and the finale throughout is genial and contented, frolicsome in a controlled way. Positive, to be sure, but not the precise note of aspiration.

Comparison with Wedding March from *A Midsummer Night's Dream*: This is nothing if not celebratory and connotes happiness achieved, with no element of want or need.

Comparison with opening of the Cello Sonata in D: This soaring, ardent theme has indeed a character not so far removed from that of Q, with its confident 3-5-1 opening, which reaches even higher on second occurrence, rising two octaves in six measures. It would not be *wrong* to describe it as having a hopeful cast, nor does its succeeding music undercut such an identification, but such a description is a *less* just summation here than it was for Q. More to the fore in the Cello Sonata's opening is a quality of drive and assertion, the faster tempo and insistent repeated chord accompaniment contributing to this in no small part; its stance to the world is more challenging than awaiting, we might say. But hope must, in some measure, *attend*.

IV

So, finally, if Q does, after all, express hope, (i) *how* does it do so, and (ii) what does a listener's *experience* of that expressiveness rightly involve? I will try, in summary, to answer both of these queries in light of the musical matters just discussed and the theoretical issues raised in Part One.

Taking (i) first, we can say this. What appears to happen in the case of the passage in question, on a general plane, is that the passage has partly isolatable features, some that relate to an inner feeling characteristic of hope, some that connect to a kind of bodily bearing or stance appropriate to hope, some that suggest certain conceptual contents definitive of hope, and perhaps some that convey a general impression of aboutness. Venturing specifics, we have the following. Some aspects of Q—e.g., the rising motive (a)—probably connect to the feeling of hope;[50] some aspects—e.g., the four-note motive (b)—to its behavioral, mainly postural, profile as well; some aspects—e.g., the leaps in (b) and (b')—to its striving, outward-directed character. And perhaps some of the pure conceptual content of hope—its favorable assessment of future in relation to present—is suggested by Q's position as general counterpoise to the worrisome tenor of the overture's first section, and as specific musical/emotive reply to the foreboding message of transition theme y. In addition, the expressive nature of Q— the fervent and faithlike hope it conveys—is helped to emerge more clearly, as we have observed, in virtue of its position as successor and intensifier of P, and perhaps even somewhat retrospectively, in virtue of the "answered prayer" character of z when it surfaces once more in the recap. It is important to emphasize, though, that this assignment of causal credit for expressiveness which we have ventured might be wrong in every particular, and only some sort of holistic judgment sustainable ("it just seems, all told, to be hopeful"), yet the passage would nonetheless express hope, and that despite the absence of its object and at most the partial invoking of its conceptual content.

---

[50] In suggesting that there is a feeling, not completely unspecific, associated with hope, I mean of course *episodes* of hope rather than the abiding *condition*, present even as one sleeps. The adage "hope springs eternal in the human breast" indicates what I have in mind.

Now for (ii). If Q expresses hope, then if I am a familiarized and properly backgrounded listener, I will readily hear Q as if it were the sui generis ("musical") expression of hope by an indeterminate individual, the persona of the passage. I will, in short, at some point hear hope "in" it.[51] But must I, in the course of that, consciously reflect on or entertain all the elements necessarily involved in that psychological state? Must all the lineaments of hope be before my mind as I hear the passage as the expression of such? We have already seen that there is no reason this should be required.[52] This or that distinguishing feature of an emotional state may or may not enter into consciousness.

What, then, *is* required for me to intelligibly hear hope in a passage as I am auditing it? Only a sense of the state I am projecting sufficient to make it hope *rather than* something else, which I then relate to the musical substance of the passage as I grasp that in audition. We must remember that a musical expression of hope is only required to somehow convey the distinctive character of hope—its feel, its bearing, its aspiration, perhaps, if the former are not individuating enough, some inkling of its specific conceptual content—but not the *object* thereof, or the *detail* of the conceptions in which the subject of hope necessarily dresses that object. Likely as not, when I hear hope in Q I subconsciously identify elements of the passage with elements of that emotion, yielding a specific interpretation of the former, but I do not necessarily use *all* of the latter in doing so, nor are even those I do use necessarily in the *forefront* of my conscious experience. Although, as Hanslick says, the emotion of hope "cannot be separated from the conception of a future state which we compare favorably with our present one," hope can come to mind, I maintain, in the way it must in order for us to hear a passage as hopeful, without that conception as it would be realized in any concrete case of hope being present to mind in

---

[51] We must not lose sight here of the difference between *hearing something* (e.g., a passage of music) *as hope* (or hopeful) and *actually experiencing hope*—whether as a result of the former or otherwise. Even though the latter requires a determinate object and specific beliefs and desires directed on it, the former requires no such object and only a partial representation of the emotion's cognitive dimension. Incidentally, I am not here saying or implying anything as to a listener's possible mirror experience (or semi-experience) of those higher emotions that are (if I am right) hearable in some music; nor has this been a concern anywhere in this present essay. Something of what I would say on that score, though, can be gleaned from Chapter 13, above.

[52] Cf. the discussion in Part One, section IV, of this chapter.

all its particulars. Yet it will still be hope in terms of which I hear the music, and not some other, perhaps more generic, state.[53]

I believe I have shown that there are no good arguments for maintaining in principle that instrumental music cannot express "higher" emotions—emotions of the sort that necessarily take objects and possess fairly complicated conceptual aspects. I have also made as strong a case as I can for the expression of one particular "higher" emotion by one particular passage of music. There *is* hope in *The Hebrides*.[54]

[53] Since I have spent so much time in this essay making a case for the expression of a particular higher emotion by a specific musical passage, a suggestion may well have arisen which I want now explicitly to cancel. Let us grant that passage Q is indeed expressive in the way I have claimed. Is this to say that the core, or even a very important part, of a fundamental understanding of this passage is being aware or consciously judging that it expresses hope? Not at all. Rather, in agreement with Roger Scruton's recent essay "Analytic Philosophy and the Meaning of Music," I would affirm that basic understanding in music is a matter of *hearing a certain way*, not of either decoding symbols or making intellectual assessments of content. (I explore this and related issues in a monograph *Apprehending Music*, in preparation.) If I am right, however, some passages *do* express specific higher emotions, and since this *entails* their legitimate hearability in a certain rather sophisticated way, *fully* understanding such passages would entail acknowledging in experience that particular emotional construals of them were especially apt, even if one had not before then arrived at those construals oneself in listening.

Finally, I would add what should perhaps not need saying, that I do not mean to suggest either that unambiguous expression of high emotions is discoverable in most, or even much, instrumental music, nor that passages in which it is present are thereby automatically expressively superior to those in which it is not. But better safe than sorry.

[54] So that the reader not be left with the impression of Mendelssohn's overture and its highlighted passage as a possibly singular case, I venture the following as possible further loci of "higher" emotion in music: Beethoven, Violin Sonata no. 10, first movement, second theme, for perhaps another expression of something like hope; Beethoven, Symphony no. 3, second movement—grief; Mahler, Symphony no. 7, scherzo—reckless optimism; Vaughan Williams, *Fantasia on a Theme of Tallis*—religious ardor; Strauss, *Metamorphosen*—sorrow and shame; Bartok, Quartet no. 4, fourth movement—apprehension; Strauss, *Don Juan*, opening—boundless heroism; Elgar, Symphony no. 1, opening—pride. (I owe this last example to Guy Sircello.) I will not here attempt to qualify or support these conjectures, and I will admit that I have not yet been struck with any likely candidates for the musical expression of embarrassment, jealousy, or resentment. But I am not for that reason without hope.

15 *Evaluating Musical Performance*

This essay has the following theme: performances of music are *legitimately* evaluated from a number of different perspectives, and thus, as a result, there is little use for the notion of a good performance *simpliciter* of a given piece of music. I call this idea the perspective relativity of evaluation of performance, or PREP for short. According to PREP, a performance that is just fair from one point of view might be quite good from another, or vice versa. According to PREP, there is no *single, overriding* point of view concerning performances such that whatever seems good from that point of view qualifies in effect as an *absolutely* good performance of the work, although there may be a *particular* point of view that is arguably most *central* to evaluative assessment, so that grading of a performance without further specification will naturally be taken to refer to that point of view. Such a perspective might have special force without being incommensurably privileged with respect to other perspectives. What I am urging is that the judgment "*P* is a good performance of *W*" is *particularly* subject to the further query: "For *whom*, or in regard to *which* purposes or objectives?" The reason is that there are several perspectives to consider, several contexts in which musical performances occur, several ends musical performance may justifiably serve. To recall that the musically involved can be sorted, first of all, into *listeners, performers,* and *composers* is only to begin to limn the multiplicity of relevant perspectives. I hope to fill out some of the detail in this picture as we proceed.

Let me begin with some preliminaries. First, I shall be concerned primarily with the evaluation of performance in that sphere for which there is a performance/work distinction—by and large, that of notated Western classical music. One has room, in this sphere, for a clear distinction between goodness of work and goodness of performances thereof. With jazz compositions, by contrast, especially those improvised and not based on standard tunes, the distinction all but evaporates. Second, I assume that when a performance is of a work, we will be exclusively concerned with evaluating it *as* a performance of that work and not as an unclassified sonic event *tout court*. I am not interested in the sort of relativity of evaluation that derives from simply *ignoring* what work a performance is of and assessing it as, say, an unusual set of noises, or something to scare children with on Halloween, or a low-key form of aerobic exercise.

Third, some terminology that will prove useful. I mean by an *instance* of a work a sound event, intentionally produced in accord with the determination of the work by the composer, which *completely conforms* to the work's sound and instrumental structure as so determined. By a *performance* I mean the product of an attempt to produce for aural perception and appreciation something that is *more or less* an instance of a work and which *more or less* succeeds in doing so. On this usage, all and only *wholly correct* performances of a work count as instances of it; thus, most performances of works are not, strictly speaking, instances of it. Finally, a performance of a work need not be wholly correct (i.e., an instance) in order to be a *good* performance of it; on the other hand, being wholly correct hardly *ensures* a performance's being good. The line between *somewhat incorrect performances* and *nonperformances* is not a sharp one. I am inclined to think of a questionable performance of a work as still a performance (albeit incorrect) if its shortcomings are largely a matter of *execution*, while inclined on the other hand to discount it as a performance at all when its shortcomings are largely a matter of substantial *modification or flouting* of defining features.[1]

---

[1] For further discussion, see Chapters 4 and 10, above.

Two further logical points about the notion of performance are worth noting briefly before we proceed. There is, first, a well-entrenched *process/product* ambiguity in regard to the concept of a performance. On the one hand, there is the *activity* of producing sounds for an audience; on the other hand, there are the *sounds* that are produced. There is, second, also a *type/token* ambiguity lurking as well. One *usually* means by 'A's performance' the *particular* action or sound event occurring or issuing on a given occasion; but one may also mean by 'A's performance' some *narrowly defined type* of sound sequence that his performance in the first sense is an exemplar of, one much narrower than the sound sequence associated with the work itself—for example, the type whose instances would be individual performances of the work more or less sonically indistinguishable from the individual performance event in question. This sense of 'A's performance' would thus be something like A's *reading* of a work, or *way of playing* a work, at a given point in his performing career.[2] It is clear that in *this* sense of performance, it is conceivable that a pianist could give the *same* performance two days in a row and that another pianist—perhaps a protegé or slavish admirer of the first—might even give this *same* performance again a month hence.

Let me illustrate these distinctions. If I remarked that Arrau's performance on the twenty-third of June was found taxing by the pianist, I would most likely be thinking of the *activity* involved. If I said that I heard Serkin's performance of the *Appassionata* at the Library of Congress last night, I would most likely be thinking of the particular *sounds* produced at that concert. And if I observed that Brendel's second recorded performance of Liszt's Piano Sonata was more reflective and yet more propulsive than his first, in all likelihood it is the specific *reading*, exemplified in a particular sonic occurrence, that I would be praising.

In the context of evaluating performances, I would suggest that the object of evaluation is standardly either the particular sequence of sounds deriving from a performer's activity on a given occasion, or else the reading (narrow performance-type) that the sequence of sounds embodies or exemplifies. In any event, the thing primarily judged

---

[2] A distinction along these lines is developed by R. A. Sharpe, in "Type, Token, Interpretation and Performance," *Mind*, 88 (1979): 437–40.

seems to be product rather than process, achieved result rather than activity of achieving it. This is not, however, to imply that one can judge the product in this case—a performance—in *ignorance* of or in *isolation* from the process that issues in it.

II

What, then, are some relevant points of view for evaluating performances? First of all, there are the various kinds of listeners performances must address. Notable among these are the first-time listener, the one-time listener, the practiced listener, and the jaded listener. Second, there is the actual performer, who has certain ends in virtue of his special positioning, and there are the other performers on that instrument or in that repertoire. Third, there is the actual composer, who is uniquely related to the work performances are of, and then there are other composers, music theorists, musicologists, and the like. Fourth, there is the point of view one might ascribe to "the work itself." I shall have most to say about the varieties of listener perspective germane to evaluation, though I shall also take up for scrutiny the putative privileged status of "truth to the work" as a yardstick of performance worthiness.

For example, what is a good performance of the first movement of the Schubert B-flat op. post. Piano Sonata like in regard to tempo? It seems that this question can receive quite diverging answers depending on whether one has in mind a familiarized or a first-time listener. For the latter, a perhaps somewhat faster tempo is ideally in order. At a somewhat brisker pace, the "heavenly" but as yet unknown lengths of the movement will not weigh on an inexperienced listener as they otherwise might, and it will probably be easier for such a listener to sense the overall progression and span without losing interest. It might also be said that the continuity and flow of the various sections, evident to a practiced listener at a moderate tempo, are more readily grasped by the neophyte auditor if the basic pulse is somewhat accelerated. Putting that point more generally, it seems there is no simple answer to how good a given performance is, how much better it is than another, if one recalls the great difference between a practiced listener, who has grasped a work's basic structure and content, and a beginning listener, who is aurally in the dark. An unusual but elevated performance might not be as good vis-à-vis the latter, as a middle-of-the-road, less exalted performance that nevertheless draws the work's outlines more clearly.

Consider the jaded listener, the one who knows a work so well that all its musical implications and realizations, as Leonard Meyer puts it, have been fully absorbed and internalized. For such a listener, a "standard" performance can verge on sleep-inducing, since no new information is being conveyed, no expectancies are generated, nothing is heard that has not been heard and reacted to fifty times before. On the other hand, a performance that *makes the most* of the fact that a performer can, as Meyer says, "shape and confirm expectations not about *what* events will take place . . . but about *how* the events will take place . . . the manner and timing of their arrival,"[3] will be a performance capable of rejuvenating a piece for the jaded listener. Such a performance, for example, might employ more rubato, might be faster, might be more pointed rhythmically than a "standard" performance, though without yet being significantly incorrect. To take a specific example, one might perform the ♩♩♩ rhythm prominent in the andante variation movement of the *Death and the Maiden* Quartet with the maximum permissible distention of the half note relative to the two quarter notes, thus imparting to the figure more of a pulsing or surging quality than it carries in more conventional readings. Such performances, while gratifying or intriguing to jaded listeners, might be rather annoying to merely practiced listeners just entering their period of maximum enjoyment of the piece in terms of its inherent structural relations and emotional qualities, and it would be undesirably confusing and misleading for listeners having their initial exposures.

There is even the situation of the one- (or two-) time listener to consider. This sort of consideration is perhaps most acute in the context of live performances of works of contemporary composers. As is well known, such compositions generally do not soon—or sometimes ever—receive second and third performances. Of course, one wants the work to come off as best it can, but if one cannot count on it being reheard with any frequency, if at all, then the question of what the best

---

[3] *Music, the Arts, and Ideas* (Chicago: University of Chicago Press, 1967), p. 48.

performance of it would be becomes complex. It seems clear, in principle, that the sort of performance that would prove most satisfying on longer acquaintance (which it might be quixotic to hope for) would not be identical to the sort of performance that would optimize satisfaction in the event of only one or two presentations that are not, we might add, recorded. To speak schematically, it might be good for a singular performance to emphasize the broadest formal and expressive features of a work while hinting at more subtle contents. In case the context I am here acknowledging as relevant to the assessment of performance strikes one as impossibly corrupt and pragmatic, I can only point out that performance of music is a practical, socially embedded, variably purposed activity and that evaluation of a performance's worth as a realization and representation of a piece of music is going to reflect this. Otherwise we are likely not evaluating *performances,* but rather concrete idealized images of musical works—in effect just fully determinate versions of works themselves.

Moving to the perspective of one performing a piece of music, we must recognize that music is not exclusively something affording aesthetic experience through pure audition, but is also a vehicle for aesthetic involvement via the production and shaping of sound events. Performers are engaged with the work they perform in a significantly different manner from listeners, but their engagement is aesthetic, by and large, if they are out to heighten and intensify their experience through performing, but without detriment to the integrity of the work in question. Performers may be after a sense of self-release in the effortlessness with which they produce cascades of sixteenth notes. Or they may be seeking a specially deep identification with the composer of the work as they imagine him or her, and so be impelled to supply more "espressivo" phrasing than others. Or they may wish to explore their capacities for rapid mood changes and so emphasize the emotional contrast between portions of a keyboard fantasy while underplaying the mediating links between them. Or they may wish to revel in the feeling of power and mastery attendant on executing passages with maximal digital independence and be thus more inclined to bring every voice out on a par with every other.

It should be obvious that a performance gratifying to a performer on one or another of these grounds will not necessarily be most gratifying to listeners of any variety we have canvassed. It may, or it may not. But even where not, its claim to being a good performance can still be sustained, it seems to me, from a certain perspective—that of the performer whose significant aesthetic ends are served by *giving* or *producing* it (as opposed to reflectively *auditing* it). Nor, one might add, is this a good only for *that* performer on *that* occasion. It is fundamentally a *kind* of performance one is approving here, as always, and so on another occasion the performer—or some other performer—could be enjoying that good again, simply by performing the work in that way. My point is this: music is for listeners, to be sure, but it is also for performers. The potential aesthetic satisfaction of the two roles are different and not entirely compatible. Thus it is that a performance's goodness can be relative to which broad musical constituency is being invoked—those on the bench or those on the couch.

I have been arguing above that the judgment that a musical performance is good, or has a certain degree of worth, must be relativized somewhat to a particular category of the musically involved. As far as listeners are concerned, what is sauce for the practiced goose is not necessarily sauce for the virginally green, or terminally blasé, gander. And a performance meet for that duck of a performer primarily concerned with exercising digital independence will not necessarily be optimific for many species of listener. Finally, there is the composing buzzard to consider—a performance might be valued from his point of view because of the light it casts on compositional process, or on high-level underlying form, without being particularly rewarding for performers or noncomposing listeners.

III

The sorts of examples I have used in my defense of PREP should not be thought to license the following kinds of extensions, whose *reductio* flavor is apparent:

  a. For a listener who wears earplugs, a very loud performance is the best.
  b. For a listener who only listens to jazz, a performance of Bach's A Minor Violin Concerto with subtle rhythm section underlining is the best.
  c. For a hyperactive individual with short attention span, a performance with all dynamic accents maximally stressed is the best.

These cases are not analogous to our earlier ones and do not provide reasonable ground for calling such performances good. This is because the perspectives from which their "virtues" emerge are *illegitimate* ones. It is incumbent upon listeners to remove physical impediments to good audition and to endeavor to comprehend unfamiliar music on its own terms. Furthermore, it is not the case that performances should be tailored to the regrettable cognitive or perceptual deficiencies of a few. On the other hand, we are *all* first-time listeners to any given piece of music at some point, however cooperative, sympathetic, and musically able we are as auditors, and so the fittingness of a performance to *that sort* of circumstance is more plausibly a ground for calling it, *without qualification or excuse,* good—though, again, good *from a certain* (legitimate) *perspective.* The posture of a first-time sympathetic and prepared listener—like that of the well-practiced listener, blamelessly satiated listener, performer concerned with digital independence, or composer interested in underlying form—is one that, even though we are not currently occupying it, strikes us as a legitimate position within the practice of music, one that is partly constitutive of what that practice is. The meeting of special demands or interests associated with such postures can thus *properly* entitle a performance to a positive evaluation.

The issue that has come to the fore is precisely that of distinguishing cases in which rewardingness of a performance for a certain kind of individual is grounds for calling it good from cases in which such rewardingness has no direct bearing on whether a performance is good. Part of the problem with the inadmissible examples recounted above is, of course, that they are significantly *incorrect* performances. But not all significantly incorrect performances are barred from being good. When, then, may a significantly incorrect performance be a good one? Perhaps, in general, such a performance can be good if it deviates from correctness in order to address a musical perspective (of listener or performer) that is at least defensible in our musical practice, and does so at not too great a cost to the integrity and import of the musical work concerned. I will try to illustrate this rough criterion by contrasting Glenn Gould's and Walter [now Wendy] Carlos's approaches to Bach.

Consider Walter Carlos's versions of the *Brandenburg* Concerti, produced by means of the Moog synthesizer. Certainly, these have their appeal. Is there, then, a musical perspective or listener whom they address, whose gratification is thus a justification for regarding them as good? The answer is yes and no. They *do* address a certain kind of audience, but (a) addressing that audience is *not* a legitimate musical objective, and (b) in addressing that audience Bach's music is *unduly* distorted and transmogrified. The Moog Bach provides an engaging musical experience to a certain kind of listener which ordinary Bach, apparently, cannot. But this is a *dull, lazy, unpracticed* listener, one who needs constant highlighting, gratuitous regular changes, impossibly rapid tempos, and a realm of sounds not too far removed from that of contemporary popular music. Enveloping a work in alien sonic dress, submerging and obscuring its basic identity, is no service to it and meets the needs of no listeners deserving consideration. The falsification of Bach's works represented by these pseudoperformances is not redeemed by the supposed end of enabling or facilitating musical appreciation "down the line." For the nature of the appreciation these caricatures lay the groundwork for is precisely in question. Extreme violence to a musical tradition seems a very suspect method of insuring its ultimate survival or preservation. One is reminded of having to destroy villages in order to save them.

On the other hand, there can be good performances that, though somewhat incorrect, achieve certain worthwhile ends or results from some defensible listener perspective, without completely undermining the character of the music involved. Glenn Gould's Bach Partita renditions are not, perhaps, in matter of instrumentation and phrasing, strictly correct performances of those works, but they answer to appropriate and even historically grounded musical interests (e.g., clarity of counterpoint and voice-leading, inwardness of expression), and they do so without *inordinately* traducing the sort of sound, performance means, and emotional domain envisaged by the composer. Many would agree with me that their musical virtues make them, as a matter of fact, *outstandingly* good performances of Bach's Partitas, even though, paradoxically, they flirt with not being performances of them at all. The Moog *Brandenburgs,* by contrast, seem to lie squarely in the limbo of nonperformances, and further, as I was urging above, even if considered as performances they cannot be reckoned good, despite their having a constituency—nor does embracing PREP commit one to so reckoning them. Of course, the Moog *Brandenburgs* may be interesting musical occurrences, with certain intrinsic merits, considered—entirely artificially—in their own light. But as I stressed at the outset, that would no longer be to assess them as *performances of Bach's pieces.*

IV

I turn now from the relativity of performance evaluation that derives from variation in the *listener* to whom performance is addressed, to the relativity that derives from variation in endorsable *performance objectives,* many of which will not be jointly satisfiable and which naturally connect with different subgroups of the musically concerned. Let me make this point via some rhetorical questions. Will a good performance make surface structure and local interrelation as transparent as possible, or will it strive for broader effects at the expense of small-scale clarifications? Will a good performance accentuate what is unusual and revolutionary about a work, or will it treat such features evenhandedly, leaving them to make what effect they will without special assistance? Will a good performance stress or highlight similarities between a given work and others in the composer's oeuvre, or will it try to present every work as sui generis?

I think it obvious there are no easy answers here, outside of a specification of a context of assessment in which certain objectives are taken as paramount. The opening of Haydn's Symphony no. 80 in D Minor can sound startlingly like the opening of Wagner's *Die Walküre.* Should a performance of the Symphony no. 80 strive to bring this out? I don't know. Are we dealing with the choice of a single recorded performance for one's record library? Is the performance occurring as a musical curtain raiser for a production of Wagner's opera? Is the Oberlin orchestra performing the symphony in connection with a musicology conference entitled "Haydn: The Music of the Future"? Would the same performance do as well for the conference the following week: "Haydn: The Rococo Roots"? Do we want to make it seem that Haydn wrote approximately the same wonderful symphony 106 times,[4] or would we rather it appear that Haydn was really 106 entirely different composers? Do we want the Symphony no. 80 to be a

[4]Nos. 1–104, plus Symphonies A and B.

succession of astonishing effects, or would we rather the organic unity of the classical symphony was to the fore?

Let me expand on the sort of relativity implicated in one of the above questions. Assessing a performance as a lone presentation of a work is different from assessing a performance as part of a *series* of performances of related works. If the radio station is broadcasting just one Brahms chamber piece that day, or the conductor has selected a single Mozart piano concerto to fill third position in the evening's orchestral program, then one's evaluation of the performance might be in some respects fairly liberal; one might be relatively tolerant of idiosyncrasy, of ahistoricity, of "interpreting" at its outer limits. On the other hand, if it is a question of a series of performances organized to present a certain corpus of works as a whole for reflective apprehension, comparison, and analysis—that is to say, in a context intended to facilitate grasp of the elusive golden ring of individual or period style—then a performance that might be judged interesting and effective on its own would here strike one as simply annoying and inept. What works as an isolated offering will not necessarily work as part of a performance cycle of all Brahms's chamber works or all of the late Mozart concertos. In projects of that sort it is appropriate to stress the underlying unity of a genre or oeuvre, the spirit that informs it throughout, the structural or technical characteristics that bind it together—and so a certain uniform and level-headed performance approach is arguably in order. Performances of the sixteen Beethoven quartets that were odd and unusual, *each in a different way,* would not, I think, make for a good cycle of the Beethoven quartets. However, this is not to deny that, assessed one by one in another appreciative context, these very same performances might be quite good—striking, perhaps even revelatory—renditions of familiar works.

I want to switch gears again and defend PREP from another angle. Earlier I invoked the situation of the work that may only receive one performance, and its correlate, the one-time listener. But it should be obvious that this is today *very rarely* our situation in regard to a piece of music. In fact, due to the recent veritable explosion in high-level musicianship and the advances in recording technology that have transformed performing and listening habits in our society, the reverse is more nearly the case. Rather than being confined to a single performance of a work on a single occasion, we have available, for numerous works, an amazing multiplicity of live and recorded performances, to which one can return on many occasions. One can roam from concert hall to concert hall, from radio station to radio station, from record to record to cassette to compact disc. The bearing of this on my topic is as follows. Often when the question is raised, "What would be a good, or a very good, or the best performance of a work W?" we seem to approach it as if we operated in the highly artificial context of being allowed only *one* performance to represent a work, instead of what is typically our actual situation, where *many* differing correct or nearly correct performances of a work will be available. The best performance from the point of view of a desert-island chooser may not have automatic relevance to the situation of the modern music lover in society. Judging a performance's value as sole representative of its work is very different from judging it as a partial contributor to the fullest picture one can have of a work via a set of significantly differing performances of it. A performance that gets highest marks as *sole* exemplar of its work might not make it into the *set* of most distinctive and revealing performances thereof; nor is it guaranteed that many of the latter would function well in the former capacity. We needn't get everything from one performance, and a performance that would count as very good if we could have no other, might be just passable in our current bountiful and amply endowed musical environment. Boult's Brahms symphonies are good, so are Solti's, so are Walter's, so are Karajan's, and so are Kleiber's, each in different ways; some individual performances are in fact transcendently good. But what if there could be only one performance of the Brahms symphonies, a sort of canonical and unique representation of those compositions in sound? Would all the aforementioned be equally good from that point of view? Would any of them be *particularly* so? Suppose we pick the Boult performances—solid, clear, straightforward affairs—as optimal in that context of assessment. It hardly follows that, *for us,* each Boult performance is better, respectively, than each of its rivals, say Kleiber's more aggressive Fourth, or Walter's more gemütlich Third. Let me switch medium, revert to the rhetorical mode, and make the point one more time. Do you want only Ashkenazy or Pollini—possibly overall the best and most balanced pianists before the public at this time—playing *everything* in your library of recorded piano music, or would you rather have some Richter, some Arrau, some Perahia, some Schnabel, some Argerich, some Berman . . . and so on? To modify a phrase of Jimmy Carter's—Why not the most? In our actual situation vis-à-vis the great tradition of Western classical music, performances are not appropriately judged as if they existed in total isolation, devoid of complementary and corrective fellows.

V

Having brought out most of the sorts of considerations that should make one a subscriber to PREP, I now turn briefly to three grounds on which, with some reason, one might be inclined to withhold unqualified subscription. First, it could be held that the ideal of truth to a work and its contents provides a commanding and perspective-free criterion for deciding whether, and to what degree, performances are good ones. Second, it could be held that there *is* a unique and overriding perspective to which defensible judgments of a performance's value are implicitly keyed and that is precisely the perspective of a *practiced and informed listener.* Third, one could cast doubt on the force or significance of PREP by maintaining that the perspective relativity being claimed for evaluation of musical performance is no more than attaches to the evaluation of musical works themselves and that neither amounts to much. I will do what I can in the remaining space to scourge (or at least scour) these pockets of resistance.

I begin with the suggested criterion for performance worth of being *true* to the work performed. What can we take this to mean? Truth to the work must be more than just strict correctness (conformity to sound and performance means structure as specified), since not all strictly correct (or virtually so) performances are good ones. Let us leave aside the fact that performances can be good even if not substantially correct, as already admitted—perhaps because they satisfy some higher-order intention we project the composer to have had[5]—and focus just on what further truthfulness to work a correct performance must evince to be good *tout court,* from no particular human perspective. What is a (correct) performance like which takes truth to the work as its fundamental aim?

The most promising move is to appeal to the work's expressive

---

[5] See Randall Dipert, "The Composer's Intentions: An Examination of Their Relevance for Performance," *Musical Quarterly,* 66 (1980): 205–18.

content and suggest that a good performance must be faithful to this.[6] But what is *the* expressive content of a work that can seem so different under differing interpretations? This is a difficult problem, which I cannot hope to settle here; but I think we can understand a work's expressive content to consist of certain broad *areas* or *ranges* of emotional quality which are delimited by the work's structure as musically defined. For example, *somberness* certainly seems part of the expressive content of the *Eroica* slow movement, since this is inherent in the composition itself and emerges on any acceptable performance. Similar remarks apply to the *defiance* evident in the opening measures of the *Death and the Maiden* Quartet; that much expression is simply in the notes. So understood, however, *any* correct performance of a work achieves an expressive result located *somewhere* within the limits of its expressive content and would thus seem to be true to it.

We need some further suggestions. Perhaps a performance is most faithful to a work's expressive content if (1) it embodies or conveys the *median* values of expression inherent in the work, or (2) it embodies or conveys the most *intense* degrees of the expression inherent in the work, or (3) it embodies or conveys the *widest* spectrum of emotional character attributable to the work. There is some merit in these criteria, but note that in endorsing them one implicitly adopts the perspective of a particular sort of listener situated in a particular way. Thus, to endorse the "golden mean" interpretation is to think of the practiced or somewhat familiar listener and probably less of the unexposed and the overexposed listener. To endorse the "extremist" interpretation is probably to reverse this priority of background concern. To endorse the "comprehensive" interpretation—if anything can in fact satisfy that conception—is implicitly to take the point of view, only infrequently appropriate, of one who knows or experiences a work entirely or primarily through a single performance.

Appealing to truth to a work's content, though it has its use in critical justification, does not seem to allow one to escape the reach of perspective relativity. Before abandoning this gambit, let me consider two further variants on it. We might suggest giving 'truth to the work' a nonexpressivist reading. Perhaps a performance is good absolutely if it

[6] See, for example, Donald Callen, "Making Music Live," *Theoria*, 48 (1982): 139–66. [I regret that the dependence of expressive content on musico-historical context, as well as musical structure, is unmarked in this and the following paragraph, but the points are unaffected.]

is faithful in the sense of *bringing out effectively the work's important aesthetic features.* Or we might say that a performance of a work is good absolutely if, in addition to being correct, it *makes the work come off well* compared to other performances—the best performance, accordingly, being one that makes the work come off best. It must suffice to point out, in response to these suggestions, that whether a work comes off well in a given performance, or whether a given performance effectively displays a particular aesthetic feature, depends somewhat on *what* variety of listener position one is assuming—indeed, on *whether* one is assuming a listener position at all, as opposed to a performer-, composer-, or theorist-oriented one.

Consider next the proposal that the perspective of the practiced and informed listener provides the only proper yardstick for judgments of performance worth. According to this proposal, to say a performance is good is to say it is good (or successful) from just that perspective. Now, while I think the practiced and informed listener's vantage point is a central one, and that the *primary* evaluation of performances is arguably with reference to that, it is hardly the *only* position of importance in the musical context. Music-in-the-world is a many-sided affair, of which performances are the main manifestation, with different sorts of involved and concerned participants, and should, it seems, be assessed in connection with a variety of ends.

Is there a way to bolster the importance of the ideal listener's perspective, securing for it not just a primary place but a paramount one? Can we identify it, say, with the aesthetic point of view or fault other perspectives for being aesthetically impure? I think not. A listener who is not ideal with respect to apprehension may still be approaching a performance in an aesthetically proper manner, and there are surely worthwhile aesthetic experiences to be had at all stages of acquaintance with a work. Yet some performances serve listeners better at some stages than at others. Furthermore, the engagement of a performer can be a species of aesthetic engagement—productive/interactive rather than receptive/contemplative—and a performance that facilitates *that* sort of engagement can be good even though not overly apt for ideal audition.[7]

---

[7] My argument here against according the ideal listener paramount status in regard to *performance assessment* is consistent with the claim that the ideal listener perhaps

Last, I take up the observation that the relativity infecting the evaluation of *performances* is no more than attaches to the evaluation of *works*. I am uncertain exactly how to counter this observation, but I do believe that the cases are not really parallel, that the relativity of evaluation of works is not as pronounced or as pervasive as the relativity of performance evaluation. I will try to give this inchoate intuition some form.

Perhaps the clearest thing one can say is that the judgment that a *work* is aesthetically good (or good as music) is *not* plausibly relativized to various kinds of legitimate *listener*. Rather, such a judgment is arguably keyed to an *ideally* attuned and prepared listener. The reason is that for a musical work to be aesthetically good is, roughly, for it to be *capable* of providing a satisfying aesthetic experience when properly apprehended, and this capacity is obviously best and most adequately *evidenced* in the experiences of one who is maximally attuned and prepared. The goodness of a musical composition *itself* is not reasonably impugned by the failure of the unfamiliar or the overly familiar to appreciate or relish it, but only by the failure to do so of the optimally positioned. In short, it seems that in judging a musical work we are justifiably more concerned with its ultimate potential as an aesthetic object than with its instrumental suitability to this or that appreciative context.

I'm not sure I can further defend the intuition that the multiplicity of perspectives from which it is appropriate to evaluate performances does not have a strict parallel in the case of works themselves. The following already partly adumbrated contrasts seem relevant, in any case: (1) the work is singular, while the number of actual and potential performances is legion; (2) the work is a permanent repository of qualities and experiences, while performances, creatures of circumstance, generally come and go; (3) the work is the primary object of

occupies a privileged place in respect of *determining that certain other perspectives are legitimate* within the musical enterprise. The point of view of ideal audition might be the one from which other musical perspectives were seen to be valid or in relation to which their validities were to be judged. But these would *still* be independent perspectives, optimization of performance with respect to which would *still* vary in the ways I have been emphasizing in this article. Thus, even if we allow such a role for the ideal listener's position, it does not follow that musical reactions *to performances* from this perspective become evaluatively decisive or overriding.

musical art, existing in relative detachment from the practical, while performances are tailored to situations and tied to concrete uses. I shall have to leave the fleshing out of these intimations for another occasion.

VI

In conclusion, I restate my main thesis, trusting it has acquired plausibility in the course of discussion. The question "Is performance *P* of work *W* a good one, and if so, how good?" can generally receive no *single* answer, but only a *series* of answers, for specifications of the question to various musically legitimate individuals, positions, contexts, and purposes.[8]

[8]This is not to deny that a particular performance of a work just *might* be good in relation to *all* legitimate musical interests and in *all* conceivable admissible contexts and thus, in that sense, *just plain good* (or good *simpliciter*). But I venture there is little reason to think this will be true very often.

Nor, furthermore, do I wish to deny that all good performances of a work may have *some* features, *some* characteristics no performance good from any legitimate perspective can be without—e.g., substantial approximate correctness, adequacy to the work's important structural properties. But these will not suffice to fix the goodness of a performance in terms of degree, will not decide as to comparative worth of similarly good performances, without perspective referencing.

Additional Notes

1. The moderate relativism of this essay in regard to ranking performances in value may, at first blush, seem to jar with the rather purist absolutism of my concluding essay (Chapter 16), on authenticity in performing. The appearance of conflict, though, is largely dispelled if one recalls that the degree of openness embraced in the present essay regarding what might make a performance good is meant to apply only *within* the class of performances that are basically authentic in the sense that is at issue in Chapter 16, that is, with respect to observance of all clearly prescribed features of a work, performing forces in particular.

   Now, it is true that, in defending Gould's Bach against Carlos's, this limitation was temporarily transcended, when I implicitly allowed that Gould's performances of the Partitas were *good,* despite being incorrect with respect to instrument and aspects of articulation. But the spirit of the restriction was still, I think, preserved— in order for a performance of a work to be a good one its departures from authenticity simply cannot be *too large,* and the performance must compensate for those departures not by providing, say, some unrelated kind of reward, but by fulfilling other desiderata or goals of the music in its authentic form *even more compellingly.*

16 *Authentic Performance and Performance Means*

I

In a recent, judiciously conducted essay,[1] Stephen Davies has attempted to trace the outlines of the notion of authenticity in musical performance, an issue that has of late much engaged practitioners and theoreticians alike. I am in substantial accord with most of Davies's positions and pronouncements on the question. Just so that the degree of agreement between us will be apparent, I will briefly recall those of his claims I can, in the main, also endorse: the authenticity of a performance of a work is a matter of faithfulness[2] to the determinative intentions publicly expressed in a score by a composer;[3] authenticity does not require reproduction of the social milieu in which a work was premiered; authenticity is not a matter of matching some particular historical performance but instead of approaching the standard of a class of ideal,

---

[1] Stephen Davies, "Authenticity in Musical Performance," *British Journal of Aesthetics*, 27 (1987): 39–50.

[2] Faithfulness here should be understood as something like *manifestly attempted* compliance with the prescriptions of a work, and not necessarily compliance that is *completely achieved*. This is because a performance that is noncompliant, and thus incorrect, in virtue of simple mistakes in execution or simple shortcomings in technical facility, is not thereby accounted inauthentic.

[3] Where these intentions are understood broadly enough to comprise what would be understood to be required in a given musical culture even when not explicitly notated in a score.

393

not necessarily actual, performances; authenticity is strictly satisfied in meeting composers' determinative expressed intentions, not in fulfilling their concurrent unexpressed wishes, nor in following their performing example; and as a consequence of these points, "different-sounding performances may be equally and ideally authentic."[4]

Where Davies goes wrong, though, is in his central construal of authenticity as consisting fundamentally in the *attaining of a certain sound for its own sake,* the sound of a piece as it would have emerged from any ideal contemporary performance of it.[5] The essence of his view is reflected in the following quotations: "the quest [for authenticity] may be characterized as aiming at the production of a particular sound";[6] "the use of such [i.e., period] instruments is justified ultimately by the resulting sound of the performance"; "in striving for authenticity, the performer aims at an *ideal* sound rather than at the sound of some actual, former performance";[7] "the closer comes a performance recognizable as such to the sound of an ideal performance of the work in question, the more authentic is that performance."[8]

It seems to be that Davies's account misconstrues, or at the least underplays, one factor that has an importance he does not explicitly recognize.[9] This is the fact that performances are partly authentic in virtue of being performed *on the instruments for which they were intended* (or envisaged), for a reason wholly *other* than, and *distinct* from, their thus procuring a *sound* that matches what an ideal contemporary performance would have delivered. What is left out of consideration is the fact that the sounds are produced *in just that manner*; that is to say, *the way in which* the performance achieves its sound result is overlooked. This, I suggest, is a serious mistake. A performance matching the *sound* of an ideal contemporary (and thus, presumably, authentic) performance is not authentic unless this match is brought about through the offices of the *same performance means or*

[4] Davies, "Authenticity," p. 44.
[5] Or the *range* of overall sounds corresponding to the set of correct performances.
[6] Davies, "Authenticity," p. 40.
[7] Ibid., p. 42.
[8] Ibid., p. 45.
[9] Using his terms, there is one crucial determinative expressed composer's intention to which he has not accorded adequate weight.

instrumental forces as were prescribed in the original score (or other composition-fixing vehicle of a composer's determinations). And one reason this is so is that if this is not done, crucial aesthetic properties of the musical work are defeated—i.e., not conveyed by the performance, and even traduced by it. Part of the expressive character of a piece of music *as heard* derives from our sense of how it is *being made* in performance, and our correlation of that with its sonic aspect—its sound—narrowly speaking; and its expressive character *tout court* is partly a function of how it properly sounds taken in conjunction with how that sound is *meant* to be produced in performance. Not only the qualitative nature of the sounds but also their specified means of production enter into the equation that yields the resultant aesthetic complexion of a piece of music in the tradition with which we are concerned.[10]

I have touched on this issue in other places,[11] and will not undertake

---

[10]I note, for the record, that one who early recognized that "the history of music is inseparable from a history of instruments and of practice traditions for playing them" is Nicholas Wolterstorff. The position he takes on instrument indispensability, however, is less firm than my own, and more important, the grounds he offers for it are more limited. Here is his most relevant statement on the matter, from which the sentence quoted above is also drawn: "Suppose, for example, that a composer tells us that his work is *for* pipe organ; and that it is clear that he means for it to be played in conventional fashion. Then to be a correct occurrence of this composition an occurrence must have the mixed-acoustic property of *sounding as if it were produced by playing a pipe organ in the conventional manner.* But is the instrumental property of *being produced by playing a pipe organ in the conventional manner* also required for correctness? . . . Until the advent of electronics this particular issue was never concretely presented to anyone. Pipe-organish sounds were produced only by pipe organs. . . . We seem, in fact, to take ambivalent stands on the matter. Almost all of us [*sic*] assume that it is possible to produce a correct performance of one of Bach's works for pipe organ on an electronic organ. Yet I dare say that few of us would regard a sound-sequence-occurrence produced by playing a keyboard to be a correct performance of some work for violin. Perhaps it is the radical difference in means of performance that is decisive for us" (*Works and Worlds of Art,* [London: Oxford University Press, 1980], p. 71).

[11]See Chapters 4, 10, and 15, above. A basic thesis that I rely on in this essay, and attempt to deploy in the particular context of authentic performance debates, was formulated and defended by Kendall Walton in "Style and the Products and Processes of Art" (in *The Concept of Style,* ed. Berel Lang [Ithaca: Cornell University Press, 1987], pp. 72–103), in the course of a general exploration of the manner in which artworks are perceived as having been made in certain ways. The specific thesis leaned on here is that the aesthetic apppearance of music is partly a function of beliefs as to how it is being produced: "much of the emotional impact of music depends on what activities sound to the listener as though they are going on. It is with reference to these

to reproduce my arguments or examples therein. Instead, I will confine myself to discussing some new examples of the kind of aesthetic import that prescribed instrumental means, as opposed to the sound they secure, can have.[12] These will serve as the core of a case for the aesthetic ineliminability of performing forces which is different from the more metaphysically focused briefs I have presented before.

II

Mozart's Serenade in E-flat, K. 375, begins with an arresting unison statement by the assembled winds (oboes, clarinets, horns, bassoons), a five-note dotted pattern with strong sforzandi. It has an assertive air, giving the impression of a call to attention. Now, this assertive, attention-getting quality is itself partly a result, I submit, of a certain *honking* quality often to be remarked in the sforzando attacks of assembled winds, especially when double reeds are included. Would this quality be present if the same sound, narrowly speaking, had been secured by other means, say, through the offices of a Perfect Timbral Synthesizer (PTS)? Of course the sound per se is, *ex hypothesi,* identical and could still be described as sustained, complex, nasal, and so on; it might even still be said to be a honking sound, *in the sense* of resembling the sound of honking, just as the noise from an air conditioner could be called a buzzing sound without implying the presence of insects. But would it have exactly the *same* honking quality as sounds actually produced by forcing air through narrow openings in tubes, in the way that geese, the originals of the honk, squeeze air through their windpipes in producing their aural trademark? Would

---

apparent activities that we describe melodies or passages of music as tender, nervous, raging, flowing, or energetic" (p. 84). In addition, the idea that the expressive content of music is closely tied to the gestures we are prompted to hear in musical sequences is a prominent theme in Roger Scruton's "Understanding Music" (in *The Aesthetic Understanding* [London: Methuen, 1983], pp. 77–100), on which I have also drawn.

[12] The examples I use in this essay, it may be noted, have a 'family resemblance' with some offered by Walton in "Style and the Products and Processes of Art," and in his earlier "Categories of Art," *Philosophical Review,* 79 (1970). My use of these examples is somewhat different, however, since my aim is to focus attention on the specific contribution of the actions imagined as involved in producing sounds to the *gestural content attributed to the music,* on which music's aesthetic, and in particular expressive, properties are most directly dependent.

those sounds—i.e., those produced on the PTS—*be* a honking in the quasi-literal sense in which the accented outputs of oboes and clarinets are such? I suggest not.[13] If it is aesthetically appropriate to take sounds in performance for what they are, and not for what they aren't, and if the opening's peculiar assertiveness is partly a matter of its properly coming across as a honking, in the sense described, then part of the aesthetic character of that opening is distorted or undercut if the performing means that Mozart directly specifies are bypassed and only the resulting sound (or timbral complex) that he indirectly specifies is adhered to.[14]

This point can now be usefully generalized. What was said of the function of being a honking, broadly speaking[15]—what geese, klaxons, oboes all do—in the generation of a piece's aesthetic content carries over naturally to a whole range of source-based characterizations of musical sounds. We hear passages as *sighing,* as *chirping,* as *sawing,* as *hammering,* as *crashing,* as *booming,* and so on, all of which make implicit reference to a kind of action connected to the passage's sonic face as its presumed source. As already noted, there is, granted, an etiolated sense in which these characterizations would still be true even if the presumption of source were to fail. Such descriptions could still be weakly applied to sounds with certain intrinsic characteristics, but a crucial semantic dimension would have been removed. A "sighing" sound, a "sawing" sound, a "crashing" sound issuing from a PTS does not sigh, does not saw, does not crash in quite the sense that corresponding sounds issuing respectively from a re-

---

[13] The dictionary's account of "honk," I think, confirms what I am urging: "*honk,* v. 1. to make the sound of a goose. 2. to make the sound of an automobile horn" (*Standard College Dictionary,* Funk & Wagnalls, 1968). The force of the second entry is roughly this: to do something *like* what a goose does in honking, with similar aural result. Clearly, the "honking" of an oboe fits under this secondary sense, whereas the "honking" of a PTS does not, being "honking" only in an even more attenuated sense.

[14] Here is a little dialogue, from extramusical life, to reinforce the point I have been pressing: "There's some barking out there." "No, there's no animal anywhere. It's just the incinerator operating." "Well, it's a barking sound." "Yes, but it's *not* barking, except in a watered-down manner of speaking. It doesn't sound the same—doesn't strike us the same—as real barking (i.e., sounds issuing from the throat of an excited canine)." "I suppose so; it certainly doesn't *seem* as fearsome as before." "I'd go further; it *isn't* as fearsome as we first thought." "Hmm. . . ."

[15] That is to say, a honking in the secondary, analogical, sense illustrated above, in note 13. The point, of course, is that the same sound image produced on a PTS is not even analogically a honking.

corder, a double bass, and a pair of cymbals do.[16] And if they do not, and if some part of the aesthetic effect of passages containing such sounds depends on their rightly doing so, then the performance of those passages on instruments or devices other than those indicated by the composer will necessarily traduce them aesthetically, even if a sonically correct result, narrowly speaking, is achieved. And such performances are thus clearly inauthentic, even if they want for nothing in matching their sound per se to that of an ideal contemporary rendition.[17]

We can reach the same conclusion from another angle, developing an argument complementary to that just given. Expressive content in music, we may assume, is centrally predicated on the construability of musical gestures as akin to, or as relatable to, human behavioral expressions of emotion.[18] But hearing gesture in music in the way we do is itself arguably predicated on taking successions of notes not as pure disembodied abstract sounds, but as sounds produced in a certain manner, by certain sorts of actions and not others: we rightly hear gesture in musical succession with full awareness of the source of what is heard. Thus, to correctly gauge the gestures inhering in a musical passage, the means by which the narrowly sonic qualities of the passage are being conveyed must be taken into account.[19] Hence, since the

[16]As an alternate way of making the point I am urging here, one could say that I am drawing attention to the broader, as well as the narrower, sense of "how a sound sounds." Two sounds sound the same, narrowly speaking, if they are aurally equivalent—i.e., indistinguishable for a hearer given just the sounds and no other information. But two sounds that narrowly sound the same might, broadly speaking, sound differently if one of them is construed, say, as a banging, while the other is not; the banging quality will then be an aspect of how it (the first one) *sounds*. (I owe this helpful clarification to Walton.)

[17]I find confirmation, inadvertent of course, of the spirit of what I have just been urging in this admiring report on the progress of Roger Norrington's Berlioz recording cycle in London: "But on early instruments, the flutes purr, the oboes squawk, the brass barks, and the strings alternately cajole and bite" (Michael Walsh, *Time*, March 21, 1988, p. 74).

[18]For suggestions along these lines, see Peter Kivy, *The Corded Shell* (Princeton: Princeton University Press, 1980), and Roger Scruton, "Understanding Music," to cite only two recent discussions. [See also Chapter 14, Part One, above.]

[19]The premise I appeal to here, note, is not that the musical gestures rightly hearable in a passage *P* are *precisely* those physical ones appropriately imagined to belong to the actual performer or performers, but rather that the former are, *in part*, a function of the latter. More loosely, the gestures we hear in music—what we hear the music *as doing*—is partly determined by what we take the producers of the music to *literally* be doing in producing it.

expressive value of a passage is partly determined by the musical gestures that are properly heard within it—in virtue of the consequent relating of that to a background behavioral repertoire of human emotional expression—expressive content in music is not detachable from the means of performance that are written into musical compositions, and authentic performance of such compositions, seeking to transmit their full expressivity, must observe instrumentation as much as resultant sonics. The total basis of that expressivity requires no less.

In order to give more flesh to this abstract argumentation, and hopefully to further clarify its dialectic, I will now consider a range of additional examples. Take the device of the rapid upward glissando as it occurs in keyboard music. Its use often conveys a small but precise impression of momentary abandon, or insouciance, if you will. Probably the best-known instances that come to mind are Chico Marx's one-finger antics in various Marx Brothers movies, but examples are not lacking in the piano scores of Ravel, Prokofiev, and Gershwin. I claim that this effect partly derives from our imaginative grasp of the flicking or sweeping gesture behind—or perhaps better, embodied in—the tonal movement itself, and our subsequent placing of that gesture within the field of expressive behavior as a whole. If this imaginative construal is in fact unsupported by performance in the apparent manner, that is, on a keyboard, and we are aware of this, the resultant effect is not that proper to the music, but rather some degree of unwelcome cognitive dissonance. Since the meaning of a keyboard glissando is tied to its being the product of physical interaction with a keyboard, a performance that yields the aural surface without the underlying action is a betrayal of that meaning.

Take the idea of a passage's being *rushed,* or giving the impression of *rushing.*[20] Whether a passage has such a quality is obviously relevant to whether it will emerge with a certain kind of expressiveness—e.g., one of exuberance, or frenzy, or anticipation. Now, our hearing of a passage as rushed pretty clearly involves human action being taken, however vaguely, as a standard of reference, and perhaps even specific common actions, such as walking, speaking, and so on. But a third term in the situation, once again, is our awareness of the kind of action that is presumably generating the passage as we hear it; how rapid we

[20] This is to be distinguished, of course, from a particular *performance* of the passage being rushed, or rushing.

feel its motion as being—a rapidity we then unconsciously correlate with some range of ordinary human actions—will depend on what we believe to be giving rise to it. *Rushed* for something understood as done with the fingers is not the same as *rushed* for something understood as done with the feet. Thus, a passage for piano right hand at a given tempo *t* might be rushed, while one for organ pedal at perhaps half that tempo strikes us as no less rushed. How rushed a passage is when instrumental means are left adrift—how rapid its motion seems in comparison to human action in general—becomes unclear and moves in the direction of increasing indeterminacy. What I have said about the quality of *rushedness* in a passage would go as well for aesthetic qualities such as *ease*, or *striving*, or *tension*, qualities that are often there to register in our experience of instrumental music. It seems clear that their determinate presence,[21] as much as that of rushedness, depends on a specification of sound maker as well as sound, and thus that a performance aiming to convey those qualities would have to regard both specifications as imperative.

One of the most vivid characterizations in all music is surely the depiction of the hypocrites in the sixth section of Vaughan Williams's *Job: A Masque for Dancing*. The suave and slimy quality of these fake comforters, the flavor of their syrupy consolations, is strikingly conveyed. The musical material that is charged with achieving this, though, is most effective, and effective to just the right effect, as it were, when the sliding, drooping seconds and thirds of the main theme, alternately major and minor, are heard as a wind effect—in particular, a saxophone gesture. For only with that does it come across as so clearly a stylization of whining, honey-tongued vocal behavior, on which the precise expressiveness of the music depends. Or consider the expressive contribution of drums to many an orchestral passage. Strokes on the timpani—it seems almost odd to call them, more neutrally, notes or tones—carry a powerful association with striking, pounding, battering in the abstract; when timpani are given prominence in a passage, this association can be overwhelming. Yet it is not timpani sound per se that is efficacious, but only that in conjunction with our belief as to the action betokened by that sound. That a phrase *sounds* a certain way (in the narrow sense) is not the only factor legitimating construing it as a

---

[21] That is to say, their presence to a specific degree.

certain sort of gesture; equally important is that it is or has been *sounded* in a certain way. In the scherzo of Beethoven's Ninth Symphony, the timpani's statements are aggressive and interruptive, while relatedly, those of the snare drum in the first movement of Nielsen's Fifth Symphony are warlike and menacing in their maddening repetitiveness. But in both cases, they are only exactly so if heard *as* strikings and hammerings—which is what they are, after all. So a performance of those symphonies without actual striking of skins—or a performance of *Job* without actual blowing into single-reed mouthpieces—is not a proper performance, whatever its sound, but an expressive diminishing of the music that was to be instantiated.

Two more illustrations. The *searing* quality of some virtuoso violin music—I am thinking of passages in Tchaikovsky's and Sibelius's violin concertos—would appear to depend to some extent on the presumption of a trenchant bow being drawn, and at times slashed, across taut, resilient strings in the act of realizing such music. Without that presumption, the specifically searing quality largely evaporates, and what remains of it on the notes left behind seems as ill poised as the colors of artificial plasticine flowers. The flowing, legato cello lines of the adagio of Dvořák's Cello Concerto, particuarly those rising arpeggiated figures in sixteenths heard at measures 16–20 and 130–34, can, I think, rightly be heard as *caressing* in character. But if so, is this not at least in part predicated on a background notion of the sort of movement cellists are called upon to produce in the rendering of those passages: an enfolding and enveloping of their instrument, almost a loving embrace? And if we cannot take it that a performance does indeed involve such movements, then what can we say of its faithfulness to the expression inherent in Dvořák's concerto?

One last observation. Even something as relatively abstract as impressions of power, force, or direction in musical lines, which surely contribute both to music's expressiveness and to the very experience of following music, cannot be completely detached from a sense of the human activities involved in recreating those lines in sounding form, and of the objects harnessed in doing so, their peculiar propensities and resistances. Such *dynamic* impressions, if one may call them that, are not solely a function of purely sonic structure, comprising tones, intervals, rhythms, tempi, phrasings, accents, timbres, and so on— that is, all determinable features of a composition *apart from* performance means. When we hear one passage or line as "thundering up and down," another as "soaring into the stratosphere," another as "leaping and bounding," another as "floating ethereally," another as "blazing forth into the tonic," and a last as "plunging into the very depths," it is implausible to suggest that such perceptions can be separated off entirely from the known fact of the first's belonging to the grand piano, the second to the violin, the third to the bassoon, the fourth to the flute, the fifth to the trumpet, and the sixth to the double bass.

Though I have emphasized the expressive content of musical *works*, and the factors operating in our *experience* of that expressiveness, the conclusion for authenticity of *performance* is plain and inescapable. If pieces in our classical tradition are for instruments, and if their expressiveness is *bound up with* the physical potentialities and gestural gamuts of those very instruments, then surely authentic performance requires performance *on* those instruments, and not *just* because a certain sound *tout court* is thereby achieved in consequence.

III

I will anticipate a reply that a "sonicist," as I shall call one who denies the thesis I have been defending, might be inclined to make to my argument so far. Granted, the sonicist will say, the apparent expressive properties, and perhaps certain other aesthetic effects, of a piece of music that we are auditing do seem to depend on what we *take* to be the performing forces behind the sounds that are reaching our ears. But still, all that *ultimately* matters is the resultant sound, for if the appropriate sort of sound is achieved at each point, the piece's successive passages either will inevitably be perceived as the product of the instruments selected by the composer, or can at least easily be so perceived at the discretion of the listener. So such passages can readily be heard to embody the right gestures, and thus to carry the right expressive and aesthetic import. All that's required is that listeners *imagine* the sounds to have been produced in the manner in which, very likely, they *seem* to have been produced. Thus, resultant sound, however achieved, would be a sufficient guarantor of authentic performance. And this, again, is because a performance with the requisite sound will be *construable* as having the right sources, and thus as carrying the right aesthetic import.

This reply, though resourceful, is not really satisfactory, for several reasons. To be convincing it relies, I think, on our not learning the real source of the performance's sounds, or else on our willingness to be fooled concerning them, neither of which is a viable stance vis-à-vis a performance.[22] So if we have access to the actual source of sounds, as we normally do in the concert setting, it will be difficult to firmly and stably imagine that source as other than what we see it so clearly to be. Suppose, though, that we did manage to achieve this, and that we were successfully construing the sounds as having arisen in a fashion contrary to what we know to have been the case; I submit that the experience we would then have of the music, believing the sounds were being produced by a PTS or other unusual means, would *not* be the same as when we straightforwardly believe the sounds to have come about in the way we hear them as having come about. In the one case our construal is, so to speak, natural; in the other, it is decidedly "against the grain."[23] A performance that enforces mental acrobatics on listeners in order that an intended expressiveness emerge, which expressiveness should emerge effortlessly and unconsciously, can hardly be thought to further authenticity. On the contrary, to ensure that a listener's experience of a performance be informed by the thought of

[22] First, it can be no part of authentic performance that it requires presenters of music to intentionally deceive audiences as to the physical sources of what they are hearing, or keep them ignorant of these sources. Second, were we somehow to manage on our own to avoid discovering the real provenance of the sounds, or to bury cognitively the discovery once made, our experience of the sonicist's performance would not be what one could call a "perceiving in the truth," to sound a Kierkegaardian note—i.e., a taking things for what they are, at least on the fundamental level. Authentic performance should presumably conduce to, rather than lead away from, that state of affairs.

[23] To expand on this a bit: If sounds are *supposed* to be produced in way σ and a listener knows, and thus believes, they are *not* being so produced, then even if they *seem* to have been produced in way σ, to a listener with a given fund of past experiences, they will not be construed *automatically and unambivalently* in terms of the actions correlated with way σ, and thus the aesthetic impression or perceived expressiveness will be subtly different. We might even say, in perhaps the broadest sense yet invoked, that such sounds will "sound differently" to listeners when they have the belief in question, in virtue of the discrepancy between the sound image, narrowly speaking, and their image of the actions behind the sounds.

certain performing actions *in the right way,* the performance should actually involve those very actions and the very instruments that make them possible.

A second, reinforcing reason is the following. The true expressive and aesthetic properties of a piece, I have argued, and not just the appearances of such, supervene on its specific tonal and timbral complexes,[24] of course, but do so with specificity only in conjunction with the specific instrumental forces through which those complexes are to be realized. An authentic performance should seek to present a piece's aesthetic substance as it *is,* to present the expressive gestures that really *belong* to the piece—and not a mere simulacrum of that substance and those gestures.[25] What we identify a passage as *doing,* in the way of expressive gesture, is a function of what we take it to *be,* in a full sense that includes its specified means of sounding. The sonicist's would-be authentic performance gives the appearances, but not the reality, of the complex of soundings that are the true vehicle of a piece's musical meaning. It is thus inauthentic in the sense that even if it manages to convey the right expressivity to a listener—which we have seen reason to doubt above—it falsifies or disguises the *basis* for that expressivity.

A third reason, not so far adumbrated, would be this. From an evaluative point of view, the natural way of comparing performances of a piece *W,* written for instruments *Z,* is to ask, roughly, how do these *Z*-ists deal with the music and the gestures it contains, given *Z*'s and their inherent natures, compared with what other *Z*-ists, in the past, have wrought in their place? If we discovered, however, that *Z*-ists and

---

[24]For more on this relation, see Chapter 7, above.

[25]It may be thought that it is often the case in art that we are to take some phenomenon or appearance as being other than it is, and other than we know it to be. For example, as when we, say, take it in a novel that a narrator of a certain sort has actually written a chronicle of events he has experienced in eighteenth-century England, or that, in the cinema, we are actually viewing from above the eruption of Vesuvius in A.D. 79. Suffice it to observe that such are, first, cases involving explicit fictions, inviting and demanding an appropriate "make-believe" response, and second, cases of appeals made by works themselves and not specifically by presentations of such works. The context of presenting works of classical music in performance cannot, in general, be assimilated to that of creative proffering of fictions for imaginative construal; even though we are at liberty to imaginatively (or metaphorically) construe the music in various ways once it is constituted in our hearing, we are not being invited to pretend regarding the real sources of the music that is being presented.

Z's weren't even involved, as would be the case with some of a sonicist's candidate authentic performances, we would be pretty much completely at sea in regard to assessing the particular expressiveness of the performance of W at hand, its particular manner of bodying forth W's inherent expression. For an important dimension of assessment would have been removed: how have the instrumentalists, given their control over and way of internalizing the gestural capacities of their instruments, related themselves, at each turn, to the demands of this music, which is conceived for and referred to those capacities?[26] A performance that generates a critical quandary of this depth gives strong sign of not being an authentic performance, whatever other virtues it might have; we would expect that any authentic performance, if nothing else, would lend itself intelligibly to critical evaluation.[27]

IV

It is time to relate our conclusions more closely to the kinds of cases that are actually involved in present-day disputes about authentic

[26]Relatedly, one might note that the whole notion of the *virtuosity* inherent in compositions of a certain sort, and not just in performances of such compositions, is made nonsense of by detaching a musical work from the means of execution that belong to it. See the intriguing discussion of Thomas Mark, "On Works of Virtuosity," *Journal of Philosophy*, 77 (1980): 28–45.

[27]For these reasons and others, I have in other essays (Chapters 4, 10, and 15, above) suggested that putative performances such as those we have been considering not even be counted as *performances*, much less as *authentic* ones. But I have naturally not wished to make such short shrift of the matter here, and have allowed them to be performances, in some sense, in order to focus on their claim to *authenticity* in that regard.

In making a case for the relevance of actual performing means I have focused the discussion on the aesthetic validity of competing realizations of a work which are completely *indiscernible* in the narrow sonic sense, though involving, by hypothesis, differing means of realization. A more realistic observation, though, suggests itself at this point. Let us recognize that, in fact, different means of production will *invariably* lead to detectable differences in sound, narrowly speaking. Why, then, are such slight differences often *quite important* aesthetically, beyond their admitted contribution to the total timbral picture? We have now a natural explanation of this, in light of the foregoing. Part of the reason they bulk larger than expected is that we are cued by those differences, however slight, to *imagine or understand* different means of production, and thus to perceive somewhat different gestural content in the music, and so eventually, differences in resultant expression. And *that* upshot is always of moment to us.

performance.[28] These are not, of course, over whether trios for basset horns are authentically performed if rendered on kazoos or a PTS, but perhaps over whether such trios can be authentically rendered on ordinary clarinets instead, and more clearly still, over whether Mozart's symphonies, written when an earlier type of clarinet was in use, can be authentically performed employing modern clarinets, with their weightier bodies and improved system of keying. We are familiar with the sonicist arguments for answering this question, regretfully, in the negative. The timbres are significantly different, thence resulting balances and blends are altered; the sound picture is thus importantly different from that which the composer envisaged—or, at least, committed him or herself to—and has a different overall aesthetic impact.

What I emphasize, in continuity with what I have argued earlier, is that there is an argument distinct from the sonicist's for denying that performances of Mozart symphonies employing modern wind instruments, insofar as the latter differ structurally in important respects from eighteenth-century clarinets, can be fully authentic.[29] It should, in outline, be familiar.

Between any two instruments or devices that differ importantly in their physical construction and mode of operation there will in effect be differences in sonic *capacity* and gestural *potential*, and thus in the expressive meaning of even qualitatively identical sounds or phrases pro-

---

[28] To avoid misunderstanding, and too deep an involvement with issues surrounding the Historical Performance Movement which are not directly germane to the case I am trying to make, it should be understood that my remarks in this section, indeed in the essay as a whole, have application in full force only to periods and genres of music in which it is fairly clear that performing means and timbral values, and their associated contribution to expressivity, are of explicit concern to composers and their intended audiences. But in Western art music, our primary concern, this is arguably so from at least C. P. E. Bach on.

[29] It is important to recognize, especially in the heatedly purist waters we are entering, that there are certainly *degrees* of authenticity, and that small failings do not condemn a performance to utter inauthenticity. Second, it must also be said that the fact that a performance would be inauthentic in some respect or respects generates no *invariable* pragmatic prescription, independent of context, as to whether it should or should not be engaged in, approved of, or pursued, all things considered. Deciding whether to perform something in a somewhat inauthentic manner, given practical constraints or special purposes, is no simple matter, and certainly there are many conceivable circumstances in which one would be justified, all told, in doing so; but this should not be allowed to cloud the prior theoretical determination of what full authenticity in performance consists of.

duced on them. In contrasting a modern clarinet with its eighteenth-century cousin these differences are subtle, nowhere near as gross as those separating a modern clarinet and, say, a PTS imitating a clarinet; but they do exist. The modern Boehm system clarinet, for example, can modulate more easily than its older cousin and has greater powers of pianissimo and diminuendo. Now, the musical gestures in Mozart's Thirty-ninth Symphony, K. 543, those that belong to it as an eighteenth-century musical composition and on which its aesthetic character is based, are presumably precisely those that are readily perceived in it against the matrix of the gestural repertoires and sonic capacities of just the instruments for which the piece was conceived—e.g., old-style clarinets—and not, say, the gestures that would be perceived in it viewed against the matrix of repertoires and capacities associated with their modern successors.[30] Thus, even if modern clarinets, given their different limits, ranges, and system of construction, could reproduce sounds *indistinguishable* from those that eighteenth-century clarinets would make in rendering the score of Mozart's Thirty-ninth Symphony, such a performance would not be expressively equivalent to *any* performance achievable on those older, and different, instruments. What expressiveness it would have is hard to say, bastardy being no simpler to deal with in the aesthetic realm than in the social one. But in any event, it would not quite be a proper representation of K. 543's own expressiveness, and hence not an authentic performance of it.[31]

[30] For example, it appears that the reed, for one, was differently placed on older clarinets—on the top rather than the bottom—thus leading to a different way of pursing the mouth in endeavoring to produce tone. (I owe this piece of information to Peter Kivy.)

[31] Compare this insightful brief for authentic performance: "Every musical idea, in a sense, is shaped by the technical means available to express it. Thus playing the Mozart violin concertos on today's long-necked, metal-stringed, power-and-brilliance-oriented instruments can be said to pervert rather than improve them. Mozart heard his own, more muted instrument when he wrote this music, and its capacity to phrase—in short, articulated sentences rather than long ones—tells us something about how he wanted the concertos to sound" (Bernard Holland, *New York Times*, Nov. 21, 1987). Indeed, it tells us that, but not *only* that, Holland might have gone on to say. It tells us something about the proper perceptual framework for assessing the expressive import of the sounds so produced in performance of these concertos; what is actually, in the music, a particularly long-breathed utterance, or a particularly pronounced dynamic emphasis, will only be heard as such if the baseline phrasing and dynamic capabilities of the older violin are held in mind.

V

To conclude: Instrumentation in traditional music is not of merely instrumental value, so to speak, in achieving a certain sound, but is rather logically tied to a piece's expressiveness and aesthetic character in its own right. Recognizing this shows us that the notion of authenticity of performance cannot be analyzed exclusively in terms of a matching of sound per se, even the sound of an ideal contemporary performance. What I have said about the involvement of exact instrumentation in aesthetic content does have the implication that, to gauge that content fully and accurately, or the expressiveness that is its major part, one must be familiar with instruments, their mechanisms, their physical potentials, and perhaps most of all with how the manipulations of which they admit stand with respect to the broader repertoire of movements, gestures, and expressions of the embodied human being; and the more familiar, *ceteris parabis,* the more full and accurate the gauging.

This familiarity can come in various ways: by observing music being performed; by noting how instruments are constructed; by handling and inspecting instruments; by studying the history of the development of instrumentation; by inducing, through wide listening, the ranges of sounds and effects of which each is capable; and of course, if one has the requisite talent, by actually practicing and playing instruments in a musical setting. Our familiarity with the producers of music—those various physical devices—is probably usually fairly imperfect, especially as our remoteness in time from the music in question increases. But *some* such knowledge, whether tacit or explicit, must be regarded as essential to the understanding of music.[32] And this, once again, testifies to a condition on authenticity of musical performance that goes beyond the purely sonic, a condition, I suggest, that Davies errs in overlooking or, at best, submerging in others that are strictly distinct from it. Music is physical activity as well as spiritual product, and the latter cannot be properly grasped—or presented—without acknowledging the specific determining role of the former in it.[33]

[32]By analogy, one could hardly be thought to understand *painting*, after all, if one had no notion of the physical reality of brushes and paints.

[33]Two essays on our topic which appeared shortly after I had written mine, and to which I am pleased to draw attention, are Stan Godlovitch, "Authentic Performance," *Monist,* 71 (1988): 258–77, and Peter Kivy, "On the Concept of the 'Historically Authentic' Performance," *Monist,* 71 (1988): 278–90. As readers of them will discover, my conclusions are more in line with Godlovitch's essay.

Index

Art (*cont.*)
ogy of, theoretical unity in, 220–21;
recursive definition of, 18–21; representational and nonrepresentational,
279–81; revolutionary, 15–17; secondary notion of, 58; theory of vs.
definition of, 54
Art-character, 182; determination of,
212; relation to art-content, 211
Art-content, 182, 186, 188, 196, 209n;
determination of, 181–82, 184, 197,
200, 201, 209, 211–12, 213n
Art forms: autographic and allographic,
89–106, 250; hybrid, 26–35; pure
(or thoroughbred), 30
Art-historical context, 181, 213n
Artist, status as, 22–23
Artistically relevant property, 194, 196,
202n. *See also* Art
Artistic attributes: and aesthetic attributes, 182–84, 239n; future-
oriented, 182, 211; permanent vs.
time-relative ways of taking, 188–89
Artistic conventions: absence of fiction-
generating ones in absolute music,
280; absence of proposition-signifying
ones in absolute music, 346; and the
identity of paintings, 178n; and reading scores, 241–42; and titling, 168
Artmaking: art-aware, 7; Duchampian,
52–54; internal vs. external views of,
21–22; intrinsical and relational
modes of, 39–40, 46–47, 49; rational
nature of, 55
Artmaking intention: art-conscious and
art-unconscious, 11, 46–47; nonpassing (or serious), 38–39, 44; opaque
and transparent construals, 11; primary and secondary, 16; and value,
53–56, 274
Artwork: component of, 166–67; concept of, 7; constituent of, 166–67;
core content of, 168; part of, 166–67,
176; time-dependence of status of,
12–15. *See also* Art
Ashbery, John, 99
Ashkenazy, Vladimir, 387
Attribute, 108n. *See also* Aesthetic attributes; Artistic attributes; Con-

textual attributes; Expressive content;
Influence attributes; Particularized attributes; Properties possessed; Structural attributes; Substructural
attributes; Ur-aesthetic properties
Austin, J. L., 82n
Authenticity, 252n
Authentic performance: degrees of,
406n; and performance means, 393–
408; pragmatic consequences of,
406n; sound of (per se), 394–95
Autographic and allographic art forms.
See Art forms

Bach, Carl Philipp Emanuel, 300
Bach, Johann Christian, 207n
Bach, Johann Sebastian, 206–7, 212,
240; *Art of Fugue*, 74n, 271; *Bran-
denburg* Concerti, 185, 383–85;
Brandenburg Concerto no. 2, 74n;
Chromatic Fantasy, BWV 903, 233n;
Concerto for Two Violins, BWV
1043, 77; Partitas for Harpsichord,
BWV 825/830, 384; Violin Partita no.
2, 99; *Well-Tempered Clavier*, 74n,
232; *Well-Tempered Clavier*, Book II,
Prelude no. 12, 150–51
Bacon, Francis, 185, 200
Bartel, Timothy, 37n
Bartók, Béla: Concerto for Orchestra,
71; String Quartet no. 4, 375n
Barwell, Ismay, 340n
Baudelaire, Charles, 106
Beardsley, Monroe, 5n, 37n, 38n, 43n,
47–48, 50–51, 109n, 110n, 112n,
121, 134n, 137, 140, 146–47, 203,
354n
Beethoven, Ludwig van: Grosse Fuge,
op. 133, 233n; Piano Concerto no. 3,
op. 37, 305n; Piano Quartet, WoO 36,
no. 2, 244n; Piano Sonata op. 13 (*Pathétique*), 271; Piano Sonata op. 31,
no. 2 (*Tempest*), 163; Piano Sonata
op. 53 (*Waldstein*), 237; Piano Sonata
op. 81a (*Les Adieux*), 167; Piano Sonata op. 106 (*Hammerklavier*), 76–
77, 86n, 240; Piano Sonata op. 111,
185, 188; Piano Trio op. 1, no. 3,
207; Quintet for piano and winds, op.